Acclaim for
SECOND OPINION
by
Isadore Rosenfeld, M.D.

"Although this book is entitled *Second Opinion,* it contains much more than a consideration of why, when, and how valuable is another opinion. It is, indeed, a pragmatic, instructive, and highly readable book for the average layman who desires authentic information about medical and health matters. In a wide-ranging discussion of medical illnesses from asthma to angina, from cataracts to cancer, and from cholesterol to contraception, Dr. Rosenfeld has provided a no-nonsense presentation of current authentic medical information that will permit the layman to understand better the judgments rendered by the physician and to determine whether a second opinion is desirable."

—Michael E. DeBakey, M.D.
The Methodist Hospital, Houston

"This is one of the best-written books for the lay public that I have read on medical treatment.... The information is current and highly accurate. I will strongly recommend this book to my patients and friends."

—Antonio M. Gotto, Jr., M.D.
Chairman, Department of Medicine
Baylor College of Medicine

"*Second Opinion* is an easy-to-read, enjoyable account of the latest advances in medical treatment, a book which finally makes it possible for the layman really to understand why, when, and where to ask for a consultation...."

—Mary Lasker

Other Bantam Books
By Isadore Rosenfeld, M.D.

Modern Prevention

SECOND OPINION

SECOND EDITION

YOUR COMPREHENSIVE GUIDE TO TREATMENT ALTERNATIVES

ISADORE ROSENFELD, M.D.

BANTAM BOOKS
TORONTO · NEW YORK · LONDON · SYDNEY · AUCKLAND

NOTE

The information contained in this book is intended to complement, not substitute for, the advice of your own physician, with whom you should consult about your individual needs. You should always consult with your own physician before starting any medical treatment or diet.

SECOND OPINION
A Bantam Book

PRINTING HISTORY
Originally published by Linden Press in March 1981

Bantam edition / June 1982
Revised Bantam trade edition / January 1988

Library of Congress Cataloging-in-Publication Data

Rosenfeld, Isadore.
  Second opinion.

  Includes index.
  1. Medicine, Popular. 2. Therapeutics—Popular works.
3. Medical consultation. 4. Patient education. I. Title.
[DNLM: 1. Decision Making—popular works. 2. Referral and
Consultation—popular works. 3. Therapeutics—popular
works. WB 300 R813s]
RC82.R67 1988   615.5   87-47787
ISBN 0-553-34478-1

Published simultaneously in the United States and Canada

Bantam Books are published by Bantam Books, Inc. Its trademark, consisting of the words "Bantam Books" and the portrayal of a rooster, is Registered in U.S. Patent and Trademark Office and in other countries. Marca Registrada. Bantam Books, Inc., 666 Fifth Avenue, New York, New York 10103.

Manufactured in Canada by Webcom Limited

WC   0 9 8 7 6 5 4 3

CONTENTS

Preface   1

1 A Second Opinion—Why, When and How   12

2 Patient Care Versus Doctor Ego   27

3 The Thyroid Gland—
   Regulating Your Thermostat   33

4 Cataracts—
   A Disorder of the Young and the Old   51

5 Diabetes Mellitus—
   When Life Is Too Sweet   63

6 Hypoglycemia—A Common "Nondisease" 78

7 Disorders of the Ears, Nose and Throat—
   Unnecessary Treatment?   83

8 Asthma—
   Preventing and Controlling Your Wheeze   94

9 The Skin—Common Problems Affecting
   the Largest Organ in the Body   104

10 Sexually Transmitted Disease
   (What We Used to Call VD)   121

CONTENTS

11   The Heart—Still Our Number 1 Killer   136

12   Hypertension—The Silent Killer   211

13   Thrombophlebitis, Varicose Veins and Blood Thinners   225

14   Your Arteries and Your Circulation— From False Alarms to True Aneurysms   232

15   Stroke—A Major Killer on the Wane   242

16   Parkinson's Disease— Many Treatments, No Cure—Yet   250

17   Myasthenia Gravis— New Hope for an Old Disease   258

18   Infertility, Contraception and Abortion   265

19   Impotence—It May Not Be All in the Head   293

20   The Hysterectomy— Our Most Unnecessary Operation   299

21   Peptic Ulcers—Down with the Diet   304

22   Viral Hepatitis— Avoiding a Jaundiced View   314

23   Gallbladder Disease— A Variety of Treatment Options   324

24   The Bowel— When and How to Treat Its Symptoms   329

25   The Prostate Gland— From Infection to Tumor   342

26   Hemorrhoids—No Laughing Matter   347

27   Cancer—New Horizons, New Hope and More Options   351

28   Arthritis—Avoiding a Laissez-Faire Approach   393

Reflections   412

Index   415

SECOND OPINION

PREFACE

It's hard to believe that seven years have elapsed since I wrote the first edition of this book. During that time *Second Opinion* has become a household term. The concept of asking for another point of view when the medical going gets tough is now widely accepted by patients, by the medical profession and by insurance carriers. Doctors are actually relieved to share the responsibility of a major decision with one of their colleagues, given the malpractice crisis, their vulnerability to lawsuits and the tremendous sums awarded for negligence. This makes it less unpleasant for patients to raise the question of getting another opinion. Many health insurers not only pay for that second opinion, they may not reimburse you unless the need for surgery was documented by another doctor. The result of all this has been a substantial decrease in the number of unnecessary operations.

Why, then, another edition if the original purpose of the book has apparently been fulfilled? Because this is not only a book that espouses a particular philosophy. It is also meant to serve as a home reference for the treatment of disease. Since 1981 there have been many important changes in the treatment of several illnesses, and new diseases have appeared. AIDS (acquired immunodeficiency syndrome) is on

I

everyone's mind these days, yet the first edition of *Second Opinion* made no mention of this terrible disorder because the very earliest cases were only just beginning to be reported. During the past seven years we have accumulated new knowledge about what causes diabetes mellitus and there are several new drugs for lowering blood sugar. We've also learned more about asthma. Herpes is no longer on everyone's mind because we're so preoccupied with AIDS, but there is also new and effective therapy for this infection. There have been many significant developments in the area of heart disease, ranging from proof that lowering cholesterol *does* make a difference, to exciting new drugs and noninvasive alternatives to bypass surgery. If you get to the hospital soon enough with the symptoms of a heart attack there is medication that can dissolve a life-threatening clot in your coronary artery. As far as high blood pressure is concerned, new drugs now make it possible to control hypertension without causing impotence in men and frigidity in women; there are vaccines against hepatitis and drugs that prevent the flu or treat it specifically after you come down with it; there are several exciting new ways to manage gallstones without surgery; major breakthroughs have occurred in the field of cancer therapy; several medications now enable you to postpone surgery if your prostate is enlarged. I could go on and on here in this introduction, but if I did, what would there be for you to read in the rest of the book?

I have brought every one of the original twenty-eight chapters up to date. However, the basic tenet of the first edition, namely that in medicine there is more than one way to skin a cat, is probably more valid now than ever before. And my basic advice stands, namely, that when you're told to undergo any treatment that is unpleasant, costly, time-consuming or hazardous, it is your right and your responsibility to ask for and get a second opinion.

SECOND OPINION—NEW CONSTRAINTS

Although most doctors are now in fact ready and willing to help you obtain a second opinion, you (and they) may find it more and more difficult to do so in the years to come. The reasons have nothing whatsoever to do with attitudes. It's all a matter of money and economics. The manner in which medicine is practiced and health care delivered is undergoing dramatic changes in this country. Solo practice, with its one-to-one relationship between you and your doctor, is rapidly being replaced by group medicine—doctors working together or in the employ of profit-making corporations. These go under various names, the prototypes of which are the HMOs (health maintenance organizations). They reflect a perceived need to reduce medical costs. Whether they will do so and still retain high-quality care in this country is a moot point. However, in the meantime, any extra expense related to your case management will be avoided by these HMOs—if at all possible. Such extra expenses include special tests deemed to be optional, hospitalization when not absolutely necessary and second opinions. When the latter are absolutely essential, a consultant is likely to be selected from the panel of doctors within the HMO to which you belong—regardless of his or her qualifications. It is important for you to remember, even in these circumstances, that you have certain inalienable rights that transcend the need for economy. If your health and life are on the line, you should not only insist on a second opinion, but get the best one available.

EVEN IF YOU LOVE YOUR DOCTOR

In my first book, *The Complete Medical Exam*, I took you step by step through the ideal physical examination or checkup. (How I wish I had entitled that volume, *Checkup—or Checkout!*) This volume is all about treatment—the natural sequel to diagnosis—what to do about any bad news given to you by your doctor. The underlying message in every one of the chapters that follows is that *for every ailment there is almost always more than one form of therapy.* You *do* have alternatives in the way your health problems can be handled, and these pages contain those alternatives.

This book tells you why, when and sometimes where to ask for a second opinion. Remember, no matter how devoted you are to your doctor or how much you dislike antagonizing him, you owe it to yourself to consult with another expert when (a) you are ill and not responding to treatment, (b) you are presented with a diagnosis or prognosis that may drastically alter the course of your life, (c) an operation is recommended, or (d) you have reasonable doubts about a treatment course you have been advised to follow.

NO RARE DISEASES HERE

A word about what you will find in this book and how it is organized: I have tried to keep the information practical and have used layman's language, not technical jargon. I have called upon my own experience to select the most pertinent subject matter. You will find advice about treatment of such disorders as asthma, overweight, hepatitis, impotence, heart trouble, blood pressure, stroke, difficult pregnancy, ulcer and circulatory problems—to name but a few of the more common troubles you are likely to encounter.

Before writing this book, I reviewed the very latest literature dealing with each topic, and afterwards I asked appropriate specialists to double-check the accuracy of the final manuscript.

YOU USUALLY HAVE SEVERAL OPTIONS (ABOUT WHICH YOU MAY NOT BE TOLD)

Your doctor frequently has several alternatives at his disposal to treat most conditions. Some may be better, more convenient or more appropriate for *you* than others. Ideally you should be made aware of *all* these options when you are sick, and you should be able to discuss them freely with your physician. Unfortunately, because he is too busy, or doesn't believe that it's really any of your business, or more commonly, because he doesn't think you're qualified to participate in making a decision vital to your own health, your doctor may not tell you that, in fact, you have a choice, or what that choice is. Such an attitude is not in your best interest, and is not likely to result in your optimal medical care.

In every one of the many disorders and diseases discussed in this book, I have listed your treatment options with enough information about each to help you judge what is best for you when a decision needs to be made. Discuss these options with your doctor. Let him know that you really *do* understand the alternatives, and then, together, decide on the course to follow. If, however, you can't agree, then it's perfectly reasonable for you to have another opinion. The preferences that I express for the management of a particular medical problem are not necessarily "better" than those of your own doctor. They simply reflect my personal experience and, perhaps, a different point of view of which you should at least be aware.

When you have finished reading this book and all about those ailments in which you are specifically interested, you will understand why your doctor has made a particular recommendation—for example, to operate or not to operate on your gallstones, to give you anticoagulants (blood thinners) or to withhold them, to use antibiotics or to avoid them, and so on. As a result, you will be more confident about that advice and less likely to worry when one of your friends tells you that *his* physician prescribed a totally different treatment for the same condition.

ONE OPINION MAY BE ENOUGH (OR ALL YOU ARE ABLE TO GET)

I'm not for a moment suggesting that a second opinion is always desirable. You don't need to see another doctor for something like a cold, a transient muscle spasm or a mild tension headache. As a matter of fact, you may not necessarily want a consultation even when you are seriously sick if the diagnosis is obvious, the treatment straightforward and, most important, you are getting better. Finally, there may not be time for a second opinion in a life-threatening emergency when every minute counts. For example, when you are in shock from hemorrhage, and the bleeding must be stopped immediately, you can't wait for a consultant to get there "in the fullness of time."

WHEN THE VERDICT SURPRISES YOU

For the many situations or diseases that may require major surgery (malfunctioning heart valves, coronary artery obstruction, aneurysms), are out of control despite treatment (diabetes, chronic backache due to a ruptured disc somewhere in your spine), impair the quality of your life (arthritis, impotence, infertility, stroke, serious emotional disorders) or affect its duration (cancer, advanced arteriosclerosis), you should ask for another opinion. Here's an example of what I mean. Suppose you consult your doctor for what you always thought was a little indigestion and he tells you something totally unexpected, like "Your electrocardiogram is very abnormal. You may need cardiac surgery. You'll have to come to the hospital for an angiogram." That may be a good time to get additional input. Or, if after a routine checkup, your doctor informs you, "I'm sorry, but there is a suspicious lump in your breast that may be malignant. We'd better get a biopsy," that too may be grounds for a second opinion.

When you suddenly find yourself on the conveyor belt of medicine, carried along into a future over which you no longer have any control, when your life is threatened and your key concern is "What are my options?" this book may fill a very important need.

SOME IMPORTANT ALTERNATIVES— WOULD YOU RECOGNIZE THEM?

There are times when the need for or the desirability of a second opinion is fairly obvious, even if you are embarrassed about asking for one, for example, when you are very sick and not responding to treatment, or after your doctor has given you some dramatically bad news that, if true, may completely change the course of your life. But would you know enough to ask for a second opinion in the following hypothetical situations, for every one of which, as you will learn in these pages, there are important alternatives in diagnosis, therapy or outlook?

One night, you are awakened by chest pressure that frightens you. It disappears in a few minutes. You visit your doctor the next day. He takes an ECG, which he says is normal. You are reassured that you do not have heart disease, because he explains to you that angina is always effort-induced and never comes at rest. (pages 168–169)

You develop a lump in the thyroid gland. Your doctor advises its removal because "no lump anywhere should ever be left alone." (page 47)

A growth has been found in your breast. The surgeon asks for your permission in advance to do whatever is necessary at the time of the biopsy, depending on what he finds. (pages 373–374)

In the course of a routine examination, your eye doctor finds that you have cataracts. Although your vision isn't all that bad, he recommends their early removal. (page 56)

You complain of chronic fatigue and lassitude. You are told it's due to low blood pressure, and you're given medication to raise it. (pages 223–224)

After suffering for years from hemorrhoids you finally decide to do something about them. An operation is advised. (page 349)

Three months earlier you had a mild heart attack from which you are recovering very well. But suddenly you develop abdominal pain and gas after eating "rich foods." A gallbladder X ray reveals some stones, and you are advised to have them out as soon as possible. (page 326)

You are sent for an upper GI series because of stomach pain, and it shows a duodenal ulcer. You are given antacids and Tagamet, and your symptoms clear up. Although you are feeling well, a few weeks later you are advised to have another X ray to see whether the ulcer has healed. (page 304)

The psoriasis you've had for so long is getting worse. Your family doctor tells you to resign yourself to the fact that there is no effective treatment for this skin disease. (page 107)

You have suffered from angina pectoris for many years, and have adjusted your life-style so that you manage pretty well. Nevertheless, you are advised to have bypass surgery to prevent a heart attack and to ensure a longer life. (pages 184–185)

One of your testes has never descended into the scrotum. You are reassured that one testis is all you need. (page 267)

You have noticed a reddish black "mole" on your skin. Your family doctor says he doesn't think it is anything to worry about, but he would like to check it again in about two months. (pages 115–116)

You have had migraine for years. You are told that the only treatment is painkillers, but that the headaches will clear up when your periods finally stop. (page 000)

You have chronic asthma, which becomes worse whenever you spend any time at home with your cat. You are advised to be desensitized to the animal, and that it is not necessary to give her away. (pages 96–97)

You have poor arterial circulation in the legs and, although you have given up cigarettes and followed all the doctor's orders, the pain has begun to cripple you. You are told there is no alternative to surgery. (page 238)

Your enlarged prostate causes you to get up three or four times a night to empty your bladder. Your doctor tells you that the only solution is to have an operation. (pages 344–345)

You are a male homosexual, but have been "monogamous" for years. Recently glands in your neck have become enlarged. You are reassured that there is no risk of AIDS because you have been sexually prudent. (pages 121–124)

You have been reading about the dangers of untreated hypertension, so you have your doctor check your blood pressure. He assures you that it is only "mildly elevated," and that mild hypertension doesn't really require treatment. (pages 156–157)

Biopsy of a lump in your breast reveals it to be malignant. You're told the safest approach is to have a radical mastectomy. (pages 371–372)

You are a woman in your thirties and know that everyone considers you a "complainer." Among your problems are migraine headaches, vague chest pains and an irregular heartbeat. Your doctor has never come up with any important abnormalities and your chest X ray and ECG are also normal. He says there is nothing wrong with your heart and refers you to a psychiatrist. (pages 139–141)

Your chronic sinusitis is being treated with frequent irrigation and drainage. (page 85)

You have been treated for rheumatic heart disease for several years, and have now become pregnant for the first time. You are advised to have an abortion to avoid undue "strain" on your heart. (page 150)

Your doctor detects an aneurysm of the aorta when he examines your abdomen. You are otherwise in excellent health. Special tests reveal it to exceed 5.8 cm in size. You are advised to come back every six months for reevaluation. (pages 240–241)

You have high blood pressure. Although you've lost weight and reduced your salt intake and exercise regularly, the readings remain elevated. The medication prescribed kills your sex drive and also leaves you very tired. When you complain to your doctor about the treatment, he tells you that side effects are the lesser of two evils, because untreated hypertension causes strokes. (pages 156–157)

You are getting a little deaf and find it especially hard to make out women's voices in a crowded room. You are told this doesn't require the services of a doctor, and to go to a hearing aid store to be fitted for a hearing aid. (pages 91–92)

Your six-year-old child had a sore throat several times last year and has just had another. You are advised to have her tonsils and adenoids removed. (pages 89–90)

You are a sixty-five-year-old man and have to get up two or three times a night to empty your bladder. You suddenly develop a stuffy, running nose and are given nasal decongestants. (page 86)

You are planning a trip to Mexico. Everyone tells you to take prophylactic antibiotics to prevent "turista." (pages 335–336)

You are a great lover and have no problem with sexual desire or the ability to have an erection. You therefore conclude that the cause of your barren marriage is your wife's infertility. (pages 266–267)

You develop swelling and pain in your right leg. It is also warm to the touch. Your doctor examines the leg, says he *thinks* you have phlebitis and recommends anticoagulation. (pages 226–228)

You are chronically nervous and tired. Your doctor cannot

find a physical basis for your complaints. You finally consult a diet specialist, who diagnoses hypoglycemia. (pages 78–82)

You are twenty-three years old, single, female, and would like to go to nursing school. But you have chest pain and palpitations, and you wonder if you are strong enough. Your doctor tells you that he hears an innocent heart murmur, which has nothing to do with your symptoms. (pages 139–143)

Your child snores and is a mouth-breather. You are advised to have his adenoids removed. (pages 87–90)

Your ulcer is not responding to medical treatment, so you are advised to have psychotherapy. (pages 312–313)

It is vital to your health that you never become pregnant again. You agree to sterilization and are advised to have a hysterectomy. (pages 302–303)

In the course of a routine exam, you are advised to have a cardiac pacemaker implanted, because even though you have never had any symptoms, your slow heart rate, together with other ECG abnormalities, makes you vulnerable to cardiac arrest. (pages 204–205)

For years doctors have been unable to cure your impotence. You have read about penile prosthetic devices, but you are told that they are only gimmicks, and that no reputable urologist would have anything to do with that sort of thing. (pages 297–298)

Your teenage daughter has acne. She is told to give up all the "junk foods" that she has been eating, because acne and pimples are caused by a bad diet. (pages 111–112)

You are told you have cancer of the ovary and that it is too late for surgery because the malignancy has already spread. (page 380)

You are found to have a small malignancy of the bowel. The surgery is successful, and the tumor is entirely removed. You are advised to have follow-up chemotherapy. (page 382)

You have had recurrent vaginal bleeding. A careful exam fails to reveal the cause, so your doctor recommends that you might as well have your uterus removed. (page 302)

You are fifty-three years old and have become impotent. A routine physical exam reveals no abnormalities, and you are advised to undergo psychotherapy. (pages 294–295)

You have diverticulitis, with periodic lower abdominal

cramping, pain and fever. You are given a strict low-residue diet to follow. (pages 334–335)

You develop pain and swelling of the big toe. It turns out to be gout. In addition to medication, you are given a strict diet, eliminating all the rich foods that cause gout. (pages 404–407)

You have a "chronic" bad back. A complete work-up shows it to be due to a ruptured disc, and surgery is recommended. (page 408)

So here are forty-seven pieces of advice or information frequently given to patients by their doctor, a friend, or the media. They cover the gamut of health concerns and diseases. In every instance the "fact" or advice is either wrong, outdated or debatable—and the following pages tell you why. This is only a representative sampling of the hundreds of other options you have in the spectrum of disease prevention and management covered in this text.

I

A SECOND OPINION— WHY, WHEN AND HOW

The medical situation that generates a second opinion need not necessarily be critical. Advice concerning diagnosis or treatment may come from a variety of sources—as the following cases illustrate.

FOUR OPINIONS FOR A COMMON COLD

Suppose you are coughing, ache all over and feel pretty awful. You know that it's just a "virus," "the flu," "the grippe" or "a bad cold," but because your chest hurts when you cough, you're worried. Could it be "walking pneumonia"? And so you go to the doctor. He examines you, and then, just to be sure, insists on a chest X ray (which you'd rather not have because of the hazards of radiation). "It's only a cold," he tells you. "Here's a prescription for twenty antibiotic pills. Take four a day for five days."

The seeds for dissension have just been sown. Some doctors routinely prescribe antibiotics for virtually every upper respiratory infection. Others don't when the patient is young and healthy and the symptoms fairly mild. Most physicians, including me, do give antibiotics when the patient is over 60 years of age and/or "fragile," that is, suffering from some chronic disorder like emphysema, heart trouble, kidney disease or impaired immunity.

On your way home, armed with your prescription, you meet a friend who, you're sure, would just love to hear all about your illness. You describe your symptoms in detail. You remind him that you never get just a mild cold like everyone else—yours always seem to border on pneumonia. This one is so bad, you tell him, the doctor prescribed twenty antibiotic capsules. Your friend looks at the prescription. (This is the beginning of a second opinion.) "Wow, that's the stuff that almost killed me last year. I'm pretty sure I heard somewhere that they're planning to withdraw it from the market. Take my advice and double-check on it." You're now somewhat less confident about your doctor and his treatment, and you've begun to wonder what you're going to do about the antibiotics you've been instructed to take.

YOUR WIFE THE SPECIALIST

You arrive home coughing and sneezing and show the prescription to your wife. (You can now depend on a third opinion.) She happens to know a great deal about medicine, and first reminds you that you are and always have been a hypochondriac. She then asserts that all anyone needs for a "plain cold" is chicken soup, fluids, a few aspirin tablets and lots of extra vitamin C (of which you have been taking five tablets a day for as long as you can remember). She shows you a clipping she saved (she follows medical literature avidly) that reports recent experiments proving that vapors from chicken soup really have a beneficial effect on the lining of the nasal and bronchial tubes. In her considered and final opinion, the antibiotic is certainly not necessary. Besides which, *her* doctor never prescribes an antibiotic for a simple cold.

Let's just analyze her advice for a moment. With regard to the chicken soup, believe it or not, serious scientific papers allege that it does help alleviate the symptoms of a cold. Don't ask me how or why, but if you're going to take the soup, make sure it's steaming. Also, don't add any salt if you have high blood pressure or other cardiac problems.

Aspirin is somewhat more controversial. If the patient is a child, and there is the possibility of a viral infection like the flu, or even early chicken pox, aspirin may lead to the development of Reye's syndrome—a serious neurological disorder. If the fever is high and the patient really miserable, you may be better off with acetaminophen, better known as Tylenol. But, in any event, don't rush to reduce the fever unless it's really troublesome. An elevated temperature is one of the body's more effective ways of dealing with infectious agents. Don't squelch it unnecessarily.

Vitamin C in megadoses remains controversial. Dr. Linus Pauling insists that very high doses (and he's talking about big numbers like 30,000 to 40,000 units per day) will prevent and/or deal a knockout punch to the common cold. Most practicing doctors don't buy that, but compromise by advising you to take a little extra vitamin C, say 1,000 mg/day, at the onset of symptoms. It does appear to help somewhat, and, at least in moderate doses, is entirely safe.

Now you're torn. Everyone knows you actually wear the pants in the family, but maybe in this instance, your wife is right. You sneak upstairs and phone "Doc" at the drugstore. (Now you are soliciting your fourth opinion.) He reassures you that the particular antibiotic the doctor prescribed is not about to be withdrawn from the market as your friend had suggested. It is perfectly safe, and he sends it right over.

CHICKEN SOUP AND ANTIBIOTICS

It's now time for dinner and you have as much of a meal as your appetite permits. It includes the chicken soup, lots of tea with lemon, and ginger ale for dessert—all of which were prescribed by your wife. But what to do about the antibiotics? You keep looking at that twelve-dollar bottle of capsules sitting there, waiting to be opened. You can't return them because it's "Doc's" policy never to take back any medicine—opened or not. (I would never deal with a pharmacy that does not strictly adhere to that rule. It's worrisome enough buying "fresh" capsules, wondering if anyone's tampered with them, without having the additional anxiety that what your druggist sent you may previously have been sitting in someone else's medicine chest!) You consider all the pros and cons, and finally, apprehensively, you take one capsule. You wait around, look at your tongue in the mirror once or twice, expecting the worst—a terrible rash, hives, wheezing or diarrhea. Six hours later you find that it did you no harm, and so you take another. But just to be on the safe side, you also swallow two Tylenol and go to bed.

In the morning, after a surprisingly good sleep, you wake up feeling much better. At this point, you have to decide about the eighteen remaining, expensive antibiotic capsules. Chances are that you will do one of the following: (a) Stop the antibiotics because you believe the two you took have already cured you. This is a mistake. Even one or two days of antibiotics, let alone just a couple of capsules, makes no real impact on any infection. At best, it does no harm. At worst, it may sensitize you unnecessarily. (You will, of course, continue for several days to have chicken soup, honey, garlic, vitamin C, mustard plasters on the chest and gallons of hot tea with lemon.) (b) Take more of the antibiotics—maybe only one or two for another forty-eight hours; the four a day prescribed was probably too many for you anyway. That's also unwise. If you're going to take the antibiotics, do so for the full five to seven days. (c) Complete the antibiotic course exactly as the doctor instructed you to. If you do that, you are in the minority.

Note that your final decision, whatever it was, was determined by four opinions—and for nothing more serious than a common cold. Aside from the question of antibiotics and vitamin C, here is some practical advice about how to deal with cold symptoms. First, remember that in addition to spreading the virus by coughing and sneezing droplets into people's faces, you can, at least as easily, give your cold to anyone who handles your soiled tissues. Whenever you have wiped or blown your nose, dispose of whatever it was you used. Have a cold mist or steam vaporizer in your room to raise the humidity. With respect to "loosening" your cough, most preparations touted for that purpose are ineffective. The only possible exception is guaifenesin, and it must be taken in large doses, like two to three tablespoons four times a day. Look for this ingredient on any bottle of cough syrup available over the counter. If you want to expectorate the phlegm causing a loose cough, avoid cough suppressants and drink plenty of water. Remember, too, if you're diabetic, that most of these syrups contain sugar, so ask for one that doesn't. If you need to stop the cough, when all you've got is a dry tickle in the throat, get an over-the-counter preparation containing dextromethorphan, rather than codeine. The former is less constipating and doesn't require a prescription. If the symptoms hang on for more than forty-eight hours and the fever remains above 102°F, if you develop any pain in the chest, especially when you breathe deeply, or if you spit up bright red blood or dark brown coffee-colored material, call your doctor, not "Doc" at the drugstore.

I believe that in the next two or three years some form of interferon (a naturally occurring substance that enhances immunity) will become available for *prevention* of the common cold. Recent experiments here and in England indicate that subjects exposed to cold viruses are protected by application of interferon into the nose.

YOUR NEIGHBOR THE DIAGNOSTICIAN

Here is another iffy problem, more serious than dealing with the common cold. You develop a pain in the calf of your left leg. You look at it, then touch it. It is slightly red and tender. You hurry over to the doctor because you are afraid there may be something wrong with your circulation. (On your way to his office, you are suddenly aware of a surprising number of amputees on the street.) The doctor examines you and says you have a mild phlebitis (inflammation of the veins). He tells you not to worry, to go home, rest in bed with your leg elevated on pillows and apply warm, moist heat to the tender area.

As you get off the bus, you meet your next-door neighbor mowing the lawn. He asks why you're limping. So you tell him your troubles. It turns out he had "exactly the same thing" last year. (Second opinion developing.) But *his* doctor, who is also his friend (they play golf together every Wednesday afternoon), took better care of him that yours did of you. He rushed him directly to the hospital, ordered many tests, and prescribed anticoagulants (blood thinners) to prevent a blood clot from traveling to his lungs (embolism). "But did you actually have phlebitis?" you ask desperately. "Or was it something worse?" "What could be worse? Of course, it was phlebitis—and in the left leg too, just like you." Now you are really worried.

After a conference with your mother (the third opinion) and several phone calls to knowledgeable people, all of whom have had vein trouble at one time or another, you get so many conflicting opinions you decide to see another doctor. (Second medical, ninth opinion in all.) Your neighbor was right because this new doctor sends you to the hospital forthwith, where your leg is kept elevated and moist heat is applied. But no one gives you the anticoagulants you expected. For this, you might just as well have stayed home. Your postphlebitic friend visits you, proud and gratified that his intervention resulted in your hospitalization. But he is appalled that you are not having your blood thinned as he did. He convinces you to get yet another opinion (your third medical consultation so far) about the anticoagulants. Thank goodness you do, because your latest doctor, in fact, recommends that blood thinners be started immediately. In a few days, you come home—cured. You are told to continue the anticoagulants for several more weeks, just in case.

All's well that ends well, but now you are convinced that some doctors don't know their business—and one of them is yours. You blanch at the thought of what might have happened if you hadn't by chance met your neighbor that day. But more importantly, you're perplexed. You can understand treatment varying in different countries; for example, the French might do things their way, differently from the Italians, and both might vary from the American approach. But here you are in a large American city, examined by several different doctors in your very own community. Why are they so far apart in *their* recommendations?

In order to understand the "differences of opinion," and their significance in your case of phlebitis, you should know something about this disorder. Phlebitis of the leg is very common—and potentially serious. It is indeed an inflammation of the veins, and it can, as you were told by all the "experts" who saw you, be associated with a blood clot. That clot, if it breaks away from the vein wall to which it is attached, can travel up the body into the lungs (where it is called a pulmonary embolism) and cause serious illness or death. In fact, about 50,000 people in this country die precisely that way every year. Another 850,000 persons annually in the United States survive blood clots in their legs but suffer damage to the leg veins in which the phlebitis occurs. The inflammation leaves the veins "insufficient"—they get big and flabby and lose their tone and their ability to move the blood up the legs to the heart. The varicose veins cause the legs to become discolored, swollen and achy, with leg ulcers developing in severe cases. You actually were lucky to have a phlebitis that gave you symptoms because you could then be treated. Half the people with phlebitis don't even know they have it! Incidentally, most cases of phlebitis develop in hospitalized patients, especially those over sixty years of age, who have been lying around waiting for an operation or who have had surgery. The likelihood of this happening can be reduced in such individuals by giving them small amounts of the blood thinner (anticoagulant) heparin before, during and after surgery, and having them wear support hose as well.

Here is how I treat my own patients with phlebitis. If the involved veins are superficial, that is, on the surface of the leg where they can be seen and felt, I neither hospitalize nor anticoagulate. Why not? Because inflammation of these superficial veins very rarely causes blood clots that travel anywhere, so there's no point in thinning the blood. I do prescribe an anti-inflammatory medication like ibuprofen (Motrin), 400 mg, four to six times a day. I advise bed rest with the affected leg raised and dressed with moist hot compresses. That usually does the trick in three to five days. If the patient has varicose veins and these attacks of phlebitis recur, I have him or her see a surgeon between acute episodes in order to have the veins removed (stripped).

If the phlebitis is deep in the leg, that is, there is pain but the involved veins are not on the surface, it's potentially more serious. This is a situation that can lead to traveling blood clots. I recommend immediate admission to the hospital, where I enforce bed rest, elevation of the leg, anti-inflammatory drugs and moist hot compresses. If there is any question at all about the diagnosis, I order some special tests first. I do so when I think there is a possibility that the symptoms may not be due to phlebitis but to a bruise, injury or muscle strain. These special tests include Dopplers (sound waves) directed externally at the leg, which can often demonstrate clots within the veins. If this procedure is not revealing, dye is injected directly into the veins of the leg (venous angiogram). This is the court of last appeal as far as the diagnosis is concerned.

Once deep vein phlebitis has been confirmed, either clinically or by the venous angiogram, I then prescribe anticoagulants—first heparin by vein for several days until the pain and swelling subside, and then an oral anticoagulant like warfarin (Coumadin). When the latter drug's full effect has occurred, I stop the heparin and send the patient home on Coumadin to resume normal activities. How long the Coumadin is continued depends on several factors—the age of the patient, the presence of other varicose veins, weight and so on—but generally anywhere from six weeks to three months.

Remember that anticoagulant therapy carries with it the risk of internal bleeding, so if you see any evidence of bleeding from the gums, rectum, lungs, stomach, nose or in the urine while on Coumadin, let your doctor know immediately. Every three or four weeks you will need to have your "pro time" measured—to make sure that, like Goldilocks and the three bears, your blood isn't too thick or too thin—but just right.

The doctor who did not prescribe blood thinners for your phlebitis must have felt that it was superficial and that you were not likely to suffer a blood clot to the lungs. He judged the risk of the anticoagulants causing an internal hemorrhage to be greater than the danger of a potential embolism (especially if you happen to have high blood pressure). The second doctor wasn't sure what you had, so he sent you to the hospital, where you could be evaluated for evidence of deep phlebitis that might cause an embolism. He too must have concluded that your phlebitis was superficial because he didn't give you anticoagulants either. The last physician decided to take no chances with the embolism and prescribed anticoagulants. In my opinion he was wrong. He should not have committed you to months of anticoagulant therapy without first making sure of the diagnosis.

LIFE WITHOUT A GALLBLADDER?

This last example may also sound familiar. You have noticed recently that an hour or two after eating fatty or fried foods, you experience an uncomfortable fullness in your "stomach" and are getting rid of enormous amounts of gas one way or another. The discomfort actually borders on pain. You finally consult the really good doctor who gave you the anticoagulants for the phlebitis. He listens to your symptoms, examines you and orders a gallbladder X ray. The verdict? Bad news—gallstones. "What do I do now, Doctor?" "We'd better make arrangements to have that gallbladder removed." "The whole gallbladder? Why not just the stones?" you ask innocently, wondering how one can live without a gallbladder. "Don't be ridiculous. We don't take the stones out and leave the gallbladder," he answers, obviously irritated by your stupidity. (Well, that will teach you to ask him medical questions in the future.) You are now intimidated, but still curious; why not just the stones? But you leave his office, all set to have the operation he suggested.

You now have visions of yourself in the operating room with the anesthesia mask over your face (you've always had a secret fear of blurting out something embarrassing as they put you to sleep). And you think of the pain, the tubes in your nose and needles in your veins, the stitches, the scars, the works—if you ever wake up, that is.

UNCLE PHIL TO THE RESCUE

When you finally get home, everyone can see that something terrible has happened to you—even though you're very brave and say nothing. A little later, you casually ask whether Aunt Millie didn't die from a gallbladder operation. Everyone pounces on you. They insist on knowing what's wrong. You finally break down and divulge the bad news. Luckily, Uncle Philip is there for dinner. He is the family medical expert, because he once thought of becoming a doctor himself. (He actually ended up as a shoe salesman but never did lose his interest in medicine.) "A gallbladder operation? Just like that? Ridiculous! No one gets operated for gallstones anymore. Don't you know there are pills you can take to dissolve them?" (A semiprofessional second opinion, but a strong one.) You wonder why your doctor didn't tell you about this great advance. Is it possible that Uncle Phil knows more than someone with an M.D. degree?

You go to bed disquieted, and toss and turn all night. The few winks of sleep you get are filled with nightmares—your surgeon is an impostor; the orderly taking care of you after the operation is a homicidal maniac; worst of all, your health insurance has expired and the hospital bill amounts to $10,000.

GOOD NEWS: THE DOCTOR'S OUT

In the morning, you call your doctor and are relieved when his secretary tells you he is not in. You are embarrassed to admit that you checked on him with Uncle Phil, and you certainly don't want him to know that you are planning to get another opinion. So you leave a message for him to hold off with the arrangements for surgery for the time being. You concoct some story about needing time to get your affairs in order, and you say you will get back to him in a few days. Then you arrange to see a consultant (second medical opinion). He listens to your story and asks to see the gallbladder X rays taken yesterday. Since you were too timid to request them from the first doctor, another study has to be done. In order to spare you the additional radiation, the consultant orders a gallbladder sonogram (sound waves are directed into the gallbladder; if any stones are present, echoes are bounced back and the stones can be easily recognized). In your case the presence of stones is confirmed. But this second physician, obviously more experienced, tells you that an operation is definitely not necessary at this time and prescribes a low-fat diet. He also advises you to forget about Uncle Phil's new medicine, the one that dissolves gallstones, because it hasn't been around very long, doesn't work in every case, and may give you side effects worse than the operation itself. You can't get over your good luck in finding this great doctor, and you conclude that he must be right.

The doctor who recommended surgery for your gallstones may have felt that you would ultimately need the operation anyway, and he preferred to do it now, when you were younger, otherwise healthy and better able to tolerate it than you might be in the future. (He should have answered your question "Why not remove just the stones?" by telling you that a gallbladder with stones in it is diseased and will simply keep making more until it is removed.) The physician who suggested that you hold off on the operation preferred to give you the benefit of the doubt, hoping that you would fall into the substantial category of patients in whom gallbladder symptoms clear up and never recur. Both points of view are perfectly legitimate. Which one you choose to follow depends on a host of personal considerations (for a more detailed account of all your options, see Chapter 23).

WHOM CAN YOU TRUST?

If you were the same person who in succession had the cold, phlebitis, and gallstones, you would now really be disillusioned, wouldn't you? Whom can you trust when you get sick? It seems that every doctor offers different advice each time something goes wrong. In this case, most of the doctors consulted for each of the problems were essentially correct. As a matter of fact, so was Uncle Phil. But the advice followed by the patient was, in the final analysis, a very personal decision. The important point is that one needs to know the options.

SECOND OPINIONS THAT MADE A DIFFERENCE

The hypothetical cases described above should not leave you with the impression that alternative treatment approaches for any given disease are always only a matter of preference (yours or the doctor's), and that it makes no real difference in the long run how your case is managed. There are times when the first opinion may well be wrong and when a correct one can, in fact, mean the difference between success and failure—even life and death. The following examples from my own experience illustrate this point.

AN "OBVIOUS" CASE OF CORONARY ARTERY DISEASE

Some years ago a colleague asked me to see a fifty-seven-year-old man for whom the diagnosis was not clear and the results of treatment unsatisfactory. The patient's major complaint was that he tired very easily and became unduly short of breath when walking quickly or climbing stairs. I listened carefully to the description of the symptoms and examined the man very carefully, but I could not find very much wrong. The electrocardiogram, however, was definitely abnormal. I concluded, as had the family doctor, that the patient had mild coronary disease. There wasn't much more I could do but make some minor changes in the dosage of the medications prescribed. I also suggested how to modify his life-style.

The patient accepted my findings and recommendations with some disappointment. After a few weeks, when it was clear that he was no better, *he* asked for a *third* opinion. The case was reviewed by another cardiologist, who disagreed with the diagnosis of coronary artery disease. He suggested instead that the patient had constrictive pericarditis—that is, formation of a thick, fibrous band around the heart. This is usually the result of a viral infection or an inflammation of the pericardium, the normally thin envelope of tissue surrounding the heart. The constriction prevents the heart from expanding fully, causing a decrease in its output of blood. This patient's symptoms were due to this diminished cardiac efficiency. The electrocardiographic abnormalities that I interpreted as being due to coronary artery disease were the result of pericarditis. It may not be easy to differentiate one condition from the other. A simple operative procedure released the band around the heart and the man returned almost immediately to a normal, active life. His electrocardiogram also became normal.

What lesson is to be learned from this particular case?

First, that if you are feeling poorly and one consultant can't help you, don't stop there. You must continue to look for help until you find it, especially when the diagnosis is vague. This man's health surely would have deteriorated slowly and insidiously if the right diagnosis had not been made and the proper treatment instituted. He knew enough to ask for another opinion, and his doctors cooperated willingly—two important ingredients for effective medical care.

THINK (AND ASK) TWICE
BEFORE YOU RETIRE

A few years ago a seventy-six-year-old man came to me for a "heart checkup." Thirty years or so earlier, in the course of a routine examination by his doctor, he was shocked to hear that his electrocardiogram was abnormal. What's more, he was assured that sometime in the past he must have suffered a heart attack. The news stunned and puzzled him, because he simply could not recall any symptoms that even remotely suggested heart trouble. Since the ECG was "diagnostic," it was concluded that his heart attack must have been "silent," as happens in about 25 percent of cases. Since he was relatively young and the electrocardiogram definitely abnormal, his doctor advised him to "take it easy." (This was thirty years ago, when we had a very different understanding and outlook on heart disease.) When the patient asked for specific advice, in particular, should he retire, the answer was "yes, if you can afford it." Fearful of the next heart attack (to which he was obviously vulnerable) and in order to prevent it, he decided to sell his factory. He ended up, however, retiring not only from business, but from life itself. He began to spend his time just sitting at home feeling sorry for himself. He walked, talked and acted like an old man. He also became impotent because of his fear of dying during sexual intercourse.

The man came to see me because his own doctor, to whom he had gone regularly, had retired from practice. He did not doubt the original diagnosis, but wanted to be reassured that in the interval since his last examination he had not sustained another silent heart seizure.

In listening to his history, I could not elicit any symptoms to suggest there was anything wrong with his heart. He had no chest pain or pressure, no unusual shortness of breath and no palpitations. Then I recorded an electrocardiogram. Now it was my turn to be surprised. I found no evidence whatsoever of any previous heart attack. Instead I saw a pattern called WPW (named after the cardiologists who first described it—Wolff, Parkinson and White). This is a variation in the form of the tracing that makes it *look* abnormal but which, in fact, in no way indicates cardiac damage. It is an electrical artifact, a freak of nature, a variant—something with which one is born and which does not per se shorten the life span. The bad news this man had been given thirty years earlier was based on an incorrect interpretation of an electrocardiogram! If he had sought a second opinion at that time, he might have been spared all his subsequent sorrow and suffering.

Remember that as newer diagnostic medical techniques become available—echocardiography, CT scanning, nuclear and magnetic resonance imaging, cardiac Dopplers, PET scanning and the like—more and more doctors may be using them before they are expert in their interpretation. Undergoing a sophisticated, expensive new test is no guarantee that the result you get will be accurate. All the more reason to ask for another opinion, especially when the news is unexpected or bad.

A "HOPELESS" CASE
WITH A HAPPY ENDING

Let me tell you about one more experience to help me make my point. The wife of one of my doctor friends developed severe headaches and attacks of double vision. She consulted a senior neurologist, who, after thorough testing, discovered a brain tumor. The patient asked for and was told the diagnosis. She was advised that surgery was not possible, and her only alternative was radiation, which would shrink the tumor somewhat and alleviate the headaches, but would not cure her. This gallant woman settled her affairs and prepared to live out her last few months in the greatest possible comfort. Her husband, the doctor, knew better than to "shop around" for another opinion. This was, after all, an open-and-shut case confirmed by an eminent brain specialist. But the patient was persuaded by a nonmedical friend to see someone else. Reluctantly she consulted another equally prestigious neurosurgeon, who agreed with the diagnosis, but not with the treatment or outlook. He recommended an operation. With nothing to lose, my friend underwent surgery, which, happily, was entirely successful. After removal of the large tumor pressing on her brain, her symptoms disappeared and she returned to a normal life in a few weeks. That was twenty years ago.

2

PATIENT CARE VERSUS DOCTOR EGO

THE SYSTEM AND THE INDIVIDUAL PATIENT

We are justifiably proud of the excellent doctors, hospitals and medical care available in the United States. These stem from our research capacity, technological skill and system of medical education. The extent to which this excellence will be maintained in future years, given our current preoccupation with "cost effectiveness" and our priority for saving money rather than lives, remains to be seen. But, in any event, high national standards are not always reflected in the kind of care an individual patient receives from any one doctor for a specific illness. Correct diagnosis and treatment depend on *your* particular physician's awareness of the latest medical findings relevant to *your* specific problem.

Every physician has a hard time keeping up with all there is to know—that's why we specialize and perhaps *overspecialize*. Furthermore, doctors are busy and chronically overworked. There simply isn't the time to attend all the important conferences where critical new information about the management of your particular disease may be disseminated. And reading the medical literature conscientiously at home may not be enough either. The lapse between when an important discovery is made and its appearance in the professional journals may often be as long as a year or more. It is entirely possible that some other doctor has the answer to your problem, and can make life a lot easier (and longer) for you. So when you are in a difficult medical situation, never hesitate to ask for the extra input of a second opinion.

The purpose of this book, insofar as it educates the lay public, is to strengthen the traditional doctor-patient relationship, which is so essential to good medical care and is the cornerstone of American medicine. But that relationship must be sound, open and healthy enough to withstand your asking for consultation when necessary.

ALL MEN (AND DOCTORS) ARE NOT CREATED EQUAL

You may occasionally find yourself in a critical medical situation in which the proper decision requires not only up-to-date knowledge and technology, but particularly good judgment and experience as well. A famous surgeon once said he could teach any student in a matter of weeks *how* to perform an operation. But to learn *when* to do it takes years. There is a wide spectrum of such skill, training, judgment and experience within the medical profession. Most patients either are not aware of this reality or fail to act on it. They may accept the first decision that comes along as final and binding, which sometimes results in tragedy.

LOYALTY OR THE FEAR OF RETRIBUTION

Why, then, despite the fact that some physicians know more than others, or have better training, judgment and experience, do so many patients still hesitate to ask for a second opinion when it is really needed? Fear. They pretend that it is because of affection or personal loyalty to the doctor. "I wouldn't want to offend (insult, hurt, anger) him," is how they rationalize it—and that is what they probably believe. However, in most cases, the truth is that they are afraid of losing his goodwill. They want to make sure that the next time they are sick, they won't get the cold shoulder instead of immediate attention.

Many doctors (usually the better ones) welcome requests for consultation and, in fact, often initiate the process themselves (especially when they are faced with a complicated problem or when things aren't going well). Also, in recent years, with the threat of malpractice suits hanging over their heads, more and more doctors, including some notorious prima donnas, actually welcome sharing the responsibility of a major decision. Their egos may not appreciate your apparent lack of confidence in asking for a second opinion, but don't worry. They'll never let on.

However, a patient's fear of "retribution" is sometimes justified, because there are doctors who make it quite clear that they believe a second opinion is unnecessary and that your request is an insult to them. So there will be times when, in order to avoid an unpleasant confrontation and a compromised relationship with your doctor (and its attendant consequences on your medical care), you may end up consulting someone else surreptitiously. I remember one man who was sorry he did. He had suffered from severe angina pectoris and consulted me after his own cardiologist had recommended an immediate coronary bypass operation. I advised him to try certain medications first. He asked me to convey my opinion and findings to his doctor, which I did. It was all open and aboveboard. A few weeks later, the patient developed severe chest pain during the night and called his physician, who refused to make a house call, on the grounds that "I'm not Dr. Rosenfeld's errand boy." He was offended that this man had asked for and accepted an opinion other than his own. In my experience, such "colleagues" represent a minority and should not deter you from doing what's right.

HOW TO ASK FOR A SECOND OPINION

Well then, supposing you've decided to solicit a second opinion. How should you go about it? First of all, avoid timidity and subterfuge. Tell your doctor what you plan to do and why. Don't have him learn at second hand that you have been to someone else. Then ask *him* to recommend the consultant. Patients often come to their doctor requesting that he consult with a particular specialist. It may be that their doctor doesn't think this man or woman is likely to be of help, in which case he won't be happy conferring with him. So let *your doctor* choose the consultant. Patients are sometimes leery about doing it that way. They believe the second doctor may be in cahoots with the first and rubber-stamp whatever his friend says. If that's something you are worried about, then by all means, make a clean break with your doctor and start over again elsewhere. Frankly, in my experience, I have rarely encountered a physician who agreed with a colleague whom he believed to be wrong.

Despite the foregoing, there will be occasions when *you* should insist on choosing the consultant rather than having your doctor do it. If you live in a small community, or one in which medical opinion is homogeneous, and you know that there exists an entirely different school of thought about how to approach your particular problem, don't hesitate to make your own arrangements. A good example is the treatment of cancer of the breast. As you will see later in these pages, there is a legitimate and very important debate about how best to deal with a localized malignant breast lump. Some specialists still insist on an extensive surgical procedure, others prefer a more limited operation, and some even recommend radiation without any cutting at all. The matter remains in flux. Data supporting each technique are still being accumulated. If *all* the doctors in your area agree on one approach, go elsewhere so that you can at least hear the other side of the story. You deserve to know what choices you have.

If your request for another opinion is turned down just because your physician objects on *principle* to having someone else in, it is time to change doctors. *In the final analysis, what medicine is all about is patient care, not doctor ego.* Should you decide to switch, be candid about it. Ask to have your complete record forwarded to your new doctor so that you won't need to repeat all the tests that you have already been through. Doctors must by law comply with such requests.

WHEN TWO DOCTORS DISAGREE

You may now wonder, "What do I do if the second opinion differs from the first? When do I ask for a third opinion? Whose advice do I finally take?" These are difficult questions to answer in the abstract. If you can't choose between two divergent recommendations, and don't know instinctively which is the better for you, then you will need to consult a final arbiter. It's a nuisance, of course, but far better than submitting to treatment that is unnecessary or wrong. Simply having been made aware that an important difference of opinion exists gives you an option, and *you* may end up having to make the final decision. That's sometimes the best way.

A word of caution at this point. Just as there are patients who take several One-A-Day vitamins every morning, because "if one is good, ten must be better," so are there individuals who are convinced that one can never have too many opinions about an illness. They spend their time and money soliciting as many consultations as they can. They do so not because of any conflict in the advice they've been given, but because no one has yet told them what they want to hear. Once they get the opinion they were looking for all along, they discontinue the search.

HOLY SURGERY

That kind of behavior is not only time-consuming and expensive, but can also be dangerous. I remember one man who consulted me because of recurring attacks of chest pain, shortness of breath and loss of consciousness. I found that the trouble lay in a severely diseased heart valve that, in my judgment, needed replacement. The patient panicked at this advice and asked to be seen by another cardiologist at my hospital. The consultant agreed with my recommendations. The patient then suggested that perhaps a specialist from another center might have a different viewpoint. In order to satisfy him, I arranged for yet another doctor to review the case. He too concurred in the need for surgery. At this point, my patient, who was deeply religious, called upon his pastor for an opinion. I don't know how the clergy make their decisions in such situations, but he advised this man not to have the operation during the next fourteen days. After that, it would be perfectly safe for him to do so.

I was delighted that the matter was now settled. In order to protect the patient, I kept him in the hospital for the prescribed two weeks while awaiting surgery. When the time had passed, my man changed his mind again and now asked to be discharged so that he could think it all over "a little more." He left my care, and finally found a physician who told him the operation was not only too risky but also unnecessary. Six weeks later, the patient died suddenly, as I feared he might. He was only sixty-eight years old, and his operative risk was less than 5 percent. This man had gone from doctor to doctor until he finally found one who told him not to have an operation—the opinion he wanted all along.

3

THE THYROID GLAND— REGULATING YOUR THERMOSTAT

THE HONEST BROKER

The thyroid has an extremely important job to do, setting the energy level of the body. It is a straightforward, honest, aboveboard gland. It sits right there in the front of your neck and, as long as it is "well," remains invisible. When something does go wrong, it is generally apparent (unlike other organs or structures that, hidden deep in the brain, chest or abdomen, make it necessary for us to call in the heavy diagnostic artillery when trouble develops). If the gland enlarges, for whatever reason, it is usually obvious. When it becomes inflamed it hurts, and you can easily identify the source of the pain; if it develops a tumor, the lump may be discernible right under your fingers or your doctor's; when it isn't working properly—that is, when it is making too much of its hormone or too little—the thyroid signals both to you and to your doctor that something is awry. Treatment of any malfunction is usually straightforward and successful, and that even includes cancer, which in the thyroid gland is uncommon, almost always slow-growing and usually curable.

BUT YOU HAVE TO LISTEN

So, in every respect—location, appearance and symptoms—the thyroid does not often hide what is going on. But it does ask in return that you pay attention to what it is trying to tell you, and act accordingly. Despite its good intentions, the thyroid's messages are sometimes so subtle they are either missed or misinterpreted. Treatment of the various diseases that affect it is also occasionally controversial. Under those circumstances, a second opinion may be desirable—as you will see below.

SETTING YOUR THERMOSTAT

Think of the thyroid gland as the thermostat controlling your body's energy level and requirements. This regulation is effected by a hormone that is produced in the thyroid gland and then released into the bloodstream. When the gland is healthy, it makes just enough to keep you functioning on an even keel. But sometimes it produces too much, in which event your body's "engine" is revving too fast, or it may make too little so your motor is barely chugging along. And these variations in the amount of hormone secreted by the thyroid gland are translated into recognizable, diagnosable and treatable disorders.

But the amount of hormone produced depends not only on the condition of the thyroid itself, but on its interaction with two other glands situated in the brain—the pituitary and the hypothalamus. The thyroid and these two "associates" are constantly exchanging chemical and nervous signals. When everything is in balance, precisely the right quantity of hormone is manufactured and released into the bloodstream. This level is in large part responsible for your energy, appearance and the pace at which you live.

There are several common disorders of the thyroid gland with which you should be familiar. These include *hypothyroidism* (when the gland produces too little hormone); *hyperthyroidism* (when it makes too much); *goiter* (a swelling of the gland that is more commonly found in women); and *lumps* or tumors of the thyroid itself, most of which are benign, but some are cancerous.

WHEN THERE'S NOT ENOUGH HORMONE

There are several circumstances in which the thyroid gland drops its hormone production. This can happen when some disease process affects the gland itself, so that it is unable to make the hormone. Or, the gland may actually be intact, but the chemical signals from the pituitary in the brain, which normally tell it to make hormone, are faulty. In either event, the thyroid does not produce enough hormone to keep you functioning properly.

Thyroid function can be impaired by some medications taken for a totally unrelated condition. For example, there is a relatively new drug called amiodarone prescribed for the treatment of serious heart rhythm abnormalities. It causes the thyroid gland to produce less of its hormone. So do lithium (an excellent agent in the treatment of certain psychiatric disorders) and iodides (found in various cough prescriptions), when taken for long periods of time. Always check your medicine chest whenever any new diagnosis is presented to you, just to make sure one disease is not being caused by the treatment of another. Finally, some infants are born with hypothyroidism, usually because of some genetic error. Here, immediate diagnosis and treatment are essential; otherwise, permanent brain damage may result from the low thyroid function.

There are specific blood tests your doctor can obtain to differentiate primary thyroid failure (trouble in the gland itself) from secondary (when it's not getting the proper messages).

When the amount of hormone produced is very low, anyone can recognize the resulting symptoms. If the condition has been present for a long time, the patient may be overweight, but not the jolly, lively, full-of-fun Santa Claus kind of fat with rosy cheeks and a glint in the eye. The individual is "sick" fat—dull and constipated. The skin is sallow, with a lemon tint, and it's dry and rough. There is little or no perspiration. The voice is hoarse and low-pitched, and speech is slow. In women the menstrual flow is heavy, and becoming pregnant is apt to be difficult. The hands are puffy, and so is the face, especially around the eyelids. Hypothyroid individuals are likely to be less alert than those around them and are often hard of hearing; they are always tired, and tend to sleep a great deal. They are usually too apathetic to complain, but when they do, it frequently is about the cold weather. They are also often depressed, and for good reason. Life isn't much fun. Although thyroid underfunction occurs in both sexes, it is more common in women than men.

SEX IS OKAY, BUT FRANKLY, THEY WOULD RATHER SLEEP

That's the picture of classic hypothyroidism (*myxedema*), in which the amount of circulating thyroid hormone is quite low and has been for some time. But when the deficiency is mild, and the patient has only a little less thyroid than normal, the evidence can be very subtle. Many such individuals go through life undiagnosed and untreated. The skin tends to be dry, despite abundant use of cream and oil; the hair is coarse and comes out in bunches when washed and brushed. These individuals are always tired; they lack energy, need lots of sleep, dress a little more warmly than everyone else, don't like air conditioning (but love the hot weather), and dream secretly of moving to a warm climate some day. They would never admit it to anyone, but although sex is okay when they get around to it, frankly, both men and women would rather sleep. When the condition is finally diagnosed, the difference a little thyroid pill makes is incredible.

If your doctor listens to your story, looks at you, examines you, and decides that you may be hypothyroid, he can easily confirm his clinical impression by a few simple tests that measure the amount of thyroid hormone circulating in the blood. In hypothyroidism this level is lower than it should be. This triggers a chain of other abnormal tests, because virtually every organ and function of the body, fueled by thyroid hormone, is operating at reduced capacity—much like a "brown-out" in an energy crisis. So, in long-standing disease we often find evidence of anemia (because bone marrow production of red blood cells is sluggish); the cholesterol is high (because there is not enough thyroid hormone to "burn it off"); the waves or complexes in the electrocardiogram are not as tall as they should be and the heart rate is slow; the chest X ray often demonstrates a swollen heart, with excessive fluid in the pericardial sac that surrounds it; the electroencephalogram (brain wave test) is abnormal too. When the doctor strikes the knees with his little hammer, the jerk response is sluggish, not brisk. At the ankle, the tendon reflex is slow, a particularly useful test.

THYROID HORMONE IS NOT A VITAMIN

When the diagnosis of hypothyroidism is made, replacing the missing hormone with a couple of pills every day is all that's usually needed. The other side of the coin is that too many people are being given thyroid supplements unnecessarily. The problem is that many of the symptoms of mild hypothyroidism occur in a host of other, unrelated states, including simple boredom, depression, nutritional anemia and gluttony. So there is a temptation and tendency to diagnose someone with these complaints as hypothyroid *without documentation.* Thyroid hormone is then prescribed to the naturally fat, slow, cold and dull among us, in order to "perk them up." Unless there is a genuine need for replacement therapy, giving such people thyroid does no good, and may be harmful.

I do, however, believe there is a gray area. Some persons with mild underfunction of the thyroid gland nevertheless have normal laboratory values. If that is what your doctor suspects, he may give you a small dose of thyroid for several weeks or months—just to see if it helps—and sometimes it does. But remember that thyroid hormone is not a harmless vitamin supplement or tonic. When taken by the wrong people for the wrong reasons (that is, by those who are not truly hypothyroid), even ordinary doses are not without danger. If you've got enough of your own thyroid, supplements can make you nervous and irritable, give you a rapid and sometimes irregular heartbeat, and cause weight loss. If you are elderly and have high blood pressure or an underlying heart condition, unnecessary thyroid hormone prescribed to make you "feel better" can create serious problems. I have seen many patients subjected to all kinds of complicated tests to explain their palpitations, nervousness and weight loss, because they didn't tell the doctor that they were taking "just a little thyroid"—and he didn't think to ask. So it is a good idea, whenever you are prescribed thyroid hormone, to request the evidence on which the treatment is based. If the data seem vague or casual, ask for a second opinion.

FEEDBACK SIGNALS TO THE GLAND

Extra thyroid hormone taken by mouth for whatever reason results in a higher level in the bloodstream, and the thyroid gland then receives a signal to make less. After all, why should the gland keep working to make its hormone, when you are swallowing in pill form all that the body needs—and more—every morning? But then, having been turned off for a while, the gland, now accustomed to working less hard, becomes sluggish. When that happens, if you abruptly stop taking the extraneous supply, you may be hypothyroid for a while, until normal glandular function is restored.

If you are being treated for hypothyroidism, you may find that you're getting a different kind of thyroid hormone pill than some of your friends. This is often simply a matter of variation in trade names. The same active ingredient is often marketed under different names. In that case, one tablet is as effective as another. But there are actually several different *forms* of thyroid replacement, and one may be better for you than others in certain circumstances.

The three main forms of thyroid replacement therapy are *dessicated thyroid*, usually extracted from the thyroid glands of animals, and two different synthetic forms. One of these is marketed as Cytomel, the other as Synthroid or Levothroid. All three do the job, but they do vary in certain ways. For example, dessicated thyroid is the least expensive and you'll usually need about 2 grains a day. I'm not aware of any advantage in taking the more expensive Cytomel, though many doctors do continue to prescribe it. My own preference among the three is Synthroid because this synthetic form most closely resembles the kind of thyroid hormone your own gland makes. Most of my patients take 0.2 mg per day.

Here's a very important warning. If you're told you need thyroid hormone and are young and otherwise healthy, it may be safe to start with the full replacement dose right off the bat. *But*, if you're older, and especially if you have some kind of heart trouble, like angina pectoris, you should build up to the required dose gradually, by small increments every two to four weeks. Doing it any faster can worsen your heart condition.

How do you know when you're taking enough thyroid? If you needed it in the first place, you'll feel a whole lot better. You can tell if you're taking too much because you'll feel nervous and irritable, develop insomnia and note that your heart beats too forcefully or rapidly, or irregularly.

HYPERTHYROIDISM—TOO MANY RPMs

When there is too much thyroid hormone in your system, because the gland is overproducing it, you may present the typical picture—nervous, can't sit still; always complaining of the heat, perspiring when everyone else is shivering; having more frequent bowel movements; losing weight despite a ravenous appetite; and finding it difficult to get to sleep. When you stick out your tongue or outstretch your hands, they have a fine tremor. Your palms are hot and wet. Chances are that palpitations due to a rapid, sometimes irregular heart action brought you to the doctor. Or you may have unexplained muscular pain or weakness. In women, the menstrual flow is very much reduced, and conception may be difficult. And even though the body motor is highly "revved," the desire for sex is usually reduced. In fact, I have occasionally seen breast enlargement in men with overactive thyroid glands. Occasionally friends will tell you that your eyes look more prominent, or even bulge, and you may notice double vision because your ocular muscles are weakened by hyperthyroidism.

WHEN THE SYMPTOMS ARE SUBTLE

The foregoing describes the patient in whom overactivity of the thyroid gland is obvious. Often, however, as in hypothyroidism, the picture is subtle, especially in older persons.

They may simply be "nervous" or irritable and report unexplained weight loss despite eating well. They may complain of palpitations or develop heart failure. Because they are old, these symptoms may be interpreted as evidence of heart disease. After all, aren't the elderly entitled to a little heart trouble? So the possibility of thyroid overactivity may be overlooked and untreated. *If you suddenly and for no discernible reason develop "heart failure," or your angina worsens, make sure to ask your doctor whether your thyroid function has been checked.*

The hyperactive thyroid gland is almost always enlarged to some extent, either diffusely or with one or more discrete lumps or nodules in it. Such nodules, when they occur, may function independently of the rest of the thyroid and produce excessive amounts of hormone all by themselves.

WHEN YOU JUST DON'T GET OVER AN EMOTIONAL SHOCK

Hyperthyroidism occurs most frequently in women between the ages of thirty and forty. We don't understand what causes it—probably some breakdown in the immune-control mechanisms of the body. I have seen it develop after a severe emotional crisis. The husband of one of my patients was convicted of tax fraud and sent to jail. Her shame, sadness and guilt were immense. Shortly thereafter, she began to lose weight and suffer palpitations. She thought these symptoms were a typical reaction to stress. She finally consulted me because she had lost some fifty pounds, and was continuing to do so even after her husband's release from prison. By the time I saw her, the diagnosis was obvious. Other women in my practice developed hyperthyroidism after the death of a child or a spouse; in one elderly woman symptoms occurred after she was mugged and robbed. So if you've become "nervous" in response to a crisis, and remained that way long after it was over, see to it that your thyroid function is evaluated before your symptoms are attributed to psychiatric problems.

Patients with mitral valve prolapse (see page 139) are also said to be more prone to becoming hyperthyroid. So if your panic attacks and forceful heartbeat suddenly (or even grad-ually) become worse, think of hyperthyroidism superimposed on your chronic valve condition.

JUST FOLLOWING ORDERS

Doctors do not always agree about the best way to suppress exaggerated thyroid function. Unlike hypothyroidism, where we simply replace the amount of hormone you are lacking, treating an overactive gland may present difficulties because the problem may not lie in the thyroid itself. At least in the beginning, the gland appears to be the victim of some disor-der in the immune system that stimulates it to make more hormone than it should. The actual command for it to over-produce comes from the brain, which secretes increased amounts of stimulating hormones. Since we don't know how to attack the underlying disorder, we vent our therapeutic fury on the thyroid gland, which is only responding to abnor-mal signals from a "higher authority." The goal of treatment is to get the thyroid to ignore these signals or render it unable to respond to them.

There are three basic methods of "cooling off" the hy-peractive gland. None, however, really gets to the root cause, but all of them do reduce the amount of hormone produced and thus control the symptoms. Whereas hypothyroidism can easily be treated by an internist, I advise you to consult a thyroid specialist for the management of hyperthyroidism. The three totally different forms of antithyroid therapy are (1) surgery (removing a substantial portion of the gland), (2) radioactive iodine (which permanently destroys functioning thyroid tissue), and (3) medications to suppress glandular activity.

SUPPRESSING THE OVERACTIVE GLAND

Treating hyperthyroidism with an antithyroid drug (propyl-thiouracil or methimazole) blocks formation of the hormone within the thyroid gland. In other words, the gland is no longer able to respond to the inappropriate signal that whips it into frenzied overproduction. But even as the drug suppresses the gland, some doctors actually give you a little thyroid hormone to make sure that you maintain *some* function.

Antithyroid drugs are probably the most desirable treatment for hyperthyroid women in the childbearing age (usually under thirty) in whom the disease is of recent onset and mild, and the gland is only slightly enlarged. If you fall into this category and any other form of therapy is suggested, get another opinion. These agents may be expected to effect a cure in about 35 percent of such cases. (The response to this medication is better when the thyroid is very large and of irregular consistency.) While waiting for the action of the drug to take effect, your symptoms, if severe, can be controlled by one of the beta-blockers like Inderal (propranolol, see page 178).

The two most commonly used antithyroid drugs (methimazole, propylthiouracil) are generally well tolerated, but may occasionally cause a rash, itching of the skin, or, more importantly, depression of white blood cell formation in the bone marrow. You should be monitored for this possibility if you are taking either of these drugs. These complications virtually always clear up when the drug is changed or stopped.

Antithyroid drug therapy is usually continued for a year to eighteen months. It is then stopped and thyroid function is assessed to see whether it will remain normal after the drug is withheld. There is some new evidence that a whole year of treatment may not be necessary, that if the propylthiouracil is stopped as soon as your gland begins to function normally—usually after several weeks or months—the cure rate is just as high as if you had continued it for a year. So if you are told to take the drug for a full twelve months or longer, ask whether this time can't be shortened.

In the majority of patients, the gland bounces right back to the overactive state after the propylthiouracil is stopped. Should that happen, you will need either radioactive iodine or surgery. Both these techniques virtually guarantee a cure, but in so doing, destroy most or all of the thyroid gland permanently—one by radioactivity, the other by the scalpel. You should be aware of the risks and benefits of both methods of treatment.

THE CASE FOR AND
AGAINST RADIOACTIVITY

There are more than 700,000 Americans who have had their hyperactive thyroid treated with radioactive iodine. It is the most popular form of therapy and works in the following way. Iodine introduced into the body, in whatever form, ends up in the thyroid. So, to get any radioactive material into the hyperthyroid gland in order to destroy it, we render some iodine radioactive and have you drink a measured amount of it. The solution itself is without taste, odor, or color—just like ordinary water. The iodine is absorbed and goes directly to the thyroid, where the radioactivity starts to destroy the overactive gland. One drink usually does the trick within a few weeks, but sometimes two or more doses are needed. This form of treatment is clean, safe and effective. It avoids the need for taking antithyroid drugs three times a day for months (which has only a 35 percent cure rate under optimal circumstances). It also spares you the pain, risk and complications of surgery.

THE EXACT RADIOACTIVE
DOSE—AN ESTIMATE

One of the complications of radioactive iodine is that in attacking the hyperfunctioning gland, it leaves some 40 to 70 percent of patients hypothyroid within ten years. It is very difficult to calculate the exact amount necessary to control the overactive gland and still not render it underactive. So be prepared to become hypothyroid after being treated this way. If and when that happens, you will need replacement hormone. That simply means taking thyroid supplement for the rest of your life—not a terrible prospect.

WHEN YOU'RE PREGNANT
OR UNDER THIRTY

Why not treat every hyperthyroid patient in this way? More and more doctors are actually doing so, with two exceptions—

pregnant women and those under thirty. We don't want to give a big dose of radioactivity to an expectant mother, because it crosses the placenta and destroys the thyroid gland of the unborn fetus too. Even if you're not pregnant, but still in the childbearing years, there is at least the theoretical possibility that the radioactivity may alter your genes in some way so as to affect a future pregnancy. There is also the matter of potential malignancy occurring later in life. As far as I know, the administration of radioactive iodine has never been proven to cause any kind of cancer. However, the suspicion exists that it can, so in order to be safe, such treatment is usually withheld from young persons of either sex.

THE PROS AND CONS OF SURGERY

All of which brings me to the pros and cons of removing the overactive thyroid gland surgically. This procedure is most widely performed in children, in adults under forty years of age and in pregnant women who have not responded to drug treatment (which may safely be given during the first seven months). None of the above should normally receive radioactive iodine for the reasons I mentioned earlier. It is not safe to have the operation while the gland is very "hot," because the surgical manipulation at that time can worsen the condition. We used to pretreat such patients with antithyroid drugs for a few weeks before surgery. We now simply give them a beta-blocker (Inderal) for a few days, and then operate.

Every patient considering thyroid surgery should have a second opinion for a very special reason—one that not every surgeon will discuss with you. Thyroidectomy is not an easy operation. It requires skill and experience to avoid several important possible complications. When I was a medical student and resident, before the widespread use of radioactive iodine for the treatment of hyperthyroidism, surgical residents did scores of these procedures every year. By the time they finished their training, they were really skilled at it. However, over 700,000 patients who would otherwise have had their thyroids removed surgically have since received radioiodine instead. Today, a surgeon-in-training may do two or three thyroidectomies a year, hardly enough to give him the necessary skill. So be sure to determine how much experience the doctor has had *in this particular operation* before you let him operate. You can do that by asking him directly, or better still, letting your internist find out.

COMPLICATIONS OF THYROID SURGERY

The risk of dying from thyroid surgery is minimal, except when the patient is very sick or old (in which case the radioactive iodine method is preferable anyway). But surgery may lead to complications short of death. If too much of the gland is removed, you will be left hypothyroid (but less frequently than after radioactive iodine). The incidence is about 15 to 20 percent in the first year and 2 percent every year thereafter. A more important danger is that the surgeon may inadvertently cut a nerve very close to the thyroid gland that supplies the vocal cords. Should that happen, you will be hoarse forever. Also, the four parathyroid glands, which control calcium and bone metabolism, may be removed by mistake, since they are very small and are situated near the thyroid gland. In that event, you will require treatment for underfunction of the parathyroid glands for the rest of your life. Finally, there is the risk of hemorrhage during the operation, because of the many blood vessels in the area. For all these reasons, the operation is considered delicate. Be sure to pick the right surgeon.

So which form of therapy should you choose? First, discuss all three with your doctor. In most cases you'll agree on the decision. Personally, my first choice is radioactive iodine for anyone over thirty years. For pregnant women in the first seven months I recommend antithyroid drugs, and propylthiouracil is my preference. Any later in the pregnancy, or if the medical treatment doesn't work, an operation is in order. If the gland is very large, surgery may be your best bet right off the bat.

WHEN THE EYES HAVE IT

There is one important exception to my earlier statement that any malfunction of the thyroid gland can be treated successfully. About 15 percent of patients with hyperthyroidism have bulging or protruding eyes, a complication that often poses more than just cosmetic problems. It can cause damage to the eyeball or the optic nerve itself—which happens from time to time—seriously affecting vision. Unlike the other symptoms of an overactive thyroid gland, the prominent eyes are caused not by excessive thyroid hormone, but by some other process that is not well understood. So treating the thyroid gland has no direct effect on the eyes, although they do tend to improve or stabilize somewhat when the hyperthyroidism is controlled.

THE IMPACT OF IODIZED SALT

Suppose you were born and raised before the days of iodized salt in an area where the soil, and consequently the food you ate, was deficient in iodine (the Great Lakes region in the northern United States, the mountainous areas of the Andes and the Himalayas). Since iodine is the major constituent of thyroid hormone, when the body does not get enough of it, the gland produces less hormone. You would think this would cause it to shrink. The reverse is true. In fact, the gland gets bigger and bigger as its cells work harder to make as much hormone as they can with less of the raw material (iodine) than they need. The result is a goiter—an enlarged and lumpy thyroid gland that may or may not produce extra hormone. When it does, it's called a "toxic goiter"; when it doesn't, it is "nontoxic."

WHO'S GOT THE GOITER

A goiter may appear during puberty and pregnancy, when the body's demand for thyroid hormone is increased. Certain drugs called goitrogens (examples are lithium, widely used in the treatment of manic-depressive states, and some of the oral antidiabetic drugs) may also cause goiters.

WHEN TO HAVE THE GOITER REMOVED

Most goiters are nontoxic—that is, they do not make extra hormone and so produce no biological symptoms. But they must nevertheless be carefully watched since a small proportion do gradually become hyperthyroid (for reasons that are not understood). Patients sometimes want the excess goiter tissue removed for cosmetic reasons. Also, the goiter may have to be excised if it becomes so large as to compress nearby structures, causing coughing, hoarseness and difficulty in swallowing. But remember, a goiter is rarely malignant. You should have it operated on only if its appearance disturbs you, if you suffer pressure symptoms from it or possibly because it's toxic. If surgery is recommended for any other reason, ask for a second opinion from an endocrinologist.

THYROID TUMORS—
BAD AND NOT SO BAD

Various kinds of growths or nodules are very common in the thyroid gland, and may be present in 40 percent of Americans. Most are asymptomatic. When a thyroid lump appears, we want to make certain it is neither frankly malignant nor potentially so. This is done first by a careful history-taking: Has the lump been increasing in size over a short period of time? (an ominous piece of information); Did you sometime in the past receive radiation to your neck for some reason or other—like for treatment of acne? (lumps in such patients are more likely to be malignant); Do other members of your family have a history of cancer of the thyroid or of any other "hormone-producing" gland? (you're more vulnerable to have a malignancy if it runs in the family). An appropriate work-up might include a radioactive scan of the thyroid gland. You drink a *tracer* amount of radioactive iodine, which is picked up by the gland; the gland is then outlined when scanned by a Geiger counter. If the nodule in question does not absorb radioactivity, we call it "cold"; if it does, it is referred to as "hot." Hot nodules are almost never malignant; cold nodules may be or become so later on in about 10 percent of cases. Hot nodules are treated with thyroid pills or, in some cases, with radioactive iodine.

We now use sonar techniques to help differentiate cancerous from noncancerous, cold thyroid nodules. Those that appear to be solid when the sound waves are directed at them are more likely to be malignant than those in which the growth is *cystic*—that is, containing pockets of fluid. But this distinction is not always reliable. So to be absolutely certain of the diagnosis, discuss the feasibility of getting a needle aspiration of the lump. This has an accuracy of 85 to 90 percent, but must be done by a trained, experienced physician. Together with the history and other tests, it usually provides the final answer. Incidentally, the chances of a single nodule being malignant are greater in men than in women or the young. The presence of more than one lump reduces the chance of malignancy. If, without a thorough evaluation, you are either reassured about a nodule in your gland and told to leave it alone *or* advised to have it surgically removed, ask for a second opinion from a thyroid specialist.

WHEN TO REMOVE THE COLD NODULE

You may be advised to have a cold nodule excised even if all tests are negative, especially if there is a family history of thyroid cancer. But this operation is rarely an emergency, since most thyroid cancers grow very slowly. If, under close observation, the nodule doesn't get any bigger for months or years, many specialists prefer to leave it alone. However, we almost always take it out in children; when it appears to be growing rapidly; if the patient has had previous radiation to the head or neck; when the nodule is so big that it causes pressure symptoms; and in men under 40 years of age.

YOUR FRIENDLY THYROID CANCER

If you do turn out to have thyroid cancer, don't panic. First, have the diagnosis evaluated by a thyroid specialist, because such cancer is rare. Then, if it is confirmed, be reassured by the fact that thyroid cancer is an infrequent cause of death in the United States. Years ago patients with such malignancies were subjected to extensive surgical procedures. A good part of the neck, its muscles, even the jaw, were removed. That is hardly ever done anymore. Almost all cases can be cured or controlled by excision only of the tumor itself and any involved glands in the area. This is followed by suppressive doses of thyroid hormone for life, in order to prevent recurrence.

I remember a very dramatic case some thirty years ago. The patient was a beautiful woman of twenty-one. In the course of a routine examination, I detected what felt suspiciously like cancer on the side of her neck—a hard, irregular, painless lump stuck to the surrounding tissues. I referred her to a surgeon, who removed the lymph gland. Under the microscope, it was seen to contain highly malignant-looking tissue. When a cancer grows wildly, it distorts the cells from which it originated so that the pathologist may have difficulty deciding whence it came. Hers was such a tumor. A thorough search of the body—the liver, the intestinal tract, the skin, the bone marrow—failed to reveal any malignancy. We suspected that it originated in the adjacent thyroid gland, but were unable to feel anything suspicious in it.

The problem we now faced was how to treat this woman, having removed a gland with a malignancy whose origin we didn't know. Several surgeons recommended a radical dissection operation. This would have meant a horrendous, disfiguring procedure—the removal of most of the jaw, as well as a search for and excision of any involved glands elsewhere in the neck.

We decided to wait for further evidence of tumor spread before doing any operation. It was my own feeling that since the abnormal lymph gland we had excised and examined already represented spread of the tumor, it probably was seeded elsewhere, and extensive surgery now would be too late anyway to make a difference. And so we waited for the next evidence of the cancer's metastasis. Thirty years later, we are still waiting, but my patient isn't. She has since had two children and remains totally free of any disease whatsoever. If she had gone to Lourdes, we would now be talking about a miracle. If she had been given laetrile, it would have represented a "cure."

Although we never did find the source of the malignant lymph gland, I suspect that it was a thyroid cancer that had involved only one lymph gland and had not spread. This woman's story represents one of the medical mysteries that we encounter from time to time, but it also attests to the rather benign course of some cases of "malignant" thyroid cancer. And, incidentally, we never did anything to the thyroid itself. The gland is still sitting there, with no evidence of any disease whatsoever within it.

KEY FACTS TO REMEMBER

Thyroid gland disorders are very common. Although their diagnosis and treatment are usually straightforward, subtle manifestation may go unrecognized. This is especially true when the gland is *sluggish*. Simple replacement of the deficient thyroid hormone will correct the symptoms of hypothyroidism. However, taking thyroid pills for fatigue and lack of energy when function of the gland is actually normal is of no benefit and not without risk.

Treatment of an *overactive* gland may be complicated, and can be done in one of three different ways—antithyroid drugs, radioactive iodine and surgery. Selecting the right one for you is crucial. You should always have a second opinion from an endocrinologist, particularly one specializing in thyroid disease, before the final choice of therapy is made. If the gland is to be removed surgically, make sure of the surgeon's skill in this particular, delicate operation.

Lumps, or *nodules*, of the thyroid gland are of several different kinds. Some are potentially malignant. Always make sure, when told that yours is or is not, that the conclusion is based on an adequate evaluation.

Thyroid cancer is uncommon, is usually slow-growing, responds to treatment, and is not often a threat to life. Proper recognition and therapy are, nevertheless, very important. The joint efforts of an endocrinologist and an *oncologist* (cancer specialist) should be obtained if you are given that diagnosis.

4

CATARACTS—
A DISORDER OF THE
YOUNG AND THE OLD

ON A HAPPY DAY,
YOU CAN SEE FOREVER

I remember, many years ago, long before I became a doctor, reading an interview given by Winston Churchill. In it, he marveled at the fact that he was "getting younger," as evidenced by a sudden ability to read fine print without glasses. I couldn't understand this "miracle" at the time, but I felt that it couldn't happen to a nicer person. Then, not long ago, one of my friends, a vigorous man in his early seventies, married a beautiful young woman. Everything appeared to be standing up to the challenges of the age difference between them. One day, in a particularly happy frame of mind, the elderly bridegroom confided to me. "Doctor," he said, "never discourage a spring-winter marriage. It has great advantages for both partners. Many women prefer older men because of their experience, stability and wisdom." (He didn't even mention money.) "As far as I am concerned, it has made me feel years younger. I know you won't believe this, but I'm rejuvenated in every respect."

At this point, I expected a discussion of his born-again sex life; I was surprised when he continued, "The most striking change of all is in my vision. I can now actually read fine print, like the phone book or the stock market quotations in the newspaper, without wearing my reading glasses." He paused, awaiting my reaction to this incredible news, certain that I would challenge it. I didn't, because although I couldn't vouch for the vigor of some of his other functions, the story of his improved vision came as no surprise. I had learned a great deal since Churchill's announcement years earlier.

This happy phenomenon is not at all, in fact, evidence of rejuvenation. Quite the contrary. The improvement of near vision described by my friend is unfortunately only temporary and usually occurs in elderly persons who were far-sighted (presbyopic) to begin with. Often referred to as "second sight," it reflects the development of myopia (shortsightedness) due to early cataract formation. As the cataract forms, the natural lens in the eye becomes more permeable and absorbs water. This thickens it and changes its shape, so that it now bends the rays of light more acutely, making the patient nearsighted (myopic). Because the degree of farsightedness is reduced by this change in refraction, near vision is improved for a while. But you can't have it both ways—it also causes increased blurring of distant vision (something my patient in his euphoria did not notice). After a relatively brief period of stability, eyesight begins to deteriorate as the cataract continues to expand.

CHANCES ARE YOU'LL HAVE THEM TOO

Although cataracts affect mostly older people (their removal is the most commonly performed surgical procedure among Medicare patients in the United States), they do occur in younger persons as well. At any given time, there are some three million Americans who have impaired vision due to cataracts. Eye doctors perform almost 500,000 operations every year to extract them. So there is a good chance that this disorder either has already affected you or will at some time in the future.

IS YOUR EYE DOCTOR UP TO DATE?

If you have a cataract, it is important to know your treatment options. In recent years, there has been major progress in eye surgery and its postoperative management. It is critical that you be able to judge whether you are being offered the best of the new procedures available. Unfortunately, not every eye specialist is trained to perform some of the more modern techniques. It is entirely possible that a doctor will suggest an older method in the name of conservatism, when the real reason is his lack of skill or experience with the newer approaches.

IT'S LIKE BOILING
THE WHITE OF AN EGG

Let me review briefly what a cataract is, how it forms and the various methods of dealing with it. The lens within your eye works very much like the one in your camera. It focuses the rays of light that strike it on the retina in the back of the eye. Here specialized cells gather this information and transmit it, via the optic nerve, directly to the brain, where the image is interpreted as the object you see. If the area of the brain making this visual interpretation is damaged, you are not able to see even if the rest of the visual apparatus—the lens, retina and optic nerve—are working perfectly. Conversely, if the brain is intact but the lens through which the light passes becomes cloudy, or if the optic nerve, which transmits the signal to the brain, is damaged, you will be visually impaired.

The normal lens is clear and transparent; but certain chemicals, diseases, infections, and injuries can render it opaque. When this happens, you have a cataract. A good analogy can be made with the white of an egg, which, like your lens, is made of protein. Raw egg white is clear and transparent. After boiling, the protein becomes cloudy. That is what happens to the natural lens of your eye when it develops a cataract; you can no more see through the full-blown, or "ripe," cataract than you can through the white of a boiled egg.

WHY CATARACTS DEVELOP

As mentioned earlier, this change in the transparency of the lens is not limited to the elderly. Anyone at any age can develop cataracts from a variety of causes—injury, radiation, infections, genetic disorders, certain diseases like diabetes mellitus, chronic exposure to infrared rays, or as a result of several different medications, notably cortisone in large amounts. However, three quarters of all cataracts occur in those over sixty-five years of age. About 20 percent of persons between the ages of forty and sixty-five have them. They may also develop in the newborn and in children. I won't discuss the mechanisms of cataract formation in the very young, because that is a complicated process. Suffice it to say that they are usually the result of some toxic effect, nutritional deficiency, injury, or infection in the mother during pregnancy (e.g., German measles). In adults, the most common cause of cataract formation is what we call "senile" degeneration.

Whatever the mechanism, a developing cataract will cause the gradual and, usually, painless deterioration of your eyesight. You may find yourself always looking for a better light by which to read, or you may keep cleaning your glasses because they frequently seem to be getting "fogged up." You may feel as if there is a veil covering your eyes, and you try to rub it away. You may notice that driving your car at night has become more difficult because the oncoming headlights cause an uncomfortable glare or halo. (This latter symptom is due to the fact that when the light rays hit the cloudy lens, they are scattered instead of passing through to the retina as they do when the lens is transparent.)

SEEING BETTER IN THE DARK

The extent and kind of visual impairment and its severity really depend on how opaque the lens has become and which portions of it are involved. For example, some patients with cataracts may actually see better in dim than in bright light. This happens when most of the lens is normal except for the central portion directly behind the pupil. Since the pupils constrict in bright light, if the clouding of the lens happens to be located mostly behind the pupil, you will have trouble seeing when illumination is good. But when it is dim, the pupils open wider, allowing more light to hit that part of the lens that is unaffected, thus improving your vision.

POOR VISION? NOT NECESSARILY CATARACTS

Just because you can't see or read as well as you used to doesn't necessarily mean that you are developing cataracts. You may simply need to have your glasses changed. Occasionally, a gradual decrease in vision is due to glaucoma, which, if untreated, can result in permanent blindness. Or your doctor may come up with other causes for impaired vision, the most important of which is vascular (blood vessel) changes in the eyes, especially common in diabetics or persons with macular degeneration—a change that entails loss of vision in the elderly. In the last few years, laser beam therapy for these latter two disorders has either arrested or slowed the deterioration of vision or actually improved it. In any event, everyone over fifty years should have his or her eyes checked once a year. The earlier the diagnosis of any disease is made, including those affecting the eyes, the better the outlook.

If the ophthalmologist does find evidence of early cataract formation, he will want to reexamine your eyes at regular intervals to see how rapidly it is progressing. Some patients with slow-growing cataracts can avoid surgery for years simply with new glasses from time to time. Unlike glaucoma, there are no drops or medications that can improve failing eyesight due to cataracts. There have been some recent reports suggesting that aspirin started early in life and taken regularly thereafter may help prevent lens clouding later in life. If you are cataract-prone or have early cataract formation, it may be a good idea to start taking aspirin if it is otherwise safe for you to do so. On the other hand, if you are beginning to develop a cataract you should probably avoid L-tryptophan. This naturally occurring amino acid (protein) promoted as a non-narcotic sleeping aid and obtainable without prescription in health food stores may accelerate cataract formation. If you have eliminated such causes of cataracts as toxic chemicals and chronic exposure to ultraviolet radiation, then there is essentially nothing else that you or your doctor can do to influence the speed with which your lens becomes cloudy.

WHEN TO HAVE YOUR CATARACT REMOVED

Unlike many situations involving surgery in which you have no say about the timing of the operation, *the timing of cataract surgery is almost always up to you.* Cataract surgery is rarely an emergency, except in some instances when the cataract has completely matured. In this circumstance the eye may become inflamed or develop acute glaucoma, mandating emergency lens removal. But in almost every other instance, you should have the operation when *you* think you need it. Age is not a factor.

I have found that patients usually decide to undergo surgery when their life-style is compromised by poor vision—for example, the surgeon who can no longer see well enough to operate, the executive who has trouble making out charts or other data, or the retired person who can no longer watch TV or read.

YOUR SURGICAL OPTIONS

Let's suppose, then, that you can't see the numbers on the bus or read the menu in a restaurant and changing your eyeglasses doesn't help anymore. Or you cannot drive a car with confidence, and driving is essential to your livelihood. It is clearly time to have the cataract out. The operation is simple and safe, and it results in restored vision in about 95 percent of cases. But there are certain facts you must know about the operation and what to expect after it is done.

Cataract surgery basically involves getting rid of the cloudy lens. The capsule that surrounds it may also be removed (intracapsular cataract extraction), or a portion at the very back of the lens may be left behind (extracapsular cataract extraction). Both procedures can be performed under either general or local anesthesia, and now require no more than an overnight stay in the hospital.

Another way of removing the cataract is by phako-emulsification (*phako* is derived from the Greek word for

56

"lens"). A needlelike ultrasonic probe is inserted through the pupil into the cloudy lens. It vibrates at forty thousand cycles a second, breaking up the lens and emulsifying it into a liquid, which is then sucked out by the same needle. The procedure is simple, provided that your doctor knows how to do it. You can usually go home the same or the next day and resume your normal activities. This ultrasonic method can be performed in about 80 percent of cases and is preferred for most patients. In the remaining 20 percent, the lens is so thick that it can't be completely broken up by the sound waves and so must be extracted in toto, the intracapsular way. *Discuss with your doctor how he plans to remove your cataract before it is done.* If he chooses not to use phako-emulsification, find out why. If you are not satisfied with the reason, by all means ask for another opinion.

Whichever technique is used, if you have two dense cataracts, they are removed one at a time, with an interval of several months. The reason is obvious. You want to be sure the first operation was a success before proceeding with the second. The poorer eye is always done first, leaving you the better one while the corrected eye is recovering.

REPLACING THE LENS

Let's assume that you have had the surgery and no longer have an eye lens of your own. You are obviously going to need something to focus the rays of light on the back of your eye. At this point you have three basically different options. Choosing the right one is important.

The oldest and, by today's standards, the least desirable lens replacement technique is spectacles. People so treated are easily recognizable as they walk about precariously holding on for support, peering through their heavy, thick eyeglasses. With such spectacles, the image from the affected eye appears to the brain to be 30 percent larger than it actually is. This degree of distortion results in double vision if only one eye has been fixed, and instability with poor balance even if both eyes are using the spectacles.

CONTACT LENSES—YOU NEED A STEADY HAND

Your natural lens can also be replaced by a contact lens, which, if you can tolerate it, is preferable to the thick spectacles of yesteryear, because it gives much better vision, with only about 6 percent distortion. However, a contact lens, especially the "hard" variety, can cause pain and irritation, especially in patients with dry eyes or abnormality of the eyelids. Newer long-wearing soft lenses represent a major advance in this field. They can be left in the eye for several weeks or months, then removed, cleaned and replaced. However, hard or soft, the fact that every contact lens does have to be taken out from time to time may constitute a serious drawback, especially for the elderly, whose coordination is less than perfect and whose hands may tremble or be unsteady. But when the contact lenses can be left in place and tolerated for several months, the doctor can remove them and clean them for the patient.

A word of caution about these extended wear lenses. They are occasionally vulnerable to changes in the environment that cause them to lose some of their water content. This, in turn, may result in damage to the eye because the fit of the lens may become too tight. Situations that may predispose to such complications are frequent long flights (the air in a plane is dry), hair dryers blowing into the eye and strong winds. Chronic use of antihistamines by persons with allergies can also cause drying of these extended wear lenses. The important thing to remember is this: If your eyes begin to itch, burn, hurt or become obviously inflamed, remove the lens and/or see your eye doctor right away.

THE INTRAOCULAR LENS: WHY THE CONTROVERSY?

We come now to the best technique of all—the plastic lens that is inserted in the eye at the time of operation and simply left there—permanently. It is not a contact lens. Despite its many obvious advantages, the intraocular lens was frequently associated with serious complications early in its development. Many patients required re-operation, some several times. The lens often became the site of infection, causing irritation and inflammation; it then had to be removed, occasionally resulting in the loss of the eye. In short, it could be a mess. These complications were due to a combination of inadequate surgical technique, poor lens design and inferior quality control. Some devices were sold with sharp edges; others fell apart in the eye after they were implanted; a few were contaminated and incompletely sterilized in the manufacturing process. Add to this the fact that there were doctors who, in their rush to compete, took crash courses in how to insert the lens, and you had the perfect setup for the early disastrous results. But things have greatly improved. For example, there is now much better quality control in the manufacturing process. Indeed, your main concern presently should be the skill of the surgeon implanting the lens. Fortunately, fewer doctors are learning to perform the operation at weekend courses in some motel (the "Holiday Inn" diploma). Properly done, the success rate of this operation is currently 90 to 95 percent. For this reason, a panel of distinguished eye specialists at the National Eye Institute has concluded that intraocular lenses have "significant visual advantages" over the other techniques and their use is "almost as safe as extraction of the cataract alone."

THE BATTLE OF BRITAIN AND THE LENS

How the intraocular lens came about is a particularly fascinating story. During the Battle of Britain, several Allied pilots were injured when bullets shattered their plastic windshields, sending splinters into their eyes. One particularly astute English ophthalmologist noted that these tiny fragments did not seem to irritate the eye, and could often be left alone without causing symptoms. Years later, during a routine cataract operation, one of his assistants commented how wonderful it would be if there were some way to replace the natural lens with a translucent, artificial one that the eye would not reject. The ophthalmologist remembered his wartime observations and set about trying to find such a material. Although his initial results were unsuccessful, a Dutch eye specialist followed through with the idea and succeeded in creating the prototype of the lens in use today.

ARE YOU A CANDIDATE FOR THE INTRAOCULAR LENS?

Intraocular lenses are not suitable for everyone. Here are the current guidelines to which you should refer if you are offered this form of treatment: Think twice about accepting an implanted lens (a) if you are under sixty years of age (because we don't yet know how long the lens will last); (b) if you have only one potentially good eye (if anything goes wrong with the lens, you've had it); (c) if you have eye disease due to diabetes; (d) if you have ever had a detached retina; or (e) if you suffer from glaucoma. There are occasional exceptions to these recommendations, but the final decision requires an expert, and that is whom you should have advising you in this situation.

FIRST JAPANESE, THEN RUSSIAN AND NOW AMERICAN—BUT WILL IT WORK?

As long as we're talking about eye operations, here's another one which may be recommended to you—and for which you should definitely get a second opinion. It goes by the name of *radial keratotomy*.

This is a surgical treatment for myopia, or nearsightedness. The usual way of dealing with this eye disorder is corrective lenses. However, some thirty years ago a Japanese eye doctor thought that he could correct this condition by operating on the eye, thus sparing people the trouble of wearing glasses. Despite the fact that within ten years of this surgery, almost all of Dr. Sato's patients required corneal transplants to prevent blindness, a Russian ophthalmologist seized on the basic Japanese idea and devised a different surgical approach. Under local anesthesia, he made a series of eight to sixteen cuts through the cornea, thus flattening the central part of the eyeball and reducing the degree of myopia.

It wasn't long before eye specialists in this country and elsewhere began refining this procedure, and making it available to persons with myopia. The purpose? To eliminate the need for eyeglasses or contact lenses. And it caught the public's "eye." So much so that the National Eye Institute sponsored a five-year clinical study known as PERK (prospective evaluation of radial keratotomy) in eight eye centers across the country. They followed exact guidelines and surgical techniques to evaluate the procedure objectively. This is what they concluded. Radial keratotomy is effective in most cases. Sometimes it works too well, so that after a while persons who started off myopic become farsighted instead. In other words, the operation may replace one kind of visual abnormality with another.

What's my personal opinion about radial keratotomy? I don't normally recommend it to my patients. If the procedure is suggested to you, get a second opinion.

KEY FACTS TO REMEMBER

Over 500,000 cataract operations are performed each year in the United States. There are now several newer and simpler surgical techniques that you should know about. It may be worth your while to get a second opinion from another ophthalmologist as to how your cataract should be removed.

The timing of cataract surgery should almost always be up to the patient. It is rarely an emergency; it needs to be done only when the patient's vision is so impaired that it interferes with his or her life-style. But remember, cataract formation is only one cause of deteriorating eyesight.

After the diseased lens of the eye is removed, it must be replaced in some manner—by thick spectacles (the least satisfactory method), by contact lenses (better, but sometimes difficult to put in and take out), or by lenses implanted within the eye at the time of surgery. The latter technique requires special skill and precautions. If you are over sixty years of age and need cataract surgery, ask for a second opinion from an eye doctor, whichever lens is offered to you.

Radial keratotomy, an operation for the correction of short-sightedness, is now widely available. When successful, it eliminates the need for eyeglasses or lenses. Many physicians remain leery about this procedure, and questions have been raised about its long-term consequences. Do not accept this procedure on blind faith. Get a second opinion.

5

DIABETES MELLITUS—
WHEN LIFE IS TOO SWEET

Diabetes is a condition characterized by too much sugar in the blood (hyperglycemia). What a simple definition for a disease whose causes, symptoms, complications and treatment are so complicated! Despite all the diabetics among us (one out of four Americans is an actual or potential diabetic, or a "carrier"—and the incidence is increasing by almost 10 percent every year), there are still a great many popular and important misconceptions about this disorder. You should know what they are because for every diagnosed diabetic in this country, there is one person who has the disease and is unaware of it. And even if you are not among the ten million known diabetic Americans, you may be one of the many who will develop the disease in their lifetime. Should that happen, chances are you will be faced with some important decisions for which a second opinion will be in your best interest.

INSULIN—THE KEY TO DIABETES

Sugar and protein in the diet are absorbed from the digestive tract, enter the circulation and raise the glucose (sugar) level in the blood. When that happens, a signal is conveyed to the pancreas, an organ situated deep in the abdomen at about the level of the belly button. The pancreas contains several different kinds of cells, one of which, the beta cell, produces insulin. In nondiabetic individuals, within minutes after receiving the news that there is some extra sugar around, these pancreatic beta cells release extra insulin into the bloodstream. This hormone then gets to work, making sure the newly arrived sugar is properly utilized. It converts some of it to energy for immediate use and deposits the rest into various organs (including the liver) for storage. Normally, insulin interacts with virtually every tissue in the body, ensuring that sugar removed from the circulation is optimally utilized.

THE DIFFERENT FACES OF DIABETES—THE CHILDHOOD OR INSULIN-DEPENDENT VARIETY

For many years, diabetes was thought to be one disease, resulting simply from a deficiency of insulin and hence too much "useless" sugar. We now know that there are at least two kinds of diabetes. *Insulin-dependent diabetes* usually begins in childhood. As compared to the adult-onset type, it is more serious and difficult to control. It is often complicated by premature "hardening of the arteries" in virtually every organ of the body—the eye (blindness), brain (stroke), heart (heart attacks), legs (gangrene, ulcers), kidneys (kidney failure). It can lead to infections and is frequently associated with high blood pressure. For all these reasons, "juvenile" diabetes may cause disability and/or death at an early age.

Insulin-dependent diabetes is virtually always due to some trouble with the pancreas. We are not sure what goes wrong. Some researchers think that this organ is damaged by a virus or some toxic agent. Others believe that diabetes is one of those mysterious disorders that we call "autoimmune" in origin. The infection, injury and insult theories all seem quite credible when we realize that only 11 percent of juvenile diabetics have a parent with this disorder. (In 85 percent of the adult-onset cases, one or both parents have the disease.)

Regardless of the underlying causes, almost every child with diabetes requires insulin. There's no second opinion needed about that.

ADULT-ONSET (NON-INSULIN-DEPENDENT) DIABETES—LIKE BECOMING GRAY

Patients who develop diabetes later in life (and that's ten times more common than onset in childhood) also have too much inert, unusable sugar and may develop the same symptoms as the juvenile diabetic. There are, however, several important differences between the two. The insulin deficiency in adults is probably not due to actual disease or destruction of the cells in the pancreas that make it, but rather to their "wearing out," much as one gets gray with age. Interestingly enough, some adult-onset diabetics who are overweight have lots of insulin in their blood—but appear to be resistant to it. Perhaps this is because the necessary interaction between insulin and sugar can take place only in certain designated cells of the body that contain "insulin receptors." But these receptors also attract fat, and they can accommodate only fat *or* insulin. So, in obese patients, the fat gets to the receptors first, leaving the insulin to float around with nowhere to go, unable to break down the sugar. That is why, even though 10 percent of adult diabetics do require insulin, the remaining 90 percent, especially those who are fat, need only to lose weight, reduce their alcohol intake and avoid concentrated sweets in order to keep their blood sugar normal. In fact, in such persons, insulin may be relatively ineffective.

COMPLICATIONS OF DIABETES

The other major difference between insulin-dependent and non-insulin-dependent diabetes is the severity and nature of their respective complications. Why these two types, in both of which there is too much unavailable sugar, react so differently is anyone's guess. In the youngster, despite every attempt to normalize the blood-sugar level with a proper balance between insulin dosage and diet, the ravages of arteriosclerosis seem inexorable and involve the small arteries of the eyes and kidneys especially. The nerves too may become involved. That is why diabetics often develop pain, numbness and weakness in various parts of the body, especially the legs.

Although adult-onset diabetics are not immune to the complications of diabetes (they have a 100 percent greater incidence of arteriosclerosis than do nondiabetics), most do attain a normal life span, especially if preventive measures are practiced. For example, if you are fifty and have just been found to have diabetes, you are less likely to develop a vascular problem (like a heart attack or stroke) if you lose weight, stop smoking, keep your blood pressure normal and get plenty of exercise. I have many diabetic patients in their seventies and eighties who are in excellent health. Even those who need insulin may have no significant symptoms of arteriosclerosis. One man, a doctor, now eighty-one years old, doesn't even need glasses.

DIABETES—FACT AND FANCY

The first myth about diabetes is that insulin, discovered in 1921, cures it. While insulin is necessary for the well-being of many diabetics, especially pregnant women and children, it is not a cure. We need no better proof of this than the fact that diabetes, with its complications, remains the third leading cause of death in this country (after heart disease and cancer). It is responsible for about three hundred thousand deaths each year, reducing life expectancy among its victims by one third. The second mistaken assumption is that diabetes is one disease—that like a rose, "diabetes is diabetes is diabetes." As indicated above, juvenile, or insulin-dependent, diabetes is not the same entity as the kind that has its onset in adult life. Not only is its treatment different, but its complications and the outlook for its victims are not the same. The third fallacy is that people who like sweets and indulge in them to excess are likely to become diabetic. What you eat has nothing to do with *causing* the disease—the wrong food can only make it worse once you already have it. Finally, there are still those who believe that everyone with diabetes is condemned forever to a stark, sparse, boring diet and destined to take insulin for life. The truth is that most diabetics may now eat virtually what they wish, provided they avoid sugar—and only one in ten adults with the disorder ever needs insulin.

GETTING THE NEWS IS NOT SWEET

Most people learn that they are diabetic when the doctor finds "too much" sugar in their blood. That news may come as a big shock, especially if, as happens so often, it is discovered in the course of a routine examination and there have been no symptoms whatsoever. On the other hand, you may suddenly develop the classic symptoms of the disease— excessive thirst, frequency of urination, weight loss and, in women, vaginal itching.

But before accepting the diagnosis of diabetes, make certain that both you and your doctor are aware of any "water pills" (diuretics) you may be taking, or oral contraceptives or pentamidine (used in the treatment of some forms of AIDS), all of which may spuriously elevate the blood sugar. A variety of other diseases can do so too, as may, in fact, any severe illness or infection, such as a heart attack or stroke. (That's the reason we don't usually measure blood sugar during such catastrophic events.)

WHAT'S WRONG WITH HAVING TOO MUCH SUGAR?

Sugar is the basic fuel that provides the energy required for all body functions—from the beat of the heart to the thought processes of the brain. However, to make that energy available, the sugar molecule must be broken down and get out of the bloodstream and into the cells. When this doesn't happen, for one reason or another (either because the pancreas isn't making enough insulin or the insulin is not working effectively), you are left with a lot of sugar just floating in the blood not doing you any good. The body then tries to eliminate it. The main way to do this is via the urine. But since the kidneys can't excrete sugar in lump form, the body must provide enough water to dilute or dissolve it in order to flush it out. The net result of all of this is that you find yourself spending more and more time in the bathroom (voiding the sugar) and at the water tap (drinking the needed extra water). That's why the cardinal signs of untreated diabetes are frequent urination and great thirst. In women, urine that is rich in sugar provides a good medium for the growth of fungus; this often results in vaginal fungus infections—hence the vaginal itching. As the volume of urine increases, so does the excretion of other substances normally retained by the kidney (for example, potassium). Finally, dehydration sets in, and, as you will see in a moment, coma.

WHEN FAT SUBSTITUTES FOR SUGAR

What alternatives does the body have when all its sugar is useless because it can't be broken down for energy? It turns to its fat stores, breaks *them* down and melts them away, accounting for another major symptom of untreated diabetes—weight loss. And when fat reserves are exhausted, protein is the next to go.

When the body utilizes fat instead of sugar for its energy needs, the end products of such abnormal fat metabolism (ketones) appear in the urine—and that's a sign of trouble. So diabetics test their urine not only to see how much sugar has been excreted by the kidneys, but also to determine if ketones are present. Finding them means that treatment must be adjusted or changed, that insulin is required or that, if it is already being used, its dosage is inadequate. When ketones are present in the blood in excessive amounts, they are toxic, sometimes literally poisonous, and may eventually render you unconscious.

TREATMENT OF DIABETES— A MATTER OF CONTROVERSY

The treatment of diabetes remains a subject of some controversy. Remember that a second opinion may differ totally from the first, not necessarily on the merits of the case, but because the physicians involved happen to subscribe to opposite schools of thought. More about that later.

INSULIN—WHEN AND WHY

Before the discovery of insulin in the 1920s, we had nothing to offer the diabetic but dietary advice. This was not enough to protect the juvenile patient from diabetic coma and death—which usually occurred within two years after the onset of the disease. When insulin became available, it was initially given to everybody with a high blood-sugar level, regardless of symptoms or the presence or absence of ketones. Such therapy prevented coma deaths in the insulin-dependent diabetic, but didn't do very much for adult-onset, non-insulin-dependent diabetics. The child, in whom there is so little natural insulin available, must receive it by injection in order to minimize the breakdown of fat. On the other hand, the diabetic adult can often be managed by diet and weight loss alone. So, if you are middle-aged, are found to have diabetes and are given insulin despite the fact that you have no symptoms, ask for a second opinion.

PILLS AGAINST DIABETES —GOOD OR BAD?

Some years ago, the observation was made that certain *oral* medications, chemically related to the sulfa drugs, could reduce blood-sugar levels. These agents were not effective substitutes for insulin in young diabetics, but were initially prescribed for almost everybody else with high blood sugar, the assumption being that such "normalization" was necessary and good for you—no matter how it was achieved. But a group of diabetologists decided to see just how beneficial these sugar-lowering pills really were. To almost everybody's surprise, it turned out that diabetics treated with tolbutamide (Orinase)—the preparation available at that time—didn't do all that well. In fact, the oral medication seemed to result in a greater number of deaths from heart disease than was the case when treatment consisted of insulin, placebo or diet alone. There was no apparent explanation for this adverse effect, which was thought to be due to some fatal disturbance of heart rhythm.

These findings by the University Group Diabetes Program (UGDP) touched off a controversy that continues to this day. There are many experts who hold that from a statistical viewpoint the study was poorly designed, that its conclusions are invalid and that the oral antidiabetic medications are very useful. Other doctors and statisticians believe that the oral antidiabetic agents really are dangerous. The U.S. Food and Drug Administration takes a position in support of the UGDP study, and has mandated that these medications carry a label stating that their use may be hazardous to your health.

WHERE DOES YOUR DOCTOR STAND ON THE ISSUE—AND WHERE DO I?

It is important for you to know your own doctor's position in this controversy. If he accepts the conclusions of the UGDP study, he is not likely to prescribe oral antidiabetic agents for you except under very special circumstances. For example, if after following a strict diet you are still thirsty, losing weight and have ketones in your urine, he may decide to give these drugs a try before starting insulin. If for some reason you cannot administer your own insulin and have no one to do it for you, he may reluctantly have you try the oral agents. But he will almost always first attempt to reduce your blood sugar by diet alone.

On the other hand, if your doctor believes the oral antidiabetic agents *are* effective and desirable, and that the UGDP study is an exercise in bureaucratic futility and its conclusions run counter to his own experience, he will probably insist that in addition to a diet regimen you take the pills straightaway.

The most dramatic proof of this difference of opinion among doctors in the United States is the fact that in the estimated 5 million Americans who have high blood sugar, about 1 million are given a pill to lower it, some 1½ million take insulin, and 2 to 3 million are treated by diet alone.

Let me tell you how I deal with the question of oral agents

in the treatment of non-insulin-dependent diabetes. When diet, exercise and weight loss alone are not enough to normalize the blood sugar, I usually prescribe oral antidiabetics. That is not to say that I completely reject the UGDP conclusions. There may be some increased risk from these medications. After all, there is a little poison in every drug. But I believe that the benefits to be derived from continued sugar control outweigh the dangers of these pills, especially in those individuals forty years of age or older who are not too overweight. (In underweight adult diabetics, insulin is often required.)

WHICH ANTIDIABETIC PILL TO USE?

There are currently six oral antidiabetics (hypoglycemics) marketed in the United States—tolbutamide (Orinase), chlorpropamide (Diabinese), acetohexamide (Dymelor), tolazamide (Tolinase), glipizide (Glucotrol) and glyburide (DiaBeta, Micronase). The first four—the so-called first-generation hypoglycemics—have been around for years. The latter two, glipizide and glyburide, are more recent, and are referred to as second-generation antidiabetic agents.

Which one is best for you depends on various factors. Don't rush to take insulin if one of the older agents doesn't seem to be working for you. A newer one may. If you have evidence of kidney disease, which many diabetics do, avoid Diabinese since its excretion from the body depends on normal renal function. Instead, use Orinase, which is "handled" by the liver. (Incidentally, the patents on both these drugs have now expired and you can save a bundle—almost half the cost—when you buy the generic rather than the brand name.) If you like to take a drink or some wine now and then, you may find that both Diabinese and Orinase give you uncomfortable flushing.

When my patients are responding satisfactorily to a first-generation drug, and tolerating it well, I leave them alone. But if their sugar levels fluctuate too much, I try one of the newer products. However, all these agents can cause too great a drop in blood-sugar levels, skin rashes and blood and liver function abnormalities. What's more, any of them can interact with other drugs you happen to be taking. As a result, the sugar-lowering properties of these hypoglycemic drugs may be interfered with—either enhanced or diminished. Also, the effect of other medications may be reduced or enhanced. So be careful if you're on diuretics, blood thinners, barbiturates (Nembutal, Seconal, phenobarbital), phenylbutazone (Butazolidin) or clofibrate (Atromid-S). Also, avoid the oral diabetic preparations while pregnant or breast feeding or if you're allergic to sulfa drugs.

THE PREGNANT DIABETIC

There is one area in which there is universal agreement. Everyone believes that rigid control of blood sugar is critical in the pregnant diabetic. Any sustained elevation of glucose in the mother is transmitted to the fetus. When this happens, the fetal pancreas responds to the elevated sugar level by making more and more insulin. This results in episodic *low* blood sugar and a high incidence of complications in fetal development and greater infant mortality.

In the past, young diabetics, especially those with any vascular disease, were discouraged from having babies, because the infant mortality rate was high (30 percent) and the mothers suffered many complications. Today, however, as a result of more successful control of blood sugar, *selected* diabetics whose disease can be stabilized are permitted and even encouraged to have children. In many such diabetic mothers there does not appear to be any worsening of the diabetic or vascular status as a result of childbearing, and the overall infant mortality is now only 4 percent. So if you have diabetes, want a baby, and are discouraged from having one, don't hesitate to ask for another opinion from a diabetologist. It may be perfectly all right for you to become pregnant.

If you do decide to have a baby, your doctor will probably do blood tests to monitor not only your blood-sugar level, but the amount of hemoglobin A_{Ic} in your blood. The latter chemical appears to be a more reliable predictor of congenital abnormalities in your baby. Also, the critical time for tight sugar control is very early in the pregnancy. So if you're going to have a baby, it's a good idea to strive for optimal sugar levels *before* you become pregnant, and to be especially fastidious during the first three months. *At no time in your pregnancy or while breast-feeding should you use oral diabetic agents.*

UNDERSTANDING THE DIABETIC DIET

Control of diabetes and to some extent the long-term outlook for the disease hinge on adherence to diet. In every case, simple sugars, the kind you might add to a beverage or put into candy, must be avoided completely, and the intake of some carbohydrates must be reduced. How much and what you may safely eat depends on your age and weight. For example, in childhood and adolescence, adequate nutrition is very important for proper growth and development. Since diabetic children are usually thin anyway, calories should not be restricted as they are in the fat adult. Any adverse impact on the blood sugar of a more liberal diet (but a carefully planned one) can be controlled by adjusting the insulin dosage. But if you are an adult diabetic and overweight, you should decrease the total number of calories to about 1,200 to 1,500 per day (people engaged in heavy labor will require more), and within that caloric limitation, you may eat virtually anything you wish except pure sugar. If you don't weigh too much, be sure you keep it that way. It's a good idea for all diabetics to add some fiber to the diet, because enough of the right fiber may decrease the amount of sugar absorbed by as much as 25 percent, and insulin requirements by as much as 20 percent. Check with your doctor about the type of fiber you're eating. They're not all equally good (oat bran is the best). Many simply leave you with a lot of gas and the same amount of sugar!

WHAT TO EAT AND WHEN

If you are an adult on a low-calorie diet and not taking insulin, you may have your meals anytime during the day. But if you are on insulin or a sugar-lowering pill, what you eat and *when* you do so are very important. Blood sugar can rise and fall precipitously if mealtime and insulin dosage are not coordinated. For example, should you miss a meal yet take the same amount of insulin at the usual time, the blood sugar may drop enough to cause a severe insulin reaction or even coma. Insulin-dependent diabetics must also be careful about the *kind* of food they eat at specific times of the day in relation to their insulin dosage, because protein, fat and carbohydrates increase the blood-sugar level at different rates. For example, a candy bar (carbohydrate) will raise it much more quickly than will a steak (protein, fat). If your insulin is geared to take care of a rise in blood sugar due to carbohydrates and you eat protein instead, you may suffer an insulin reaction because the protein has not delivered as much sugar as the insulin was expected to neutralize.

Since vigorous exercise also burns up sugar, a diabetic taking insulin or oral medication who works out should either eat more or reduce his insulin dosage, in order to avoid a low-blood-sugar reaction. This, however, is not true for the diabetic who is neither on insulin nor on drug therapy.

Whatever kind of diabetic you are, if you have been given a diet that makes life almost intolerable, discuss it with your doctor—or get a second opinion from a diabetes specialist. In view of today's new knowledge, it is no longer necessary for you to endure a lifetime of boring, tasteless food. Almost anything is permitted—in moderation—except simple sugars. The inflexible high-protein, low-fat, low-carbohydrate diet of yesteryear is rarely needed anymore. In fact, today most diabetes specialists prescribe a very tolerable diet with 60 percent complex carbohydrate (that is, starches), 20 percent protein and 20 percent fat—with liberal amounts of fiber. If you're not satisfied with the scope of your diet, ask your doctor to obtain for you the list of interchangeable foods prepared by the American Diabetes Association—or write to them directly at 1660 Duke Street, Alexandria, Virginia 22314.

HOW SAFE ARE SUGAR SUBSTITUTES?

Many of my diabetic patients ask me about using sugar substitutes and which among them are the safest. Your best bet is really to do without them if you can and simply avoid all concentrated sweets. Most persons can easily develop a taste for sugar-free coffee and tea. If you like carbonated beverages, club soda is what you should drink. If, however, you simply must have the "sweet" taste, saccharin and aspartame are available to you. The former carries a warning of possible cancer risk. Although aspartame has been judged to be perfectly safe by the FDA, there are still some islands of dissent within the medical community. My advice is to go as easy as possible on both products.

Many diabetics use sugar-free gum, mints and candies. Many of these contain a nonglucose sugar called sorbitol. A word of caution about consuming such products in excess. Sorbitol sucks water out of the bowel and can result in chronic diarrhea. So if you're diabetic and being very good about the "candies" you're eating, but suffer from watery stools, ask your doctor about the possibility that sorbitol may be the cause.

BETTER SUGAR CONTROL— A WORTHWHILE GOAL

A key question that remains unanswered is whether all the devastating chronic complications of diabetes result from the high blood sugar, from excessive ketones or from other causes not as yet identified. In other words, if we were able to keep the blood sugar normal at all times, would diabetics still have all these problems?

Most experts now think that rigid sugar control at or near normal levels would greatly reduce the debilitating, crippling and lethal consequences of this disease. So do I. But even when the blood-sugar level is "acceptable" in random measurements, there are often peaks and valleys throughout the day and night. You can identify these fluctuations by checking your own blood sugar at regular intervals at home or at work, and adjusting your medication accordingly. This can now be done very simply, accurately and almost painlessly by one of the several home testing kits that have become available. You simply prick your finger, put the tiny drop of blood on a chemically-treated paper strip, and insert it into the "glucometer." In a few seconds, your blood level appears on a light-emitting diode. Ask your doctor about it. I advise all my diabetic patients on insulin or pills to buy one of these devices. They cost less than $200 and are much more accurate than urine analysis.

Another recent device is the insulin pump, developed to avoid swings in blood-sugar levels. Especially designed for use in young diabetics, the pump is worn on the belt and releases insulin into a vein or the tissues of the abdomen or chest at preset intervals through a permanently placed catheter. Such a pump permits you to regulate your insulin dosage up or down, depending on your sugar level, or in anticipation of changes in your diet. For example, do you intend to lose your will power over a scrumptious-looking dessert? After all, you're only human! If you do, just have the pump squirt a little more insulin. However, I wouldn't make a habit of it!

I have been less than overwhelmed by the reliability of these pumps. They are useful sometimes, but I do not prescribe them routinely because they can be fraught with complications—excessively low blood sugar from too much insulin, infection at the site of the catheter and battery failure.

FRONTIERS OF RESEARCH IN DIABETES

Efforts to transplant a healthy pancreas, the organ containing the cells that make insulin, into diabetics have not as yet been widely successful, although a few "cures" have been reported. The major problems with this technique are blood clotting within the transplanted organ and its rejection. Hopefully, these difficulties will one day be overcome.

Another area of research involves the injection of healthy insulin-producing beta cells into the vein of a diabetic. These cells settle in the liver, where it is hoped they can produce insulin, as they did in the pancreas. The problem with all these theories is that no one knows whether simply replacing the insulin by whatever route will provide the basic solution to everyone suffering from the complex disease we call diabetes.

KEY FACTS TO REMEMBER

Diabetes mellitus, the presence of excessive sugar in the blood, is the third leading cause of death in the United States. It probably represents more than one disease. The two forms currently identified are the insulin-dependent type, more serious and usually found in children, and the adult-onset or non-insulin-dependent form, which often can be managed by diet, weight loss or oral medication.

Major immediate complications of diabetes result from the body's burning of its fat stores in lieu of the normally available sugar. The end products of such metabolism (ketones) are toxic when present in high concentrations in the blood.

The major area of disagreement about the treatment of diabetes relates to the use of the antisugar pill. Many doctors believe that it is beneficial; others think it is dangerous.

Insulin is almost always needed by diabetic children. It is much less commonly required in adults. The latter should ask for a second opinion when advised to take insulin, especially in the absence of symptoms.

Careful management of the pregnant diabetic has reduced complications of the disease in the mother and has significantly reduced infant mortality. Diabetic women should not *pro forma* be denied the right of childbearing. If you are, ask for a second opinion from a diabetes specialist.

Diabetic diets need not be severely restricted. If yours is, ask for an opinion from a diabetologist. The goal, however you manage it, must be good sugar control over the years. Almost everyone now agrees that avoiding prolonged high sugar levels is the most effective way to prevent the serious complications of diabetes.

▼

6

HYPOGLYCEMIA
—A COMMON
"NONDISEASE"

In contrast to the excessive amounts of sugar in the blood (hyperglycemia) that characterize the diabetic, a reverse situation may also occur—*hypo*glycemia—in which the sugar level is actually too low. By definition, this is said to happen when the sugar reading is 40 mg percent or less. This figure is, however, arbitrary. You may in fact experience symptoms of hypoglycemia even when your blood-sugar level is higher.

We know for a fact that millions of people in this country have diabetes. Many of them have the typical symptoms described in Chapter 5, and *all* of them have a demonstrated, measurable increase in blood sugar. It's interesting that vast numbers of individuals are convinced they have hypoglycemia despite the fact that its symptoms are mimicked by a wide variety of conditions ranging from simple anxiety to mitral valve prolapse. What's more, in only a small fraction of these cases is the blood sugar ever found to be low!

The scenario is played out countless times in the offices of doctors across the country, including my own. A patient, usually female, and most often somewhere between thirty and sixty years of age, comes in. "Doctor," she says, "there's something very wrong with my metabolism (or circulation). I feel well one minute and then I suddenly develop a headache and become very weak (or cold, nervous, depressed, exhausted). My heart races (or pounds). I begin to sweat, feel like fainting, and then suddenly it's over."

Such complaints, including a feeling of hunger, usually generate a battery of tests to rule out the possibility of thyroid trouble, mitral valve prolapse and hypoglycemia.

If the doctor suspects the latter, he will ask the patient to come to his office as soon as the "attack" begins, and measure the blood-sugar level then and there. The diagnosis of hypoglycemia is made if the sugar is actually low at the time of symptoms and these are quickly relieved by the administration of sugar in one form or another. If coming to the office immediately during an attack is not feasible, the doctor may order a glucose tolerance test, in which the patient is given a measured amount of sugar to drink. Blood samples are taken every hour for five or six hours, or longer. If the symptoms are reproduced at any time during the test and can be correlated with an abnormally low blood sugar, that is, 40 mg percent or less, or with an abrupt drop in sugar in a relatively short time, or again, are relieved when the patient takes some sugar, then the diagnosis of hypoglycemia is confirmed.

If the results of all the tests performed, including the sugar measurements, are completely normal, the doctor may well conclude that the patient has some underlying emotional disorder. She leaves the office with a prescription for a tranquilizer, quite unhappy with the diagnosis and convinced that the real cause of her symptoms has been missed. It rankles her and she looks for a second opinion, and a third opinion, and even a fourth. She searches until she finds a doctor who tells her what she wants to hear, that her symptoms are *not* psychological, but have a physical basis—hypoglycemia. Rarely is that diagnosis made by actually demonstrating a low blood sugar—but no mind, the patient is given a high-protein, low-sugar diet, and lo and behold, she soon feels better, at least for a while. Repeat this experience thousands of times and you witness the birth of a nondisease called hypoglycemia.

If you are convinced that you have hypoglycemia even though all the objective tests are normal, and you feel better following the prescribed diet, I suggest you continue exactly what you are doing. Don't ever argue with success!

All the above notwithstanding, true hypoglycemia does exist, but much less frequently than is supposed.

WHAT MAKES THE BLOOD SUGAR DROP?

You may become truly hypoglycemic under certain special circumstances. For example, if you're diabetic and you take too much insulin, either by mistake or because you fail to eat in time, your sugar may drop. Also, if you've gone without food or drink for too many hours, your glucose level may be low, leaving you feeling faint. But that doesn't happen too often because with the reduced sugar intake the pancreas makes less insulin. If for some reason the pancreas continues to secrete an inappropriately large amount of insulin, low blood sugar with its attendant symptoms can develop.

In addition to the pancreas, the liver also helps the body maintain a normal blood-sugar level. It does so by acting as a reservoir, storing sugar and releasing it when levels are low. So if you have severe liver disease, and that extra amount is not available to you when you need it, you may become hypoglycemic in circumstances when normal individuals would not. This is also true for heavy drinkers—their livers may still be functioning normally in most parameters, but excessive alcohol poisons the enzyme system that allows that organ to release its sugar into the circulation.

Low blood-sugar levels are sometimes found in pregnant women due to the increased requirements of nourishing the fetus.

If you have some illness, are running a low-grade fever and have lost your appetite, the increased metabolism resulting from the fever together with impaired nutrition may reduce blood-sugar levels. (Remember grandma's advice to "feed a fever"?)

WHEN TOO MUCH
SUGAR IS TOO LITTLE

The foregoing is a description of some of the ways in which an inadequate food intake can result in low blood sugar. But you can also develop hypoglycemia *after* eating sugar. It happens this way. You take something sweet and delicious. It's digested and the sugar enters your bloodstream. The pancreas is now stimulated to produce more insulin. The sugar level drops and no more insulin is made. However, if this feedback mechanism is impaired so that the pancreas continues to produce insulin when it's no longer needed, you end up with an abnormally low blood sugar. This phenomenon is called reactive hypoglycemia, and is sometimes the forerunner of diabetes. You can avoid this particular kind of hypoglycemia by eliminating sweets from the diet and thus preventing the insulin "overshoot."

Normally, sugar is digested in the stomach, from which most of it goes into the bloodstream. But if you have had a portion of your stomach removed, for example, because of an ulcer, the sugar you eat passes directly into the small bowel. Here it is more rapidly absorbed than in the stomach. The resulting sudden increase in blood sugar causes insulin overshoot and hypoglycemia.

If you are found to have low blood sugar and are taking any of the following drugs, be sure to tell your doctor: sulfas, oral antidiabetic agents, aspirin, Darvon or Thorazine. These are only some of the medications that may cause hypoglycemia, as can alcohol in large amounts (tolerance varies from person to person).

A very uncommon cause of hypoglycemia is a tumor of the pancreas (called an insulinoma), which produces large amounts of insulin regardless of the blood-sugar level or how much you eat. Surgical removal of the tumor cures the hypoglycemia.

TREATING HYPOGLYCEMIA

After all is said and done, there are a small number of patients who really *do* have hypoglycemia for reasons we do not understand. We call this state functional hypoglycemia. Treatment in such cases consists of dietary manipulation. If you fall into this group, you will feel better if you eat smaller meals more frequently, avoid sugar, reduce carbohydrate intake generally and eat more protein. This will result in a more gradual absorption of sugar, and therefore less insulin overshoot. A high-fiber diet is also useful. But these cases of functional hypoglycemia are all documented by low blood sugars.

KEY FACTS TO REMEMBER

Hypoglycemia is probably the most overdiagnosed "non-disease" there is. If you are told that this is what you have, and a low-sugar diet helps, stay with it. It can't hurt you. But ask for a second opinion from an endocrinologist anyway.

True hypoglycemia may occur in liver disease, among alcoholics, after surgical removal of large portions of the stomach, and in diabetics taking insulin. It may also be associated with the use of certain medications and, in rare cases, with an insulin-producing tumor.

7

DISORDERS OF THE EARS, NOSE AND THROAT— UNNECESSARY TREATMENT?

No one wants to undergo unnecessary surgery. There is widespread suspicion that some of the organs we allow doctors to remove might better be left alone. Procedures most suspect are the hysterectomy, prostatectomy, cataract removal and the group discussed in this chapter, in the area of the ears, nose and throat.

Deciding whether or not to have one's tonsils and adenoids removed or the nasal sinuses repeatedly drained is not usually critical, but the right choice may reduce unnecessary pain, suffering and expense. If you have had your sinuses perforated or drained at regular intervals, or can remember your own tonsillectomy, you know how miserable these procedures can be.

IT'S MY SINUSES AGAIN

Chronic sinusitis affects about 25 percent of the adult population of the United States. Those affected are plagued by recurrent cough, fever, headache and yellowish green or bloody nasal discharge. Millions of us every year have our nasal bones cracked to release trapped pus; we pop expensive antibiotics down our gullets, or we sit at home bent over a humidifier instead of going to work. So it behooves you to know about some recent progress in the treatment of this condition.

WELL PROTECTED BUT HARD TO TREAT

The nasal sinuses are air pockets surrounded by bones (the skull). They are designed by nature to resist infections originating in the nose and mouth. And they are pretty efficient, considering all the dirt and contaminants we breathe, as well as the many dental and gum infections we have. But the same protective structures that render the sinuses fairly resistant to infection also deny access to treatment once infection has set in.

There are three main sets of sinuses—the maxillary, the frontal and the ethmoid. The maxillary sinuses, situated in the general area of the cheekbones, are the largest and the most likely to give you problems. I have found that when they are infected, they are irrigated either too frequently or not often enough. The frontal sinuses, above the eyes, and the ethmoid sinuses, very small multiple air pockets in the skull, can also become infected and require treatment.

BLAME THE WOES ON YOUR NOSE

Sinus trouble is most frequently the result of an allergic condition affecting the lining of the nasal passages. Allergy, as for example, to pollens, causes the interior of the nose to become boggy, swollen and therefore more vulnerable to infection. All kinds of viruses and bacteria can more easily penetrate the irritated lining of the nose. Unless eradicated in time, the infection becomes chronic, and the bacteria make their way into the nearest sinuses, where they create a pocket of pus. Also, if you have a deviated nasal septum that interferes with proper drainage and breathing, or if you have polyps in your nose due to chronic infection and allergy, you are a natural target for sinus trouble. Infected or abscessed teeth and gums, contaminated bathing water and a head injury can also leave you with sinusitis.

WHICH ANTIBIOTIC TO USE AND WHEN

So the key to preventing sinus infection in the first place is to nip in the bud any abnormal process in the immediate vicinity of the sinuses, that is, in the nasal passages. Once the symptoms of sinusitis have set in and you have begun to blow greenish yellow mucus out of your nose, or you've developed a tickle in the back of your throat because of the material dripping down from the sinuses, you should use steam inhalation and take nasal decongestants to shrink the lining of the nasal passages so as to improve drainage from the sinuses. Then promptly take an antibiotic. Theoretically, which one you take should be determined after the mucus is analyzed and subjected to the killing action of various antibiotics in a test tube. Most doctors, however, will right off the bat give you ampicillin, doxycycline (Vibramycin), penicillin, erythromycin or one of the cephalosporins like Ceclor without actually making such an analysis.

WHEN IS SINUS IRRIGATION JUSTIFIED?

Acute sinusitis usually responds well to antibiotics within forty-eight to seventy-two hours. But if you continue to have facial pain, headache, postnasal drip and chronic nasal discharge after treatment of the acute attack, *occasional* washing of the sinuses is helpful. Also, when sinus X rays reveal clouding and the radiologist is not sure whether it is due to an old burned-out infection or the presence of fresh pus, the doctor may irrigate the sinuses in order to find out. But *repeated* washing out of sinuses with all its pain, cost and inconvenience is not usually necessary. If you've had it done three times and are advised that further irrigation will be necessary, discuss with your doctor the advantages of an "antral window." This is an artificially created permanent opening in the maxillary sinus that permits natural drainage without the need to crack the bones repeatedly.

A STUFFY NOSE AND A FULL BLADDER

A chronically stuffy nose is usually the result of an allergy, irritation, deviated septum, local infection, certain medications, glandular or hormonal problems, nasal injury or tumor. When it develops, one is tempted to use a nasal decongestant right away. Remember that some of these agents may give you a rebound effect if taken frequently and for prolonged periods of time. While they do shrink the lining (mucous membranes) of the nose, the congestion may return with a vengeance as their effect wears off. Also, most nasal decongestants contain ephedrine, pseudoephedrine, phenyl-propanolamine or related ingredients, all of which may increase heart rate, raise blood pressure and initiate disturbances of cardiac rhythm. Most healthy persons can tolerate these effects without any problem, but be careful about using them if you have any heart problem, a thyroid disorder or hypertension. Most decongestant preparations also contain antihistamines, which have drying and antiallergic actions. They may make you very drowsy, so take them just before retiring, when you can get a good night's sleep, not in the morning when you're about to drive your car. These same antihistamines can cause problems in older men, especially those with some enlargement of the prostate gland. In such cases they interfere with the ability to empty the urinary bladder. I have seen more than one man in agony due to sudden urinary retention after taking a "harmless" decongestant. For all these reasons, if you fall into any of these categories and have a stuffy nose, it's a good idea to try some simple steam inhalation first. If that doesn't help, then you may use one of the many nasal sprays, drops or oral decongestants available over the counter.

In some persons antihistamines, taken for whatever reason, seem to lose their effectiveness with time. It's almost as if one becomes "immune" to them. Before abandoning this group of drugs and going on to more powerful agents like steroids, you should know that there are at least seven different groups of antihistamines from which you can choose. Tolerance to one does not necessarily mean you will not respond to any of the others. So if you have a chronic allergy and need antihistamines fairly regularly, it's a good idea to switch brands from time to time, say every two months.

If the kind of antihistamine you've been taking makes you sleepy, ask your doctor to prescribe Seldane. It comes in 60-mg strength and you require only two tablets a day. Seldane's advantage over the competition is that it doesn't leave you drowsy, and in most cases permits you to carry on your normal activities. But try it first before going out to drive a car or operate some potentially dangerous piece of machinery. Remember, however, no matter what kind of antihistamine you use, don't take alcohol with it. The sedating effect of the two together may "knock you out."

Your allergic symptoms may flare up after prolonged exposure to a pollen or other offending substances. Under these circumstances, you may need something stronger than an antihistamine-decongestant combination for a few days. The usual medication prescribed is likely to be a corticosteroid (e.g., prednisone). You can take it in tablet form, or via a slowly absorbed injection, or by aerosol. If steroids are prescribed, be sure to tell or remind your doctor if you're pregnant, have high blood pressure, an ulcer history, diabetes or a psychiatric problem.

Remember, too, that not all stuffy noses are due to infection or allergy. Medication may be the culprit, so if there is no apparent reason for your symptoms, check to see whether you are on any drug to lower high blood pressure. Common offenders include the following: reserpine, hydralazine (Apresoline), guanethidine (Ismelin), methyldopa (Aldomet), prazosin (Minipress), propranolol (Inderal), nadolol (Corgard) and metoprolol (Lopressor). Certain tranquilizers also cause nasal stuffiness, so it's a good idea to check out *any* drug you happen to be taking if you have this symptom.

TONSILLECTOMY—AS AMERICAN AS THANKSGIVING TURKEY

Tonsillectomy has for decades been a ritual performed on most American children. At the very first complaint of a sore throat, parents rush to consult the pediatrician about scheduling to have the tonsils removed. Seduced and distracted by promises of ice cream and ginger ale after their operation, over a million youngsters are subjected every year to this barbaric rite in which the lymph glands in the throat are extirpated. The adenoids are also usually removed for good measure.

There is now a very real difference of opinion concerning the need for this operation. After all, we don't remove a kidney simply because it is infected. We treat it with antibiotics. We do our best to save a tooth, and pull it only as a last resort. Why then, after a sore throat or two, are tonsils immediately condemned to extraction?

Tonsils *do* have a function. They consist of lymph tissue and constitute the first line of defense against infection in the throat. They act as filters that trap invading bacteria and prevent them from getting into the bloodstream. An infected tonsil is one that has been doing its job. Of course, after repeated infection, the tonsillar tissue is finally destroyed and may then have to be removed. But it doesn't make sense to remove tonsils simply because they are inflamed, especially when one can now treat them with antibiotics, restore their integrity and retain their protective function.

DOES TONSILLECTOMY REALLY MAKE A DIFFERENCE?

Those still in favor of the routine tonsillectomy in children with a history of only a few sore throats argue that after the operation the incidence of these attacks decreases. I wonder. There have been several reports in recent years that show that in most cases, removing the tonsils makes no difference whatsoever on the subsequent incidence of sore throats in these children. So if your child has some sore throats in his or her first year of school, that does not mean that they will recur. The sore throat in childhood is probably a naturally occurring phenomenon that is self-limited and usually does not require removal of the tonsils. If you're advised otherwise, ask for a second opinion.

MY SON, THE MOUTH BREATHER

Should we be as conservative about removing the adenoid

glands too? Like the tonsils, they are collections of lymph tissue, but are situated in a different part of the throat area. They are routinely removed with the tonsils (that's why the operation is called T and A—tonsillectomy and adenoidectomy). Parents are rarely asked for permission to remove the adenoids when a child has a tonsillectomy. It is part of the package, kind of a "might as well" operative procedure. The justification? Your child often has his mouth open and snores, doesn't he? When the results of large series of T and A's were analyzed and the removed adenoids examined, they were rarely found to be infected. What's more, there was little if any correlation between snoring, mouth breathing and the size of the adenoids. So even if the tonsils have to come out for some reason, ask the surgeon what he plans to do about the adenoids.

TONSILLECTOMY—ONLY UNNECESSARY OR ALSO HARMFUL?

Are these T and A operations merely painful and unnecessary, or can they possibly cause some harm in the long run? I'm not really sure. In one study, persons who had had their tonsils and adenoids out in childhood had a higher incidence of Hodgkin's disease (a form of cancer of the lymph tissue) later in life than did a matched group in whom the operation was not done. That is not enough to permit any definite conclusion, but it does at least raise a question.

Recently, a potential problem has arisen for those individuals actually requiring a tonsillectomy. It relates to the growing trend to avoid hospitalization whenever possible. As a result, ambulatory surgical centers have sprung up all over the country in which you can have same-day procedures done—minor or cosmetic surgery, diagnostic cardiac catheterization or angiography, electroshock of the heart to restore normal cardiac rhythm, blood transfusions, cataract extirpations, hernia repairs and the like. The list is constantly increasing, and now also includes tonsillectomies. Many third-party payers, the people who pick up the tab for your medical care, are insisting that they will pay for your child's T and A only if it's done in one of these day centers. That may be safe most of the time, but discuss with your surgeon your child's particular risks for this operation, or your own if you are an adult with some other underlying medical disorder. If there is any question about safety, or the emergency facilities in the outpatient facility leave *anything* to be desired, tell your insurance carrier and your doctor both that you want to be admitted to the hospital for your operation. Paying premiums all these years entitles you to that.

All this adds up to the following: If your child has enjoyed good health except for recurring sore throats and plans have been made to remove his tonsils the following spring or fall, even though he has been free of attacks in the interval, get a second opinion. If during the next year or two, attacks don't recur, your child may be free and clear, and may avoid the surgery forever. If, on the other hand, the throat infections persist, he may fall into the small group that actually needs the operation. Even then, ask whether the adenoids must come out too.

HOW WE HEAR

Sound is conducted through the external ear canal (that's where people who live dangerously poke things to get the wax out), reaches the eardrum and makes it vibrate. This moves three little bones attached to the drum, which then send messages to the hearing apparatus in the inner ear. The sound signal is subsequently transmitted by nerves to the brain, where it is interpreted. Deafness can result from a wad of wax in the ear canal blocking passage of the sound wave. A hearing aid obviously won't do you any good in this situation, because the sound can't get through. Or the trouble may be due to an eardrum scarred by previous infections and therefore unable to vibrate normally when the sound waves strike it. Or, the three little bones behind the drum may become fused and thus unable to transmit the vibrations of the drum to the hearing apparatus in the inner ear, which may itself be diseased or injured. Finally, the nerve (acoustic nerve), which carries the impulses to the brain, may malfunction—occasionally because of a tumor pressing on it.

These various potential mechanisms of deafness permit us to divide hearing loss into two major types. The first is *conductive*—due to some obstruction of the transmission of sound in the external canal, or to disease of the drum or bones. This embraces the entire route the sound travels until it finally reaches the inner ear and the acoustic nerve. Any trouble beyond that point, involving the inner ear or the acoustic nerve itself, is termed *sensorineural,* or nerve, deafness.

People with nerve deafness don't hear high-pitched sounds very well. They have trouble understanding a soft-spoken female, especially at a noisy cocktail party. At home, they may go about their business unaware that the phone is ringing. (I often wonder why the pitch of the bell has not been lowered by the telephone company in order to make it more audible to subscribers with nerve deafness.)

Conductive deafness is usually treatable—by simply removing wax or a foreign body from the ear canal, or by operating on the eardrum or the little bones behind it if they have become fused. A hearing aid may be helpful too.

Deafness due to an acute infection in the middle ear will improve strikingly after treatment with antibiotics. However, if you have chronic middle ear disease, you may require surgical treatment.

A disorder called Ménière's disease, in which there is buzzing and other noises in the ear, dizziness and a fluctuating hearing loss, will sometimes respond to medications, including antihistamines, tranquilizers and diuretics, or to a low-salt diet.

By contrast, *sensorineural deafness* is more difficult to treat. In my experience, no medication results in measurable improvement. Some doctors, out of desperation, have prescribed nicotinic acid and high doses of other vitamins. I have never seen them work. Neither do the so-called cerebral artery vasodilators, which are supposed to widen the blood vessels going to the brain. Nor is there any surgical procedure for sensorineural deafness. There are some experimental techniques for those individuals who are completely deaf, which permit them to appreciate sound, but none of these is currently applicable for the elderly "hard of hearing," most of whom are basically nerve deaf. It has been suggested that a low-fat diet may slow down the rate at which hearing is lost. I suggest you follow such a diet anyway, regardless of its effect on hearing. A high-fat diet is bad for you in other ways.

What about hearing aids? Until recently they weren't much good for nerve deafness. There are some new ones that are. If you are missing much of what is being spoken, sung or played, consult a good ear specialist and have him or her then refer you to a competent audiologist. Chances are that between them, they can help you. But make sure you get a money-back guarantee for any hearing aid you buy. They're expensive. And never purchase one except when prescribed by a hearing specialist.

DEAF WITH HEALTHY EARS

Deafness need not originate in the hearing mechanism. For example, as many as 10 percent of patients with hypothyroidism have a hearing loss that will improve, often dramatically, when the deficient thyroid hormone is replenished. Rheumatoid arthritis may cause a conductive type of deafness that sometimes responds to steroids (cortisone-type drugs). About 10 percent of patients with fluctuating hearing loss are found to have diabetes mellitus. Unfortunately, reducing the sugar doesn't always improve the hearing in these cases. Certain disturbances in fat metabolism, characterized by high triglyceride and cholesterol levels, may result in hearing loss. In such cases, weight loss and a reduction in the intake of saturated fats and concentrated sweets may help. Patients with kidney disease may become deaf. Certain medications (antibiotics) may cause hearing loss that is frequently permanent. I have several patients who became stone deaf after taking the antibiotic streptomycin or ethacrynic acid, a diuretic. I know of heavy smokers who became deaf and whose hearing was at least partially restored when the cigarettes were stopped. (I suppose this can best be explained either by nicotine toxicity or spasm of the blood vessels in the ear.) Aspirin in large amounts has been known to produce a hearing loss, which fortunately clears up when the drug is stopped. Allergic reactions to food or inhalants also can cause deafness that may or may not be permanent. So, it's a good idea, when your vanity finally permits you to accept the fact that you're deaf, to consult your doctor first and then an ear specialist. Don't rush off to buy a hearing aid. You may not need one.

KEY FACTS TO REMEMBER

Chronic sinusitis is a disabling disorder affecting 25 percent of the population of the United States. It usually results from chronic allergy and/or infection of the nose. The acute attack can often be managed by antibiotics, but the sinuses may *occasionally* have to be drained. However, repeated irrigation and washing is rarely necessary, and you should see another ear, nose and throat specialist if you're told that's what you need.

Chronic nasal stuffiness is usually, but not always, due to allergy. Most cases can be managed by antihistamine-decongestant pills, but certain precautions should be taken. Some people become "tolerant" to antihistamines. Switching to another type may be all that is necessary to restore the efficacy of these agents. In more severe cases, short-term use of steroid hormones may become necessary.

Tonsillectomies are probably unnecessary for most children. Recent evidence suggests that their sore throats usually clear up without operation. Removal of adenoids probably has little impact on mouth breathing or snoring.

There are many different causes of deafness. Various diseases and drugs may induce hearing loss, which is often temporary but sometimes permanent. Deafness due to disorders of the hearing apparatus are of either the "conductive" or the "nerve" type. The former may benefit from surgery and hearing aids, but the latter usually do not. Never buy a hearing aid from a commercial establishment without first checking with your ear doctor—and always ask for a money-back guarantee.

8

ASTHMA—PREVENTING AND CONTROLLING YOUR WHEEZE

MUSICAL, BUT NOT A COMEDY

Some three million Americans—twice as many men as women—suffer from some form of asthma. Most asthmatics, perhaps 60 or 65 percent, develop this disorder before the age of five; some outgrow it, others don't. Despite all the drugs we have for its treatment, many of which are new, five thousand people still die from asthma every year in the United States. Many of these deaths are unnecessary. If you or a loved one has asthma, read this chapter carefully. Compare your treatment with what's available, and if you're not doing well, ask for a second opinion.

ACUTE, CHRONIC OR BOTH

Any process that narrows the air passages (bronchial tubes), be it spasm, infection, allergy or mucus, results in wheezing. In asthmatics this constriction is sporadic, so that there are usually symptom-free intervals of varying duration. Attacks may be sudden and for no apparent reason, or provoked by an obvious cause. They may be mild or severe, and are characterized by coughing, wheezing, excessive mucus production and some degree of respiratory distress. After treatment breathing becomes normal again. In other words, acute asthma is completely reversible.

IT'S EITHER INTRINSIC
OR EXTRINSIC, OR BOTH

In order for you to understand how best to manage your asthma, you should know a little about what causes it. There are basically two distinct forms. The first is called *extrinsic,* because it is induced by an environmental substance to which one is "allergic." It's the kind infants and children get when they inhale something their system doesn't like—a pollen, certain dusts or other irritants. Occasionally food will also cause an asthmatic attack. By contrast, in *instrinsic* asthma there is no apparent external provocation. Patients are usually adults and present with chronic respiratory infections, colds or sinusitis, and repeated attacks of asthmatic wheezing. There is no apparent relationship to the external environment or to diet.

The distinction between extrinsic and intrinsic asthma is an oversimplification of a complex biological process, but it is a useful guide. In actual fact many cases of asthma are a blend of both forms. (There is no evidence that asthma is an emotional disorder, despite the fact that many people mistakenly think so.)

Presented with this "insult" or "challenge," either intrinsic or extrinsic, the body responds by throwing the airways to the lungs into spasm and having them make more mucus to entrap any invading organisms that may be present. The end result is an attack of wheezing (because of the airways' constriction) and coughing (because of the mucus secretions). In time and with experience, vulnerable patients begin to dread certain places or seasons of the year (where and when offending agents are found); they try to avoid friends who wear perfumes that trigger asthmatic crises or who invite them to dinner in a home filled with dander from furry pets.

EXERCISE, ASPIRIN AND ASTHMA

Sudden attacks of asthma, in individuals who have had them before, can also result from acute emotional stress—fear, anger or sorrow, as well as from vigorous exercise, especially in cold weather, and abrupt exposure to cold. You may become asthmatic because of the kind of work you do (exposure to fumes, dusts and other "allergens"—occupational asthma) and even from medication. Some thirty years ago I reported in the medical literature near-fatal asthmatic attacks in two patients with chronic asthma who had taken aspirin for some minor pain. (Other doctors have described similar reactions to this agent in persons without any previous asthmatic history.) So, if you have chronic asthma or are prone to acute attacks of wheezing, be careful about *any* drug you use, including "benign" ones like aspirin.

Regardless of any classification, every asthmatic should know precisely what it is that makes him or her sick. Sometimes that's easy, as for example, exposure to cats, dogs, grasses or pollens from other plants. When it is not, you may have to be tested—for allergy to house dust, pollens (ragweed in particular) or animal dander, to mention but a few of the common offending inhalants; or to nuts, seafood, tomatoes, a dye called tartrazine, widely used in such food products as hot dogs and margarine, sulfites (recently banned from most foods, but still present in alcoholic beverages and some medications) and other foods. Most patients have more than one allergy.

Whatever the offending stimulus, it should be avoided whenever possible. When that's not practical, then you should have at your disposal those agents that can effectively forestall or end the attack.

ANYONE WANT A CUTE SIX-YEAR-OLD?

I have found that patients often know what makes them sick, but hide that information from the doctor and so kid themselves. I was a "denier" myself once. Years ago, when my children were very young, I bought a German shepherd puppy for them. He turned out to be an extremely protective, fun dog. He was very intelligent too, preferring me to anyone else in the family. But Christopher was huge, and he shed all over the place. My oldest son, who had heretofore enjoyed excellent health, suddenly began to suffer frequent "colds" —coughing, wheezing and shortness of breath. These symptoms seemed to come on whenever he played with his favorite pet. It never occurred to any of us, least of all to me, the doctor, that the boy's trouble could be due to the dog. That would have been unthinkable—almost like being told that you are allergic to your wife, husband or child. My son was also unaware of any association between the dog and his new illness, not only because he loved the animal, but probably too because he subconsciously feared the animosity of the rest of the family should the dog have to go on his account. As the asthmatic attacks became more frequent, serious and prolonged, I asked several of my colleagues what they thought the cause of the boy's respiratory distress could be. Each one pointed to the big dog—hair and dander and all! I couldn't imagine how so many experts could all be so completely wrong. Seven allergists later, all of whom were in agreement on the diagnosis and recommendation ("Get rid of the dog"), I still resisted. I was sure there *must* be some other way, especially since Christopher was now protecting me on my house calls at night. I conferred with a host of veterinarians and visited dozens of pet shops, looking in vain for something to spray on the dog's coat. There is, of course, nothing that can neutralize the dander from a one-hundred-pound dog in a five-room apartment, or prevent it from affecting the lungs of a susceptible six-year-old. After I had tried all the sticky, smelly, useless sprays I could get my hands on, and as the child became sicker, I made the inevitable, overdue decision to give the dog away.

It is easy to become emotionally trapped by a pet, no matter who you are and how much you know, or how bad it can be for your health. (An interesting sidelight to my own story is that having been deprived of his dog and all other furry pets, my son developed a great interest in reptiles. He is now a knowledgeable herpetologist and has recently published a book for allergic persons on how to enjoy nonfurry pets.)

AN ENVIRONMENT THAT DEFIES CONTROL

The first objective, then, in managing allergic asthma is to identify the offending allergen and get rid of it. *Promptly.* Of course, except for pets, that is not always possible. There are too many aspects of our environment beyond the control of any individual. You can and, indeed, *must* stop smoking, and you can choose the no-smoking section of an airplane, but there are no no-perfume areas, nor can you always find a haven from certain noxious industrial fumes, pollens and dust. As civic awareness becomes more widespread, perhaps these areas will be available.

Supposing, then, that you have asthma—mild, moderate or severe. (Incidentally, if it's mild, that is, the attacks occur infrequently and don't cause serious symptoms, they won't necessarily get worse with time.) Whether the asthma is of recent onset and you are visiting a doctor about it for the first time, or it has been chronic and you consult another physician because treatment has not been satisfactory, here are some tips. First of all, ask for enough time from the doctor to permit him and you to delve into your history and identify precisely what it is that *triggers* your attacks. This is especially important in children, where allergy is such a common cause of asthma.

After you've analyzed the factors possibly responsible for your asthma, make sure the physical exam your doctor performs is thorough and focused. If it isn't, see someone else. There's a great deal to be learned about your asthma from a careful checkup. For example, your throat should be thoroughly examined. The presence of glandular tissue there suggests that you have chronic postnasal drip, such as occurs in sinusitis. The doctor should take a good look up your nose to search for polyps (20 percent of persons with intrinsic [adult] asthma have such polyps). Even your thyroid function should be reevaluated because from time to time an overactive thyroid can throw your air passages into spasm, causing a worsening of the asthma. Lung function should be tested. A chest X ray should be obtained. Sinus films are especially important since chronic sinusitis is present in about half the patients with nonallergic asthma. Skin testing may also be necessary. In other words, the onset of asthma is an important landmark in your life, and should be approached seriously and thoroughly, not with just a five-minute visit and a few prescriptions.

HOW EFFECTIVE IS DESENSITIZATION?

In the typical asthmatic attack, the body is challenged by a substance called an *allergen,* which provokes an immunological or "defense" response. This consists of the release of certain chemicals, one of which is histamine, that constrict the bronchial tubes and cause asthma. Desensitization, or hyposensitization, involves injecting under the skin tiny amounts of whatever it is you are allergic to. We don't give you enough of the material to precipitate an attack, but sufficient to stimulate the body gradually to build up resistance to it. Theoretically, when that is achieved, the adverse reaction to the allergen will either be entirely prevented or rendered less severe.

Desensitization usually takes years, is expensive, and occasionally is uncomfortable. Does it work? There is an 80 percent success rate in hay fever caused by pollens, ragweed, dander and dust. Don't expect results for at least two years after starting the shots. As far as foods are concerned, desensitization is probably of no value. You simply have to avoid eating anything that makes you sick.

BLUE CROSS WON'T PAY

In cases of *intrinsic* asthma, the kind that develops not so much from allergy as from chronic lung or sinus infections, attempts to desensitize patients to their own bacteria led to the administration of vaccines made from those bacteria. Although this technique remains popular and sounds logical, in actual fact, there is no evidence that it works. Most insurers, including Blue Cross, will not reimburse you for it. Should this regimen be offered to you, get a second opinion, unless you're willing to pay for the treatment out of your own pocket.

THE ANTIASTHMA ARMAMENTARIUM

So you've done everything *you* can to manage your asthma. You've tried to live in an allergen-free environment, you've stopped smoking, you've identified and now avoid foods that might induce an attack; you're careful about exercise, aspirin and the newer nonsteroidal anti-inflammatory drugs (Motrin, Naprosyn, Clinoril). You also take antibiotics at the very first sign of any respiratory infection. You even try to spare yourself unnecessary emotional crises (but you now know that your asthma does not reflect a disturbed personality). You also make certain to avoid beta-blocker drugs like Inderal (used mainly in the treatment of high blood pressure, cardiac rhythm irregularities and angina pectoris) or Timoptic (in the form of eye drops to control glaucoma) since these can bring on an acute asthmatic attack in vulnerables. But despite all this, you're still getting attacks of wheezing for which you clearly need medication. There has been a great deal of progress in this area, so that no asthmatic should really have to suffer anymore. Here is how I treat my asthmatic patients.

TREATING ASTHMA—
THERE ARE CHOICES

In my opinion, the best way to treat asthma is to prevent it. But, if you find yourself in a setting where an attack is inevitable, as for example, when you're visiting a friend to whose cat you're allergic, or prior to some exercise that you know will throw your airways into spasm, you have a choice of preventatives. My favorites are the "beta-adrenergic agonists"—marketed as metaproterenol (Alupent), terbutaline (Brethine, Brethaire, Bricanyl) and albuterol (Ventolin, Proventil). The best way to take them is by inhalation using a nebulizer. They break the airway spasm in seconds, and are especially effective in preventing exercise-induced asthma in children. They also come in oral form, but I have found the side effects to be more troublesome via this route. The forerunners of the beta agonists, Isuprel and Bronkosol, were good products in their day, but in my opinion not nearly as effective or as well tolerated. The beta agonists do the job with much less effect on heart rate or blood pressure, an advantage that becomes very important if you have high blood pressure or any cardiac condition. They can be used three or four times a day, virtually indefinitely.

Many asthmatics can go for long periods without any antiwheezing drugs. Others need something almost continuously to keep their airways open. You can use the beta agonist inhalers for that purpose. Another type of medication, the xanthines (theophylline), is also useful. These drugs are marketed in tablet form as Slo-Phyllin, Theo-Dur, Quibron or Uniphyl, to name but a few of those currently available, as a liquid (Elixophyllin) to be taken by mouth, as an enema preparation, or as suppositories. I avoid this latter route because of the rectal irritation it produces. A recent formulation of theophylline has made possible a one- or two-per-day dosage.

Although the xanthines have been the mainstay of chronic antiasthmatic treatment for years, more and more doctors are now using the beta agonists. Very often both are necessary and when that is the case, they may be taken together. Theophylline can cause several problems, including gastric irritation, stomach pain, nausea and vomiting; the rate of absorption may also vary from person to person. Elderly patients don't do too well with it. There may be other toxic side effects like rapid heart rate, nervousness and even convulsions that may preclude their use in any given patient, but these are usually dose-related. Theophylline should never be given with food.

PREVENTING THE ATTACK
IN THE FIRST PLACE

One medication, cromolyn, blocks the formation or release of the adverse chemicals ("mediator substances") when the provoking agent strikes the lungs. Cromolyn, when it works, is particularly effective in allergic children or young people and those patients at any age whose asthma is induced by exercise. Remember, however, never to use it for the treatment of an acute attack—only for prophylaxis. It comes in a powder-filled capsule, which is put in an *inhalator* that pierces the container and propels the powder into the air passages. Children sometimes find this route of administration inconvenient, and their parents find it relatively expensive. Also, youngsters generally don't like to take medication prophylactically. But you're in luck if it works, so be sure to ask your doctor about cromolyn, especially if he tells you he's planning to use steroids, which should be the last resort therapy for chronic use.

STEROIDS WHEN NECESSARY

Steroid hormones are potent dilators of the bronchial tree, and therefore very effective in the treatment of asthmatic spasm. They should, however, be used only after other treatment has failed. Throughout this book you will find notes of caution and dire warnings about taking the cortisone-type drugs capriciously. Their long-term use is fraught with potential danger. But in some asthmatics, the situation can become so bad that the doctor has no choice. When these steroids are necessary, they should be taken for a short period of time, no longer than seven to ten days, and prescribed in declining doses. In other words, you start off with a large amount the first two days. This has an almost immediate effect on symptoms (in association with other bronchial-dilating drugs), and you can begin to taper the dosage on the third day. The schedule is so planned that by the tenth day at the latest, you're off the medication completely. And that's usually all you need. If steroids are prescribed for a longer time than that, get a second opinion, especially if you have a history of hypertension, heart trouble or ulcers.

After the short course of oral steroids, you may safely continue taking the cortisone now available in an aerosol mist. It acts directly on the walls of the bronchial tubes, and is *not absorbed* into the bloodstream. This drug, beclomethasone, is marketed in the United States as Vanceril. It is effective for the acute attack and can also be taken in small doses as a preventive during a vulnerable phase, for example, the hay fever season. The combination of beta agonists mentioned above and Vanceril is excellent for most chronic asthmatics.

DRUGS ARE NOT ENOUGH

You must live by two cardinal rules if you are asthmatic. First, stop smoking. Tobacco smoke is irritating to the lining of the air passages. Second, any respiratory infection, no matter how minor, should be treated promptly with antibiotics and eradicated. If you fail to do so, although you started with a "cold," you will end up spitting yellowish or greenish sputum. Then you will begin to wheeze and will be sick for weeks, coughing and wheezing. Doctors hesitate to prescribe antibiotics for patients who have only a "simple cold." If you are asthmatic, that conservatism doesn't apply to you.

Finally, remember that the long-term outlook for asthma is good since it does not per se cause emphysema or chronic lung damage.

KEY FACTS TO REMEMBER

Asthmatic wheezing results from narrowing of the bronchial tubes by spasm, mucus, infection or allergy. Asthma may be acute and paroxysmal, or chronic. Its causes, external or internal, must be identified and eliminated from your environment. Determination of the responsible factors may require the aid of an allergist.

A number of drugs, some very old, others quite new, are available for the prevention and treatment of asthma. They must be carefully selected and combined for optimal effect—something that may require a second opinion from an allergist or a chest specialist.

9

THE SKIN—COMMON
PROBLEMS AFFECTING
THE LARGEST ORGAN
IN THE BODY

This chapter contains a discussion of some of the more common and difficult skin problems. Since so many are chronic and a few are even life-threatening, you should be alerted about when to get a second opinion and why.

THE EASY LIFE

When I was a medical student, my friends and I used to sit around and muse about our future as practitioners. We speculated with some animation about what each of us might be doing twenty-five years down the pike. Most of my classmates expected to end up as family practitioners. Others hoped to be specialists in one field or another—endocrinology, cardiology, gastroenterology or surgery. Many, especially those who thought they lacked the necessary technical talent or dexterity, opted for psychiatry. Interestingly enough, anyone who expressed the desire to become a dermatologist was accused of taking the easy road, of avoiding a career with real physical or intellectual challenges. After all, whoever heard of a skin doctor getting an emergency call in the middle of the night? Where was the glamour or challenge in treating an itch, a rash or a pimple?

THE LARGEST ORGAN IN THE BODY

How times have changed! The specialty of dermatology, which my classmates and I used to think was dull, is actually one of the more exciting fields in medicine. We now appreciate the fact that the skin is as vital to health as any other body tissue. One of my dermatologist friends reminds his patients that he treats the largest organ in the body. The skin often mirrors important disease processes taking place internally. Do you have a "simple" rash? There is probably more to it than meets the eye. In some cases the heart, lungs, liver or kidneys may also be involved. If you have an unexplained sore, it may be due to syphilis—a disease that can spread throughout your body. A peculiar tightness of the skin may reflect a disorder that also "scars" the heart and the gut. Almost every serious malady has skin manifestations—tumors, arthritis, heart trouble, kidney disease, liver malfunction and glandular diseases, to name but a few. So the dermatologist is no longer perceived as the chap who wanted the easy life. A good "skin man" is an astute biological detective, tracking down the clues that lead to proper diagnosis. In addition to that, however, he is also confronted with the problem of treating some of the most troublesome symptoms known to man. If you have ever been plagued by a serious, persistent itch, you know exactly what I mean. It can be worse than pain. But happily, today's dermatologist has at his disposal a wide range of treatment options (from sophisticated radiation to ointments that eradicate skin cancer), none of which were available to his predecessors a generation ago.

PSORIASIS—IT'S MORE THAN JUST DANDRUFF

Psoriasis is a chronic, troublesome skin disease that is newly diagnosed in as many as 250,000 Americans each year. It's a bore, it's embarrassing, it's uncomfortable, it's expensive, and occasionally, it can be serious. You can't always spot psoriasis victims because the silver-red, scaly plaques that are its hallmark are often hidden under their clothes. But if it affects the scalp, you'll see more "dandruff" on the patient's shoulders than you thought was possible—a veritable snowfall.

The superficial cells in the skin respond to everyday wear and tear by shedding and then replacing themselves. These two processes normally occur at equal rates. In psoriasis, however, these "top-layer" cells are formed much more rapidly and prematurely than necessary, and so the superficial skin is scaly and sheds very easily. No one knows why these cells multiply so enthusiastically. It's obviously due to a breakdown in the mechanisms that regulate cell division.

Psoriasis is easy to diagnose, but difficult to treat. It not only involves the scalp, where it simulates a bad case of dandruff; the typical scaly, silvery patches can occur anywhere—on the elbows, knees, penis, back, between the buttocks and around the anus (which, like the scalp, is one of the few areas where they are likely to be itchy). Nails are commonly affected too. In about 7 percent of cases, psoriasis not only involves the skin, but is also accompanied by a severe form of arthritis.

INHERITED, BUT NOT
FOUND AMONG BLACKS

Some four in every hundred whites living in the United States have psoriasis, but it is rarely found in the dark-skinned races. It appears to run in families, and may develop at any age. Although patients can occasionally tell me exactly when their skin problem started—triggered by a bad cold, a sunburn or some other illness—such a relationship is not usually apparent. In about one third of the cases new rashes appear on areas of the skin that have been hurt in some way.

TREATMENT, YES; CURE, NO

Psoriasis is difficult to treat. Fortunately, most cases are mild and localized to small areas of the skin. But the disorder can become sufficiently widespread to require vigorous management. Patients so affected go from doctor to doctor looking for a cure. If you are one of them, remember that there *is no cure* at this time, but the disease *can* be treated. The regimen that is best for you will depend on the size of the area of skin involved, how long you have had it and whether it is complicated by arthritis. Even if you do respond to treatment, chances are that you will have a recurrence sometime in the future.

FIRST DO NO HARM

Before thinking about therapy, you should know that there are certain drugs you may be taking that can make your psoriasis worse. Unless the doctor who prescribed them for you is a skin specialist, he may not be aware of their potential adverse effect. For example, the widely used beta-blockers can worsen psoriasis. So can lithium, frequently taken for control of certain psychiatric disorders. Even the nonsteroidal aspirin-like medications (e.g., indomethacin [Indocin]) are thought by some to exacerbate psoriatic patches.

If you have psoriasis, pamper your skin. Try not to injure it. Remember that new lesions may appear at the site of trauma. Keep it soft and moist with mild lubricating jellies, mineral oil or Vaseline.

Psoriatic patches are most commonly treated with topical creams, ointments, lotions and shampoos containing cortisone, tar, phenol, salicylic acid or even simple salt water. Among these, the most effective, at least in my experience, has been hydrocortisone. It's also the most expensive. Strengths that require prescriptions should usually be tried first. They need be applied only once a day, or even less frequently. Use creams and lotions in hairy areas. In nonhairy areas like the elbow or knee, ointments covered overnight with Saran Wrap, Glad Wrap or some similar product reduce scaling and redness.

There are literally scores of these topical steroid preparations now commercially available without a prescription. These weaker strengths can be applied after the initial stronger therapy. They should be used three times a day and rubbed in thoroughly.

Indiscriminate application of the more potent topical steroids can cause damage to healthy skin, leaving it very thin and sometimes painful. Avoid the chronic use of any cortisone cream or ointment over large areas of the body, since, in addition to its local effect, there is the possibility of its absorption into the bloodstream. And keep it away from your eyes.

Occasionally, an injection of a diluted cortisone solution into individual plaques of psoriasis yields very good results, but this should be done only by a qualified dermatologist. Finally, let me emphasize that almost never should anyone with psoriasis take hydrocortisone by mouth. First of all, massive doses are required to achieve any effect and the risks involved in such a regimen are simply not worth it. What's more, in some cases, the psoriasis gets much worse after the drug is withdrawn.

COAL TAR—MESSY, BUT IT MAY BE WORTH IT

Crude coal tar is a form of topical therapy in use today that dates back some fifty years, and which is also fairly effective (but remember, like every other treatment of psoriasis, it is not a cure). If it alone doesn't do the trick, then daily exposure to ultraviolet rays (the Goeckerman method) is usually tried. This therapy is usually limited to patients whose disease is severe, because the treatment is messy, time-consuming and requires hospitalization. The coal tar ointment is applied every two to four hours to the entire skin surface, except the body folds and head. It is removed twice a day and followed by the ultraviolet treatment. Plaques usually clear after two to four weeks in most cases, and you may remain free of disease for many months, or even years, thereafter. So if your disease is severe enough, and not responsive to topical or injectable hydrocortisone, ask for a second opinion about the Goeckerman method. But be sure the dermatologist doing it is experienced with it, since the proper dosage of the ultraviolet rays is very important.

SUNLIGHT, SUNLAMPS AND THE IRS

I am sometimes asked to write a letter to the Internal Revenue Service to justify a patient's going to a warm climate for the winter. I do so happily with a clear conscience in cases of severe heart disease, where cold weather worsens symptoms, and for patients with psoriasis who benefit from exposure to sun and salt water. One of the best places for getting both is the Dead Sea in Israel, where in addition to sunlight, you can bathe in water with a very high salt concentration.

If it is not practical for you to go South, West, or to the Middle East in the wintertime, and if your psoriasis is extensive and severe, you may benefit from ultraviolet light therapy. Ultraviolet radiation often helps patients with severe psoriasis when the methods described above have failed.

Ultraviolet radiation covers a spectrum of light emission. The first kind to try is the midrange type, or UVB. This is usually combined with some kind of topical moisturizer. It results in a "sunburn" effect on the skin and the risk of cataracts if you look directly into the lamp (so never do so and make sure to wear sun goggles anyway). Some skin doctors think this phototherapy may impair immunity against cancer, but I don't believe this has been proved.

If you're really in trouble with your psoriasis, you can go one step further and receive a different spectrum of light therapy, UVA. This is combined with an oral drug called psoralen. This combination treatment is called PUVA, referring to the psoralen and UVA.

I worry particularly about skin cancer after PUVA therapy, especially if you had such cancer in the past or have previously been exposed to significant amounts of ionizing radiation. For example, if you were treated for acne in the days when doctors recommended superficial X rays to the skin, PUVA therapy increases your chances of developing skin cancer or cancer of the thyroid gland. But one has to balance the good with the bad. Whether or not you decide to take PUVA depends on the severity of the psoriasis. In any event, after the treatment is completed, have your skin checked very carefully over the years in order to detect the earliest evidence of cancer. The risk of this happening is about 2½ times normal.

For patients with severe psoriasis, there is available a strong and potentially toxic drug called methotrexate. It is often given instead of psoralen with UVA treatment. Methotrexate is a chemical used in the treatment of various cancers; it slows the growth of rapidly multiplying cells, and in psoriasis such rapid, nonmalignant growth is the basic problem. Since methotrexate may damage the liver, it should be used only by highly trained specialists, in the lowest possible doses, and for the shortest time necessary to get results. But it does work, and has been approved by the Food and Drug Administration for cases of severe psoriasis.

WHAT'S NEW—AND FAR OUT

Patients with psoriasis, desperate for relief, may end up trying some "far out" recommendations. These include dietary changes, sleep therapy, tonsillectomy or antibiotics, none of which I have ever known to make any difference whatsoever in the course of the disease.

I have been reading scattered reports of the use of dialysis in the treatment of psoriasis. Dialysis is the process in which body wastes are washed out of the system via an "artificial kidney." I know of no convincing evidence that it works. If this fairly drastic approach is recommended to you, be sure to get a second opinion.

The FDA has recently approved the release of Tegison, a new drug for the treatment of very severe psoriasis. It is said to be highly effective, but also toxic. Ask your dermatologist whether you qualify to receive it.

ACNE—A PLAGUE AT ALL AGES

Acne is the most common of all skin diseases. Although it occurs predominantly among teenagers and young adults, affecting some fifteen million of them between the ages of twelve and seventeen, I have also seen it persist into the thirties and even the forties. Although not a threat to life, acne may be cosmetically and socially disastrous, especially to youngsters. I have written this section to help separate fact from the folklore surrounding the causes and treatment of this disorder.

A MATTER OF HORMONES, NOT INFECTION

Acne *looks* like a skin infection but it is essentially a hormonal disorder. Infection when present is a secondary complication. Usually beginning in puberty, it is worse in girls, and flares up before their menstrual periods. It may have its onset after a young woman has started on the "pill," or more importantly, when she discontinues it. But acne affects boys too and in both sexes tends to clear up in adult life. However, it sometimes reappears in a slightly different form at the time of the menopause—again presumably because of altered hormonal status.

HOW ACNE DEVELOPS

The sebaceous glands in the skin, which produce the oil that gives the skin its normal texture, are under the influence of the sex hormones. As the production of these hormones fluctuates, so does the amount and quality of the oil made by the glands. Bacteria normally present in the ducts of the hair follicles (which receive the secretions from the sebaceous glands) can alter the chemistry of the waxy stuff. Under certain circumstances, they produce an irritating chemical, which then causes the inflammation and the pimples that we call acne. Blockage of the hair duct is the final and crucial element in the causation of the disease.

Acne most commonly involves the face, back and chest, because this is where the greatest concentration of sebaceous glands is found. In adult men, lesions frequently concentrate on the back, while in women the lower part of the face is more commonly affected. Cosmetics, especially greasy moisturizing creams, can aggravate or even trigger the disease.

So the three preconditions necessary for acne to develop are (a) hormonal changes that increase the secretion of the glands, (b) the action of normal bacteria on these secretions, and (c) obstruction of the hair ducts.

OLD MYTHS DIE HARD

The subject of acne is still permeated by old wives' tales, the most important of which concerns diet. There is a commonly held but mistaken view, even among some doctors, that acne is your punishment for eating "junk food." The fact is that diet has almost nothing to do with acne; changing it usually will not make any difference. There are only two exceptions to this statement: (1) A high intake of seaweed and kelp (not favorite snacks of American teenagers) may produce an elevated iodine content that can occasionally worsen the condition; (2) some dermatologists believe that a drastic reduction in the amount of fat consumed will improve acne. I don't have any personal experience with kelp eaters, and I'm not sure that the claims about fat reduction are valid.

Other misconceptions and half-truths about acne implicate masturbation and poor personal hygiene. These are totally false. The belief that squeezing the pimples will spread the infection is only partially true. The admonition not to do anything for the acne because "you'll outgrow it" is not only wrong but dangerous. Although superficial blackheads or whiteheads sometimes do clear up spontaneously (presumably because of a change in the patient's hormonal status), failure to treat acne can lead to permanent scarring due to the rupture of pus-filled cysts deep in the skin.

YOUR TREATMENT OPTIONS

So treatment of acne has very little to do with your diet, sex habits or personal hygiene, and is basically of two forms, topical ointments (creams or solutions), and oral medication. Mild cases in which there is little or no inflammation or infection usually respond to topical therapy.

Tretinoin (retinoic acid—a derivative of vitamin A) in cream form opens up the plugged glandular ducts and thus improves acne. It is probably the most effective of the topically applied agents. Since it renders the skin more sensitive to sunburn, always apply sunscreen with it if you're going to be exposed to strong sunlight. You're better off applying the tretinoin every other day, rather than daily, since that will give you substantially less irritation.

Topical application of tetracycline or clindamycin is also beneficial. However, topical tetracycline causes the skin to "glow" under the black light used in discotheques, a side effect that is of particular concern to some teenagers! Another effective topical antibacterial (but not antibiotic) is benzoyl peroxide, applied to the skin in a gel form. There are several soaps and lotions that help peel and dry the skin. These contain salicylic acid, resorcin and sulfur products.

When topical treatment is not effective, especially in the presence of considerable inflammation, infection and blockage of the ducts, antibiotics are required. Oral tetracycline is the one most widely prescribed. It is relatively inexpensive and safe, and that's important because you may have to take it for years, until your hormonal balance "straightens itself out." When tetracycline is not well tolerated, erythromycin (taken with meals) is effective too. In my experience, however, it is more apt than tetracycline to cause intestinal symptoms.

If pus has accumulated behind the blocked ducts, the doctor may have to drain it, or he may inject a weak solution of cortisone directly into the inflamed areas to prevent scarring.

The really big breakthrough in the treatment of severe acne, the kind that doesn't respond to any of the topical or oral preparations described above, is isotretinoin, marketed as Accutane. It has changed the lives of many thousands of young people. It is taken by mouth and treatment is continued for several months. Improvement is often dramatic, and may continue for years. Sometimes the course of therapy needs to be repeated, but wait a few months before doing that.

Unfortunately, those who need Accutane most are apt to

be women in the childbearing years—and this drug can cause serious deformities in the fetus of a pregnant woman who uses it. So before you start treatment with Accutane, be sure to have a pregnancy test. And while you're on this medication, be very fastidious about your contraception. Do not try to conceive for at least two months after ending a course of treatment with Accutane. Men taking it need not worry. It does not affect the sperm.

Another interesting consequence of Accutane treatment has recently been reported, namely, significant elevation of triglyceride levels. Since this may be a risk factor for vascular disease, you should have your triglyceride levels checked before therapy is begun. If, after you've been taking Accutane for a while, the levels are indeed found to be higher than at the onset, then you should avoid alcohol and reduce your sugar intake. Both these substances raise triglyceride levels in their own right. Also, tetracycline and Accutane often have adverse interactions. Avoid taking them together. Because of its many potential complications, be sure to discuss all the pros and cons of Accutane therapy with your doctor if he prescribes it for your acne.

POCKS ON YOU

When pockmarks develop in patients with severe acne, *dermabrasion,* a kind of sandpapering of the skin to smooth out the crevices, may help. This treatment is somewhat involved, and the results are not always good. If you are black, think twice about dermabrasion because the resulting keloid (scar tissue) formation can be worse than the scarring from the acne. Also, if you are dark-complexioned and are exposed to the sun after dermabrasion, you may end up with areas of too much pigment, or too little.

Other forms of therapy for acne are sometimes recommended. There are dermatologists who prescribe the "pill," especially those preparations that contain high doses of estrogen. This will reduce the amount of wax produced in the hair glands. You won't, however, see any results for at least three months.

Other doctors will advise you to take zinc tablets. You're

probably better off without them, especially if you have ulcer problems, since too much zinc can cause gastrointestinal bleeding.

JUST LYING IN THE SUN

Acne does improve in the summertime, but no one is really sure why. It may be that the irritation of the solar ultraviolet radiation results in increased blood flow to the skin, or perhaps it's the tranquilizing effect of just lying in the sun.

SKIN CANCERS— YOU CAN RARELY BE SURE

Hardly a day goes by without my being asked whether a mole, wart or some other kind of skin change is "suspicious" for cancer. To be perfectly honest, there are times I just don't know for sure. Even my dermatologist colleagues admit that they cannot always be certain what to make of a growth on the skin. To be sure it isn't either malignant or potentially so, they do a biopsy. I agree wholeheartedly with that approach. You should never refuse the suggestion of a biopsy to exclude the possibility of skin cancer.

The wisdom of that position was driven home to me very dramatically not long ago. One of my patients complained of an itch in the middle of his back. He couldn't see the involved area because of its location, but his wife told him she saw a "pimple" there. He consulted a dermatologist, who "doubted" that it was anything serious, but suggested another look in one month. About six weeks later, my patient returned to the doctor, who happened to be very busy that day. After waiting impatiently for more than an hour, he left in a huff to "teach that guy a lesson." It was a case of cutting off his nose to spite his face, for a month later he complained to me that the itch was worse than ever. When I looked at his back, I now saw what was obviously a malignant melanoma, one of the most dangerous cancers one can have. Two precious months had been lost—the first because the dermatologist failed to do a biopsy when he wasn't sure, and the second because the patient was impatient. The cancer was finally removed. Fortunately, six years later there has been no recurrence. That man is very lucky!

FACT AND FOLKLORE ABOUT SKIN CANCER

There are several popular misconceptions about skin growths. "A growth that's painless can't be serious." Not true. Pain has absolutely nothing to do with the diagnosis. "Removal or biopsy of a tumor causes a growth to spread or others to appear." Also obvious nonsense. We used to think that the hairy elevated mole is always benign and that the flat, brown variety is a potential troublemaker. That's not true. *Any* skin cell with pigment in it has malignant potential. If in the slightest doubt, check it out with a skin doctor.

Most skin tumors are, in fact, benign. They include the common freckle, mole, and what we call keratoses. The latter, which develop as we get older, are small areas of heaped-up skin with a brownish discoloration. They are important only cosmetically. Skin tags, especially frequent around the neck and armpits, are completely innocuous.

Here is a good general rule to follow. *Any bleeding or ulceration on the skin, any growth that itches or changes in color or size, is suspicious.* Show it to a dermatologist without delay.

THE SPECTRUM (AND SPECTER) OF SKIN CANCER

Skin cancers can be divided into three major types. The first and most common, the basal cell cancers, or *epitheliomas,* originate in the lowermost cells of the epidermis (the superficial layer of the skin). They usually occur in areas of the body chronically exposed to sun, like the face. They grow very slowly and often bleed spontaneously or after slight irritation. They don't really constitute a threat to your life once they have been completely removed.

Another kind of skin cancer is the *prickle-cell epithelioma.*

It originates a little more superficially in the epidermis than does the basal cell cancer, and it is much less common. Unlike the latter, which is almost always curable, no matter how late it is treated, the prickle-cell cancer must be eliminated immediately because it spreads very quickly.

Malignant *melanomas* are among the deadliest of all human cancers, but some forms are more threatening than others. The kind that spreads soonest and most rapidly, the nodular melanoma, may be black or brown in color, frequently ulcerates or bleeds and may be tinged with red, white or blue. It is usually more elevated than the less deadly varieties. Another type, the superficial spreading melanoma, is highly curable when treated early. Redheads and blondes are more susceptible to the above two forms of melanomas. The black, mottled and large pigmented lesion constitutes the third type of melanoma. Usually appearing on the face of the elderly, it is also frequently curable if removed early. *Excision, as wide and as deep as necessary, is the sole preferred therapy for all melanomas.*

There are several different ways to remove malignant skin lesions. Some do not require surgery. This is never true for malignant melanomas. There are, however, skin tumors that can be burned, scraped, irradiated or even treated with topical anticancer preparations (5-FU). Cryotherapy, using liquid nitrogen, is also effective in some circumstances. Chemosurgery with potent topical anticancer drugs is also often successful. So if you are told that you have a skin cancer that has to be cut away and you want some options, ask for a second opinion from an experienced dermatologist, especially if the lesion is on your face. But never reduce your chances for a cure by opting for therapy that has the best cosmetic results—and leaves you in danger. A scar, even a highly visible one, is a small price to pay for your life.

SHINGLES—NOT FOR DOCTORS ONLY

Herpes zoster (also known as herpes varicella), or shingles, as it is commonly referred to, is a painful skin eruption caused by a virus belonging to the herpes family (see Chapter 10). Although rarely a cause of death, shingles is responsible for a good deal of pain and suffering. The zoster virus can cause two "different" diseases—chicken pox in childhood and shingles in older patients. In addition, cancer victims, or anyone taking immunosuppressive drugs (used in the treatment of certain malignancies and also to prevent rejection of transplanted organs), or those who have received excessive radiaticn are all particularly prone to shingles.

When the zoster virus is acquired in childhood, as is usually the case, it causes chicken pox, with its typical blister-type rash. The virus itself then travels from the skin surface up the nerve fibers, and settles down for a more or less permanent residence in the nerve cells near the spinal cord. There it remains for years and years and usually gives you no further trouble. But then, in some three to five unlucky persons per thousand, something reactivates the virus, which then leaves the nerve cell, travels back down the nerve to its endings in the skin and causes the characteristic painful blisters called shingles. For a few days before the sores actually appear, the area of skin involved becomes tender or sensitive. Symptoms may be mild, but occasionally the pain is severe, especially if the eye or ear are involved. So if you suddenly develop pain over a localized area of your body, and there's nothing to see on the skin surface, look again and again over the next few days. If it's shingles, the rash will appear. One other characteristic of the disease will help you make the diagnosis. The rash almost never crosses the midline of the body. So if you develop any kind of eruption on *both* sides of your chest, or back, or face, chances are it's not shingles.

Fortunately, in most patients, the painful skin lesions clear up after a few days—and that's that. Sometimes, however, the complications may be disastrous. This is most likely to happen during pregnancy, or if the eyes or ears have been involved. The most common serious consequence of shingles is persistence of the pain—for weeks, months or even years—after the rash itself has disappeared (postherpetic neuralgia). The affected nerve endings remain exquisitely sensitive and can make life very miserable for the unfortunate patient.

There has been a good deal of progress in the treatment of shingles in recent years. Should you be unlucky enough to be stricken, there is now a wide variety of options available that you should know about. Be sure to discuss them with your doctor. You should also be aware of therapy that is *not* effective—B$_{12}$ shots, gamma globulin injections and antibiotics.

The treatment goals for shingles are first to provide relief of pain. This can usually be accomplished during the acute stages by applying various topical substances—calamine lotion with or without phenol, wet dressings that evaporate, giving a cooling effect, and a host of over-the-counter analgesic creams. For painkillers, start with aspirin or acetaminophen (Tylenol), gradually working up to more serious analgesics like codeine. Other measures that may be effective in some cases include a form of electrical therapy called transcutaneous nerve stimulation, a drug marketed as Tegretol (normally used as a painkiller and anticonvulsant), and certain antidepressants like Elavil and Sinequan. Dilantin, carbamazepine, and the antiulcer drug Tagamet have also been reported to be effective pain relievers.

Once you've started local treatment, you should do all you can to reduce the likelihood of the pain becoming chronic. The best way to avoid that is, in my opinion, to take steriod hormones orally. Your doctor will know the dosage. The drug should be started within five days after the onset of symptoms, and continued in decreasing amounts for about three weeks. There is no guarantee that this will prevent a long, drawn-out siege of pain, but it often does. Remember, however, there's no use starting the steroids well into the course of the disease. You've got to do it early.

The big news in the shingles story is the availability of antiviral agents that can modify the severity of the acute attack and protect those individuals with lowered resistance (immunocompromised) in whom the zoster virus can be life-threatening. The best antiviral drug now available for shingles is Zovirax (acyclovir)—the same agent used for the treatment of genital herpes (see Chapter 10). It comes in topical, oral and intravenous forms. The most predictable route of administration, when the threat is serious, is via the vein. Otherwise, the oral form is preferred. I prescribe it to all my patients as soon as the diagnosis of shingles is made. This treatment speeds up the healing process and reduces pain.

KEY FACTS TO REMEMBER

Diseases of the skin often mirror serious internal disorders ranging from infection to cancer. Their correct diagnosis and management is, therefore, more than a matter of appearance and comfort.

Psoriasis, a very common skin disorder, may affect the joints in its more serious form. There is no cure for this disease at the present time, but several kinds of therapy may result in relief and remission. These include topical ointments, ultraviolet light and a variety of drugs, some of which are also used in the treatment of cancer. Too much exposure to ultraviolet rays increases the risk of cancer of the skin in later years. Anticancer agents have potential toxicity.

Acne is basically a hormonal disorder, not an infection. It has very little to do with life-style, what you eat, masturbation or personal hygiene. Fundamentals of treatment consist of oral or topical antibiotics and measures to prevent scarring.

The great majority of *skin cancers* are easily recognized, removed and cured. A few, especially the malignant melanomas, are among the most virulent cancers known to man. It may take an expert and skin biopsies to differentiate the relatively harmless from the malignant kind. The management of malignant melanoma demands early and aggressive surgical removal.

Shingles, a form of herpes infection, is the chicken pox virus operating in a different setting. Most cases are characterized by skin pain of limited duration. Various treatments are available for management of symptoms. To prevent pain from persisting long after the skin rash has cleared, many doctors use steroids orally early in the course of the disease. The big breakthrough, however, in the treatment of this disorder is acyclovir (Zovirax), which is especially useful when the infection threatens immunocompromised patients.

10

SEXUALLY TRANSMITTED DISEASE (WHAT WE USED TO CALL VD)

AIDS—THE NEW GREAT PLAGUE

It's hard to remember when AIDS wasn't with us. It's even difficult for me to accept the fact that when I wrote the first edition of this book in 1980, this disease was not included. Today, it is a pandemic of major proportions that may ultimately dwarf the Great Plague, which was responsible for the death of millions the world over. Unless we come up with some treatment or vaccine in the near future, hundreds of thousands in this country alone will suffer and die from AIDS in the next decade. At the present time, it is primarily an affliction of a few vulnerable categories, for example, homosexuals, prostitutes, intravenous drug users, children of infected mothers, Haitians and perhaps those requiring frequent blood transfusions (I say perhaps because we've developed techniques that can quite effectively, though not with 100 percent certainty, screen infected donor blood). However, the threat of AIDS spreading to the heterosexual community looms large on the horizon. This is due to the fact that the virus responsible for AIDS appears to be mutating, that is, changing some of its vital characteristics. Therefore, in the future, transmissibility may not be limited to the routes followed by the current virus.

AIDS (acquired immunodeficiency syndrome) is actually a group of diseases caused by a virus variously referred to as HIV, LAV (coined by its French discoverers) and HTLV-III (used by the American scientists who found it). It is believed to have had its origin in Africa among monkeys, and over the years apparently altered its infectivity to assume its present virulent state. It kills by destroying the body's defense mechanisms (the immune system), leaving the patient vulnerable to a host of different infections and malignancies for which there is no treatment. Normal persons are usually able to ward off such attacks. AIDS victims cannot and ultimately die from some form of cancer, pneumonia or meningitis.

There are various stages of AIDS. In the first, the patient is infected by the virus, but the immune capability has not yet been impaired. Such individuals can, however, transmit the virus at this time (the carrier state). The diagnosis is made by finding the antibody to the virus in the blood. The next level of disease is called ARC (AIDS-related complex), in which the "opportunistic" infections that kill have not yet begun. Finally, there is the full-blown illness, so tragic to watch—and uniformly fatal at this time.

We estimate that almost two million people already have AIDS in some form or other, all the way from the still quiescent stage to the advanced disease. There is no cure at present, even at the earliest stage. This is one of those unusual situations in which early detection does not make a difference to the outcome. It is nevertheless important to recognize the disease so that others yet unaffected can be protected, for example, a homosexual's lover(s).

If you are told you have AIDS, you should, of course, obtain a second opinion to make sure the diagnosis is correct. Put yourself in the hands of a specialist in infectious diseases, not because he has any treatment to which someone else is not privy, but because he is apt to have experience in making you more comfortable as symptoms of the disease evolve. Such a specialist is also apt to be the first to know of any breakthrough in treatment or prevention.

The key to the control of AIDS at the moment lies in education—teaching the public at large how to avoid contracting it. Today that means prudence in sexual activity, avoidance of promiscuity, the use of condoms whenever the background of one's sexual partner is in doubt, never sharing a needle or syringe with anyone if you're a drug user, accepting blood transfusions only when absolutely necessary, and stockpiling your own in preparation for certain surgery on a fixed data (antilopas transfusion).

It is important for all of us, physicians and laymen alike, to avoid hysteria at this time. The threat of AIDS is great enough without adding unfounded and unwarranted panic. Casual contact—eating, touching, keeping or living with an AIDS patient—is not hazardous. Receiving their blood is—so is sexual activity. Short of that, there is no danger.

Although we are now able to screen all donor blood for the presence of AIDS *antibody,* it takes about two to three months after infection for that antibody to develop. So if someone donates blood shortly after becoming infected with the AIDS virus, that virus can be transmitted even though the antibody, the marker for which we test, has not yet appeared. This makes the screening procedures about 95 percent effective—small comfort if you're in the remaining 5 percent and have received AIDS in your transfusion.

A new category of potential AIDS victims is emerging—individuals who received blood before we knew how to identify the AIDS antibody. Anyone who was transfused because of anemia due to any cause or during surgery between 1980, when AIDS was first diagnosed, and 1986, when screening procedures became routine, may have been infected. (There were hundreds of thousands of heart operations, for example, during this time.) Most hospitals have now begun a "look back" program, searching for recipients of blood whose donors were subsequently found to have AIDS. Two of my own patients have been so identified. You have no idea how terrifying it is for them to receive such news and how stressful it is for me to impart it. We are trying to identify these unfortunate persons not because there is anything we can do for them, but to protect those with whom they come in contact, especially if they're still sexually active. I have no idea what percentage of those so innocently infected will ultimately develop clinical evidence of the disease because the AIDS virus sometimes lies dormant years before it causes symptoms. We must assume, however, that almost everyone so affected will ultimately manifest the full-blown disease. But even before they do so, they are carriers and can transmit it to those with whom they are in intimate contact.

The only cause for optimism in the depressing scenario of AIDS is that we have in fact made great progress against this disease in a very short time. Scientists suddenly confronted with the specter of a new and deadly infection have in short order found a causative agent and developed techniques to identify its presence. That's at least half the battle won. What remains to be done is to discover a vaccine to prevent AIDS and to find some agent(s) to treat the disease once it has been contracted.

VENEREAL, NOT VENERABLE

An infection transmitted from one person to another during any kind of sexual act, even an innocent kiss, is technically a venereal disease. For most people the term "venereal" brings to mind only the traditional syphilis and gonorrhea, with which my generation grew up. Today, however, "venereal disease" includes several other common infections, which affect many more people than syphilis or gonorrhea ever did (and the term itself is giving way to the designation "sexually transmitted disease"). There is, for example, *Trichomonas,* a "benign" organism harbored by as many as one quarter of all normal women (and their sexual partners) that causes vaginal discharge, itch and sometimes local pain. *Chlamydia* is another extremely common infectious agent, a bacterium that may also affect the eyes. It is responsible for a great deal of sterility and chronic PID (pelvic inflammatory disease) in women, as well as a penile discharge that raises fears of gonorrhea in men (even though it is watery and not purulent like that found in the typical "dose"). Finally, there are *viral* infections, the most important of which are *herpes* and *venereal warts.*

Chlamydia and herpes run neck and neck in terms of incidence, and even consequences, but the herpes virus has received more attention because it is not curable and recurs unpredictably. Chlamydia, on the other hand, can be eradicated by several antibiotics, the most widely used and effective being tetracyline.

In the first edition of this book, I said, "At this time there is no compelling reason to ask for a second opinion if you have a genital herpes infection, except to confirm the diagnosis. There is no effective treatment." I then went on to ignore this extremely important disease! Things have changed considerably in the last seven years. Although herpes is still "incurable" in the sense that the recurrent sores cannot *predictably* be prevented, the severity of symptoms and the rate of recurrence can be reduced. So let's take a closer look at genital herpes.

Although there are several herpes viruses, the one we're interested in here is the herpes simplex virus (HSV), of which there are two types—I and II. They differ mainly in respect to which part of the body they infect and the seriousness of the resulting illness. Type I is almost always found *above* the belly button. It is especially common in children, in whom it causes painful sores in the mouth, eyes, and the lining of the upper airways and food pipe. Type II herpes, on the other hand, hits *below* the belly button at any age and is related to sexual contact.

Types I and II will both "take" at the site of their inoculation, wherever it may occur. For example, if someone with a Type I infection of the lip or mouth engages in oral-genital sex, the virus will cause sores in the genital area. Because of the greater frequency of such sexual activity, some 30 percent of genital herpes cases are now actually of the Type I variety, the kind that rarely used to be found below the belly button!

Anywhere from 30 to 90 percent of Americans are believed to harbor the genital herpes virus. The figures vary so much because herpes is not a reportable disease. Whatever the incidence, it is increasing annually. The Centers for Disease Control estimate there are three hundred thousand *new* cases per year. In addition to those who develop symptoms when infected, there is a large number of carriers, individuals who harbor and can spread the virus, but who themselves don't suffer from it.

HOW YOU GET HERPES
AND WHY IT RECURS

After sexual activity of one kind or another with someone who is infected, the virus lands in the area of contact, the mouth, vagina, penis or anus. Some three to seven days later, one experiences a burning at that site, followed by the appearance of the typical blisters. These usually persist anywhere from two to six weeks. They then heal completely, without scarring. But that's by no means the end of the story. As is the case in shingles, after the blister clears, the virus travels along the nerves whose fibers terminate in the area of skin affected. This pathway ends in the nerve cells near the spinal cord where the virus settles down. And there it sits until it's ready to make the return trip back to the skin. That usually takes place within one year in most patients. Such "reactivation" usually occurs after a fever due to any cause, exposure to excessive heat or sunlight, menstrual periods, sexual intercourse, emotional stress or physical debility generally. That's a pretty wide spectrum of provocative factors, some of which are unavoidable.

The natural history of genital herpes infections then is a primary lesion followed by recurrences at varying intervals. One is most contagious when the sores, teeming with viruses, are visible. However, some individuals, especially women, can transmit the disease even when the sores are not apparent.

Despite the pain and psychological problems associated with any sexually transmitted disease, genital herpes is not often life-threatening or dangerous. There are two exceptions. Herpes is associated with an increased incidence of cancer of the cervix. Also, a newborn emerging through the mother's genital tract can develop the disease, become very sick and sometimes even die. As a result, many physicians now recommend a cesarean delivery when the mother is known to be harboring the virus. So if you are pregnant and have had recurrent herpetic attacks, make sure that you are under the care of an expert in the identification and treatment of this infection. He should work closely with your obstetrician. If the virus is found in your genital tract near the time of delivery, all three of you should discuss the question of a cesarean. Unless you are given a reasonable explanation as to why it shouldn't be done, ask for a second opinion.

PREVENTION AND TREATMENT OF HERPES INFECTION

It is obvious then that in order not to infect their partner individuals with recurrent herpes should abstain from sex while sores or blisters are present. Even *between* recurrences, men should always use a condom, and women a contraceptive foam.

Once the symptoms appear, the purpose of treatment is to control pain and shorten the attack as much as possible. That can now be done safely and effectively using acyclovir (Zovirax). The sooner this drug is started, the better the results. It is usually taken orally in a dosage of 200 mg five times a day for several days. In critical cases, where the infection is widespread and life-threatening, the intravenous route is preferable. For local therapy of the lesions themselves, drying agents should be used *only* in the early wet or blistery stage. I tell my patients to compress the blisters with salt water. I also recommend dabbing them with rubbing alcohol a few times a day if that's not too uncomfortable. I avoid prescribing calamine lotion because it almost always causes crusting, making the sores more vulnerable to infection.

Herpes, because it recurs, is by definition a chronic disease. So keep away from potent painkillers. You don't want to end up addicted. Use aspirin instead. Two will not only afford relief, but may also retard the spread of the virus.

Acyclovir not only reduces the severity of symptoms and shortens the course of the disease, it also delays recurrences. When these happen frequently, you may have to take this medication for months at a time.

TRADITIONAL VD

Gonorrhea and syphilis have plagued mankind for centuries. Despite the fact that they are easily curable with antibiotics, they are by no means extinct and, indeed, continue to infect many thousands each year. There have been some important changes in their treatment, of which you should be aware.

HOW DO I LOVE THEE?
LET ME COUNT THE WAYS

Gonorrhea is much more common than syphilis, although the latter is a more serious disease. You are not likely to get gonorrhea from using someone else's towel or from a public toilet. (I'll have more to say about that later.) The bacterium that causes gonorrhea (the gonococcus) is spread via the vagina, penis, anus or throat—but not the mouth. If you use your imagination you can see how "indulging in the pleasures of Venus" (as Hippocrates put it) can transmit gonorrhea between homosexuals, "innovative" heterosexuals, or plain old-fashioned lovers.

GONORRHEA, MY KNEE!

Although the portals of gonococcal infection are the penis, vagina, throat (gonococcal pharyngitis from fellatio but rarely cunnilingus) and anus (gonococcal proctitis), the organism does not always remain at the site of contact. It sometimes enters the bloodstream and can involve almost any part of the body—especially the heart (if you have a diseased valve from old rheumatic fever) and the liver. It may even cause arthritis, usually of a large joint, like the knee. So if you have contracted typical gonorrhea, with discharge from the penis or vagina, and days later develop a hot, painful, swollen joint, the symptoms may be connected.

THANK GOODNESS FOR ANTIBIOTICS

The consequences of gonorrhea ("dose," "clap" and other colorful synonyms) have, of course, been modified by the availability of treatment. Before the era of antibiotics, it was a miserable business. Women were frequently left sterile from scarring of the pelvic organs. (Many, untreated, still are.) In men, the penile urethra would become obstructed, requiring repeated, uncomfortable stretching, or dilation, in order for them to be able to urinate or copulate. In the acute stage, with pus coming out of the penis, the only treatment was painful irrigation. Then, in the middle 1930s, sulfa drugs were discovered, and initially they cured the disease. But the gonorrhea bug soon became resistant to them, and within a few years less than 25 percent of cases responded to those agents.

THE RESISTANT BUG

The phenomenon of *resistance* to antibiotics is an interesting one. It is not the patient who becomes resistant to an antibiotic, but the infecting organism. It happens this way. When an antibiotic works, it eradicates *most* but not all of the offending bacteria. Some resistant strains remain, but are too few to cause symptoms. With time, however, they multiply, and their subsequent generations are also resistant. When transmitted to someone else, they are not sensitive to the original antibiotic. In order to eradicate them a different drug must be used.

The genes that confer resistance on an organism are not only passed on to the next generation, they also spread, by a process called transduction, to other bacteria with which they are in intimate physical contact. It is a kind of good-neighbor policy among bacteria, and it is effected and enhanced by bacterial viruses that go from bug to bug, passing along this "resistance factor." The degree of resistance and the length of time it takes to develop depend on the organism and the antibiotics involved. For example, consider two very common bacteria originally sensitive to penicillin— the streptococcus and the staphylococcus. The former are still sensitive to this antibiotic, even after forty-five years, while only half of the staphylococcus infections today now respond to it. Generally speaking, the longer an organism has been around and the more people it has infected (gonorrhea is an "old" disease with a multitude of victims), the greater the problem of resistance.

When penicillin was discovered in 1943, it was extremely effective against the gonococcus. All one needed for a complete cure in virtually every case of gonorrhea was one shot of 160,000 units of penicillin G. Gradually, resistant strains began to emerge, so that more and more penicillin was required. To make matters worse, in the late 1970s, we began to observe another phenomenon, which complicated treatment. Some of the gonorrhea organisms were making an enzyme called *penicillinase*, which inactivated and rendered ineffective any penicillin with which it came into contact. (The ending "ase" identifies an *enzyme*—a protein that breaks complex chemicals into simpler compounds. For example, lactase works on lactose, lipase splits fats [lipids], and so on.)

So now there were two obstacles to treating gonorrhea. As a consequence of the widespread use of penicillin over the years, the development of relatively resistant strains made it necessary to increase the dose of penicillin from the original 160,000 to the 4,800,000 units used today to cure the infection. And now there were penicillinase-producing gonococci totally untouched by penicillin.

IT SHOULD BE REPORTED, BUT OFTEN ISN'T

The combination of changing sexual mores and penicillin resistance has resulted in a worldwide gonorrhea epidemic. In the United States alone, it is estimated that 1 of every 108 persons is infected. (No one can be sure of the exact number since gonorrhea is not usually reported, even though the law requires doctors to do so.) There are between three and four million new cases every year, but the incidence has begun to level off, largely because of more prudent sexual habits stemming from the fear of contracting AIDS.

NO LONGER A DISEASE OF MEN

In the "old days" gonorrhea was basically a disease of men, and its reservoir was the prostitute. That's no longer true. In the British Isles and Scandinavia, for example, the ratio of males to females with gonorrhea is now a little less than two to one. This change of incidence is probably due to the increased frequency of sexual activity in women resulting from modern contraceptive techniques. In addition, the "pill" contains hormones that alter the chemical environment of the vagina, making it, in fact, more hospitable to any gonococcus that is introduced. The result is a 50 percent greater vulnerability to infection in exposed women taking the pill. When a woman with an intrauterine device (IUD) contracts gonorrhea, the risk of it spreading within the pelvis is also greater. This is probably due to the changes induced in the lining of the uterus by the IUD—a phenomenon that may also be responsible for its contraceptive effect.

The following is an example of your treatment options in the event your own gonococcus is penicillin resistant. You have just had a sexual encounter with a new "friend" (male or female), and a few days later you come down with gonorrhea. You receive a shot of penicillin and are sent on your way—ostensibly cured. But the yellowish discharge and burning during urination do not clear up as expected. A few days later you go back to the doctor to complain that the treatment didn't work. A look at the pus under the microscope indicates that you are still infected. Chances are that you will now be given tetracycline capsules, four a day for five days, for a total of 10 grams (g). (Remember always to take tetracycline either one hour before or two hours after eating, since food—especially dairy products—interferes with its absorption from the stomach. Also try to avoid this antibiotic if you are pregnant, because it may have adverse effects on the fetus.)

Some doctors now prefer to use oral tetracycline in the first instance when treating gonorrhea, because of the resistance problems with penicillin, the pain of the injection and the ever present possibility of a sensitivity reaction to penicillin. (Remember, however, that 30 to 40 percent of the penicillinase-producing gonococci are also resistant to tetracycline.)

There are physicians who treat gonorrhea with ampicillin or amoxicillin (related antibiotics) in one big dose by mouth. These are effective, but not quite as dependable as penicillin or tetracycline.

If none of these four drugs does the job, you will have to be treated with spectinomycin, administered in a single, intramuscular injection. This antibiotic is effective against penicillinase-producing as well as resistant gonococci. It costs considerably more than penicillin and doesn't work too well in cases of gonorrhea of the throat. It has not been shown to be safe for pregnant women. Also, if by any chance you just happen to be incubating a syphilis infection contracted at the time you got your gonorrhea, spectinomycin will have no effect on that infection. (Penicillin, tetracycline, ampicillin and amoxicillin, on the other hand, will probably cure both infections.)

Here are a few additional tips about gonorrhea and its treatment. Before you opt for tetracycline rather than penicillin, remember that (a) tetracycline has a 25 percent failure rate when the infection involves the anus, which it frequently does in homosexuals; and (b) if you are pregnant, the drug may adversely affect the fetus. Also, if you are not always compliant about taking pills prescribed for you, a single shot of penicillin is much more reliable than five days of "maybe" treatment with capsules.

When you are given a shot of 4,800,000 units of penicillin G for the treatment of gonorrhea, you should also take probenecid, a drug that blocks the excretion of penicillin by the kidney, thus ensuring adequate blood levels for long periods of time.

If penicillin and probenecid fail to cure your gonorrhea, and you later develop a discharge again, before blaming it all on a penicillin-resistant organism, you should think of two other possibilities. First, if you are sexually active with the same sexual partner and didn't think to have him or her treated as well, you may have simply gotten yourself reinfected. Then again, maybe you didn't have gonorrhea in the first place. I mentioned earlier that chlamydia, transmitted the same way as gonorrhea, also results in a urethral discharge (although it is watery and not mucus). In fact, in the United States, 80 percent of white males and 30 percent of black males who visit the doctor because of a discharge from the penis after sexual contact have chlamydia, not gonorrhea. Tetracycline will cure both diseases (one of the reasons some doctors prefer to start with this drug rather than penicillin). So if your doctor prescribes penicillin for your discharge *without examining it under the microscope to make sure it's gonorrhea,* ask whether he's considered chlamydia.

YOUR ALIBI—THE PUBLIC TOILET SEAT

Let's get back to the question of the toilet seat. Earlier I said that you can't get gonorrhea from using somebody else's towel or from a public toilet. Recently, some scientists who were curious to know whether the gonococcus could, in fact, survive on a toilet seat long enough to infect anyone reported the results of a study they carried out. They commandeered several different men's and ladies' rooms, and put live gonorrhea organisms on the toilet seats. (I presume the facilities were closed to the public for the duration of the experiment.) To their surprise, they found that the bugs survived for periods of up to two hours—long enough for the next several users to contract the disease. Even so, how the gonococcus, alive or dead, could get from the toilet seat into the penis or vagina is not clear to me.

Did that "scientific study" really prove anything? Not necessarily, because in its next phase, a random examination of several toilet seats was made to search for any gonococci that had *not* been put there by the researchers. You will be relieved to know that none were found. So the experiment was inconclusive, but if you ever develop gonorrhea and need an alibi about how you got it, you might refer to this work.

GONORRHEA VACCINE?

There is talk about the possible development of a gonorrhea vaccine in the foreseeable future. If successful, this might well eradicate this disease. But it hasn't happened yet.

SYPHILIS—EVERY LITTLE BREEZE
SEEMS TO WHISPER "LUES"

Syphilis (lues) is a much more serious, but far less common, venereal disease than gonorrhea. It disseminates throughout the body more vigorously from the point of contact than does gonorrhea. If left untreated, syphilis can affect almost any part of the body—the brain, heart, liver; you name it—years after you contract the infection.

Penicillin remains the most effective antibiotic agent against syphilis. However, since the causative organism (*Treponema pallidum*) divides very slowly and penicillin is active only against the dividing forms and not the fully developed ones, a single shot of the type of penicillin given for gonorrhea is not enough. To cure syphilis, you will need either several such shots over a period of time or one injection of a slowly absorbed, long-lasting preparation that remains in the blood for a prolonged period. If you are allergic to penicillin, you can be treated with oral tetracycline for fifteen days or erythromycin for thirty days.

Remember that when you get gonorrhea, there always is the chance that you contracted syphilis at the same time. Penicillin in doses that will cure gonorrhea may not eradicate syphilis, which will then continue its insidious spread. So, if you have been treated for gonorrhea, even successfully, always have your blood checked for syphilis a month or two later—just to be sure.

How reliable are the blood tests for syphilis (VDRL, Wassermann)? If you think you were infected and noticed on your mouth or genitals a suspicious sore that cleared *without* treatment, bear in mind that a blood test may be negative for a few weeks after exposure.

If you are completely sexually "innocent" and, in the course of a routine blood test, are told that you have syphilis, don't panic. A widely used test (VDRL) sometimes gives "false-positive" results. Don't let your doctor convince you that you are syphilitic. Hold your ground. When your blood is sent for a very specific test that does not lie, the truth will out. (The interesting thing about the false-positive test for syphilis is that the disease such a result reflects [lupus erythematosus] is usually much more serious than the easily treatable syphilis.)

KEY FACTS TO REMEMBER

AIDS is a new disease of pandemic proportions for which there is presently no cure. The only means of prevention are sexual prudence and dependence on the condom. The virus responsible for the infection is not transmitted by casual contact.

The term "venereal disease" used to conjure up images of gonorrhea and syphilis among the promiscuous. We are now aware of several other infections of equal or greater importance that can be transmitted sexually. These include genital herpes and chlamydia.

Syphilis and gonorrhea are both curable if recognized and treated adequately—and in time. Penicillin is the drug of choice for both, but penicillin-resistant gonorrhea organisms are emerging. In such cases there are effective alternative antibiotics.

Vaginal and penile discharges are not necessarily due to gonorrhea. The majority are caused by chlamydia, which can be cured with tetracycline.

Syphilis, if untreated in its acute form, may go "underground" for many years, surfacing later in a lethal form. Expert consultation is desirable in such late cases because of the complexities of treatment.

Genital herpes is among the most common of the sexually transmitted diseases. While not usually serious, it can be life-threatening to the newborn and may also increase the risk of cervical cancer. Pregnant women with this infection should consider a cesarean section. If this is not suggested, a second opinion should be obtained.

Oral acyclovir is the treatment of choice for herpes infections. It is not, however, a cure.

11

THE HEART—STILL OUR NUMBER 1 KILLER

This is the longest chapter in the book, not because I am a cardiologist, but because heart trouble is the number 1 killer in our country. In the pages that follow you will read about the major types of heart disease and the various options available to you to prevent and treat them.

Chances are that when your "number is up" (and even long before it should be) you will die from some disease or disorder related to your heart or blood vessels. The condition that, statistically speaking, is most likely to do you in is called *arteriosclerosis*, or "hardening of the arteries." There are, of course, other cardiac nemeses such as birth defects, rheumatic fever, infections, spasm of the coronary arteries and various heart injuries, but these are of relatively minor importance as compared to arteriosclerosis.

THE "EXPERTS"

As a result of our justifiable preoccupation with vascular disorders, we are swamped by suggestions, dicta and warnings about what we should and shouldn't be doing in order to prevent disability and death from heart disease. This advice comes from a variety of "experts"—the media, friends, government agencies, the food industry, countless do-gooders and the medical profession. The current focus is on control of certain risk factors—high blood pressure, cigarette smoking, obesity, cholesterol and other dietary constituents, personality characteristics, elevated blood sugar and the sedentary life. The abundance of theories about what is responsible for arteriosclerosis—some valid, some still conjectural—stems from the fact that we have not as yet identified its real, fundamental cause(s). In this chapter, I will review the status and validity of the most important concepts presently in vogue, and discuss the extent to which understanding and acting on them may affect your health and longevity.

WHO GETS "HEART SICK"?

Most of us think of heart trouble as something old folks get. But infants and children are also vulnerable, usually because of some error in development while still in the womb. For example, their mother may have provoked their cardiac abnormality by contracting German measles while she was pregnant. (She should have deliberately exposed herself to this otherwise harmless viral infection *before* she became pregnant, or she should have taken the vaccine that is now available against this disease. And if she wasn't sure whether she had ever had German measles, she should have been told that there is a blood test that could have given her that information.) Or she may have smoked excessively, drunk too much, or taken some "harmless" medication, all of which increased her chances of giving birth to a child with congenital heart disease. The classic example was thalidomide, a very effective sleeping pill once widely used in Europe for a period of several years. Children of women taking it were born not only with incompletely formed limbs (the most dramatic and obvious consequence) but also with serious heart deformities.

The bottom line is that every year there are at least 25,000 children born in the United States alone with one or more of thirty-five different cardiac defects. Most of them will die unless the abnormality is corrected surgically. If the surgery is performed in time, 15,000 of those lives can be saved, and the number continues to grow as operative techniques improve. Nevertheless, if your baby is born with a heart defect and an operation is recommended at or shortly after birth, it is still a good idea to get a second opinion from a pediatric cardiologist to make sure that the surgery is in fact necessary, and that this is the best time to do it.

SURGICAL TIMING—AND ALTERNATIVES

Some cardiac malformations are so severe that the infant will die unless an operation is performed immediately. But some of the congenital abnormalities do not require surgery right away, and it may in fact be better for the repair to be performed when the child is older, stronger and better able to withstand a major heart operation. Also, in some types of congenital heart disease, for example, *ventricular septal defect* (a "hole" in the wall between the two ventricles), the defect may close spontaneously later on. Even when closure of this hole is advised, it can sometimes be done without surgery. There is a new technique in which a small umbrella-like device is slipped into the heart in the closed position by means of a catheter introduced through a vein in the leg. After the catheter is in place at the site of the defect, the "umbrella" is opened, sealing off the hole.

Another fairly common congenital heart condition, *patent ductus arteriosus,* can actually be cured by medication—without surgery. In such cases, a large artery (called the ductus arteriosus) that should have closed off at birth remains open. During its development, while the fetus is still in the womb, its lungs are not functioning because the fetus cannot breathe. Oxygen necessary to sustain life is delivered to the embryo or fetus from the mother's placenta via this ductus. At birth, when the infant starts breathing on its own, the ductus arteriosus begins to close, since it is no longer necessary, a process that takes several weeks. However, if closure fails to occur and the ductus remains open, the result is an abnormal shunt of blood between the heart and the lungs. Clinically this produces a "blue baby." For years we treated such infants by tying off or cutting this "extra" artery. Then one day an astute scientist observed that Indocin (indomethacin, a drug used in the treatment of arthritis) actually caused this vessel to constrict and close of its own accord. But this therapy works only when started early, a good reason why every newborn baby should be carefully examined at birth. If a suspicious murmur is heard, a pediatric cardiologist should be called in for consultation.

Years ago, prospective parents waited with bated breath to learn whether their newborn child was "perfect." Today the guesswork has largely been replaced by readily available techniques that can predict, during pregnancy, the presence of important developmental defects. This information may help prepare you for important decisions, ranging all the way from whether or not to terminate the pregnancy to what kind of intervention may be necessary at birth (and even sometimes within the uterus) to save your child's life. Some conditions, formerly lethal, can now be surgically corrected. And there is hope even for infants born with a single ventricle, an abnormality not compatible with life (remember Baby Fae, who was given a baboon's heart to replace her own?), if they can receive a heart transplant.

THE "FLOPPY VALVE"
(MITRAL VALVE PROLAPSE)

A very common abnormality that has literally burst onto the cardiac scene, and which is keeping cardiologists busy dispensing reassurance, is mitral valve prolapse. This disorder was only recently recognized, although it has long been responsible for a host of symptoms. The disorder may be present in as many as 20 percent of "healthy" women, and a somewhat lesser number of "normal" men. The diagnosis is usually made when the doctor hears a little click when he or she listens to the heart with a stethoscope. There may or may not be an accompanying murmur (a sound produced under many different circumstances when blood flows in a turbulent manner through the heart). We used to think that this "click" and murmur were simply variations of the normal heart sounds, of no significance, and that the complaints of individuals with these findings were neurotic. But the introduction of echocardiography (in which sound waves bounced off interior heart structures are carefully analyzed) has enabled us to "view" the inside of the heart noninvasively. As a result, we now know that these sounds result from one of the heart valves, the mitral, closing somewhat abnormally. We are still not sure what causes this condition. It is sometimes present at birth, or it may first be heard during adolescence or early adult life. It goes by a variety of names—Barlow's syndrome, floppy valve and mitral valve prolapse. In the vast majority of cases, this variation in valve motion neither interferes with normal heart function nor reduces life expectancy. However, it can be associated with a variety of symptoms that are disturbing to the patient—chest pressure or pain, palpitations, migraine headaches, fainting and panic attacks.

Although the floppy valve is not usually a threat to survival, in a small number of cases where the valvular distortion is severe and the leak a major one, the valve may need to be repaired or replaced. Occasionally the rhythm disturbance associated with this disorder is serious, potentially lethal, and requires medication to bring it under control. The best drug for this purpose is a beta-blocker like Inderal. Don't hesitate to accept this prescription from your doctor unless you are asthmatic. Also, if you are taking Inderal and become pregnant, it's probably all right to continue this medication until a week or two before you deliver. Inderal has not been implicated in any cases of fetal birth abnormalities, but it may lower the pulse and blood pressure of the fetus close to parturition.

In addition to their antiarrythmic effect, beta-blocker drugs have another beneficial action. They help control the migraine headaches with which some floppy valve patients suffer.

A word about panic attacks associated with mitral valve prolapse: These are real, frightening and often very troublesome. However, they usually respond to repeated reassurance *and* some kind of tranquilizing or antianxiety agent. I have found Tofranil, in a dose of 25 mg three times a day, to be very effective. BuSbar, a newer drug, promises to afford relief as well. These medications are sometimes required for weeks and months at a time in order for the patient to be able to function normally.

Women who have been told they have mitral valve prolapse frequently worry that it will interfere with childbearing. It almost never does. There is, in fact, no reason for you to change your life-style in any way, except to take antibiotics when you're having any dental work or gynecological or urological intervention. I usually prescribe such antibiotics only when the click is accompanied by a murmur. Other cardiologists, however, recommend them to all patients with this disorder. This prevents the most dangerous and common complication of mitral valve prolapse, subacute bacterial endocarditis (SBE). This occurs when the distorted and/or leaky mitral valve becomes infected by bacteria circulating in the bloodstream. These organisms usually originate in the mouth, whence they have been released during some innocuous dental procedure such as teeth cleaning or gum massage, or during an operative procedure.

If you develop a persistent or recurrent low-grade fever for which there is no apparent cause and you have a mitral valve prolapse, think of SBE—and suggest that diagnosis to your doctor if he hasn't thought of it himself. SBE is confirmed by finding bacteria in your blood in a routine blood culture, and the treatment is fairly standard—several weeks of antibiotic therapy.

THE SPECTRUM OF SYMPTOMS IN MITRAL VALVE PROLAPSE

You might wonder how this mechanical derangement of the mitral valve can cause such a spectrum of symptoms. We are not quite sure, but according to one theory, persons so affected may secrete too much of an adrenaline-like substance, which may account for the palpitations, nervousness, headache and chest pain. There may also be an association between the floppy valve and other congenital heart lesions. Unless your doctor listens to your heart very carefully, he may miss the diagnosis and you may go through life incorrectly and unfairly branded a neurotic. (But remember, there are many more real neurotics than there are floppy valves.)

HEARTS NOT EASILY BROKEN

The heart has a very special place in our culture and folklore. Even though it is probably the toughest organ in the body, working constantly every moment of our lives, day and night, we still regard it as fragile. In recent years, with increased survival and a better quality of life due to newer medications, bypass surgery and balloon angioplasty, the adult cardiac patient has been accepted into life's mainstream. But a heart problem in a child, no matter how trivial, still generates fear and anxiety in its parents. These children are stigmatized as "different" by family and friends. Physical and emotional overprotection can be devastating to a youngster, even more so than the consequences of the cardiac condition itself. I know many adults who, because of some harmless heart murmur in childhood, are now cardiac neurotics because of unwarranted anxiety instilled by their loving parents. So if your child has a heart murmur due to whatever underlying condition, find out what it's all about. If it is a harmless or a "functional" murmur, leave the kid alone. If it's something that requires an operation, it's better to get it over with than to pamper and protect the child over a lifetime. Today's sophisticated surgical procedures can usually permit a virtually normal life.

RHEUMATIC FEVER—"IT LICKS THE JOINTS AND BITES THE HEART"

Hearts normal at birth may become diseased as we go through life—sometimes early on. In adolescents and young adults, the coronary arteries in the heart are not yet significantly narrowed. Therefore, heart attacks are uncommon in this age group. However, the valves that control the flow of blood in, through and out of the heart may be distorted by rheumatic fever. The trouble begins in childhood, usually after a series of sore throats followed by an acute attack of painful joints, "growing pains," or "arthritis." The child usually has no cardiac symptoms at this point, although the heart has often already been affected. The joint symptoms clear up, and the patient is seemingly free of disease. Then years later, usually during a routine physical examination, an abnormal heart murmur is heard. When asked about a history of rheumatic fever, many patients do not even remember the early episode of "arthritis." What is the connection between joint pains and the heart?

During the acute attack, while attention is focused on the "growing pains," the lining of the heart valves becomes inflamed. This results months and years later in the formation of scar tissue. Now, instead of moving freely to direct blood flow within the heart, the scarred valves are rigid and their component leaflets are stuck together. When, as a consequence, they fail to open properly, blood is prevented from *leaving* a given heart chamber, a condition called *valvular stenosis*. On the other hand, when the valve leaflets open normally, but do not shut tightly upon closing, blood *leaks back* into a chamber from which it had been squeezed out, a condition called *valvular regurgitation* or *insufficiency*.

Stenosis and insufficiency may often occur together in the same valve, or one set of valves may be stenotic and another insufficient. When valve distortion is severe enough, the heart muscle must pump harder to get the blood through a narrowed opening, or dilate in order to accommodate the extra volume of blood that has leaked back. During years of such malfunction, the heart enlarges progressively, and finally weakens. When this occurs, "heart failure" has set in. This late consequence can be avoided by timely surgical correction or replacement of the diseased valve or valves.

Your doctor will usually recommend valve surgery when he begins to see evidence that the heart is laboring, and it becomes apparent that stressing it further may cause irreversible damage. The decision is reached in several ways and includes your description of how you feel, the physical examination, and an array of tests. What you tell the doctor and how he interprets the story are most important. Some of the special procedures are easy, painless and relatively inexpensive, like the ECG, chest X ray and electrocardiography. Others are more costly, uncomfortable and, on occasion, risky. You should know what tests are available to you, the information they yield, and in what sequence they should be done. It is obviously foolish to start with the most complicated, uncomfortable, dangerous and expensive ones.

DIAGNOSTIC CARDIAC TESTS

The most important aspects of the heart examination are the complete history and thorough physical examination. Then there is the ECG. You never need to balk at that. It tells the doctor a great deal—whether your heart rhythm is normal, whether its muscle is damaged or getting any bigger as a result of whatever cardiac problem you have and whether it is under strain.

The *chest X ray* is also informative, because it indicates heart size and shape, as well as the presence of congestion (fluid) in the lungs—evidence of heart failure.

You should also know about *echocardiography,* which is as easy to do and as painless as the ECG (although more expensive). This sonar technique has in very recent years become so highly developed that it can in many cases replace the more complicated, invasive techniques described below. We used to look at the heart in only one plane with echocardiography. We now usually do so in two dimensions (the 2-D echo). These machines used to be too big and expensive for most cardiologists' offices. They are now much smaller and affordable. Adding Doppler techniques (blood flow analysis) to echocardiography now yields such accurate information about the valve that if cardiac catheterization is recommended to you in order to evaluate valve function, ask for a second opinion to see whether it is really necessary. In many cases, a good Doppler provides all the data we really need.

Another method of evaluating the heart, and more specifically valve function, is the radionuclide cineangiogram (RNCA). Like echocardiography, this test does not involve "breaking and entering" as far as your body is concerned. Nor does it require your checking into a hospital. You simply go to a laboratory as an outpatient. There you are given intravenously a tiny tracer dose of a short-lived radioactive substance (usually technetium), which goes to the heart. A computerized gamma camera, in effect a big Geiger counter, is swung over your chest, and the activity of the radioactive particles in the heart is monitored at rest, as well as during and after exercise. This provides additional useful information about valve function, and to what extent its distortion is hurting your heart. (As you will see later in this chapter, it is also extremely valuable in assessing the status of your coronary circulation.)

CARDIAC CATHETERIZATION

If all the data thus far accumulated noninvasively suggests to all concerned that "it looks like go" as far as surgery is concerned, more detailed information about the interior of the heart and its functioning may be required, and that means coming into the hospital for cardiac catheterization. You are usually admitted the night before and leave the day after the test. You should, however, know that some cardiologists are now performing these studies in day centers where you remain for a few hours after the procedure and then go home. Avoiding admission to the hospital can save you (and/or your insurance company) a bundle of money. Whether it's as safe as hospitalization is yet to be determined.

Cardiac catheterization involves the passage of a thin tube (catheter) into one of your veins or arteries (depending on which side of the heart is being studied—veins go to the right side, the arteries to the left), and threading it under fluoroscopic monitoring up into the heart. This procedure does not require general anesthesia. The area where the skin is broken in order to introduce the catheter is frozen with a little Novocain, so you feel no pain whatsoever. Nor do you have any discomfort once the catheter is in the heart, where it measures oxygen content and blood flow, and records the pressures on either side of the diseased valve. When these data are obtained, iodinated dye is injected through the catheter into the heart, and the size and thickness of the various cardiac chambers are determined, and photographs are taken. If you are over fifty years of age, the radiologist or cardiologist doing the procedure will usually for good measure also take a look at your coronary arteries. If they are diseased (blocked), then before any valve surgery is done, these diseased arteries are either ballooned open or bypassed in order to minimize the risk of the subsequent heart surgery.

It's a good idea to have your cardiac catheterization in

the hospital where you will be undergoing surgery, should that be necessary. And always ask about the experience of the team who will be performing the test. The fewest complications occur in those institutions where the procedure is commonplace and not an occasional event.

WHEN TO OPERATE AND WHEN TO WAIT

Suppose that after all the studies have been completed, you are told that you need an operation. How *soon* to have it will depend not only on the objective findings, but also on how you feel. If you have become increasingly short of breath after less and less exertion, that's an indication that your heart muscle is weakening and cannot expel all the blood returning to it. This extra volume of blood then backs up into the lungs, leaving you breathless. When that happens, there's no point in delaying surgery. But you can buy some time, if you must, with medications that decongest the lungs (water pills), strengthen the contraction of the heart (digitalis) or reduce its work load (Minipress, Apresoline, ACE inhibitors like Capoten and Vasotec, or nitroglycerin derivatives). Some of my patients have been able to delay surgery for varying periods of time, but once failure has set in, an operation is virtually inevitable. However, if you feel good, don't rush into surgery just because the *test results* are bad. Consult another cardiologist first.

You might well ask, "Why wait? Why not replace the valve as soon as it's found to be diseased?" My personal philosophy about any heart surgery is that the longer you can delay it *safely,* the better off you are—provided that a reasonable quality of life can be maintained. There are risks inherent in any operation, risks that are constantly decreasing as newer anesthetic and surgical techniques are developed. For example, valve prostheses in the 1980s had fewer long-term complications than did those inserted in the 1960s. Also, there are now alternatives to valve replacement that were not available just a few years ago.

PICKING THE SURGICAL TEAM

After the decision to operate has been made, there are still some very important options to be exercised. Where are you going to have the operation? A small institution may have very modern surgical equipment and an excellent cardiac surgeon or two, but successful heart surgery requires an experienced team that consists of trained nurses, trained respiration therapists and various technicians who work together day in and day out. A "name" surgeon without such a team is not enough. Can you depend on the "track record" of the institution as far as its cardiac surgical statistics are concerned? Not entirely. A hospital with a superb cardiac surgical capability may have higher mortality figures than one less good because it is tackling more difficult, high-risk cases that have been turned out elsewhere. But there is no harm asking about the numbers and discussing what they mean before you decide.

ALTERNATIVES TO VALVE REPLACEMENT

Options to valve replacement depend on the kind of surgery that needs to be done. For example, if your mitral valve is diseased, it may not have to be replaced at all. If you are young and the valve is not yet rigid due to deposition of calcium, the surgeon may be able to perform a *commissurotomy,* in which he cuts into the valve, frees the leaflets and enlarges the opening. This takes less time and is not as hazardous as replacing the valve. Except in special circumstances, it does not require subsequent anticoagulation. These are three very important advantages. Several of my patients have had this commissurotomy done, some as long as fifteen years ago, and for some the valve is still working well. In others, the valve cups became stuck again and needed repair or replacement, usually some five to ten years later.

Diseased aortic valves generally require replacement, although currently some are being ballooned open without surgery. The repair is carried out during cardiac catheterization, when a collapsed balloon is inflated, dilating the narrowed opening. This procedure is already available in several centers here and abroad.

OF HOMOGRAFTS AND HETEROGRAFTS

If the diseased valve needs to be replaced, an artificial device is usually inserted. Such prosthetic man-made valves work very well, but require anticoagulation for reasons described below. Alternatives are heterograft valves made from pig (porcine) or cow (bovine) tissue, and homograft valves fashioned from other parts of your own body. Although these have the advantages of not requiring permanent anticoagulation, we are unsure about their long-term durability. If you are about to undergo valve replacement and for some reason cannot take anticoagulants, ask about these alternative materials.

WHY PROSTHETIC VALVES
NEED CAREFUL WATCHING

Artificial heart valves require indefinite anticoagulation ("thinning") of the blood in order to prevent little clots from forming on their surfaces. These clots can break off and travel to different parts of the body (embolism)—the brain, for example, where they cause strokes. When your blood is being thinned, you must have it tested at least once or twice a month for the rest of your life, because the correct dosage of anticoagulant varies virtually from day to day. It can be affected by your diet, the weather, transient infections or other medications you happen to be taking. The amount that was just right last week may now leave your blood too thin, putting you at risk for an internal hemorrhage. Or it may not be thin enough, leaving you vulnerable to an embolism.

A prosthetic valve can become infected very much like the diseased rheumatic valve it replaced. That is something you will have to be extremely careful about for the rest of your life. A minor dental procedure, putting a catheter into your urinary tract, a simple curettage, manipulation of the prostate—indeed, any situation in which bacteria are released into the bloodstream—can result in their settling down on and further distorting the valve. These infected clumps may also be seeded throughout the body. This condition, called *bacterial endocarditis,* is often difficult to control once it develops on an artificial valve and may require a second operation to replace the valve.

A word here about preventing infection, not only on prosthetic valves, but in floppy valves and those diseased by rheumatic fever. I have found a great deal of confusion among patients (and doctors) as to which antibiotic should be given, in what circumstances, in what dosage, and how soon before and after the "event" that is being covered.

If your valve is vulnerable to infection for any reason whatsoever, here are some vital guidelines:

▶ You should have antibiotic prophylaxis whenever you undergo *any* operation.

▶ No fever should go undiagnosed and untreated for more than 48 hours.

▶ Antibiotics should be prescribed for sore throats associated with temperature elevation.

▶ If you need catheterization of your urinary bladder for any reason, you should take an appropriate antibiotic.

▶ As far as dental work is concerned, no matter what problem brings you to the dentist, you should have an antibiotic aboard before you open your mouth. Some patients dose themselves with a drug several days before and after cleaning and extraction of their teeth. That's unnecessary. All you need is 2 grams of an oral penicillin preparation like Penicillin VK (it comes in ½-gram tablets), and you take them all at one time, thirty minutes to two hours before the procedure, followed by 1 g six hours after the procedure is finished. That's all. If you're allergic to penicillin, you may use erythromycin; take 1 g (the usual tablet is 250 mg or 500 mg, that is, ¼ g or ½ g) one half to two hours before the dental work, and 500 mg six hours after it's over. If you have a prosthetic valve, the antibiotic should be given by injection. I know of several patients with prosthetic valves in whom the oral route failed to protect against endocarditis subsequent to dental procedures.

Endocarditis can also disrupt the suture lines that hold an artificial valve in place, so that it can no longer open and close normally. Even in the absence of infection, an artificial valve can degenerate and break down. (This was especially true in some of the earlier models used in the 1960s and 1970s, which soaked up fats in the blood and became swollen and cracked.) Or, as blood rushes across the artificial surfaces, the red blood cells may disintegrate, releasing their pigment and causing jaundice and anemia.

In short, valve replacement means lifelong vigilance and monitoring. It is not like having your appendix or your gall-bladder out. But despite these potential problems, when you really need to have it done, there is no alternative to a spanking new heart valve. The dire consequences just mentioned happen in only a relatively small number of patients. I can't emphasize often or strongly enough that the matter of timing is a delicate and critical one. You must not wait too long, because then the heart may become irreparably strained or damaged. The final judgment is one that must be made by you and your doctor, and you may both want to share that responsibility by asking for another opinion from an experienced cardiologist.

DISEASED HEART VALVES AND PREGNANT WOMEN

An important question often raised by young women with rheumatic valvular disease is whether it's safe for them to have a baby. They worry that their gynecologist may be either too conservative or not cautious enough in his advice. This decision should always be made in consultation with a cardiologist, regardless of how the gynecologist rules. We have come a long way in the medical (and surgical) management of rheumatic heart disease, so that today many women so affected may safely give birth. But they bear special watching.

HARDENING OF THE ARTERIES— ANYWHERE IN THE BODY

Let's go on to the major problem of vascular disease— *arteriosclerosis* (or "hardening" of the arteries)—which though declining in incidence since the early 1960s still causes about a million deaths every year in the United States alone.

Before middle age, arteriosclerosis is mainly an affliction of men. But when women reach the menopause, the two sexes are affected in approximately equal measure. Wherever in the body this disorder occurs, the interior of the affected artery is narrowed by plaques lining its walls. These plaques are rich in cholesterol, calcium and other fats. They become progressively larger until complete occlusion of the vessel takes place. In a smaller number of cases, total blockage follows transient spasm of the diseased artery or bleeding into one of the plaques.

When arteriosclerosis involves the coronary arteries, the result is a heart attack; when it takes place in blood vessels of the brain, a stroke ensues; it causes kidney disease when it strikes the renal artery; aneurysms of the aorta and vascular disease of the extremities result from involvement of those blood vessels; and blindness is often the consequence of diseased arteries in the eye.

The two major theories concerning the nature of arteriosclerosis are that (a) hardening of the arteries, like fever, is a manifestation of many disorders (this explains why it affects different arteries with varying rates of progression and severity, so that some patients survive for years while others die quickly), and (b) it is, in fact, a single disease due to several contributing causes.

Regardless of which of these diametrically opposite concepts is correct, your vulnerability, as you will see, depends on several factors.

Suppose that you were to consult me because one or both of your parents, various aunts and uncles, and perhaps one or two grandparents had all died before the age of sixty from heart attacks. You are now forty years old and feel perfectly well, but you have been reading all about the prevention of heart attacks and want to know how you can avoid succumbing prematurely to the disease that runs in your family. The following pages contain the same advice I'd give you if you consulted me in my office. It is based on my interpretation of current medical opinion.

WHERE THERE'S SMOKE, THERE'S HEART DISEASE

My first question to you is whether or not you smoke cigarettes, how many and for how long you've been doing so. If you use more than ten per day, you are "playing with fire." So many of my patients who have suffered heart attacks in the prime of life have had "good" family histories; their exercise level was normal; they were not overweight; they exercised, and their blood pressure was "perfect." But, alas, they smoked cigarettes.

I could write a short monograph about the excuses people make when they continue to smoke. "But, Doctor, I don't really inhale." (Nonsense, everyone inhales.) "Cigarettes are not bad for *me*. I only smoke them halfway down." (That's still bad because a half is worse than none.) "What you're telling me doesn't apply to my brand of cigarettes, because they are very low in tar and resin, and have a marvelous filter." (A cigarette is a cigarette is a cigarette.) "If I stop smoking, I'll get as big as a house. Wouldn't that be worse for me than cigarettes?" (If one must choose between overweight and smoking, in my opinion the former is less dangerous.) "But a cigarette relaxes me so much. Isn't nervous tension worse than tobacco?" (Decidedly not.) "Okay, I'll stop using cigarettes, but I'd like to smoke a pipe or cigars because I hear they're pretty safe." (Less hazardous, but not "safe," and it would depend on how many you smoked anyway. Many cigarette smokers switch to pipes and cigars and continue to inhale, in which event they might just as well have stayed with the weed. But more about that later.)

HOW CIGARETTES NAIL THE COFFIN

After I dispose of all these excuses, the reluctant patient petulantly demands to know exactly why and how cigarette smoking is dangerous. My answer is that regardless of the mechanism(s) (not all of which are fully understood) cigarette smokers are at fifteen times greater risk of developing heart attacks than nonsmokers, especially if they also have high blood pressure and an elevated cholesterol level. (And, by the way, women who smoke also have an earlier menopause.)

There are several theories about how tobacco does you in.

▶ Experiments in humans and animals have shown that when cigarette smoke is inhaled, blood vessels in various parts of the body constrict, presumably due to the nicotine. When such spasm affects the coronary arteries, the blood supply to the heart muscle is reduced. If these vessels have already been somewhat narrowed by arteriosclerosis, this additional constriction can be critical.

▶ Cigarette smoke also releases a substance that promotes clotting of the blood within the arteries.

▶ Smokers generally have higher cholesterol levels than do nonsmokers.

▶ Persons who have an irregular heartbeat often tell me that their palpitations are worse when they smoke. (Remember that sudden death may occur when the rhythm of the heart becomes abruptly disordered, even if the coronary arteries are not completely blocked.)

▶ As you puff away and inhale the carbon monoxide, there is less oxygen available to the heart. This too may play a role over a period of time in the causation of angina and arteriosclerosis.

▶ Finally, it has been postulated that women who continue to smoke heavily during pregnancy may predispose their children to arteriosclerosis at an early age. Analysis of the umbilical arteries in infants of such mothers reveals evidence of damage to the vessel walls. It may be that this kind of injury also occurs in other blood vessels in the fetal heart or brain and lays the groundwork for premature arteriosclerosis in adult life.

If you need any further inducement to stop smoking, let me remind you that cigarettes are an important cause of lung cancer and osteoporosis in women; they also aggravate stomach ulcers. Tobacco is responsible too for low birth weight babies, with all the problems that that entails.

Whatever the underlying mechanisms, almost every doctor I know is convinced that cigarette smoking significantly increases vulnerability to heart attack. In the unlikely event that your own doctor doesn't agree, I'd not only get a second opinion, I'd also find another doctor.

THE CIGARETTE ADDICT

Most people actually do know that smoking is hazardous. Every time they light up, the Surgeon General's message is right there for them to see. So why don't they stop? Why, indeed, doesn't the very same doctor who pleads with you to break the habit always follow his own advice? Why do some patients who have already had a heart attack or lung disease continue to smoke?

The answer to all these questions is that cigarette smoking is more than a bad habit—it is an addiction. Heavy smokers tell me that when they try to quit, they can't sleep, feel nervous, are depressed, suffer from headaches and eat compulsively. I believe them because these are all classic symptoms of nicotine withdrawal. The heavier the habit, the more difficult it is to kick it.

IS ANY CIGARETTE "SAFE"?

Smokers and the tobacco industry continue to search for the "safe cigarette," one that can be smoked with impunity. No such cigarette has yet been made, the ads emphasizing less tar and nicotine in some brands notwithstanding. These are meant to assuage the fear, guilt and anxiety of the tobacco addict—and to sell more cigarettes! In fact, there is evidence that these "milder" cigarettes may be more harmful, not safer. Given a weed with less nicotine, the addict puffs it more frequently, smokes it down to a shorter butt, and lights up more often than he would with the high-nicotine brand. A report by the Medical Research Council in Britain has reaffirmed the suspicion that the "weaker" the cigarette, the more it is smoked, and the more you smoke, the more carbon monoxide you inhale.

Some scientists believe that carbon monoxide, not tar, resin or nicotine, is the most harmful substance in cigarettes. Cardiac patients driving cars on congested freeways, and guards working in heavily trafficked tunnels, have decreased exercise tolerance, presumably because of the greater concentrations of carbon monoxide to which they are exposed. So, in the long run, you may be doing yourself more harm with these "safer" cigarettes.

Pipe tobacco and cigars do contain less tar and nicotine, but they actually give you more carbon monoxide, because of the manner in which the smoke is delivered to your lungs from the bowl of the pipe or the leaf of the cigar. Also, as I mentioned earlier, when a cigarette smoker switches to pipes and cigars (whose main "benefit" is that he inhales them somewhat less), the smoking technique to which he became accustomed when he used cigarettes leaves him inhaling the pipe and cigar smoke very much as he did the cigarette smoke.

Given the apparent dangers of smoking, it has been suggested by some that smokers should substitute nicotine tablets or chewing tobacco for cigarettes, thus at least eliminating the risk of carbon monoxide. But there is little consolation even in these alternatives. Persons who chew tobacco have a high incidence of cancer of the mouth, throat and pharynx. So "you pays your money and you takes your choice."

COLD TURKEY IS BEST

If you have decided to quit cigarettes, it is probably better to do so abruptly—cold turkey—than to taper (although Smokenders reports considerable success with their method of gradual withdrawal). It's true that sudden cessation may leave you temporarily with more intense symptoms of nicotine deprivation, but then in a matter of days, if you can hold out, you are through with it. Oh, you may continue to yearn for the weed now and then, especially after a heavy meal, but most people can handle that. On the other hand, when you "cut down," rather than quit, you are more likely to return to the full-blown habit.

THE RISKS OF PASSIVE SMOKING

We used to say (and think) that if someone wouldn't or couldn't stop smoking—well that was *their* problem. Unfortunately, that's not the whole story. True, it *is* their problem, but it's ours as well because you and I breathe in what they breathe out. Many studies have now shown the dangers of such passive smoking at home and at the worksite. Women whose husbands are heavy smokers have a higher incidence of lung cancer than those married to nonsmokers. Infants whose parents smoke have more respiratory disease and suffer from impaired growth as compared to those raised in a smoke-free environment. Absenteeism is higher in industries where smoking at work is permitted. Airline personnel assigned to the smoking section of transatlantic flights excrete nicotine in their urine. In my view, society owes it to itself to see that the right to breathe clean air supersedes permission to smoke.

THE RISK OF HYPERTENSION

Tobacco, then, is a key risk factor for arteriosclerosis. High blood pressure, which is the most important cause of strokes, is another. We could probably reduce heart attacks by at least 30 percent if everyone in America stopped smoking and had a normal blood pressure. *In my opinion, hypertension of any degree, from mild to severe, should always be treated and normalized.* Weight reduction, regular exercise, and in appropriate cases, a decrease in salt intake are all important in managing elevated pressure. Quite frankly, however, what it almost always boils down to in the end is medication. Since this involves a lifelong commitment, it should never be made casually. But be sure that the diagnosis of hypertension is based on several recordings taken over a three- or four-week period. And if, after you have started the medication, you find it gives you unpleasant side effects, don't just stop taking it. Your doctor has several alternative agents at his disposal with which to normalize your blood pressure in a tolerable manner. If he doesn't seem to be able to do so, get a second opinion from someone specializing in the treatment of hypertension.

CHOLESTEROL—THE GREAT PREOCCUPATION

Let's get back to the hypothetical case of someone with a strong family history of premature arteriosclerosis. He will listen politely to the data implicating cigarettes and high blood pressure, but for some reason, what really impresses him most is his cholesterol level. The Western world, particularly America, is totally preoccupied with blood fats and diet. The other day, I sent a man to the hospital with an acute heart attack. Hovering between life and death, he was concerned with only two things: when his bowels would move and his cholesterol level.

The world is full of cholesterol "authorities," each with his own theory about its role in the causation of arteriosclerosis. Every doctor has *his* own opinion and offers *his* own brand of advice on whether to avoid eggs like the plague, eat them at will, or simply be "prudent" and consume them in moderation. Before telling you what I think, let me first present the available data to you objectively and let you decide whether or not cholesterol is a precipitating or causative factor.

INDIVIDUALS VERSUS POPULATIONS

There is no question that many people with "too much" cholesterol do attain old age. Conversely, individuals with normal or even low levels suffer heart attacks early in life. What's more, among my own patients with heart disease, cholesterol levels seem to bear little if any relation to *individual* dietary habits. For example, someone who eats lots of cheese, butter and eggs (anathema to the cholesterol purist) may not have any more cholesterol in his artery walls than a person on a more "prudent" diet. This may reflect the fact that two thirds of our cholesterol is manufactured in the body regardless of diet, and only one third is derived from what we eat. Yet, among *populations* (as opposed to individuals), cholesterol levels *do* appear to reflect eating habits. What's more, the higher that level, the greater the statistical association between arteriosclerosis and heart disease.

THE CLINCHING EVIDENCE?

In the first edition of this book, I was more or less on the fence as far as the relationship of cholesterol to heart disease was concerned. I had a feeling it was important, but I was not convinced by the objective evidence at that time. Since then, however, some impressive new data have been collected that really make a strong case to justify lowering one's cholesterol, either by diet or by one of the more effective new drugs now available. There have even been several studies demonstrating actual reduction in the size of some of the obstructing plaques when cholesterol levels have dropped as a result of intervention. The most impressive demonstration of the validity of the "cholesterol hypothesis" was the NHLBI (National Heart, Lung and Blood Institute) project involving several thousand individuals at risk. When their cholesterol levels were reduced by a medication (cholestyramine, Questran), there was a demonstrable decrease in the death and heart attack rates—1 percent for every 2 percent reduction. Most but still not all cardiologists now accept this relationship.

CHOLESTEROL— THE MINORITY VIEWPOINT

There are still some very distinguished scientists (not all of whom are spokespersons for the dairy, egg and cattle industries) who reject the alleged hazards of dietary cholesterol and the benefits of lowering it. They believe that the high levels of cholesterol in the blood of patients with heart disease is but a *symptom* of some underlying disorder whose real cause is not known. They point out that arteriosclerotic plaques begin to form in the arteries early in life, and initially do *not* contain cholesterol. Even later, when hardened, fully formed and already narrowing the arterial channels, only 50 percent of these plaques have cholesterol in them. Also, there are two noncardiac conditions—one in the kidney (nephrotic syndrome) and the other in the thyroid (underfunction of that gland)—that are associated with very high cholesterol levels but with no more coronary artery disease then in the "normal" population. In some cultures where very little fat is eaten, there is no less heart disease than where fat consumption is high. When confronted with the evidence that experimental animals fed massive amounts of butter develop "lesions" in their arteries, these critics reply that the "unnatural" changes due to forced feeding in the laboratory are different from the plaques of arteriosclerosis that develop in humans.

How do these nay-sayers counter the evidence of the NHLBI studies referred to above? They claim the statistics are faulty, that the differences between the "treated" and the "control" subjects were the result of some elegant figure-juggling and that the alleged benefits of lowering cholesterol are more apparent than real. They continue to maintain that we should pursue research into the *real* causes of arteriosclerosis, and not waste our time, money and effort on a wild goose (cholesterol) chase!

The "anti-anticholesterol" buffs conclude by warning against tampering with cholesterol levels, especially by means of drugs. They point out, for example, that clofibrate, a drug that lowers the amount of cholesterol in your body, may produce cholesterol gallstones. Changing the composition of the bile in any way, they believe, may also account for the higher incidence of cancer deaths in some studies in which cholesterol was lowered by drugs. They even condemn the excessive use of polyunsaturated fats, which was once the basis of all cholesterol-lowering regimens, on the grounds that these substances may damage the lining of the arterial wall and also may increase the risk of cancer.

IF NOT CHOLESTEROL,
WHAT IS THE CULPRIT?

So what *do* the nonbelievers of the cholesterol theory think is the cause of arteriosclerosis? Most are convinced that the plaques form in the arterial wall at the site of some prior injury caused by any one of a number of possible factors, including increased blood pressure, infection (perhaps some virus early in life), an altered immune response, or abnormal architecture or angulation of the particular artery involved.

WHOM SHOULD *YOU* BELIEVE—
AND WHAT SHOULD *YOU* DO?

How should one react to this controversy in practical terms? This is what I recommend to my own patients. If you are healthy, have a cholesterol level of 220 mg percent or less, and do not have a bad family history, there is no need to change your eating habits. With a cholesterol level that low, you (or your body) must be doing something right.

But if you are *under* sixty-five, have a cholesterol level above 220 mg percent and there has been a lot of heart disease in the family, you should follow a "prudent" diet. That means cutting down on your consumption of butter, cheese and other dairy products, and limiting your intake of eggs to four a week, or less. In addition, beef should be replaced by chicken, veal and fish, and all visible fat should be avoided.

I also urge my patients to eat lots of fish, especially the fatty, cold water varieties like salmon, mackerel, halibut, cod and sardines. These fish are rich in the Omega-3 polyunsaturated fatty acids (ECA, DCA), which have been shown to have a beneficial effect on the lipid profile (see below), and which, in addition, tend to lower blood pressure a little and reduce the tendency of blood to clot. For salad dressings and cooking, I recommend olive oil (a monosaturated fat) rather than polyunsaturated vegetable oils.

This dietary advice also has some psychological impact. Together with weight reduction and exercise, it helps to allay patients' anxieties, makes them feel that they are at least doing *something* to reduce their vulnerability to heart attack—and they probably are.

If you are older than sixty-five, regardless of whether you have heart disease, paying homage to the cholesterol hypothesis is, in my opinion, probably futile—too little and too late to have any significant impact on the disease or its prevention. I permit my patients of this age to eat whatever they like, as long as they maintain a good weight.

SHOULD YOU BOTHER MEASURING YOUR TRIGLYCERIDE LEVEL?

I do not believe that triglycerides, another blood fat, constitute an important independent risk factor for arteriosclerosis. When triglyceride levels are elevated, it is often in conjunction with some other abnormality like a high blood-sugar level. If your triglyceride level is being checked, make sure that the blood sample is taken only after you have been fasting (had nothing to eat or drink except black coffee, tea without milk or sugar, or water) for at least fourteen hours. Many individuals who worry about a high triglyceride level detected in a screening survey are found to have normal levels when the test is repeated after appropriate fasting.

Tests for triglycerides may, however, be useful in determining the *kind* of blood-fat abnormality you have. For example, when the cholesterol is high, its dietary management depends to some extent on whether the triglycerides are normal or elevated. If both cholesterol and triglycerides are up, it is more important to restrict sugar and carbohydrates than to limit cholesterol and fats. But when the triglycerides are normal and the cholesterol high, the consumption of cholesterol and fat should be cut.

GOOD GUYS (HDL) AND BAD GUYS (LDL)

A better way to evaluate your lipid or blood status is to measure the *lipoproteins* in the blood, as well as the cholesterol. Let me explain what these lipoproteins are all about.

Lipo means "fat." Since fat and water don't mix, in order for the fatty cholesterol to circulate in solution, or dissolve, in the watery bloodstream, it must be "transported." The vehicle that does the carrying, the lipoprotein, attaches itself to the cholesterol molecule.

Lipoproteins are made in the liver and are of three kinds—high-density lipoproteins (HDL), low-density lipoproteins (LDL) and very-low-density lipoproteins (VLDL)—according to their chemical weights and composition. The *kind* of lipoproteins you have, and their amounts, appear to be more important than the cholesterol level. The reason for this is that the artery wall does not respond in the same manner to each of these lipoproteins. For example, when a cholesterol molecule attached to HDL approaches the arterial wall, it is rejected and turned back into the bloodstream where it doesn't do you any harm. Only when cholesterol is absorbed into the wall of the artery can it eventually cause arteriosclerosis. In addition to being rejected by the lining of the artery, the HDL is also thought to attract cholesterol already in the wall, sucking it out—a sort of chemical Roto-Rooter. So the more HDL you have, the better off you are. That is why HDL blood levels are now routinely measured by many doctors. However, cholesterol molecules transported by the LDL or VLDL lipoproteins are deposited into the blood vessel wall. As more and more of them settle there, the artery becomes progressively narrower and may finally close.

HOW TO GET THE HDL UP

There are ways to elevate your HDL level. Stop smoking; cigarettes lower HDL. Exercising and losing excess weight raise HDL. So does eating fish, garlic, brewer's yeast and lecithin. (It is interesting that in many "primitive" cultures garlic is intuitively thought to be beneficial.) Absolute teetotalers have a somewhat higher incidence of heart attack than the social drinker who takes one or two drinks a day. It seems that alcohol, in moderation—a couple of drinks a day—raises HDL. (But if you are a reformed alcoholic and have had a lot of trouble getting and staying on the wagon, don't throw it all away just to elevate your HDL. Alcoholism is in my opinion a greater threat than too little HDL.)

THE CHOLESTEROL–HDL RATIO

Analyzing both the cholesterol and HDL levels is probably more revealing than considering either number alone. When we calculate the cholesterol–HDL ratio, the lower the value, the smaller the statistical risk. Below a ratio of 4½ to 1, you are in good shape; between 7 and 9 to 1, you are at twice the risk of having a heart attack; a ratio greater than 13 to 1 triples the danger.

PRITIKIN'S PROGRAM

A few years ago there appeared in the lay press glowing reports of "miracles" being wrought by the "Pritikin Regimen"—a tough diet coupled with a substantial daily walk. This program is now being administered in "live-in" centers throughout the country. In addition, thousands of patients with heart disease (or a vulnerability to it) are following the regimen on their own.

If you choose to go to a Pritikin Center (there are now several in the United States), you'll sign up for a three- to four-week program (at a cost of about $5,000). You will be put on a stringent low-fat (5 percent to 10 percent of daily intake), low-cholesterol diet (no more than 100 mg (*milligrams*) per day), consisting basically of complex carbohydrates. These are, for the most part, whole grains, fruits and vegetables. Processed or refined foods are taboo. Within the permissible categories, you can eat as much as you want. Tobacco, alcohol, coffee and tea are forbidden. You will use no sugar and only tiny amounts of salt. When packing your bags for the trip, you might just as well leave all your vitamin and mineral supplements at home. They are considered "no-no's" by the Pritikin people.

You will also walk at least thirty to sixty minutes twice a day.

Soon after Pritikin began getting publicity, a few of my patients enlisted in his program. They returned reporting much less angina, normalization of previously high blood pressure without the use of drugs, significant lowering of cholesterol and triglyceride levels, weight loss (usually twelve to fifteen pounds) and, among the diabetics, reduction of their blood-sugar levels to the point where insulin was sometimes no longer required. Patients who hadn't been able to get "from here to the door" without chest pain were now able to walk several miles a day. And age was apparently no barrier. People in their eighties, some of them "too far gone" to have heart surgery, were coming back rejuvenated.

I asked among my colleagues whether they too had heard such reports, and what they thought of them. Very few knew anything about Pritikin and most of those who did said it was just "ballyhoo." Formal comment from the medical establishment was also negative.

HOW TIMES HAVE CHANGED!

Since then, much of the initial skepticism about the rigorous Pritikin regimen has waned. It's too bad that Mr. Pritikin wasn't a doctor. Had he been, I don't doubt that his ideas would have been accepted much sooner by more physicians. Today, the dietary recommendations of the prestigious American Heart Association (AHA) come very close to those made by Pritikin years ago. And it's all so logical! After all, what can be bad about cutting out cigarettes, losing weight, going for long walks, avoiding salt and sugar, eating lots of fresh vegetables together with some chicken and fish? The only problem is that not many people, at least in my experience, can or will adhere to this regimen long enough to make a difference. The spirit is willing, but the flesh is usually weak. After a few months, most of my patients began to "cheat" a little, then a little more, and soon are back to their old eating habits. But some end up in the middle road following the "prudent" diet now advised by the AHA.

So I encourage all my patients to follow the Pritikin program. Those few who can make a lifelong commitment to it do benefit. The seeds of healthy dieting and exercise are at least planted in the rest.

WHAT MAKES SAMMY JOG?

So much for modifying risk factors like hypertension, tobacco and abnormal blood fats. What about the relationship between exercise and arteriosclerosis?

Millions of people the world over are into jogging, running and "working out" in other ways. They are convinced that exercise makes them feel better and will help them live longer. Such individuals are also more "health conscious" and so most have stopped smoking and lost weight, and have their blood pressure checked regularly. Believe me, no matter how enthusiastic you are about running, doing so with a cigarette hanging out of your mouth isn't going to help you much. In fact, one study showed that men who smoke heavily and exercise vigorously are at greater risk of developing a heart attack than is the "normal" population.

The impact of exercise on the *prevention* of arteriosclerosis and heart attacks remains to be proved but there's nothing to match the feeling of a good workout, regardless of whether or not it will prevent heart attacks sometime in the distant future. Mind you, there are some data to suggest that the physically fit withstand a heart attack or major surgery better than those who are not. Also, when hundreds of Harvard graduates were asked about their exercise habits years after graduation, those who said they were dedicated to ongoing, *very* rigorous, regular workouts, without lapse or respite, year after year, did manifest definite protection against heart attacks. But the level of exercise required was so strenuous as to preclude its performance on a sustained basis by more than a small fraction of the population. So I encourage young healthy people who enjoy jogging to do so if they have no orthopedic problems (muggings and traffic accidents en route are another matter). However, young women, classically immune from the ravages of arteriosclerosis, may find that the athletic life can cause menstrual irregularities. This is particularly true when they become lean and "hard" and lose body fat. Nature endows potential mothers with a certain amount of fat to nourish the fetus and make lactation possible. When this store of energy is lost, so too is the ability to conceive. If you've been exercising vigorously, feel great, but can't become pregnant, tell your doctor about your physical activity program before submitting to a complicated work-up.

A NORMAL ECG IS NO GUARANTEE

So exercise is great for the young. What about "healthy" middle-aged people? Again, I think that if it makes you feel better, you should do it. However, never start on such a program without seeing your doctor and getting clearance. Such an evaluation should include a thorough history, physical exam, and a treadmill (or other equivalent) stress test. As many as 75 percent of people with *underlying heart trouble* have normal electrocardiograms taken at rest. (That is why insurance companies require a stress test when you apply for a particularly large policy.) Only when the tracing is taken *during* and *after* exercise can the presence of coronary artery disease be excluded, and even then the test is not foolproof.

After you get the green light, you may begin to exercise, but always follow these cardinal rules: Start at a low level and increase it gradually to whatever goal you have in mind. You must commit yourself to doing it routinely at least forty minutes a day three times a week. Should your program be interrupted for longer than two weeks, you must start again at a lower level.

From time to time, joggers drop dead on the run. Sometimes they are young, but more often they are middle-aged. Most had previously been given a clean bill of health. When their hearts are examined at autopsy, the majority are found to have some form of heart disease that was either undetected during life or whose symptoms were denied or ignored. Rarely, the victims' hearts appear normal. The precise cause of death is never really established but is presumed to have been a sudden coronary artery spasm or electrical instability of the cardiac muscle.

The recent publication of a book called *The Exercise Myth* by a New York City physician was attended by national publicity and comment. The author concluded that most exercise programs are at worst excessive and dangerous, and at best of very little benefit. He also deprecated the routine use of electrocardiographic stress testing as hazardous, excessive and of little clinical value. If you happened to read this book or hear about it, and are puzzled or depressed by its message, don't be. In my opinion, much of what was written is anecdotal, and the viewpoint expressed is that of a small minority of the medical profession.

CAN FAT BE HEALTHY?

Obesity is a definite risk factor for arteriosclerosis (and a host of other disorders like hypertension, diabetes and gallbladder disease). Some doctors are more permissive than others with respect to what constitutes "optimal" weight. The heavier the doctor, the more tolerant he is apt to be. After all, people in glass houses shouldn't throw stones! Most of us instinctively know when we need to slim down. Here is a handy rule of thumb. A man five feet tall should weigh approximately 115 pounds. Add 5 pounds for every additional inch. This formula is not quite applicable to women because of differences in bone size and structure, as well as for cosmetic and cultural reasons. For example, my wife, who is five feet eight inches tall, weighs a "perfect" 122 pounds. Can you imagine her reaction were I to tell her what she ought to weigh according to the male formula?

CAN YOU EVER RESIGN FROM TYPE A MEMBERSHIP?

Your *personality type* may also be important in determining vulnerability to coronary disease. There is a cadre of cardiologists who believe that tense, aggressive, time-conscious individuals who are always working on a tight schedule—in short, those who make the world go round (or think they do)—are more vulnerable to heart attacks than are easygoing, more placid persons. The former are said to have a Type A personality, and the latter, Type B. Considerable data were presented to support this hypothesis, which for some years went essentially unchallenged. After all, it made sense that aggressive, angry persons were more likely candidates for heart trouble than their calm and collected counterparts. And so doctors started sending their coronary patients, even those without apparent emotional problems, for behavioral counseling. Type A modification clinics began to spring up all over the country. But then dissonant voices were raised. Some studies refuted what were termed simplistic concepts. The most recent criticism of the Type A-B theory is a very interesting one. It was observed in one large number of men who had survived heart attacks that survival during the first twenty-four hours was no different for the Type A's than the Type B's, but *late* deaths were substantially greater among the B's than the A's! There is no immediate explanation for this observation, except perhaps for the fact that the Type A's are better organized, know what needs to be done when the chips are down and do it. What makes this particular study so interesting and important is that among the doctors carrying it out were the two men who first postulated the personality theory of heart attacks—and they disagree completely with each other about this study. One says the findings are valid. The other denies it.

So where do we go from here? I'd advise you to be wary of advice to attend a behavioral modification clinic unless you yourself, your spouse or someone else who knows you very well thinks you should. Don't buy it on the basis of a psychological test that puts you into a "category" that needs treatment. If you have angina or have suffered a heart attack, try to lead a "normal life," especially psychologically. Get your priorities in order. If you are a workaholic, if you get up at the crack of dawn and don't come home until late at night, or if you frequently find yourself in situations of chronic stress, tension and anxiety, try to modify those aspects of your life-style.

WELCOME TO THE CORONARY CLUB

Let's assume that you have done what you could to prevent or delay heart disease and were unsuccessful. You have become a "cardiac." Usually it happens like this. You have been perfectly well. Then, one day, while rushing home in the evening, running to catch a bus some cold morning, in the setting of a severe emotional reaction, or for no apparent reason, you experience a sense of oppression, tightness or pressure in the center of the chest. It may last only a moment or two. You ignore it at first, and the symptom may not recur for days, weeks or months. But then it returns, again and again, until you finally come to realize that there is something seriously wrong.

Sooner or later, depending on how willing (or unwilling) you are to face reality, you consult your doctor. Chances are that, on the clinical exam, he will find nothing amiss, and even your electrocardiogram may be entirely normal. An unsophisticated doctor will then reassure you, but *you* know deep down in your "heart of hearts" that all is not well. If you're not advised to have a stress test at this point, ask for one. You may otherwise fail to be correctly diagnosed as having angina. Remember, persons with angina frequently have a normal resting electrocardiogram and a diagnostically abnormal stress test.

YOU MAY DIE BEFORE YOU KNOW IT

Although angina is usually due to narrowing of one or more coronary arteries (either by plaques or by spasm), and a heart attack results from their complete obstruction (by the same mechanisms), the time between your first chest pain and your heart attack is entirely unpredictable. My father, for example, first experienced symptoms of coronary artery disease at the age of forty-seven, did not have a heart attack until he was eighty and lived three years after that. In other individuals, the first anginal attack may herald progressively more severe episodes and culminate in a heart attack within days or weeks. That's why early correct diagnosis is so important. Even though angina is often the first indication of coronary artery disease, many patients suffer a heart attack without any previous symptoms, and sudden, instantaneous death is frequently the first (and last) objective evidence of trouble.

NOW THAT YOU HAVE ANGINA

If you're one of the lucky ones who gets a warning signal of trouble in the form of an anginal attack, your doctor will start drug treatment immediately. He may even hospitalize you if he feels you're heading for an imminent coronary. He will also carefully review any contributing risk factors and try to eliminate them. For example, he will harass you constantly about your smoking; if your blood pressure is high, he will reduce it with medication; if you are overweight, he will prescribe an appropriate diet; if your cholesterol is high and your HDL is low, he will institute remedial measures.

SHOULD YOU BE TAKING
CHOLESTEROL-LOWERING DRUGS?

Because of the new and convincing evidence that lowering cholesterol, either by diet alone or, if necessary, with medication, does make a difference, most doctors have become aggressive in their attempts to do so. They recommend the American Heart Association diet, whose objective it is to reduce the cholesterol level to below 200 mg percent. Your total consumption of cholesterol should be less than 300 mg per day (the contents of only one whole egg). Your fat intake will also be cut to under 30 percent of your total caloric intake, with no more than 10 percent in saturated or animal fats. You'll be advised to limit your alcohol intake to two ounces of hard liquor per day, or two four-ounce glasses of wine, or two bottles of beer. Salt consumption will also be reduced to less than a level teaspoon per day. Many cardiologists are excited too about the beneficial effect of the fat found in certain cold-water fish like salmon, cod, halibut, mackerel, and sardines, and will encourage you to eat as much fish as you can afford. These fish fats, called Omega-3 fatty acids, seem to have protected Eskimos against coronary artery disease. If you don't like or can't afford to eat all the fish you should, then these Omega-3 fats can be purchased in capsules in pharmacies and health food stores. Their actions are multiple and varied, but from the cardiac point of view, they lower cholesterol, raise HDL, decrease LDL, lower blood pressure and make the blood less sticky. What a package of benefits for the angina patient!

If diet and the Omega-3 fatty acids don't bring your cholesterol down to the desired level, should you use drugs? Personally, I don't think so, unless your cholesterol level is above 250 mg percent and/or you have either severe angina or an impressive family history of premature heart disease. The drugs currently available to lower cholesterol are cholestyramine (Questran), colestipol (Colestid), nicotinic acid, probucol (Lorelco), Cytellin, Choloxin, neomycin and gemfibrozil (Lopid). A new and exciting agent, lovastatin, will probably have been marketed by the time you read this. All these drugs work differently, but each can render your blood fats less abnormal. The first two, *Questran* and *Colestid*, cause increased excretion of cholesterol in the stool. They often produce annoying intestinal side effects—notably gas and constipation—so much so that many patients just won't take them as prescribed!

Nicotinic acid lowers cholesterol and triglyceride levels and offers the additional bonus of raising the HDL. It's also very inexpensive. Unfortunately, in doses large enough to be effective, it causes profound flushing and itching, which become less intense with time and which can be minimized if you start with a low dose, such as 100 mg two or three times a day and increase it every few weeks. Also, an aspirin taken with nicotinic acid helps control these symptoms, which are frightening and annoying, but not dangerous. Nicotinic acid may raise the blood-sugar and uric acid levels, so avoid it if you're diabetic or have gout.

Probucol has very few side effects, but it lowers the HDL as well as the cholesterol, and how desirable that is over the long run, I'm not sure. *Cytellin* has been around a long, long time. I remember hearing about it when I was a medical student! It simply sits in the stomach and prevents the absorption of any cholesterol you eat. Because it has a mild laxative effect, some doctors prescribe it together with Questran or Colestid, which have a tendency to constipate you. *Choloxin*, a thyroid derivative, is one drug I wouldn't advise you to use for lowering cholesterol. In the large Coronary Drug Project run a few years ago in this country to determine the impact of reducing cholesterol levels in patients who had had heart attacks, this agent was withdrawn from the study because it was associated with an *increased* number of cardiac deaths and heart attacks. *Neomycin* is an antibiotic which, because it is poorly absorbed, sits around in the gut and interferes with cholesterol absorption by acting on the bacterial composition of the intestine. Do not use it if your kidneys are not working properly.

At the time of writing, a new drug with profound cholesterol-lowering effects has just been approved by the FDA. Called *lovastatin*, it allegedly is relatively free of toxicity and may lower cholesterol levels by as much as a third. It also raises HDL (a good thing) and lowers LDL (also a desirable effect). It works by interfering with the cholesterol-producing mechanisms in the body.

ANGINA AND EXERCISE— A SAFE COMBINATION?

Earlier I discussed the role exercise may play in the *prevention* of heart disease. How important is it in someone who already has a "condition"? Remember that heart muscle is supplied by a network of blood vessels that course through it very much like the branches of a tree, and which become narrowed by arteriosclerosis. Heart muscle also contains "collateral circulation," a mesh of new channels that can increase blood supply. When we inject dye into the coronary circulation and take X rays to visualize the blood flow within the heart (angiogram), we can actually see these collaterals.

Many cardiologists recommend exercise to patients with angina in the hope that it will provide a further stimulus to the development of an effective collateral circulation, improve exercise tolerance and create a sense of well-being in patients worried about their future. Indeed, I am more enthusiastic about exercise as a treatment than as a preventive measure. Suitable supervised programs are widely available in cardiopulmonary rehabilitation centers throughout the country. If your doctor tells you that you have to "take it easy" because you now have angina and must not engage in any physical exercise, or shouldn't "strain yourself," ask for a second opinion.

THE EXERCISE PRESCRIPTION

If you have heart disease, it is very important for you to determine the right *kind* of exercise, how much and how intense, and to obtain the proper supervision by trained personnel. A workout should be prescribed for you as carefully as a potent drug, and you should follow the instructions for it no less conscientiously. A doctor would never give you any medication and tell you to take as much of it as you want as often as you like. The same should be true of exercise. Every cardiac patient should perform an exercise program under medical supervision, at least until his or her clinical status is stable and predictable. The work load and pace should be selected after a careful physical exam, followed by a treadmill or other standardized stress test. This helps determine the heart rate at which your ECG becomes abnormal, and whether or not any life-threatening disorders of heart rhythm are provoked. Armed with this information, your doctor can prescribe a level of exercise that is safe for *you*. Remember, what is right for your friends and neighbors may be too much (or too little) for you.

THE RIGHT AMOUNT
AT THE RIGHT PLACE

After you have decided to embark on a cardiac rehabilitation or preventive program, make sure that the exercise facility you choose has the personnel trained to handle any complication or emergency, as well as the necessary equipment to do so (defibrillators, intravenous sets and cardiac drugs). Accidents can and do occur, although fortunately, they are uncommon. Such treatment and resuscitation capabilities should be available not only in exercise centers, but also wherever stress tests are done, and that includes your doctor's office. If you are scheduled for a stress test, don't be shy about asking whether emergency facilities and trained personnel are immediately at hand.

Some forms of exercise are not only more fun than others, but safer too. For example, I have not found isometric exercises, in which pressure is exerted against an immovable object, to be well tolerated by patients with angina. This type of exercise usually raises blood pressure. Patients do better with dynamic exercise, for example, walking (the best of all), biking or running. One important exception is vigorous swimming, which seems to induce angina more easily than other types of physical stress, at least in my experience. Remember that any program, once started, must be continued on a regular basis, at least three times a week. *Always begin your exercise with a warm-up period and end it by tapering off.* Never get right into it and never stop abruptly. A few deaths have been reported among persons taking hot showers after vigorous exercise, presumably because of a sudden drop in blood pressure. So take a tepid shower when you're through, not a hot one.

JOGGING IN THE PARK WITH YOUR TAILOR

I have found that my cardiac patients who perform exercise regularly and conscientiously do become more physically fit, and can attain a higher level of energy expenditure before the onset of chest pain or electrocardiographic abnormalities. Thus, if at the start of a program, it took a certain amount of effort to raise the heart rate to 110 beats per minute, and induce angina, after several months of training, much more work can be performed before those end points are reached.

To be perfectly honest, I am among the minority of cardiologists who remain nervous about their cardiac patients running or even jogging. I much prefer them to walk briskly or to exercise under the supervision of trained personnel. In my opinion that's a whole lot safer than running around the park with their stockbroker, lawyer or tailor. I know that many doctors are jogging enthusiasts and do not share this point of view. In the final analysis, *you* must decide what is right for you, physically and emotionally.

One of the downsides of exercise even when properly prescribed and performed is that it is truly addicting. You feel great doing it, probably because of the release of natural opiates from your brain. You literally "feel no pain," and that may explain the admittedly small number of deaths that occur during running. Also, most runners must keep running in order to maintain their high—and the amount of exercise required to do so seems to increase progressively.

THE GOLD STANDARD AGAINST ANGINA, THE LITTLE WHITE PILL UNDER THE TONGUE

Most patients with angina pectoris require medication to prevent, control or minimize their symptoms. Let me tell you what drugs are available so that when they're prescribed for you, you'll understand how they work and what side effects, if any, you can expect.

The hallmark of medication against angina is nitroglycerin—the little tablet you slip under the tongue either when you expect the typical chest symptoms induced by exertion or after you develop them.

There are several *noncardiac* causes of chest discomfort that very closely mimic true angina. These include hiatus hernia, chest wall pain, various neuralgias, muscle strain, arthritis in the neck, peptic ulcers and gallbladder disease, to name but a few. And it's not always easy to be sure which of these disorders is responsible for the symptoms. Since nitroglycerin specifically relieves angina but not distress from these other sources, it is useful in the differentiation of cardiac from noncardiac pain. But you should know that when this drug does in fact abolish your angina, it does so within three seconds to three minutes. Patients often tell me that their "nitro" worked because it eliminated their pain in twenty minutes! Under those circumstances the credit should definitely not go to the nitroglycerin; the pain likely would have disappeared by itself and was probably not angina to begin with.

Nitroglycerin works by dilating the blood vessels—not only the coronaries, within the heart, but arteries elsewhere. So when you get a headache after taking nitroglycerin, it's not an indication of toxicity. It simply means that the drug is working, in this case by dilating the cranial arteries in the head. Unfortunately, we do not have a medication that widens the coronary arteries and no others. Don't give up the nitro when it gives you a headache. Just take a couple of aspirin tablets and stay with it. After a while the headaches will become less frequent and disappear. If, however, you cannot tolerate the headaches, ask your doctor for a weaker strength nitroglycerin.

IF YOU FAINT AFTER TAKING NITROGLYCERIN

Since nitroglycerin dilates the arteries, large and small, your blood pressure may drop after taking it. If you happen to be standing at the time and the fall of pressure is substantial enough, you may faint. So always sit down before using this drug.

The life span of most preparations of nitroglycerin is fairly short, between six and twelve months, after which they lose their potency. Be sure always to ask your pharmacist how long he's had on his shelf the bottle that he sells you, and better still, request that the medication be dispensed in its original bottle. That permits you to check the expiration date yourself. Remember too, to protect the bottle from light and to keep what you're not carrying in your pocket in your refrigerator.

I have had very good results using a relatively new delivery system for nitro—an aerosol inhaler marketed as Nitrolingual Spray. It keeps for three years without losing potency and using its container is easier than fumbling in your pocket for a small tablet to be placed under the tongue. Each dose is metered. You simply squirt it under the tongue. It works within thirty seconds.

THE "NITRO" COMPLEX

Don't develop a complex about taking nitroglycerin. So many patients think that to use it is to "give in," to admit to some weakness of character. That's nonsense. Nitroglycerin, when needed, is good for you. It is not habit-forming; it does not worsen your disease; you do not become "used" to it or dependent on it, and it can, in fact, save your life. Take it as freely as necessary. However, if your chest pain persists after using three tablets within fifteen minutes, call your doctor. You may be having a heart attack. Also, if your angina was always brought on by effort of some kind and now comes on at rest or during the night, or if nitroglycerin is less effective than it used to be, let your doctor know. Any of these symptoms may indicate that one or more coronary arteries are closing off faster than your collaterals are opening up.

WHEN LONGER ACTION IS NEEDED

Unfortunately, the effects of sublingual nitroglycerin last for only twenty or thirty minutes. For a longer duration, other agents are available. Some are related to nitroglycerin. Others are not. For a more prolonged effect, nitroglycerin can also be applied topically as a paste, a cream, an ointment, or on an adhesive patch. It works best when put anywhere north of your belly button—the arms, the chest or the back. Apply it at bedtime, changing the patch every twenty-four hours. Used in this way, it has a prophylactic action, that is, it will *prevent* pain. Its effect persists anywhere from four to twenty-four hours. If one of the many patches available irritates your skin, try another brand.

The mainstays among the longer acting antianginal preparations in the nitroglycerin family are the nitrates. They are marketed under a variety of names in the United States, the best known of which are Isordil, Sorbitrate, Peritrate, Cardilate, and Nitrobid. They can be swallowed, chewed or dissolved under the tongue. These oral preparations come in several strengths, with different rates of absorption from the stomach and varying duration of effect. Like nitroglycerin, they usually cause headaches at first, and for the same reasons. But as you continue to use them, this side effect gradually disappears.

REVOLUTION IN TREATMENT—THE OLDER BETA-BLOCKERS AND THE NEWER CALCIUM CHANNEL BLOCKERS

The beta-blocking drugs are extremely important in the treatment of angina. The first to be marketed in this country was Inderal (propranolol). Seven are now available in the United States (Inderal, Lopressor, Corgard, Tenormin, Blocadren, Visken and Sectral). More are on the way.

This group of drugs controls angina by reducing the heart rate and the oxygen requirements of the heart. The net result is an increase in the amount of exercise that you can do before the onset of pain. They also lower blood pressure, and so are especially useful in patients who have both angina and hypertension—a common association. Finally, they help regularize disturbances of heart rhythm that frequently complicate arteriosclerotic heart disease.

The symptomatic improvement resulting from the use of the beta-blockers is not due to a "painkilling" property. These agents don't merely mask angina. Patients taking them feel better because they really do help the heart.

BETA-BLOCKERS ARE NOT FOR EVERYONE

There are certain circumstances in which, despite all their virtues, beta-blockers should be very cautiously prescribed, if at all. Beta-blockers can worsen heart failure by reducing the force of cardiac contractions. So, if your legs are swollen and you suffer from shortness of breath, they are probably not good for you.

These medications may also mask the symptoms of an insulin reaction. So diabetics who use them must be very careful to avoid low blood sugar.

Beta-blockers can provoke spasm of the bronchial tubes in asthmatics. Although those agents have many actions in common, there are individual differences among them. For example, two of them, Tenormin (atenolol) and Lopressor (metoprolol), are "cardioselective," that is, their main action is on the heart and they constrict the airways to a lesser extent. So if you are asthmatic and *must* have a beta-blocker, either of these would be the one to try (but still with great caution and in the smallest dosage necessary). Visken and Sectral are also said to have characteristics that lessen their impact on the pulmonary tree and might be useful for asthmatics as well.

Some cardiac patients have a very slow heartbeat—either because they are taking some drug like digitalis, or because the area of the heart that controls the rate is diseased. Under these circumstances, beta-blockers should also be avoided. If for some reason these drugs are absolutely necessary, then a cardiac pacemaker may be required to permit one to take them safely.

In my view there are so many other agents to do the available job that I virtually never prescribe a beta-blocker for asthmatics, anyone in heart failure or those with a dangerously low heart rate.

A word of caution about timolol (Timoptic) and Betoptic. These are beta-blocker eye drops that are extremely effective in the treatment of glaucoma. It is not always appreciated, however, that as little as one or two drops instilled in the eyes each day can slow the heart rate, aggravate heart failure and precipitate an acute asthmatic attack. These drugs can also enhance the effect of oral beta-blockers prescribed for cardiac reasons. So if you have glaucoma, ask your eye doctor whether the eye drops he's prescribed are beta-blockers. If they are, let your primary care physician know about them too.

THEY ALSO PREVENT HEART ATTACKS

The beneficial effects of a beta-blocker drug soon become apparent to those patients who need them. But in addition to controlling symptoms, these medications also reduce the incidence of recurrent heart attacks and sudden cardiac death by nearly 50 percent. They should be administered during the acute attack and continued for at least three years thereafter—unless, of course, there is some reason not to do so.

BETA-BLOCKERS—SOME
IMPORTANT SIDE EFFECTS

So beta-blockers are wonderful. They've had an enormous impact on the treatment of heart disease, hypertension and several other disorders. But they have their share of side effects, including impotence in men, decreased libido in women, fatigue, weakness, impaired memory, bad dreams, intestinal problems and coldness of the extremities. If the particular beta-blocker prescribed for you results in any of these complications, remember, you have six more from which to choose. There are enough differences among them so that if one gives you a particular side effect, another may not.

THE CALCIUM CHANNEL BLOCKERS

A relatively new family of drugs has joined nitroglycerin, the nitrates and the beta-blockers in the medical management of angina. These are called calcium channel blockers and are represented by nifedipine (marketed in the United States as Adalat and Procardia), verapamil (Calan, Isoptin) and diltiazem (Cardizem). As with the beta-blockers, new and better ones are on the way.

The calcium channel blockers are every bit as phenomenal as the beta-blockers. They too have multiple useful actions. In addition to their antianginal properties, these drugs also lower blood pressure, ameliorate spasm (not only of arteries, but of such organs as the esophagus and the uterus), control certain cardiac rhythm abnormalities, and help prevent migraine headaches. One of them, Cardizem, probably retards the entire atherosclerotic process.

The calcium channel blockers exert their effect by impeding the movement of calcium in and out of cardiac cells. Unlike beta-blockers, these agents are not virtually interchangeable. Although they do have many actions in common, the three calcium channel blockers currently available are quite different one from the other. In certain circumstances you may benefit from, say, nifedipine, but should not take verapamil. Their prescriptions to every patient with angina pectoris should be carefully and individually determined.

Unlike my experience with the beta-blockers, I have not seen much impotence among patients using calcium channel blockers. They may, however, have other untoward side effects—swelling of the legs (particularly with nifedipine), excessive slowing of the heart rate (most apparent with Cardizem and verapamil), too great a drop in blood pressure, fatigue and constipation. All of these undesirable effects are, as a rule, reversible. When you stop the drug, they clear up.

THE "HASTY" ANGIOGRAM

After your doctor makes the diagnosis of angina, he will and should prescribe a drug regimen using one or more of the agents previously described. But every now and then, the first "anginal" encounter with the doctor may be frightening. The following scenario is not uncommon:

You visit your physician because of exertional chest pain or pressure. You are not even sure that you have heart disease. You're hoping it's indigestion or a hiatus hernia, about which you had been reading lately. But by the time he has finished evaluating you, your doctor has not only told you you have angina, which is bad enough, but he has also scared you out of your wits by raising the possibility of a coronary angiogram and even bypass surgery. All this and you haven't even had a heart attack!

Why would any physician spring this on you at your very first visit, and what should you do about it if he does? Clearly, this is the kind of situation for which second opinions were made. No matter how mild or severe your symptoms, you owe it to yourself to have another opinion from a cardiologist at the first hint that cardiac surgery is being considered— even though your own physician may be perfectly correct.

THE THREAT OF A
MAIN STEM OBSTRUCTION

What is it your doctor suspects that would raise the question
of heart surgery right off the bat? Several things. He may, for
example, be so impressed with the severity or abruptness of
onset of your symptoms, or the magnitude of the electrocardiographic abnormalities (either at rest or after exercise)
that he feels it necessary immediately to determine the extent and location of obstructive disease within the coronary
arteries. In order to understand that, think of your cardiac
circulation in terms of a tree. When the main trunk is so
severely affected that the nutrients coming up from the roots
cannot pass beyond it to reach the branches, the entire tree
dies. By contrast, if the same disease affects not the trunk
but only a limb, a branch or two may fall off but the rest of
the tree will remain intact. And so it is in the heart. If the left
main stem coronary artery (from which most of the coronary
blood supply derives) is critically narrowed (and this can
often be suspected from your symptoms and other tests), you
are at great risk if and when that artery finally closes. For at
that time, most of your heart muscle will suddenly lose its
life-sustaining nutrition. The result? A serious heart attack
and possibly death. If your doctor believes that you have
such "left main" obstruction, he will urge you to undergo
further testing. But that shouldn't necessarily mean invasive
angiography. There are intermediate steps of which you
should be aware.

THE RADIONUCLIDE ANGIOGRAM

If your doctor suggests a coronary angiogram, ask about a
radionuclide angiogram first. This is a painless, relatively
risk-free, noninvasive cardiac diagnostic technique now in
fairly widespread use. It renders invasive angiography unnecessary in some cases. This technique involves the intravenous administration of a small amount of a radioactive
tracer element (similar to radioisotope scanning of any organ of the body—the brain, liver, thyroid, etc.). The radioac-

tive material goes to the heart, where its pattern of distribution is assessed by a special computer camera positioned over the chest. We look to see whether the injected radioactive material is uniformly distributed through the heart. A gap, or "hole," in the cardiac image suggests the presence of dead tissue—evidence of an old heart attack. Then a stress test is performed, and the nuclear scan is repeated. When one or more coronary arteries are narrowed and unable to deliver adequate amounts of blood to the exercising heart, gaps not present at rest appear in the distribution of the radioactivity. Abnormal cardiac contraction, another reflection of interference with coronary blood flow, can also be detected with this test.

A properly interpreted radionuclide scan usually reveals whether or not there is significant disease of the coronary arteries. If the scan is very abnormal, then a coronary angiogram is usually necessary, since that's the only method presently available that actually permits us to see the arteries and to pinpoint the exact location of the areas of obstruction.

THE CORONARY ANGIOGRAM

The coronary angiogram (some doctors use the term arteriogram) involves passing a thin catheter from an artery near the groin (or in the arm) to a point very near the heart where the openings to the coronary arteries are located. Dye is then squirted into them. The procedure is done under local anesthesia, although the patient is usually sufficiently sedated to allay the normal anxiety one feels in such circumstances.

The procedure may be uncomfortable and involves an overnight stay in the hospital. In these days of great preoccupation with cost cutting, clinics are springing up in which you can have the angiogram done in the morning and, if there are no complications, go home a few hours later. It sounds good, but quite frankly, I have not had any of my patients studied this way.

One of the problems with coronary angiography is the consent form you are legally obligated to sign. In order to protect patients from undergoing procedures whose consequences they do not fully understand, the law stipulates "full disclosure" by the doctor. He must explain to you everything that can conceivably go wrong no matter how remote the likelihood. More than one of my patients has gotten dressed and left the hospital when the angiographer indicated that patients do occasionally die of a heart attack, sustain a stroke, develop blood clots in their limbs or have their hearts damaged by the catheter. All these terrible things can happen, but they do so very rarely when the angiogram is performed by experts. What's most important for you to remember is this: If the test was necessary in the first place, then the risk of having it done is much, much less than not doing it at all.

That brings up another point. Unfortunately, angiography is sometimes recommended not because of any imminent threat but because there *are* doctors who believe that *all* patients with angina should have surgery, that a bypass procedure protects virtually everyone against heart attack and death. Although our considerable experience with such surgery indicates that successful bypass surgery done by expert teams does reduce the risk of heart attacks and, in fact, does prolong life in *properly selected cases, not every patient with angina needs the operation.* In my judgment, one should have an angiogram and consider heart surgery only after a fair trial with all the medicines that are now available. But if you continue to have frequent, debilitating chest pain despite vigorous treatment, you should not hesitate to consider surgery. However, this is a recommendation that should not be made at the time of your first visit unless there is a very strong suspicion of left main stem blockage or serious obstruction of all three major coronary arteries.

CORONARY BYPASS SURGERY— PROTECTIVE OR ONLY PALLIATIVE?

The entire subject of bypass surgery—when, why and where it should be done—is something that every patient with heart disease should fully understand. The decision to operate is one that you must share with your own doctor and a cardiologist. It should be based on the severity of your angina, the extent to which it interferes with your life-style and your response to *optimal* treatment with medication. Other factors to be considered include the presence of certain ECG changes, your response to exercise testing and the results of the radionuclide test and coronary angiogram. But remember, given the same tests and even the same interpretation of the results, doctors will not always agree on the question of bypass surgery.

MY OWN POSITION ON BYPASS SURGERY

I now recommend bypass surgery to the following patients: (a) anyone who has angina so severe that it interferes with the quality of life and in whom medication has not been effective, (b) those with left main stem obstruction, regardless of age or symptoms, (c) those whose angina is getting worse despite all efforts to control it with medication and (d) those who have already had one or more heart attacks, continue to suffer from angina and have severe disease of all three coronary arteries. Make sure that your own doctor is not too conservative or too liberal in his viewpoint. But whatever his stance, it's always a good idea to get a second opinion about surgery if you have angina, whether or not it has been recommended.

A word here about the operation itself. The very first patient I sent for bypass surgery had it done back in 1970, when the procedure was in its infancy. It was a triple bypass—three of the coronary arteries were severely obstructed. The operation lasted more than twelve hours and was a tour de force. (Incidentally, the man is still alive and well.) Today, with newer surgical techniques, the same procedure is finished in about two hours, and the risk is much lower too. Properly selected patients whose surgery is performed by a skilled team face a risk of about 1 percent! The majority can leave the hospital in seven to fourteen days and can resume normal activities shortly thereafter. More than 80 percent become pain-free, and are able to discontinue most of their antianginal medication. There are, of course, some operative failures, and sometimes surgery is necessary a second or even a third time. But such unfortunate results constitute a minority of the several hundred thousand bypass procedures done in the United States each year. Nor is age a critical factor. The decision to operate should be based on the criteria I have discussed and on the patient's ability to withstand the bypass, regardless of age. We've had great success in persons in their eighties, and even in a few "well-preserved" patients in their nineties. Age is neither a disease nor a contraindication.

CORONARY SPASM—HEART ATTACK DESPITE "CLEAN" ARTERIES?

No discussion of angina is complete without reference to *coronary spasm*. For years doctors have encountered patients whose angina comes on at rest, not with exertion. Some of these individuals have died suddenly, and when their hearts were examined, the coronary arteries were virtually clean, with little or no evidence of arteriosclerosis. It was assumed that spasm of the coronary arterial tree rather than its obstruction by plaques was responsible for the angina and death. This theory has now been proven by angiography. However, although spasm can occur in coronary arteries that are otherwise normal, more frequently it is superimposed on vessels already narrowed by arteriosclerotic plaques.

Why coronary arteries go into spasm is not clear, but patients with this problem do not usually respond to the beta-blockers, which are so effective in treating angina due to obstructive disease of the coronary arteries. In fact, these drugs may worsen the symptoms. Here, the drugs of choice are the calcium channel blockers and the nitrates.

LOFTY GOALS FOR THE LOWLY ASPIRIN

In the chapter dealing with strokes, you will read about the prophylactic value of aspirin in arterial disease of the brain. It offers the same protective action in the heart. Anyone with coronary artery disease (history of a previous heart attack or ongoing angina pectoris) should take one aspirin tablet per day (unless you are allergic to it, have ulcers, are on anticoagulants or have some bleeding disorder). Aspirin prevents the platelets (formed elements in the blood) from clinging together and forming a clot.

Aspirin is not the only substance that has such a beneficial action. Persantine (dipyridamole) also has an antiplatelet effect. Many doctors prescribe these agents together. I'm not sure that adding the Persantine really makes a difference, and whenever one drug can do the job, I prefer not to use two. But in persons who musn't have aspirin for one reason or another, then Persantine should certainly be taken.

The Omega-3 polyunsaturated acids (ECA and DCA) mentioned earlier, found in cold-water marine fish like salmon, cod, halibut, mackerel and sardines, do all kinds of wonderful things for the Eskimos who eat them. As I indicated above, they reduce the stickiness of the blood by their antiplatelet, aspirin-like effect. The best way to get them is to eat at least a pound of fish a week. If for some reason you can't or won't do so, you can buy these same oils in capsule form at a health food store or pharmacy. How many Omega-3 capsules one should ideally take has not yet been established. I recommend, quite arbitrarily, about three a day of the 1-gram strength.

Eating more Chinese food, at least the cuisine that features black tree fungus (called "tree ears" or mo-er) may also be the thing to do. Tree ears apparently have an antiplatelet action similar to that of aspirin.

BLOWING UP THE PLAQUES—BYE-BYE BYPASS?

Recently, there was reintroduced and popularized a concept and technique first used in 1964 in the United States— *percutaneous transluminal angioplasty*. A very thin catheter is inserted into a partially obstructed artery. Once it is in place, another small catheter with a soft, flexible balloon at its top is threaded into it. This balloon, when inflated, compresses the plaque obstructing the artery, thereby widening the lumen or diameter of the vessel and permitting more blood to flow through it. When it can be done, this technique is obviously preferable to surgery.

Although a very major development, and one that is being

used much more frequently as new and better balloon cathe-
ters are produced, balloon angioplasty is not risk-free. It still
cannot be done in most cases—as for example, when the
artery is totally blocked or when the diseased vessel is at
such an angle that the catheter cannot reach the obstruction. Still, you should always ask about angioplasty whenever
bypass is recommended. Sometimes patients are denied a
procedure only because no one in their particular hospital
knows how to do it!

Because of the possibility (4 or 5 percent of cases) of the
balloon rupturing the wall of the artery, or a piece of the clot
breaking off and completely obstructing the vessel farther
down and thus causing a heart attack, there should always
be a surgeon standing by ready to operate on an emergency
basis.

POOF GOES THE LASER

In 1981, I wrote in the first edition of this book: "Angioplasty
. . . must still be considered experimental," and it was at the
time. Today it is making progressive inroads in the number
of bypass operations being performed. I predict the same
outcome for laser beam therapy for coronary plaques. Today
this technique remains experimental. Three or four years
ago it was being done only in animals. Today, a handful of
human subjects have already been treated this way, some
successfully, others not. I fully expect that within five years
lasers will be used in many centers throughout the country
to vaporize obstructive plaques, and together with angioplasty
and other currently evolving techniques to dissolve fresh
coronary artery clots, it will further reduce the number of
cases requiring open chest bypass surgery.

WHEN YOU'RE ABOUT TO
HAVE A HEART ATTACK

Let's move along, then, from the patient with chest pains
who has not yet had a heart attack to one who has. Although
many heart attacks occur suddenly without any prior symp-

toms, others are preceded by a progressive worsening of angina. Symptoms that may have been present and stable for years become more and more severe and are provoked by progressively less effort or begin to occur at rest (especially at night), and the number of nitrogylcerin tablets consumed increases significantly.

Angina that becomes "unstable" in this way is as much an emergency as is a frank heart attack. Patients with such symptoms are in a "premonitory" or "impending" phase of a heart attack. Under these circumstances, your doctor will restrict your physical activity, keep you at home or preferably send you to the hospital for observation. Your medication will be adjusted and/or changed. With rest and a bit of luck, you may be able to avert the threatened attack. If you don't, then if you were sent to the hospital, you have the added protection of having the necessary treatment administered without delay when the final closure of the diseased coronary artery takes place. If you have "unstable angina" and your doctor recommends this regimen, don't argue. It is sound advice, the kind that does not normally require a second opinion.

If, after you are hospitalized, you continue to suffer chest pain at rest, despite the change in your medical regimen, you will very likely be advised to have a coronary angiogram. This is good advice.

Depending on what the angiogram shows, bypass surgery may then be recommended. A second opinion is desirable at this point, even if all the pieces as I have related them fall into place. The purpose of a consultation now is to determine that this is the hospital in which to have the operation, and that the surgical team is experienced. If there is any question about these two preconditions, have yourself transferred elsewhere if it is still safe to do so.

A bypass operation is "open chest" and not really "open heart" surgery. The coronary arteries on which the surgeon does his work are actually on its surface. The heart is not entered as it is, for example, in valve surgery. For these reasons, the risk of bypass surgery is considerably less than for valve replacement.

If you're satisfied with the hospital and the surgical team and agree to undergo surgery, make sure everything to be done is fully explained to you. That's extremely important for many reasons. First, ask about getting an internal mammary artery graft, if possible, rather than a saphenous vein graft. The former is an artery located in the chest wall. Long-term follow-up of patients whose hearts have been revascularized indicates that internal mammary grafts last longer, and do not clog up as often as do saphenous veins taken from the legs. Such internal mammary artery grafts are not always technically feasible, but when they are, they should be used. Also, it's important to know what to expect when you awaken from anesthesia. A strange, frightening environment may lead you to believe you're in heaven or —! Also, the gadgetry, the noises, the needles, the strange faces, the pain, and most important, the tube going down your throat into your lungs (necessary to ensure adequate ventilation while the anesthesia wears off) may all terrify you. It won't be long before you're feeling comfortable, but your initial anxiety can be managed if you're not taken by surprise. Also, the speed of your recovery and the incidence of important complications is apt to be very much reduced if you are taught *before surgery* how to breathe properly and expand your lungs in the first few days after surgery.

IN THE EVENT OF A HEART ATTACK

Suppose that instead of developing a premonitory, warning, impending or unstable phase of your angina, you simply continue to have your usual symptoms. Then one day, and for no apparent reason, you develop a heart attack.

Here is a typical scenario: It is the middle of the night. You are awakened by a more severe heaviness, pain or pressure in the chest than you have ever had before. Unlike your usual angina attack, this time nitroglycerin offers no relief. You feel faint, nauseated, and begin to perspire. The symptoms increase in intensity and your jaw may begin to ache, or the pain spreads to either arm (more commonly the left one) or through to the back.

Interestingly enough, statistically, all this is more apt to happen on a Monday. It's not clear whether that's due to too much revelry and drinking on the weekend or to the re-exposure to occupational stress after a period of relaxation.

NO TIME FOR HEROICS

Whenever it happens, a heart attack is no time to be unselfish, a hero or a diagnostician. As I wrote in *The Complete Medical Exam*, a host of different conditions may mimic an acute heart attack. These include a pinched nerve in the neck, a blood clot in the lung, a hiatus hernia, gallbladder disease, ulcer, gastritis, inflammation of the sac surrounding the heart (pericarditis) and arthritis of the chest wall. But whatever *you* think the symptoms may be, don't fall into the trap of the "denial mechanism." So many patients are convinced that if they don't call the doctor, the trouble, whatever it is, will go away. This unwillingness to face reality is responsible for many deaths. Remember, delay during the first critical hour after the onset of symptoms may be fatal. Wake your spouse and *get to the hospital the fastest way you can.* I encourage my patients to call my office immediately, but not to wait for a response in the event my associates or I cannot be reached instantly. When I receive the message, I do not waste precious time making a house call if I believe a heart attack is in progress. Remember, the first hour is critical. Have someone call for a hospital ambulance with a paramedical team, or the local police emergency squad. As soon as you arrive at the hospital emergency room, the personnel there will institute the necessary treatment. Here, time, not a second opinion, is of the essence, because of the threat of sudden death.

SHOULD YOU GO TO THE HOSPITAL OR STAY HOME?

There are "experts" in this country—doctors, statisticians, accountants and politicians—all looking for formulas to reduce medical costs. One of their targets is "unnecessary" hospitalization. To that end it has been suggested that some persons with "mild" heart attacks might be safely treated at home. Despite the statistics offered, I insist on sending my own patients to a coronary care unit in the hospital. I do not believe that it is always possible to distinguish a "mild" heart attack from a "serious" one early on, although it is very easy to do so in retrospect. If someone experienced only minimal pain of brief duration, and the blood pressure never dropped, and there were no life-threatening arrhythmias, I can look back and say with confidence, "You had only a mild heart attack." But in many individuals, symptoms start with some nondescript pain that persists and worsens, and only later is attended by serious complications requiring immediate expert intervention. When that happens it's good to be in the proper environment, which is a hospital, and not your home. So it's a matter of hindsight, and I have found it virtually impossible to tell in the first thirty minutes or one hour, when the decision about hospitalization must be made, which patient will have a mild attack and which a serious one.

But there are other compelling reasons for *all* heart attack patients to be admitted to the hospital. Modern technological advances responsible for the great reduction in mortality from heart attacks are not available at home. Not so many years ago, there was little one could do for a "coronary." We prescribed medication to control pain, administered oxygen, insisted on prolonged bed rest—and hoped for the best. If that were all we could do today, I would agree that home was not only as good as a hospital, but perhaps even preferable. If one is going to die anyway, it's nice to be surrounded by familiar faces and loved ones. But very few patients die during an acute heart attack these days, and as you soon will see, we now energetically go after the fresh clot that is causing the attack, dissolving it chemically within hours after its formation. This not only saves life, but by reducing the amount of muscle damage within the heart, improves its quality later on.

So if you're having chest pain or pressure, a diagnosis of an acute heart attack is made, and you are told you can be treated safely at home, ask for a second opinion. Better still, simply insist on going to the hospital. Don't get shortchanged at one of the most critical times in your life.

TREATING THE HEART ATTACK

Once you're hospitalized, treatment will depend on your symptoms and what the doctors find in their examination. You will immediately be given something for your pain, usually a narcotic like morphine. At the same time you will receive oxygen via little prongs in the nostrils. You will be hooked up to a monitor, a screen or console on which your electrocardiogram is continuously displayed within view of the specially trained personnel caring for you.

To improve your coronary flow, and to reduce the work of your now (or about to be) damaged heart, nitroglycerin is administered either by paste on your chest or intravenously. You will usually also be given a beta-blocker by mouth and/or a calcium channel blocker to reduce spasm of the diseased coronary arteries.

DEALING WITH AN
IRREGULAR HEARTBEAT

If your heart is beating irregularly, too quickly or too slowly, you will be given one of a variety of drugs, usually intravenously. For example, to suppress the irritable foci arising in the injured tissue, the most important and widely used medication is lidocaine (which, interestingly enough, is also a local anesthetic). Other agents include procainamide (Pronestyl), quinidine, verapamil and digitalis. There are additional, more specialized drugs that are occasionally necessary.

If the cardiac rate becomes very rapid, it can cause your blood pressure to drop quickly and decrease the blood supply to the brain. In that event, your doctor may decide not to wait for medication to take effect, but will apply direct-current electroshock to the chest (cardioversion). This usually normalizes the rhythm disorder immediately. If you're an anxious relative in the anteroom of the coronary care unit, wondering about a loved one inside, and are told that cardioversion was necessary, don't despair. It does not necessarily mean a poor outlook. The electroshock was needed simply to pull the sick heart through what is often an acute, *temporary* emergency. Availability of the equipment for this technique has significantly reduced the early death rate from heart attacks in hospitalized patients.

Occasionally, especially when blockage of the *right* coronary artery caused the heart attack, the cardiac rate drops to dangerously low levels. Again, this is usually temporary, but even so, a pacemaker may need to be inserted for a few days. This, too, is not a catastrophic event. As soon as healing begins, the pacing wire can usually be removed. This is not a kind of intervention that normally requires a second opinion, since it is made on an emergency basis.

WATCHING THE BLOOD PRESSURE

Your blood pressure too will be checked frequently. If the injury to the heart muscle is very extensive, it may not be able to pump enough blood to keep the circulation going through the body. Under these circumstances, the blood pressure may become dangerously low. We then try to maintain it at appropriate levels. Under these circumstances, drastic measures are sometimes required. We may have to insert an artificial auxiliary pump into the aorta near the heart to help that ailing organ pump the blood more adequately. We leave this auxiliary pump there for a few days to help sustain the circulation, buying time for the stricken heart to regain some of its strength. However, a modest *reduction* of pressure in response to injury is often a natural protective mechanism that reduces the work of the sick heart. So sometimes during a heart attack, we now deliberately lower the blood pressure with medicines (especially if it is elevated) in order to ease the burden of the heart.

If, upon admission to the coronary care unit, your attack is evaluated as being serious, certain other procedures may be instituted to help manage your case or offer extra protection. In order to evaluate the state of your heart, a Swan-Ganz catheter may be inserted through a vein in your arm or neck to the right side of the heart, where for the next few days it measures pressures. This information guides your doctor with respect to your fluid needs. Too much or too little can stress the circulation. The Swan-Ganz catheter is very useful. I'm not sure, however, that it isn't inserted more often than is necessary.

Perhaps the most dramatic change in the management of acute coronary occlusion has been the development of enzymes (streptokinase, tissue plasminogen activator, or TPA), which, when injected either intravenously or directly into the obstructed artery via a catheter, can dissolve the fresh clot within minutes. This must be done within the first two to three hours after the onset of symptoms. In many cases, dissolution of a clot is followed by balloon angioplasty, which compresses the underlying arterial plaque. These two maneuvers can drastically minimize the extent of cardiac damage in a heart attack, and constitute additional compelling reasons for everyone with this diagnosis to be admitted to a hospital. If you are offered the choice of "thrombolysis" (clot dissolution) and angioplasty, take it, but only if the institution to which you have been admitted has a successful track record with such cases.

When the heart attack is very severe and thrombolysis, with or without angioplasty, is either not feasible or has been unsuccessful, emergency bypass surgery may be necessary. There is growing evidence that an operation at this time can be life-saving. This decision, however, is so important that it should never be made without adequate consultation.

The vast majority of heart attacks are not fatal. In most good hospitals, among every hundred patients who are admitted with that diagnosis, almost ninety survive. Before the introduction of the coronary care unit, more than 30 percent died.

Much of what I have described above—treatment of arrhythmias, maintenance of dropping blood pressures, management of shock, use of intra-aortic balloons (auxiliary pumps) and emergency surgery are not usual in a heart attack. Furthermore, none of these measures, when necessary, usually allows time for a second opinion. You're going to have to depend on the first one. It therefore behooves you, *before you get sick*, to make sure of your doctor's credentials and his skill at doing the right thing in a crisis. But in any event, regardless of that assessment, it is a good idea to ask for a cardiology consultation as soon as you are admitted to the hospital if your own doctor is not a heart specialist, in the event of any unexpected emergency that requires extra skill and expertise.

The more usual course of events in a heart attack is not very dramatic. You have pain for a few hours, it responds to medication, and the rest of the time is spent badgering your doctor to send you home. No drama, no resuscitation, no shock.

HOW LONG IN THE HOSPITAL?

Until fifteen years ago, we used to keep heart attack patients in the hospital for at least six weeks. Then we became aware that prolonged bed rest itself was hazardous, mostly because of clots forming in stagnant blood in the veins of the immobile individual. Today, I generally discharge my patients who have had an uncomplicated heart attack in about ten days.

BEFORE YOU GO HOME

All right, you've had your heart attack, and recovered nicely. Your outlook is good, especially if you are really serious about quitting smoking, losing weight, watching your diet, getting enough exercise and generally following doctor's orders. But before you leave the hospital, there are certain tests that should be done. Ask your doctor about them if he fails to recommend them. First, I think every postcoronary patient should have a low-level stress test. This gives us a very good idea of how much you will actually be able to do when you get home. In the old days, we'd simply tell patients, "Take it easy." Neither the doctor nor the patient knew exactly what that meant. We can be somewhat more precise these days after looking at the stress test. You should also have Holter monitoring, in which your ECG is continuously recorded for a twenty-four-hour period. This may reveal your vulnerability to dangerous disturbances of heart rhythm. Of course, if you continue to have angina after your heart attack while still in the hospital, you will probably be advised to undergo cardiac angiography. It's better to know where you stand *before* you go home.

LIFE AFTER YOUR HEART ATTACK

What kind of life can you look forward to after a heart attack? Years ago, you would have been "finished"—unemployable and treated like an invalid in every respect. Today, the question is not *whether* you will go back to work, but *when*; not *if* you will make love again, but *when*? We have had this change of heart (no pun intended) because in most cases the damaged cardiac area forms a tough scar that will not likely cause you any future symptoms. You should now focus on preventing another heart attack, not worrying about the one you have already survived. The world is full of people who have had "coronaries." The great majority enjoy normal, active lives. In about six weeks to two months, most patients can return to work. You may not be able to resume your former job if it involves an inordinate amount of physical and emotional stress, but that does not mean that you have to stay home and do nothing. Your local medical society or heart association can direct you to job retraining programs in your community.

If your doctor advises you to retire, despite the fact that you feel perfectly well, get a second opinion. There is nothing worse than forced and unnecessary retirement.

CARDIAC REHABILITATION

I usually advise my patients who have recovered from an uncomplicated coronary to enter a cardiac rehabilitation program, one that is individually tailored. Such a program is conducted under close supervision at least three times a week, for three or four months after discharge from the hospital. You should then be able to continue it at home or at a local gym. There's nothing better for morale than physical fitness.

SEX AFTER YOUR CORONARY— UP THE STAIRCASE AND INTO BED

Unfortunately, most doctors fail to advise their patients about sexual activity after a heart attack—and most people are too embarrassed to ask. If you want to remain sexually active (and who doesn't), be sure to request *specific* instructions. Since intercourse, regardless of how it is done—up, down or sideways—requires effort, I advise my patients to abstain for about one month or until they can climb a couple of flights of stairs at their own pace, without chest pain or undue shortness of breath. If they continue to have angina, I insist that they take nitroglycerin *before sex*. And, even though I am not a Masters or a Johnson, it is clear that the traditional "missionary" position, with the male on top supported by his elbows, involves more work for the man, because, in addition to performing the sex act, he has to support the weight of his own body. It is easier to assume the side-by-side position or have the woman on top. Also, try to avoid intercourse right after eating or drinking alcohol, when it is too hot or too cold, when you're overtired or when you've been having more than the usual number of angina attacks.

When advice about sexual activity after heart attacks is given, it is usually addressed to men, a reflection of the fact that this illness strikes males with alarming frequency in their prime of life and is uncommon in women before the menopause. But any woman who has suffered a heart attack should follow the same guidelines with respect to sexual activity as is offered to men.

DEATH IN THE SADDLE (*MORTE D'AMOUR*)

The actual risk of dying while making love is very small. You may take comfort in the fact that fewer than 1 percent of all sudden deaths occur "in the saddle," but I always remind my patients that of these, 80 percent occur when the action is extramarital!

FEAR OF SEX

Although most patients are anxious to resume their sexual activity, they usually need to be reassured that it is safe to do so. Seventy-five percent of men suffer at least some temporary interference with sexual performance after a heart attack.

In at least 10 percent, impotence becomes permanent—for psychological, not physical, reasons. And of those who do resume sexual activity, two thirds permanently decrease its frequency to less than half of what it was before they took sick. The attitude of his spouse is critical to a man's sexual enjoyment and performance. Many women are terrified of killing their husbands by loving them physically. Their caution becomes counterproductive and renders the husbands impotent. If your husband or lover has had a coronary, discuss his condition frankly with him and the doctor. After being instructed in the do's and don'ts of your relationship, proceed accordingly.

Female patients are woefully neglected with respect to their future sexual activity—so much so that more than 50 percent of women who engaged in lovemaking prior to their heart attack stopped doing so afterwards. In most cases, there were no other reasons than fear and/or ignorance. Never let this happen to you.

WHEN SYMPTOMS CONTINUE AFTER A HEART ATTACK

In some patients, cardiac symptoms persist after a heart attack. I discussed earlier the indications for corrective angioplasty or bypass surgery. If you are managed medically, treatment will be very much like what it was before your heart attack. However, if a substantial amount of heart muscle was damaged, the remaining portion may not be able to pump well enough to meet the demands of the body. This is called "heart failure," and is treated mainly by prescribing adequate rest, a low-salt diet, diuretics and digitalis. All beta-blocking drugs are usually stopped. In more severe cases, we now use a combination of agents that act to reduce the work load of the heart by dilating the arteries and veins. These include the nitrates, hydralazine and a more recently available group of drugs called ACE inhibitors, of which captopril is the prototype. You will also have to delay or postpone indefinitely any exercise program until your heart has been substantially strengthened.

Another chronic problem with which we sometimes have

to deal after a heart attack is some *disturbance of heart rhythm*. But remember that not every "palpitation" or "extra beat" is serious or requires treatment. When it does, the drugs currently available for that purpose are often toxic and potentially dangerous. So, if you have a heart rhythm disorder requiring medication whose side effects make you miserable, do not hesitate to ask for a second opinion from a cardiologist experienced in their use.

Before you take any agent, however, make sure you have eliminated from your diet those substances that render the heart more irritable—caffeine in coffee, tea, and many cola drinks; liquor in all its forms; most nasal decongestants; appetite suppressants; and, of course, cigarettes.

DRUGS FOR THE IRREGULAR HEARTBEAT

Cardiac agents now available for oral use in the United States for restoring or maintaining a regular heartbeat include some form of digitalis (digoxin [Lanoxin], digitoxin [Crystodigin]), quinidine (Quinidex, Cardioquin, Quinaglute), procainamide (Procan, Pronestyl), Dilantin (not for epileptics only), the various beta-blockers, disopyramide (Norpace), amiodarone (Cordarone), flecainide, tocainide, mexilitene and several others still in research. If you have a rhythm problem that *must* be treated, yet you seem to be unable to tolerate any of the agents that your doctor prescribes, request a second opinion from a cardiologist who is experienced in this area.

The following is a brief discussion of the most important antiarrhythmic drugs currently available, so that you may know what benefits and adverse side effects to expect and how to recognize them.

First there is *digitalis*, of which there are several forms. They are not all interchangeable, since each has its own rate of absorption, duration of action and route of excretion from the body. The major use of this agent is to slow a speeding heart. Its greatest application is in the control of atrial fibrillation and flutter, cardiac rhythm disturbances whose major threat to you lies more in their tendency to cause a rapid rate than in their irregularity per se.

WHEN YOU HAVE TOO
MUCH DIGITALIS ON BOARD

Digitalis in the proper dosage is safe and usually without side effects. Older persons generally require less than younger individuals. When "normal" doses are given to older persons, they may end up with toxic side effects. This is especially likely if there is impairment of kidney function. The first evidence of such toxicity is distaste for food—especially meat. The appetite may be so severely impaired as to cause significant weight loss. When the digitalis is stopped for a few days, then restarted in a lower dosage, these symptoms disappear. So, if you have been given a digitalis preparation for whatever reason and find that you are gradually losing your appetite, tell your doctor about it. Don't be shy about suggesting to him the possibility of digitalis excess. He will be grateful to you (especially if you are right).

You are more likely to develop such digitalis toxicity if, after you have been taking it for a while, a quinidine preparation is also prescribed. This is a recent and important observation. Whenever quinidine is added this way, the digitalis dose usually should be reduced by half immediately. If there is any question about the dosage, the amount of digitalis in your blood can be measured by a technique called radioimmunoassay.

THE BETA-BLOCKERS
AS ANTIARRHYTHMICS

Beta-blocking drugs like Inderal (used for the treatment of hypertension and angina pectoris) also help to regularize heart rhythm. But if you are being treated for heart failure or asthma, they must be taken under close medical supervision or not at all.

QUINIDINE—LOTS OF SIDE
EFFECTS, BUT EFFECTIVE

Quinidine is perhaps the most useful antiarrhythmic drug we have, but is difficult for many patients to tolerate. It frequently causes diarrhea or soft stools, skin rashes, hearing problems and blood disorders. But certain commercially available forms are less troublesome than others. So if you are given a quinidine preparation and you experience any of these problems, let your doctor know. There are alternatives to going through life with chronic diarrhea. If you are able to tolerate the quinidine, but it doesn't seem to be helping the rhythm problem, your doctor can obtain a quinidine level from your blood to see if you need a higher dose of the drug.

PRONESTYL—EFFECTIVE
BUT POTENTIALLY TOXIC

An alternative drug to quinidine is procainamide (Pronestyl). It is about as effective as quinidine, but also potentially toxic. Unlike quinidine, which just makes you miserable, Pronestyl can cause persistent, severe arthritis, a serious disease called lupus, and a host of other symptoms. I try not to prescribe this agent over the long term, but often find I have little choice. If you are taking it and you develop arthritis, fever, malaise or other unexplained symptoms, advise your doctor immediately. If he doesn't take your complaints seriously, get an opinion from another cardiologist. As with digitalis and quinidine, Pronestyl drug levels in the blood can also be measured. In addition, there is a special test (ANA) that indicates whether the Pronestyl is having adverse effects on your body.

NORPACE, BUT WATCH
YOUR PROSTATE

The antiarrhythmic agent Norpace (disopyramide) is used in circumstances similar to those in which quinidine or Pronestyl might be prescribed—for the prevention or treatment of certain kinds of "extra beats" originating in the ventricles. Although Norpace appears to be better tolerated than quinidine and Pronestyl, it can depress heart function. So be careful if your heart is weak. It should also be used with caution in men over sixty years of age because it can cause difficulty in urination.

Among the plethora of new antiarrhythmic drugs, the one I have found most useful is amiodarone (Cordarone). It has long been available in Europe, where for some reason its toxicity appears to be somewhat less frequent and serious than in the United States. In any event, the untoward effects to watch for are abnormal chest X-ray findings, visual changes and thyroid underfunction, all of which are reversible. Sensitivity to sunlight may also be a problem.

The bottom line with respect to treating abnormal cardiac rhythm is that it is a tricky business requiring a doctor with solid experience in the field. Not every rhythm variation or brief palpitation needs to be dealt with. Most such variations are perfectly harmless, and in fact, the therapy is often more uncomfortable and dangerous than the arrhythmia. Once a decision is made to institute drug therapy, you will find that some work and others do not. It requires a real rhythm virtuoso to select the right medication, its dosage and timing.

Sometimes your doctor, no matter how sophisticated his background in the field, may not be certain whether or not a particular disturbance of heart rhythm is potentially life-threatening. He may then suggest programmed stimulation of your heart to be sure. This involves introducing a catheter with an electrode at its tip into the heart, in other words, a cardiac catheterization of sorts. The electrode is then stimulated to see whether your arrhythmia can be reproduced, and if so, whether or not it is potentially life-threatening. If it is, specific drugs are tested then and there. The net result of this intervention is to indicate whether your rhythm problem in fact needs therapy, and if so, what the most effective drug is apt to be. I suggest that since this is an invasive procedure, you should get a second opinion if it is recommended to you.

There are certain life-threatening cardiac arrhythmias that come on unpredictably, and are not responsive to any available drug. This is an uncommon and drastic situation for which two new forms of therapy have recently become available. One is an operation in which the irritable focus within the heart is actually surgically excised. In the second an implantable, internal defibrillator is programmed to recognize the onset of a dangerous rhythm. It then does spontaneously what the personnel in the coronary care unit do under similar circumstances. It shocks the heart into normal rhythm. This is a most fascinating and impressive development, which fortunately is not required by too many patients. However, if you are a candidate for sudden death, this device should be made available to you.

THE CARDIAC PACEMAKER
—NO BIG DEAL

Virtually all rhythm abnormalities requiring drug treatment are those in which the heart beats too fast. Appropriate medication can slow the rapid rate to levels that do not exhaust the heart. There are, in addition, certain rhythm disturbances in which the rate is not too fast, but too slow—so slow that the brain and other body tissues do not receive enough blood to function normally. There is no drug for such disorders. Treatment requires a cardiac pacemaker.

There is a tiny piece of tissue within the heart that is responsible for regularizing the rate and rhythm of the beat. It is called the sinus node. When it becomes damaged, either by a heart attack or the formation of scar tissue, its malfunction results in intervals during which your heart alternately beats very rapidly and then too slowly. Because the sinus node isn't working properly, medication to decelerate the rapid rate may slow the heart too much. When the dose is reduced, the heart speeds up again. This slow-fast situation, which puts the doctor between a rock and a hard place as far as treatment is concerned, is called a sick sinus syndrome. Under these circumstances, a cardiac pacemaker is usually required. It can be programmed so as to guarantee that your heart will beat no more slowly than a predetermined rate. For example, it can be set so that the cardiac rate will never be less than, say, fifty beats per minute. With this protection, we can then give you medication to control the rapid heartbeat without worrying that it will reduce the rate too much.

The heartbeat may also slow down excessively without

the rapid component seen in the sick sinus syndrome. This is usually due to a condition called heart block. (The block is an electrical one, not in an artery.) Symptoms depend on how slow the heart rate actually becomes. If it is below thirty beats per minute, you may suffer attacks of light-headedness, dizziness or even loss of consciousness. If that happens, you may need a cardiac pacemaker.

A pacemaker is no "big deal" anymore. Your life may depend on having one, but it will not prevent you from carrying on normally. There are throughout the world more than 500,000 patients who have pacemakers, and thousands more are implanted every year. The surgical procedure itself entails little risk, and is usually done under local anesthesia. The chest is not opened. A small electrode slipped into the heart through a vein (just like a catheter) takes over the job of regularizing the heartbeat from your own diseased sinus node. It is triggered only when your own heart fails to beat—in other words, it functions on demand. (That is why it is called a demand pacemaker.) It can be set to ensure any heart rate considered desirable for you. The electrode that stimulates the heart is powered by a small generator sewn under the skin.

A cardiac pacemaker does nothing for the heart muscle itself. Nor does it prevent heart attacks, or permit you to live forever. It simply guarantees that your heart will never again beat too slowly.

While a pacemaker is great if you need one, it shouldn't be inserted without a valid reason. Occasionally, the heart beats too slowly because of some medication you are taking. I have seen patients referred for an opinion about a pacemaker, when their problem was simply that they were getting too much digitalis, Inderal, reserpine or even lithium—medications that decrease the heart rate. Simply stopping the responsible drug, or reducing its dosage, restored the heart rate to a satisfactory level. The generator powering the pacemaker electrode formerly had to be changed every two or three years. Newer technology has permitted us to extend that interval to at least seven or eight years—and longer.

SELECTING YOUR PACEMAKER

The field of pacemaker technology is changing rapidly. Before you have one put in, make sure that the surgeon who will be doing it discusses with you and your cardiologist which one he plans to insert. Ask for a programmable model, one in which the heart rate can be varied *after* the unit has been inserted. This can be done simply by holding a potentiometer next to the body. (In the older devices, it was more difficult to change the heart rate once the pacemaker generator had been sewn under the skin.) So, in the event that the original heart rate at which the device was set is not the best for you, it can be slowed down or accelerated.

The pacemaker impulse as it appears on the ECG does not permit interpretation of what is going on in the heart. All we can tell is whether the pacemaker itself is working. If your chest pain has changed in character and we suspect some heart damage, a pacemaker ECG is of no help. But if you have a programmable one, it can be temporarily slowed so that your own heartbeat shows up on the tracing and can then be interpreted.

You have several other options when selecting a pacemaker. Ask about the *size* of the battery pack. If you are going to be spending time on the beach, or at the health club, and don't want to advertise your pacemaker, get one of the smaller ones.

Then there is a matter of the *power source* itself. The first generation of pacemakers had mercury-zinc batteries, which lasted only two to four years. The most important recent improvement in the energy source is the lithium battery, currently the most widely used, which can last as long as ten years.

Finally, there are *nuclear pacemakers* powered by plutonium 238 with a life span of ten to twenty years. The isotope itself is encased in metal, which prevents the emission of its radiation. There are some three thousand of these nuclear pacemakers now in use, but not in any of my patients! I prefer the lithium-powered models.

HEART TRANSPLANTS

The four scientific achievements in my lifetime that I consider most significant were the detonation of the first atom bomb, the launching of Sputnik, man's first step on the moon and Christiaan Barnard's heart transplant operation.

The drama of removing someone's heart and replacing it with the beating organ of a "dead" person was to me an event of staggering technological and emotional proportions. Some cardiac surgeons I know were not so overawed. Technically, this procedure is apparently not difficult to do, given the kind of skill and backup teams available at most cardiac centers. Christiaan Barnard had both and, in addition, more than the usual share of imagination, vision and courage. After his initial operations, followed by a flurry of "me-too" procedures throughout the world, heart transplants fell into disrepute because survival was so short due to rejection, the cost was prohibitive and suffering of transplant patients was so great. But despite the fact that the headlines stopped, serious interest in heart transplantation continued in several centers here and abroad. Without the original hoopla and fanfare, hundreds of transplants have now been performed throughout the world, most by the team at Stanford University at Palo Alto, California.

Advances in two areas have made cardiac transplantation feasible. The first is better tissue typing, so that the replacement heart is less likely to be rejected by the recipient's body. The second major factor is the development of cyclosporine, a suppressant of the immune system. While not without its own toxicity, this drug renders rejection much less likely, especially when tissue typing is carefully done. In any event, the only limitations on heart transplants now are cost and the availability of donor hearts. Improved retrieval of intact hearts from accident victims and the establishment of regional surgical centers now make heart transplantation an obtainable objective for hundreds of individuals each year. Although children whose heart muscle has been damaged by a virus or some other toxin are prime candidates, anyone whose other organs are intact and who does not have an underlying serious disease, physical or emotional, may be a suitable candidate. We used to limit the operation to those under fifty years of age. More recent experience has shown that heart transplants work and are worth it even in persons in their sixties, provided the rest of the body, especially the brain, lungs and kidneys, are intact.

THE ROLE OF THE ARTIFICIAL HEART

Where does the artificial heart fit in to all of this? It may hold greater promise for the future, but in my opinion, the Jarvik model presently available is only suitable as an emergency measure for someone waiting for a donor heart, where availability of the replacement organ has been delayed and death is imminent.

KEY FACTS TO REMEMBER

Heart disease is still by far the number 1 killer in most Western countries. A better understanding of the factors that contribute to "hardening of the arteries" has resulted in a significant and impressive decline in the cardiac death rate. There are many far-out theories about how to prevent heart attacks, but the only proven ones are control of high blood pressure, reduction of cholesterol levels and elimination of cigarettes. There is growing evidence, but no definite proof, that exercising regularly, watching your weight, modifying your behavior so that you are less tense, angry and frustrated, may all delay the onset of arteriosclerosis.

There are three major kinds of heart disease—the kind you are born with (congenital); forms that result from infections acquired in early (or later) life (rheumatic fever); and arteriosclerosis.

Congential heart disease often results from some toxic effect in the mother during pregnancy (thalidomide is the classic example) or infection (German measles). The child may be born with various cardiac malformations—a hole in the heart, deformed valves, or other structural abnormalities. Almost all can now be corrected surgically, but the decisions about if and when to operate, and who should do it, are critical. These should be made only after appropriate consultation with a pediatric cardiologist. Some congenital disorders can be corrected nonsurgically.

A recently recognized common cardiac disorder involving the mitral valve (floppy valve) is now believed to account for many of the symptoms we used to attribute to "nerves," especially in young women. Make sure that isn't your problem before you sign up with a psychiatrist.

Acute rheumatic fever, a disease of children and young people, follows streptococcal infections. The development and use of penicillin has resulted in a marked decline in its incidence in the last forty years. The cardiac consequences of rheumatic fever may not be evident during the acute stage of the disease, appearing only years later, when the heart valves become scarred and distorted. Eventually, these damaged valves must be repaired or removed. As in surgery for congenital heart disease, the timing of the operation is critical. This depends on a careful description of your symptoms to the doctor, together with his use of appropriate diagnostic heart tests. Make sure that the invasive, uncomfortable and costly ones are done last.

With regard to preventing arteriosclerosis, we are currently limited to the control of risk factors. Cigarette smoking is a major hazard. There is no such thing as a "safe" cigarette, since reduction in nicotine may result in increased use of "less toxic" tobacco with increased exposure to the harmful carbon monoxide in the smoke.

High blood pressure is never "benign." *Any* elevation has been shown to be dangerous over the long term, and should be normalized.

The cholesterol controversy is for the most part resolved. Impressive research data indicate that lowering blood levels of this fat can reduce the risk of heart attacks.

It is now widely believed the concentration of HDL (the kind of protein that transports cholesterol in the bloodstream) may be more revealing and prognostic with respect to heart disease than the cholesterol level, and that raising HDL levels may be protective.

Regular exercise is the best "tranquilizer" there is. Evidence is accumulating that it *may* reduce the risk of heart disease when done in the proper way and right amount. However, no one with any history of, or particular vulnerability to, heart disease should embark on an exercise program without prior medical clearance and ongoing supervision. For cardiac patients, the amount and kind of exercise should be as carefully prescribed as any potent medication.

Angina pectoris refers to chest symptoms due to too little blood reaching the heart muscle. It is usually the result of narrowing of the coronary arteries by arteriosclerotic plaques, but may also be caused by coronary spasm—an old theory whose validity has only recently been proven.

The most important drugs for the prevention and control of angina are members of the nitroglycerin family, beta-blockers and calcium channel blockers. The proper dosage and selection of the best antianginal agents may require expert consultation. The side effects of these drugs can usually be minimized.

Coronary bypass surgery is an important advance in the treatment of reduced blood flow to the coronary arteries. When done by experienced surgical teams, in properly selected patients, the risk of the operation is near 1 percent. In the great majority of cases, this operation eliminates or substantially reduces the severity of angina pectoris. There is a growing belief that bypass surgery also protects against heart attacks and prolongs life. Defining the need for such surgery requires a careful history-taking, physical exam, ECG stress tests, radionuclide scans and, ultimately, coronary arteriography (angiogram).

Percutaneous transluminal angioplasty (balloon angioplasty) is a newer technique that also relieves coronary artery obstruction, but without surgery.

Most heart attacks are uncomplicated and are followed by excellent recovery. However, some are severe, require expert care and leave the patient with symptoms that may require treatment later. Patients in both categories can benefit from sound advice about life-style, medication and cardiac rehabilitation.

Cardiac pacemakers are easy to implant, with only minimal risk. They are used when the heartbeat is too slow. The decisions as to when to implant a pacemaker and what kind to use may require a second opinion.

Heart transplants are now feasible in selected patients at virtually all ages. Survival is increasing, and the procedure is now being done successfully in many centers throughout the world.

12

HYPERTENSION—THE SILENT KILLER

Untreated high blood pressure (hypertension) is one of mankind's most important afflictions. Over the years, it pounds away silently at key arteries throughout the body, weakening their walls, helping to clog them up and occasionally causing them to burst. In most cases, while all this is going on, the patient has no telltale symptoms until it is too late. Then, after a "free ride" of several years, the ravages become apparent with a stroke, heart attack, ruptured aneurysm, blindness, kidney failure, cardiac weakness or hardening of the arteries in the legs or elsewhere in the body. The only way you can know, before it is too late, whether you are destined to suffer or die this way is by having your blood pressure measured. If it is high, it must be treated effectively.

BLACK AND WHITE

The incidence of hypertension is substantially higher, and its complications likely to be more severe, in blacks than in whites. Our genes determine the diseases to which we are susceptible, and genes do differ among races (for example, sickle-cell anemia, which occurs in about 0.3 percent of blacks in its full-blown form, is never found in whites). Genetic factors endow blacks with lower amounts of renin, a hormone that helps flush salt out of the body. This renders them more sensitive to dietary salt and more susceptible to hypertension.

WHY NOT JUST LOWER THE PRESSURE? WHY GET A SECOND OPINION?

If it is simply a matter of treatment, why am I devoting a chapter to hypertension in a book dealing with second opinions? For the following three reasons: (1) Not all physicians are as vigorous as they should be in their attempts to normalize elevated pressures; (2) there is still some disagreement as to what numbers constitute high blood pressure and when to start treatment; and (3) the optimal combination of drugs, one that effectively lowers pressure without intolerable side effects, may be difficult to achieve, and may require consultation. I will elaborate on each of these points as we go along.

It is hard to believe that only a few years ago many doctors did not believe that high blood pressure needed any therapy at all. In their opinion, as long as you had no symptoms, you could safely be left alone. That's why the condition used to be so called benign essential hypertension—"benign" because so many people, especially women, *seemed* to be none the worse for it; "essential" because that's what we call any disease whose cause(s) we don't fully understand. The term "benign" has been abandoned in describing hypertension.

In all fairness, I think this laissez-faire attitude was to some extent influenced by the fact that doctors did not have the drugs with which to lower blood pressure safely, effectively and for long periods of time. But we do now. If you are being treated by someone who has not caught up with the times (and there are still a few such physicians around), who pats you on the back and says the high pressure is "normal" for you, run, don't walk, for a second opinion.

DR. FREIS AND MRS. LASKER

Although most physicians at least suspected that normalizing blood pressure might delay or prevent its terrible consequences, it remained for Dr. Edward Freis and his colleagues to prove it in the Veterans' Administration study in 1970—the first large-scale controlled trial of this hypothesis. When their data showed how important it was to treat every case of high blood pressure, Congress was further motivated to do something about the problem by Mary Lasker (America's own Florence Nightingale). As a result, the National Heart, Lung and Blood Institute embarked on an intensive educational campaign directed at doctors and the public alike, a campaign that has been and remains eminently successful.

THE IMPACT OF ACTION

The truth about hypertension has spread like wildfire among health care consumers everywhere—in government, industry and the private sector. In just a few short years, the number of cases detected and treated has increased substantially. The result has been a dramatic and continuing drop in deaths from strokes and heart attacks in the United States during the last decade.

In view of this experience, and given the increasing number of effective new drugs available for the treatment of hypertension, there is no excuse for anyone to be walking around with an elevated pressure.

WHAT IS HIGH?

The *definition* of what blood pressure levels are abnormal and require treatment remains a matter of some controversy. In my opinion, there are still too many doctors who accept as normal readings that are too high to be left alone. There are probably two main reasons they do so. Even though Dr. Freis and his colleagues showed the benefit of treating hypertension, they did so only in patients with pressures that were quite high. It was not until the beginning of this decade that the need to treat even "mild" elevations was also demonstrated. Furthermore, doctors do not like to give potent medications to patients who feel well and many persons with high blood pressure have no complaints at all. However, leaving them be, because they are without symptoms, is a dangerous game.

IMPORTANT—BUT BORING

Suppose you are in "excellent" health (as far as you know) and have gone to the doctor only for a checkup. To your surprise, he tells you that your blood pressure is high. If you both act on that information, things will never be the same for you. From now on, you will be constantly reminded about matters that were never important to you before—what you eat and how much you weigh; the hazards of tobacco; the risks of salt; the perils of cholesterol; the need for exercise and the benefits of equanimity. It's all a bloody bore, and most people resent such massive intrusion into their life-styles, especially when they feel perfectly well!

Initial reaction to these fiats varies among hypertensive individuals. Those who are intelligent and understand the implications of untreated hypertension follow the advice conscientiously. Many "behave" for a few weeks and then revert to their old habits, subconsciously denying their high blood pressure ("After all, I feel so *well*"). Others refuse to cooperate at all ("I'll just take my chances. Life is too short for me to follow that sort of regimen").

I wouldn't sell life insurance to anyone in the latter two categories, and I would suggest that you defer trying to buy any yourself until your pressure is down—unless you are prepared to pay a stiff extra premium. You see, the insurance companies know the score. In statistics accumulated over the years from millions of subscribers, they have found that even for persons with "borderline" readings, for example, 138/88 (we still consider 140/90 the cutoff point for the normal range), the chances of death are 36 percent higher in men and 22 percent higher in women. When we look at numbers like 158 to 167, the risk is 110 percent greater in men and 67 percent greater in women—and the premiums are rated accordingly.

IF YOU COMPLY

Suppose you are a complier. You realize that lowering your blood pressure is important, especially since you have read the projections that if all thirty-five million Americans with high blood pressure were adequately treated, the overall death rate from strokes and heart attacks would probably drop another 20 percent. You are also impressed by the fact that 68 percent of patients who develop a heart attack and 75 percent of those who sustain strokes have a prior history of untreated high blood pressure. So you faithfully follow the advice given you. You adhere to your diet, you exercise, lose weight, reduce your salt intake and try to "relax" as best you can. You come back a few weeks later expecting your blood pressure to be normal. So you are disappointed when your doctor tells you you will need medication. As you leave the office, armed with a prescription for pills that you will probably have to take for the rest of your life, you are a little resentful—toward yourself, your bad luck and your doctor. The pills cost money, as will the revisits to check their effectiveness. And the irony of it all is that you actually feel very well despite the numbers on the blood pressure machine.

GETTING ANGRIER AND ANGRIER

In the next few weeks, your anger and frustration increase. You are nervous as hell because you are no longer smoking. You fantasize about forbidden foods. And now, to top it all off, you have begun to notice some side effects from the drugs. At this point, some patients throw in the towel. They quit the regimen and simply stop visiting the doctor. Their displeasure doesn't exactly leave the doctor happy either. He, after all, has lost a patient! This scenario happens so often that many doctors delay prescribing drugs for the control of high blood pressure until they "really have to"; they leave borderline values, which are also dangerous to you, untreated. To protect yourself against that possibility, always ask your doctor what your pressure is and write the numbers down. Be prepared to discuss with him the pros and cons of treatment. Pressure readings are not a secret to which only your physician and your insurance company are privy.

THE NUMBERS GAME

What are the numbers for which you require treatment? There is still no unanimous agreement, but the definition of optimal blood pressure is coming down with every new study reported. The lower the pressure, the better your outlook. For example, even though 140/80 is "normal," and nobody would give you medication to lower it, if you happen to have a pressure of 110/70, you are less likely, at least statistically, to develop a complication of hypertension at some future date.

MY PERSONAL TECHNIQUE

I use the following criteria in my own practice. If there are three successive readings, on different days, greater than 140/90 in persons under sixty years of age, I begin treatment. Beyond age sixty, as the arteries become more rigid and less flexible, I accept 160/90 as the upper limit of normal and treat any persons with values above that on any occasion.

Sometimes, especially in the course of an insurance examination, the "friendly" doctor who finds a borderline blood pressure will turn the light out and have you rest so that your pressure will drop to an "acceptable" level. Such "tranquil" pressures are good for purposes of reducing the insurance premium. They should not, however, constitute the basis for any decision about treatment. Your pressure response in the real world is what counts, not readings taken while you're relaxing on a couch in a darkened room.

Some patients, when told that their blood pressure is high, have even pleaded for "another chance," after which they go home, load up on tranquilizers and come back a few days later looking like zombies. They are surprised when I tell them their readings are still high. Although stress and anxiety do raise the pressure, true hypertension is not a consequence of emotional disturbance. It is a complex biological disease involving many factors—chemical and hormonal. Tranquilizers and other sedatives may help you deal with a particular crisis in your life, but they are not antihypertensive drugs and should not be used as such over the long term.

HOW MUCH TESTING
BEFORE TREATMENT?

At this point, you may be confronted with another problem that requires a second opinion, the matter of how thoroughly the *cause(s)* of your hypertension should be evaluated. Although we know what happens in association with high blood pressure—the arterial walls are in spasm, arteriosclerosis is accelerated over the years, the blood level of certain hormones, like renin, is sometimes increased—the basic, underlying mechanisms are not understood in the great majority of cases. But in about 5 percent of patients with hypertension, specific curable causes *can* be identified and eliminated, after which the blood pressure usually remains normal without need for any medication. These forms of hypertension include certain tumors of the adrenal gland and particular types of kidney disease. In order to diagnose such unusual situations, a fairly extensive and expensive work-up—chemical, hormonal and radiographic—is required.

Should you submit to such a complex diagnostic evaluation? Years ago, most physicians, especially the "purists" among us, insisted that *everybody* with hypertension be studied in order to identify the meager 5 percent with the curable form. That approach is impractical. There just isn't enough money in the public treasury to pay for all those tests, and most people are either unwilling or unable to spend it personally. However, since the majority of those with surgically curable hypertension are for the most part relatively young, most doctors compromise and undertake a thorough work-up for anyone under forty years of age. In conclusion, if you are a hypertensive in your fifties, sixties, or older, and are advised to undergo CT scans, kidney X rays and sophisticated biochemical testing, ask for another opinion from a hypertension specialist.

HOW TO COPE WITH SIDE
EFFECTS OF MEDICATION

Now let's get back to the hypothetical situation in which you find that modifying your life-style does not significantly lower your pressure. (Chances are, mind you, that if you are over-weight, and do succeed in losing a substantial amount of weight, you will not need any drugs.) Medication is then prescribed that results in some undesirable effects. These are almost always either temporary or tolerable. But if they are not, there are other drugs you can try. If you continue to be unhappy with various regimens prescribed and your doctor informs you that it is the unavoidable price you must pay for normalizing your blood pressure, that "every blood pressure medication has side effects," get another opinion. It is possible to adjust your treatment so that you are virtually symptom-free.

HOW ANTIHYPERTENSION DRUGS WORK

In order to understand which agents lower blood pressure and how they work, you must first appreciate what happens to the circulation in the presence of hypertension. The level of the pressure depends, to a great extent, on the *caliber, or width, of the arteries.* You know from fishing or boating that the narrower the stream, the more quickly it seems to flow. In the disease we call high blood pressure, the arterial walls are taut, and it is this tension that is largely responsible for the elevated pressure within the vessels.

Since nerve endings in the arterial wall keep it tense, agents that neutralize these reflexes reduce blood pressure. Such drugs may counter the nervous influences where they actually originate, that is, in the brain itself, or where they end up, in the nerves that supply the tiny muscles within the arterial wall that constrict or narrow the vessel.

In some patients with hypertension, there is an excess of a hormone called *renin* that throws the arterial wall into spasm. This spasm can be neutralized by beta-blocking drugs, like Inderal, Tenormin, Lopressor and several others. Newer agents, captopril (Capoten), and enalapril (Vasotec), belong-ing to the family of drugs referred to as angiotensin converting enzyme (ACE) inhibitors, prevent the formation of renin. If your renin is measured before any therapy is begun and is found to be high, you can immediately start therapy with one of the antihypertensive agents that prevent renin formation, which are most likely to be effective in your case. Most doctors, for reasons that are not clear to me, prefer the trial and error approach.

The *volume of blood* in the circulation also determines pressure. Blood volume is increased by salt. So, treatment of high blood pressure involves reducing the blood volume by a low-salt diet and/or diuretics, which eliminate excess fluid. (It is not always easy to reduce your salt intake. Avoiding salty foods is obvious, but how is one supposed to know that Vichy water, for instance, is loaded with salt, as are many packaged foods?)

COMBINING SEVERAL DRUGS IN SMALL AMOUNTS

I prescribe small amounts of each of several drugs in combination, rather than large doses of any one medication. This approach reduces the incidence of side effects, most of which are determined by the size of the dose of any given drug.

DIURETICS—NO WONDER THEY'RE CALLED "WATER PILLS"

Unless you are diabetic or suffering from gout, the first drug your doctor is likely to give you is a diuretic. There are several different brands available, most of which are thiazides. They lower pressure by causing a loss of salt and water in the urine. As a result, you have to empty your bladder frequently. You not only lose salt in the urine, but also potassium. This doesn't usually create a problem, especially if you take extra potassium (which is found in orange juice, bananas and figs). Potassium depletion may, however, cause generalized muscle weakness. Also, if you happen to be taking digitalis (digoxin, digitoxin) with the diuretic, low potassium levels do become important, because they enhance digitalis toxicity. You will recognize that by the onset of nausea and palpitations.

An additional consequence of low levels of sodium, potassium and other trace minerals like magnesium is leg cramps. Diuretics may also elevate blood sugar; stopping them usually results in a return to normal values. So if you are told that your blood sugar is high and that you may be diabetic, the thiazide preparation you've been taking may be the cause. Diuretics also frequently increase the uric acid content of the blood. That doesn't usually cause any symptoms, but it sometimes precipitates an acute attack of gout, especially if you have a history of this disorder. Patients taking diuretics also develop higher levels of blood fats (cholesterol and tri-glycerides). As many as a third of the men taking them become impotent and/or fail to ejaculate. But before blaming impotence on this medication or any other pill, remember that hypertension itself can cause sexual problems in men.

Aldactone and Dyrenium, both diuretics (but not thiazides), are sometimes used alone or in combination with other water pills, because they minimize the loss of potassium. Men taking Aldactone may become impotent and notice enlargement of their breasts. In women, the suspicion that this drug may cause breast cancer has also arisen. If you have been given this agent, discuss these possible consequences with your doctor.

Anyone reading this list of side effects from the diuretics might easily conclude that they are horrendous drugs to be avoided and that it is preferable to take one's chances with the high blood pressure. That is not so. Most of the adverse reactions are mild and can be eliminated by reduction of the dose. One way to make this possible is to *really* cut down your salt intake. The less salt you eat, the less of the diuretic you will need.

MY FIRST CHOICE, THE BETA-BLOCKERS

Although most doctors still start with diuretics when treating hypertension, many prefer beta-blockers. In the United States, there are currently seven beta-blockers available—Inderal, Lopressor, Corgard, Tenormin, Blocadren, Sectral and Visken, with several more on the way. Their action is at least in part due to the neutralization of the hormone *renin*, which is responsible for some cases of high blood pressure.

Beta-blockers have certain advantages over diuretics. For example, they do not raise blood sugar, lower potassium, increase uric acid or keep you going to the toilet. However, they slow your heart rate, make you feel more tired and frequently leave you impotent or frigid. Also, bear in mind that if you are asthmatic or have any degree of heart weakness or failure, these drugs are not for you.

If the beta-blocker you are taking interferes with your sexual function, try switching to another brand. For example, Tenormin, Sectral and Visken are said to cause less impotence than do some of the others. Beta-blockers may also give nightmares, painful enlargement of the breasts, cramps, diarrhea, and cold hands and feet.

Should you want to discontinue a beta-blocker for any reason, do not stop it suddenly, especially if you have angina pectoris. Doing so may induce a heart attack. Despite the foregoing, the beta-blockers are extremely useful, effective and well tolerated in the treatment of high blood pressure.

A third group of drugs only infrequently prescribed these days for lowering blood pressure is derived from an Indian herb called *Rauwolfia*. A purified form, reserpine, is available, either alone or in combination with other drugs. I have never liked it much, because it can cause serious depression, especially in older persons. I don't think this particular drug should be in your medicine cabinet unless you absolutely have no alternative, and that's hard to imagine.

Another agent, still widely used but which is not among my first choices, is methyldopa (marketed as Aldomet). Although it does lower blood pressure effectively, it also causes impotence in at least 40 percent of men; retrograde ejaculation (during orgasm, the sperm is ejected back into the bladder instead of out of the penis); breast enlargement and tenderness; and untoward effects on the blood. Never take Aldomet if you have any form of liver trouble. If this drug has been prescribed for you and you find that you have lost all interest in sex, or can't do much about it even if you still have the desire, ask your doctor to replace it with another medication. So many patients are afraid to make such suggestions to the doctor, especially when the side effects are in the sexual area. They suffer unnecessarily in silence, because they are too timid or ashamed to talk about it.

Clonidine (Catapres), another blood-pressure-lowering agent, is chemically related to methyldopa. Its possible side effects include dizziness when you stand up suddenly (postural hypotension), impaired sexual function and a rebound of blood pressure when it is abruptly discontinued. Do not take beta-blockers with it.

Clonidine is unique in that it is the first antihypertensive drug that can be taken not only by mouth, but also via the transdermal route. A patch applied to the skin once a week results in a slow, steady absorption of the drug, avoiding the peaks and valleys often associated with oral medication.

An interesting, important and totally unrelated effect has serendipitously been noted with clonidine. Heroin addicts receiving this medication can apparently withstand abrupt withdrawal of the narcotic (cold turkey) without the usual agonizing symptoms. This is a most important pharmacologic observation.

Then there is guanethidine, useful in cases of hypertension resistant to other forms of therapy. I don't prescribe it much anymore because patients often suffer a sharp drop in pressure when they change position suddenly, as, for example, when leaping out of bed in the morning. Guanethidine also frequently results in poor sexual function.

Your doctor may prescribe prazosin (Minipress) and hydralazine (Apresoline), both of which are very effective, especially when used in combination with beta-blockers or diuretics. I like both these agents very much, and neither causes significant impotence. In fact, I often start therapy with Minipress. This drug has another salutary effect. In men whose sleep is frequently disturbed by the need to empty their bladder because of prostate enlargement, Minipress often reduces the number of necessary trips to the john. But there is one important caveat. In some individuals, Minipress may cause a profound drop in blood pressure. So always take the very first capsule in its weakest strength (1 mg) at bedtime. If you experience no dizziness during the night after that initial dose, you may then safely take it in the prescribed amounts two or three times a day.

Captopril (Capoten) and enalapril (Vasotec), which block the formation of renin, are the newest antihypertensive drugs. When Capoten was introduced a few years ago, the Food and Drug Administration recommended its use only when other medications failed to lower blood pressure significantly or tolerably. That is no longer the case. Many doctors, including me, are using these ACE inhibitors as first-line drugs, especially when renin levels are high, because they are often free of many of the side effects of the beta-blockers and diuretics. It is often necessary to add small amounts of a diuretic. The combination of ACE inhibitors and diuretics is a potent one and usually well tolerated. But no medication is *always* free of side effects. In some cases, ACE inhibitors can compromise kidney function, so they should be used with caution whenever renal function is abnormal. ACE inhibitors may also reduce the number of white blood cells your bone marrow makes, rendering you more susceptible to infection. There is not enough experience with these drugs to warrant their use by pregnant women and nursing mothers.

Sometimes patients whose blood pressure has been normalized for months or years ask me about terminating medication to "see what happens." I usually hesitate to do so, especially if they are feeling well and the drugs are causing no problems. I hate to rock the boat. However, if they insist, I will go along with their request, because it has been shown that in about 20 to 25 percent of patients with mild or even moderate elevation of blood pressure that has been under good control for a year or more, the pressure remains low even after medication is stopped. So it's worth a try, but if the pressure shoots up off therapy, resume medication without delay.

LOW BLOOD PRESSURE IS NOT A DISEASE

Many patients complain of "nonspecific" symptoms whose causes are rarely identified. They have no energy, are chronically tired, nervous, weak and sweaty, and they are troubled by cold hands and feet. Thorough investigation often fails to reveal an underlying cause. It's almost as if there is a constellation of symptoms in search of a disease. After such a negative work-up, there is a great tendency (and temptation) to ascribe these complaints either to low blood sugar (*hypoglycemia*, discussed in Chapter 6) or low blood pressure.

If you learn nothing else about blood pressure, remember this: *Low blood pressure is rarely abnormal or a disease*. That obviously does not refer to the low blood pressure (hypotension) induced by medication or to the drop that sometimes occurs in the course of a severe heart attack or in certain chronic neurological disorders. People with underfunction of the thyroid gland or Addison's disease (an inadequate production of hormones by the adrenal glands, from which President Kennedy suffered) have low pressure, but this is a symptom of another disease. If you don't have another condition that causes hypotension, *leave it alone.*

If you are weak or dizzy and all your doctor can find is a "low blood pressure," for which he recommends hormone treatment, ask for a second opinion. Such therapy is rarely needed or justified.

KEY FACTS TO REMEMBER

High blood pressure is an important "silent killer." It is the major cause of strokes, and may lead to heart failure, kidney malfunction, and manifestations of arteriosclerosis elsewhere in the body. Although it sometimes is responsible for headaches and nosebleeds, it usually produces no symptoms and is detected only during routine blood pressure measurements. It tends to be more prevalent and severe among blacks.

The importance of treating all cases of elevated blood pressure has begun to be appreciated only recently. Because of the "free ride" the patient has for so many years, during which there are no symptoms, some doctors and many patients still tend to be permissive about this serious disease. National educational and treatment programs relative to hypertension have already resulted in a 40 percent decrease in the incidence of strokes in the United States since 1972.

Weight loss, regular exercise and reduction of salt intake are all beneficial in controlling high blood pressure, but most people require drugs for the rest of their lives. When properly selected and in the right dosage and combination, these agents are well tolerated. Anyone who simply "can't take blood pressure pills" should ask for help from a specialist in this field.

Except in very rare circumstances, low blood pressure is not a disease but a blessing. Never agree to having it raised artificially without asking for a second opinion.

13

THROMBOPHLEBITIS, VARICOSE VEINS AND BLOOD THINNERS

In the first chapter I described a hypothetical case of thrombophlebitis and the seemingly conflicting advice the patient was given for its treatment. Let us now look at this disorder in greater detail.

Thrombo means "clot," *phlebitis* is an inflammation of a vein. When the interior lining of a vein becomes inflamed, the blood no longer flows smoothly within it. Little clots form and stick to the vessel wall. Thrombophlebitis can be caused by anything that injures the veins in your legs or causes the blood within them to flow more slowly—an infection, a blow to the leg, prolonged bed rest, diseases in which the blood is more viscous than it should be and various kinds of hormones (especially estrogens, found in "the pill"). Also, in anyone who develops "migrating" phlebitis for no apparent reason, that is, phlebitis in one leg or arm and then in the other, we often find a cancer somewhere, most commonly in the pancreas or the lung. Such tumors probably produce a substance that affects the circulation in the veins.

THE DANGERS OF PHLEBITIS

The threat of thrombophlebitis lies in the possibility that a piece of the clot attached to the vein wall will break off and

225

travel along the circulatory pathway. Since almost all the veins in the body (except those from the brain and the heart) return to the lungs, we worry about a blood clot ending up there. (A traveling clot is called an *embolus*; the organ in which it finally lodges is said to have an *embolism*; damage caused by the clot is called an *infarction*.) So, an embolus from phlebitis in the legs that goes to the lungs gives you a pulmonary embolism with infarction. If the fragment is tiny and the size of the infarcted area is small, your symptoms will consist only of some pain in the chest when you take a deep breath, a little cough and perhaps some bloody sputum. You are sick, but you are not likely to die. On the other hand, if a big clot ends up in the lung and obstructs a large blood vessel, you may be in serious trouble.

Pulmonary embolism is an important cause of death and disability in patients with thrombophlebitis. Since we can never predict the size of an embolus, it is very important to diagnose thrombophlebitis correctly and treat it properly— and in time. For some reason that I don't fully understand, phlebitis in the arms, the kind that sometimes follows intravenous therapy, rarely if ever sends clots to the lungs. It does not require the same treatment as does phlebitis in the legs.

HOW PHLEBITIS IS DIAGNOSED

When you show the doctor your painful leg, he must first decide whether you have phlebitis. The diagnosis is often, but not always, obvious. The leg hurts; it is swollen, red, warm and tender to the touch. When the doctor abruptly jerks your foot up and back toward your knee, that worsens the pain in the calf of your leg. If, in addition, he can feel a swollen, tender vein in your leg, then you almost surely have phlebitis. But such classical clinical evidence is not always present, and the diagnosis based on that evidence is accurate in no more than 50 percent of the cases. *Whenever phlebitis is suspected and the doctor is less than absolutely certain, objective testing is necessary.* Make sure you get it before any commitment to therapy is made.

The need to be certain about the diagnosis is well illustrated by the following story. A fifty-eight-year-old man came to see me because of pain in the calf of his left leg. He had just returned from a trip to Europe. In the preceding few weeks he had done a lot of flying, walking and climbing—a perfect setup for thrombophlebitis. The sore leg looked a little larger than the other, and did, in fact, measure one quarter of an inch more around. But such minor variations in leg girth are not uncommon. It also felt a little warm, and it hurt, especially when I pressed on it. One fairly reliable test for thrombophlebitis was also positive—when I jerked the foot back toward his knee, the patient winced.

ON BEING LED DOWN THE GARDEN PATH—BY SHINGLES

The diagnosis seemed fairly straightforward, and I sent the patient to the hospital for treatment of thrombophlebitis. Intravenous heparin, a potent blood thinner, was started immediately. The patient's family then asked for a consultant whom they had used in another instance of vascular disease—"just to be sure." The consultant examined the patient, and he too was impressed by the findings. He nevertheless performed a Doppler test to evaluate the blood flow in the veins. It was completely normal. "How accurate is that machine?" I asked. "Only about 60 to 80 percent," he replied. "Well," I answered, "in that case, I think we should continue the anticoagulants since the picture is so typical of phlebitis." And we did. Some three or four days later, while reexamining the leg, I noticed a few little pimples behind the knee. Within the next twenty-four hours, the patient developed shingles. This disease accounted for all the pain, redness and warmth in the leg. I had been led down the garden path by the herpes zoster virus. The Doppler test was right, and I was wrong.

TREATMENT DEPENDS ON
DIAGNOSIS AND JUDGMENT

The basic treatment decision to be made in any case of phlebitis is whether or not to use anticoagulants. The answer will depend on whether the involved veins are deep or superficial. When the phlebitis is only superficial, the veins and redness are visible, and the condition rarely results in embolization. It therefore does not usually require thinning of the blood. Therapy involves resting the leg, keeping it elevated and applying warm soaks. For disabling pain, I usually prescribe a nonsteroidal agent like Indocin or Motrin. Symptoms usually subside in a few days. If they do not, or if they appear to be getting worse, anticoagulants may be necessary. They should always be added if there is any question about the presence of coexisting deep vein involvement. In such cases withholding anticoagulants can be disastrous. Not long ago I saw a patient who had a typical superficial thrombophlebitis for which I had her rest the leg, elevate it and apply moist heat. Two days later she called to tell me that she was coughing, had a pain in the chest and was spitting blood. She had, in fact, thrown a blood clot from a deep-vein phlebitis that had gone unrecognized. The point to remember is that even when the phlebitis is superficial, objective testing is a good idea to make sure the deep, threatening form is not also present.

WHEN OBJECTIVE TESTING IS
BETTER THAN CLINICAL JUDGMENT

There are several diagnostic techniques to determine whether the deep veins of the leg are involved and, indeed, whether the leg pain is due to a vascular problem at all. The most definitive procedure is called a venogram, an X ray of the veins taken after a contrast medium has been injected into them. But most vascular specialists first evaluate blood flow in the leg noninvasively by the Doppler method described earlier, as well as by a procedure called venous outflow plethysmography. Don't hesitate to ask your own physician about these techniques in order to be absolutely certain about the diagnosis in your case.

WHEN PHLEBITIS STRIKES THE DEEP VEINS

When the deep veins are inflamed, the risk of embolism is high and you will usually be sent to a hospital for several days to have your blood thinned. For an immediate effect, we start with intravenous heparin. Then, after a few days, we give you an oral preparation (warfarin). How long the anticoagulants are continued depends on several factors. If this was your first attack and it was not complicated by a blood clot to the lung, anticoagulation is usually continued four to six months. If, however, you have varicose veins, suffer from recurrent phlebitis and have already had a pulmonary embolism, you may well be kept on anticoagulants for a year or longer.

PROBLEMS OF ANTICOAGULATION

Aside from the cost and the inconvenience (you need to have your blood tested at regular intervals, usually every three to four weeks, to make sure it is not too thin), anticoagulants can create their own problems. You may, for example, be allergic to them and develop a rash. If you have high blood pressure, anticoagulants increase the risk of a brain hemorrhage. And then there always is the danger of internal bleeding when the blood gets too thin, something that may happen spontaneously or after an accident. Remember, too, that the level of anticoagulation can be affected by some other medication you're taking—a sleeping pill, antibiotic, or painkiller.

TREATING VARICOSE VEINS

While on the subject of veins, let me tell you how I manage patients with varicose veins. One in five Americans and half the population over fifty years of age have this condition. It occurs most commonly in women who have had many children, and in persons who stand a great deal. The main symptoms are aching and tired legs, especially at the end of the day.

In some women, varicose veins may become more tender during the menstrual period; in others, they are simply unsightly. Patients often ask for their removal for cosmetic reasons. When the varicose veins are very small, so that you see little red streaks in the legs but can't really feel them, an operation does not usually help. The best thing to do in such cases is to wear an elastic stocking, many of which are now cosmetically acceptable. Varicose veins do not usually require surgery. If you have them, keep off your feet whenever you can, avoid crossing your legs, elevate them when you sit (using an ottoman or footstool), raise the foot of the bed at night and wear support hose. Also get into the habit of taking long walks at a brisk pace. Wherever possible, do so barefoot (not so easy in the city!). There are also some simple leg exercises that can improve the circulation in your veins. Ask your doctor about them. If you do all this, chances are that you won't require surgery or injections.

THE EXPENDABLE VEIN

Sometimes dilated varicose veins need to be removed. The term surgeons use for this procedure is "stripping." How can the blood continue to flow normally in the legs after large veins are cut out? The answer lies in the fact that there are so many of them. This also permits their use in coronary bypass operations.

If your symptoms are really troublesome but you prefer not to have surgery, the offending veins can be injected with a "sclerosing" solution, that is, one that closes them up. I am not sure that this is as safe and long-lasting as vein stripping, the operative approach. If you are advised to have injections, make sure that your doctor is skilled in this technique.

KEY FACTS TO REMEMBER

Thrombophlebitis is the formation of a clot within a vein which is inflamed. This can result from a number of causes, ranging from simple injury to cancer somewhere in the body.

Thrombophlebitis produces pain, redness and swelling, and may be difficult to distinguish from several nonvascular causes, such as a simple injury. Correct diagnosis is imperative because, unless properly treated, phlebitis can result in a portion of the clot breaking away and traveling to the lung (embolism)—a dangerous complication.

When the diagnosis of phlebitis is made, a second opinion from a vascular specialist should usually be obtained for confirmation. He has at his disposal several techniques, some of which are not invasive, to determine whether or not a clot is actually present. If there is a clot, anticoagulants are usually prescribed.

In most cases, varicose veins can be managed conservatively, without surgery. If "injection" of the veins or an operation is recommended, consult a vascular specialist.

14

YOUR ARTERIES AND YOUR CIRCULATION— FROM FALSE ALARMS TO TRUE ANEURYSMS

Many people are too quick to attribute almost any symptoms in the arms, legs, hands and feet to poor circulation. "My toes are numb. They're probably not getting enough blood." Or "I know my circulation is bad because I spend half the night walking around the room to get rid of the terrible cramps in my legs." The first complaint may be due to a circulatory disorder, the second probably is not.

Pain, weakness, cramps, numbness, tingling or coldness of the extremities can all be due to several different causes, only a minority of which reflect problems of blood flow. The list of these *noncirculatory* disorders is long and includes arthritis (of the limbs themselves or of the spine), diseases that render the nerves irritable or interfere with their function (diabetes, syphilis), medications (diuretics) and muscular injury, strain or spasm.

MIMICKING VASCULAR PAIN

You may not always know whether your symptoms are due to poor circulation, but your doctor will. Take *arthritis* of the spine, for example, in which nerves to the legs are either irritated by the diseased bone or displaced by a disc pressing on them. The net result is pain down the leg when lying in bed, or sitting or standing. Even though you perceive the pain along the pathway of the compromised nerve—in the toes, heels, buttocks, calves, shoulders, elbows, hands or chest—the trouble actually originates in the spine.

In *diabetes* too the nerves are frequently diseased (diabetic neuropathy), not by mechanical pressure as in spinal arthritis or disc disease, but because of some chemical effect due to the diabetes. These "sick" nerves cause pain in the legs (or elsewhere, depending on which ones are affected). Again, these symptoms have nothing to do with circulation (although diabetics are, in fact, also prone to vascular problems).

You may suffer pain in the legs due to *muscle spasm* from any number of causes—injury, strain, inadequate arch support, too soft a mattress, bad posture or excessive jogging.

"Feeling cold" in the hands or feet often reflects temporary constriction, *spasm* or narrowing of perfectly healthy arteries from which the blood has been shunted when the body needs it more urgently elsewhere—in such vital organs as the kidneys, heart, brain and liver. Also, diseases that have nothing to do with poor circulation, such as hypothyroidism, can give you cold extremities. But patients with low thyroid function may not only *feel* cold, they *are* cold. The beta-blockers, like Inderal, can also induce these symptoms. Switching from one of these drugs to another may improve matters.

The symptoms resulting from actual arterial disease depend on which organ(s) the obstructed vessel was meant to nourish. Poor circulation in the brain, for example, results in stroke; in the eye, blindness; in the heart, a "coronary"; in the kidneys, renal failure; in the intestines, severe pain after eating. When the penis is deprived of its normal blood flow, the result is impotence.

HOW *YOU* CAN DISTINGUISH ONE KIND OF LEG PAIN FROM ANOTHER

Symptoms of inadequate circulation in the legs are almost always associated with effort. Pain at rest during the night, or while standing or sitting still, is not likely to be circulatory. But a cramp or "charley horse" in the calf while walking that disappears within minutes after you stop is almost certainly vascular. It may actually occur higher or lower in the leg, but the calf is the most common site. (In angina pectoris—pain in the chest due to coronary artery disease—there is a similar relation to effort. Angina occurs on exertion because the narrowed coronary arteries are unable to deliver enough blood to the heart muscle.)

HOW YOUR DOCTOR
MAKES THE DIAGNOSIS

If you have pain in the legs when you walk a given distance at a certain pace, your doctor will perform the appropriate tests to confirm the presence of circulatory insufficiency. He will first inspect the feet to see whether either or both are blanched. Also, when blood supply is inadequate, men often lose the little tufts of hair on the top of their toes. He then touches various parts of the leg looking for temperature differences. Any area deprived of blood feels cold to the touch. The pulses in your groin and legs are also checked to see whether they are full, diminished or absent.

If your doctor is particularly interested or skilled in vascular disease, he will probably examine the circulation by the Doppler method, which employs an ultrasonic probe to assess the blood mass flowing in the artery beneath it.

HOW MUCH COLLATERAL
DO YOU HAVE?

If the diagnosis of vascular disease is made, don't worry about losing your legs. There are countless thousands of people with this problem, only a tiny number of whom eventually require amputation. This is so because patients with arteriosclerosis are protected by collateral circulation. And the best way for you to develop such a backup system is to *keep walking*. The demand for blood in the muscles of the leg is increased by exercise. Since the narrowed arteries cannot supply the extra amount needed, the ever resourceful body forms new channels or widens smaller ones already there, providing collateral flow. So, if you have pain when you walk, don't retreat to the armchair; the best way to improve your circulation is to keep moving as much as you can.

YOU MUST STOP SMOKING

There is something else that you will have to do, whether you like it or not. *You absolutely must stop smoking*. Not cut down, or change the brand, or avoid inhaling the smoke—all the old excuses—but *never* touch another weed, stogie or pipe. Tobacco causes the arteries to go into spasm. This further constricts the already narrowed vessels, worsening your symptoms despite anything medical we can do for you.

BUT DON'T GO OFF THE WAGON

According to tradition, a little alcohol at bedtime is good for you, because it supposedly dilates the arteries. That theory has been questioned recently, but it is such a pleasant form of therapy that nobody challenges it very seriously. But if you have a problem with alcohol and have finally gone on the wagon, don't start drinking again in order to "improve" your circulation. I remember one patient with exertional leg pain to whom I recommended a brandy at bedtime. He never told me he was a recovered alcoholic. My well-meant advice, which he had accepted with great pleasure and alacrity, nullified the results of months of psychiatric treatment.

Whether or not you take that nip, there are other things to be done for the arterial circulation in your legs. Warm compresses or a heating pad applied near the groin or lower abdomen for a few hours at bedtime will reflexively dilate the vessels lower down in the leg and may improve your symptoms. But make sure that you don't burn yourself in the process, and never apply heat directly to the affected limb.

More advanced cases of circulatory disease in the legs sometimes benefit from the use of an oscillating bed, which very gradually rotates a certain number of degrees up and down, thus stimulating the circulation.

Until quite recently, despite all the hype and medical advertising, there has been no medication for the treatment of poor blood flow to the legs (or the brain, for that matter). However, in 1985 Trental (pentoxifylline) was approved by the FDA for this purpose. It works by making the red cells (the formed elements in the blood that carry oxygen) more malleable, permitting a greater number to squeeze through a narrowed portion of the artery. Trental comes in only one strength (400 mg) and is taken three or four times a day. It's not a cure, but it often increases the distance patients can walk before the onset of leg pain.

HOW TO WASTE YOUR MONEY

Too many doctors still indiscriminately prescribe vasodilator drugs for circulatory problems. They may help when symptoms are due predominantly or solely to *spasm* of the arteries (Raynaud's disease) rather than obstruction by arteriosclerotic plaques. But most arterial disease is due to blockage of the arteries, and here the vasodilator drugs are of little or no benefit. As a matter of fact, theoretically at least, they can make things worse. The blood vessels they end up widening are not the narrow ones that need it, because those are too rigid and diseased to respond. So the healthy ones dilate. As a result, blood is shunted to them and away from the critically narrowed ones.

IS YOUR CAST TOO TIGHT?

If the arteries in your legs are diseased, avoid wearing tight or elastic stockings, which further compress them. Also, protect any limb with a poor blood supply against injury. Even a trivial blow, especially if it breaks the skin, may cause serious problems.

I remember one elderly woman who fell and fractured her kneecap, requiring a minor operation to remove the broken fragments. A cast was then applied from the knee to the ankle. Shortly thereafter, she kept telling anyone who would listen that the cast felt too tight and was hurting her, but she was assured by her orthopedist that the pain was to be expected and that if the cast were any looser, it would not support the injured knee securely enough. She continued to complain of a terrible burning under the cast until finally the surgeon cut a little window in it to see what was going on. He found the underlying skin cyanotic (blue) and discolored, due to poor blood supply. It subsequently broke down, leaving a painful ulcer, which took many months to heal. All this because the patient's circulation was poor to begin with, and it didn't take much compression by the cast to diminish the flow below a critical level. Fortunately, in this particular case, the ulcer cleared up. However, I know another elderly woman with vascular disease whose pleas about a tight cast were ignored until it was too late. She lost her leg!

SURGERY IS UP TO YOU

In most patients with vascular disease, such simple measures as stopping tobacco, regular walking, alcohol in moderation, reflex heat to the lower abdomen or groin, weight loss if called for and Trental usually make the symptoms tolerable. But if your walking is so limited that your life-style is really compromised, your doctor may propose an operation. Remember that such surgery is usually done for your comfort and not because the arterial disease is a threat to life or limb. In other words, the decision regarding an operation is almost always up to you. If you are satisfied with being able to walk only one or two blocks (and some people are, especially if they have some other physical problem that limits their activities), think twice about an operation.

WHAT KIND OF OPERATION IS BEST FOR YOU?

If you agree to surgery, an arteriogram must first be done. This is a special X-ray procedure performed in the hospital. Dye injected into the arteries of the legs, usually at the groin, outlines the portion of the vascular tree in question and indicates the site of narrowing or obstruction, how extensive it is and whether it can be corrected. Surgery involves either replacing a portion of the diseased artery with a Dacron graft or bypassing it by attaching the graft above and below the obstructed segment. In some cases, the artery can be reamed out (*endarterectomy*) and left in place.

AN ALTERNATIVE TO SURGERY

There is a newer technique of which you should be aware—*percutaneous transluminal angioplasty*. It may make surgery unnecessary in some cases. It is done by a radiologist (with a vascular surgeon standing by in case anything goes wrong). The usual arteriogram is performed, with the following difference. The catheter through which the dye is injected has an inflatable balloon at its tip. After the obstructed area in the artery is located, the catheter is carefully guided alongside it and the balloon is blown up, compressing the material blocking the blood vessel. This procedure not only works in the legs, but also in the coronary arteries.

Angioplasty, when it can be done, is obviously preferable to surgery. But it is not risk-free. It is possible that the arterial wall will be ruptured by the balloon or that a piece of plaque may break off as the balloon is distended, totally obstructing the vessel further down.

Whenever arterial obstruction must be relieved, whether you are a poor surgical risk or a good one, balloon angioplasty should be considered before an operation is performed.

HEADING FOR A BLOWOUT

The popular term for arteriosclerosis is "hardening of the arteries." Its main effect is to narrow the interior channel of the vessel and so deliver less blood to whatever organ it is nourishing. But this "hardness" does not strengthen the artery. In fact, the reverse is true. The wall becomes progressively weaker, so that a portion of it may begin to balloon out. This is most apt to happen in cases of long-standing, untreated high blood pressure.. Such ballooning is referred to as an aneurysm, and it is dangerous because it may burst or "blow out," much like a damaged car tire.

Most aneurysms form in the aorta, the large artery that comes out of the heart and from which all arteries branch off. It may occur anywhere in the course of that vessel, from its origin at the heart to its termination in the lower abdomen. The most common site, however, is in the belly. Aneurysms can develop in vessels other than the aorta, for example, in smaller arteries of the brain. Here the main cause is some congenital or developmental defect in the artery itself. The consequences of rupture of an aneurysm depend on its size and location, but death, often instantaneous, is a common result. So it is very important that any aneurysm anywhere be detected and treated in time.

UNLESS YOU FIND AND TREAT IT

An aortic aneurysm is not always easy to find because it often does not cause any symptoms. It is frequently picked up on a routine X ray, or, if large enough, felt by the doctor examining your abdomen. Once diagnosed, the critical question is whether and when to remove it. Most specialists agree that when an abdominal aneurysm attains a size of 5 cm, or roughly 2 inches, across, it should be taken out and the removed section of the artery replaced by a Dacron tube. This number was arrived at after years of experience revealed that almost half the patients with aneurysms greater than 5 cm die from spontaneous rupture. There are some surgeons who recommend operation no matter what the size, but they are in the minority.

A FALSE-NEGATIVE EXAMINATION

I remember one man, sixty years old, who twenty years earlier had had a mild heart attack. His blood pressure had been "modestly" elevated, but came down nicely with treatment. One night he developed pain in his belly. He went to a hospital emergency room where the intern diagnosed "indigestion" and lectured the patient about his dietary indiscretion. (He had had a "fabulous" meal with great wines at a famous French restaurant earlier that evening.) The patient was sent home, reassured by the normal physical examination, but still experiencing abdominal pain.

Two hours later he returned to the emergency room. The pain was now agonizing. A thorough examination again gave no clues as to the cause. The man was overweight, with a paunch, so that the belly was not easy to evaluate. In order to be safe, an X ray of the abdomen was done. It did not reveal any significant abnormalities either. This was before the days of the CT scan and sonography. Because the pain was intolerable, an exploratory operation was performed. The surgeon found a large aortic aneurysm that had ruptured. It must have been there for years—silent and undetected—until it suddenly burst. The patient survived the operation and returned to his normal eating and drinking. He subsequently became very friendly with the intern, who is now a better diagnostician—and a gourmet himself!

So one can have an abdominal aortic aneurysm for a long time, yet feel perfectly well with it. But if it is detected, and is 5 cm or greater in diameter, you should have surgery if you are able to withstand it. Your chances of living another five to ten years are doubled if you do.

HOW BEST TO DETERMINE ANEURYSM SIZE

Since the size of an abdominal aneurysm is critical, it must be determined as accurately as possible. That cannot be done without technological help. Conventional X rays of the abdomen are not enough. You need either abdominal sonography, which is accurate, safe and simple, or a CT scan. Be sure to ask for either one of these procedures if you are told that you have an abdominal aortic aneurysm, no matter how small it is estimated to be.

HOW SHOULD SMALLER ANEURYSMS BE MANAGED?

Abdominal aneurysms less than 5 cm in diameter are usually left alone, but must be reassessed at frequent intervals to see if they are increasing in size. The best way to slow such progression is to make sure your blood pressure is kept at a normal level.

Too conservative an approach—waiting too long to remove an aneurysm—can be disastrous. But so can premature surgery. That is why an additional opinion from a qualified vascular specialist is so important whenever an aneurysm is discovered.

KEY FACTS TO REMEMBER

Arteriosclerosis, or "hardening of the arteries," reduces the amount of blood delivered by an artery to whatever organ or tissue it supplies. Symptoms will depend on where this obstruction takes place. In the legs, it causes pain (usually in the calf) on walking quickly, which promptly subsides with rest. But there are many different causes of leg pain that may mimic pain due to vascular disease. When the latter diagnosis is suspected or made, it is wise to ask for a second opinion from a vascular specialist. He has at his disposal sophisticated techniques to measure blood flow.

Arterial disease in the extremities may severely limit your ability to walk any distance at a normal pace, but only infrequently does it progress to gangrene. This favorable course is the result of the natural development of a collateral circulation. "Dilator" drugs are usually a waste of money in such cases, exercise being the best stimulus for the formation of collaterals. But you *must* stop smoking. The most recent medication for this problem is Trental, which relieves symptoms to some extent.

Should surgery be recommended, ask about percutaneous transluminal angioplasty, a nonsurgical method of relieving arterial obstruction.

An aneurysm is a "bubble" developing in the weakened wall of an arteriosclerotic artery. The most common cause is long-standing, untreated high blood pressure. If you are found to have an aneurysm, consult a vascular surgeon. The best way to determine aneurysmal size is by sonography or CT scan. Abdominal aneurysms that attain a diameter of 5 cm or more should usually be removed.

15

STROKE—A MAJOR
KILLER ON THE WANE

ENDING UP A VEGETABLE

Older people often worry about having a major stroke. They are terrified of the prospect of being unable to control their bowels, of having to be lifted from bed to chair or toilet, of being unable to communicate with others—hearing, seeing and usually understanding, but unable to respond.

This fear of stroke is not unjustified, since it is the third leading cause of death and disability in the United States, following close on the heels of heart disease and cancer. There are about 750,000 new cases and 175,000 deaths each year. Among those who survive, 16 percent spend the rest of their lives in a hospital; another 20 percent never walk again without help; an additional 31 percent remain permanently dependent on others wherever they end up. Yet most of these victims were in good health just moments before the catastrophe.

That's the bad news about stroke. Here's the good news: The incidence is declining dramatically in this country because its leading cause—hypertension—is being so successfully identified and treated.

THE ORIGINS OF A STROKE

There are three kinds of stroke. The first, *cerebral hemorrhage,* occurs when an artery in the brain suddenly bursts after having its walls pounded year after year by high blood pressure. The key to preventing such a blowout is treatment of hypertension *as soon as it is discovered.*

Instead of rupturing, a cerebral artery may develop a clot (like rust in a pipe), which shuts off the blood supply to the brain (*thrombosis*). Keeping cholesterol levels down, controlling blood pressure and avoiding cigarettes will reduce the incidence of this disorder.

Finally, an artery may become obstructed by an *embolus,* a traveling blood clot that usually originates in the left side of the heart or in an arteriosclerotic plaque in one of the larger vessels in the neck. Clots tend to form within the heart when the cardiac rhythm is very irregular, a condition called *atrial fibrillation.* Many otherwise normal individuals have chronic atrial fibrillation. They can be protected against a brain embolus by having their blood "thinned." Unfortunately, some physicians still fail to institute anticoagulant therapy in such cases. If you are a "fibrillator" due to whatever cause (and there are several), discuss prophylactic anticoagulation with your doctor.

THE "STROKELET"

There is a very common group of neurological symptoms called TIA (*transient ischemic attack;* "ischemic" means inadequate blood supply). A TIA is the result of a sudden but temporary reduction in blood flow to the brain. When it occurs, any of the following may develop suddenly: dizziness (vertigo), double vision, numbness, tingling or weakness in an arm or leg and temporary slurring of speech. These symptoms persist anywhere from a few minutes to several hours (but definitely not more than twenty-four hours), then completely disappear, leaving you as well as you were before. It is critical that a TIA be correctly diagnosed, because it may herald a stroke. Indeed, 40 percent of patients with TIAs who are not treated have a stroke within five years. Although the symptoms of a TIA are classical, similar symptoms occur with migraine headaches.

ASPIRIN TO THE RESCUE

How do we treat such warning symptoms? Not long ago, there was little that we could do to avert a stroke after the warning TIA. Today, one to three aspirins a day have been shown to reduce the incidence of a subsequent stroke by about 50 percent in men. Strangely enough, it doesn't seem to work as well in women or in diabetics (who should nevertheless take it). Remember, however, it must be aspirin, and not a substitute like Tylenol. Aspirin affords this protection by interfering with the blood clotting mechanism. And if you can't take aspirin because you are allergic to it or have an ulcer, Persantine (dipyridamole) has similar properties. So use that instead, although the evidence of its effectiveness is not quite as convincing as that of aspirin.

ALL TIAs ARE NOT ALIKE

If you are having TIAs, consult a neurologist. It is important to determine their cause. These transient interruptions in blood supply to the brain may occur in either of the two major arterial trunks that supply the brain. One is the carotid system, which goes up the side of the neck, and which your doctor feels and listens to when he examines you. The other is the vertebrobasilar artery, situated in the back of the neck, which cannot be examined except by X rays and other procedures. Symptoms vary depending on the location of the vascular problem, because these arteries feed different parts of the brain. The carotids supply the retinal artery in the eye and the gray matter of the brain; the vertebrobasilar system feeds the back and undersurface of the brain.

When the carotid artery is involved, you may develop a constellation of visual disturbances in one eye, black out for a few minutes, or experience weakness, numbness or tingling of a hand or a leg; you may drop something that you are holding, or lose coordination, or your speech may become slurred. Blockage of the vertebrobasilar artery, on the other hand, usually results in a graying of vision, or you see double or become totally blind for the duration of the attack. There may be weakness of all four limbs rather than only one arm, and you may lose your balance or suddenly keel over. Nausea, vomiting and speechlessness are also common.

HOW A NECK COLLAR CAN PREVENT A STROKE

The distinction between these two kinds of transient ischemic attacks is important, because they may have to be managed differently. For example, when the carotid artery is involved, the arteriosclerotic plaque obstructing it can often be removed surgically. This affords an 80 percent chance of cure, assuming that the operation is done by an experienced surgeon. But the vertebrobasilar artery system is inaccessible to the surgeon. A clot there is best managed by aspirin. Make sure also that your blood pressure, if it is being treated, doesn't get too low, since a TIA may occur in patients with hypertension whose pressure drops too much—especially when they get up suddenly after lying down. When that happens, blood flow to the brain is decreased below a critical level. On rare occasions, the vertebral artery is narrowed by external pressure from arthritic changes in the bones of the upper spine, especially when you move your neck from side to side, extend it, or throw your head back. For that reason, I always order neck X rays in patients with vertebrobasilar artery symptoms. It is amazing how many "strokes" can be prevented by wearing a neck collar.

THE ANTICOAGULANT CONTROVERSY

Anticoagulants are required when a stroke has resulted from an embolism. Although there is no hard evidence that anticoagulants in fact reduce the incidence of stroke in patients with TIA, most doctors favor their use when aspirin doesn't do the job. They are usually prescribed for two or three months. However, some experts advise that they be taken indefinitely. Remember never to take aspirin while taking anticoagulants, because the blood can then become too thin, and you run the risk of bleeding internally. It is a good idea to ask for a second opinion when long-term anticoagulation is recommended, especially if you have hypertension.

DEFINING THE CLOT

If your symptoms and the clinical evidence point to obstruction somewhere in the carotid artery, you should be investigated to see where the clot is situated and to what extent it interferes with blood flow. This can almost always be done noninvasively. The available techniques include Dopplers, sonography, CT scans and magnetic resonance imaging (MRI). Injecting dye directly into an artery, an invasive procedure with a small but definite risk, should only be done as a last resort just prior to operation so that the surgeon can see where he is going.

If you are found to have a large plaque in the carotid artery and you have recurrent TIAs, you may need to have the artery "reamed out." Endarterectomy should only be done by a neurosurgeon or a vascular surgeon in a hospital where such procedures are frequently performed. And let me reiterate, do not have the operation simply because the plaque is there. In a neurological center, the risk of dying from an endarterectomy is about 1 percent, but it may be twenty or thirty times higher in a nonspecialized institution. So don't be shy about asking for another opinion before the surgery, and be sure to inquire about the performance statistics of the neurosurgical team that will be doing the operation.

A NOISE IN YOUR NECK

Occasionally, in the course of a routine physical exam, your doctor may detect a murmur or *bruit* (the French word for "noise") in one or both sides of your neck when he places his stethoscope over the carotid arteries. This sound may be transmitted there from a narrowed heart valve, or it may originate in the carotid artery itself. In the latter event, it represents an area of narrowing in that blood vessel. You may be entirely without symptoms, or you may be experiencing TIAs. In the former event, some doctors will want to pursue the investigation to see if the blockage is significant. (The extent of narrowing isn't related to the intensity of the bruit, since a minor narrowing can create a great deal of noise.) Other physicians will choose to ignore it, especially if the pulse itself is good and strong. If neurological symptoms are present the cause of the bruit should be investigated. Otherwise, I usually leave such patients alone.

RECOVERING FROM A STROKE

Suppose that you develop a full-blown stroke either after a TIA or suddenly without any warning. You may now be paralyzed in one or more limbs; your speech may be impaired; your face may be distorted because of muscle weakness; or you may even lapse into a coma. Whatever the symptoms, there is usually gradual improvement during the subsequent few weeks in most cases. So no matter how bad it looks at first, never lose hope. I have seen many people completely "stroked out" (to use a favorite phrase of interns) who have gone on to full recovery.

Every patient who suffers a stroke should immediately be admitted to the hospital—for two reasons. First, and most important, expert nursing care is needed in the early stages, while the stroke is still evolving. The biggest threat in the early hours and days is to the breathing and swallowing mechanisms, which may have to be assisted if the stroke has involved the muscles responsible for those critical functions. Tiding you over then may mean the difference between life and death. Second, every stroke patient should have a CT scan (the computerized brain X ray) to determine the kind of attack it was—hemorrhage, clot or tumor—and how to treat it. Sometimes a curable tumor may result in a stroke, as can various types of blood disease. The outlook and management of strokes due to these disorders differ greatly from that for strokes due to hemorrhage or clot, which are more common. Sudden disturbance of heart rhythm can also cause a stroke, and this can be identified by cardiac monitoring.

If you have suffered a stroke, you may also be given medication to prevent brain tissue swelling that occurs immediately after a cerebrovascular accident (which is what doctors call a stroke). These drugs are called "osmotic agents," and the standard one is mannitol. Some neurologists prefer to administer steroids in high doses during the acute phase to reduce this swelling. You may also be given Dilantin to prevent seizures. (When the brain is damaged, it becomes irritable, resulting in epileptic-like fits.)

TOTAL COMMITMENT
CAN MAKE A DIFFERENCE

Always insist on total commitment and an aggressive, optimistic approach in the medical and nursing care of a loved one who has had a stroke, especially during the initial phase. After the first week or two, we have a fairly good idea of what the residual disability will be. But even if it appears to be substantial, do not "pack it in." Today's sophisticated physiotherapy and rehabilitation techniques using newer electronic appliances are able to effect miracles for paralyzed patients. What seems like only insignificant improvement to someone in good health may, in fact, make a major impact on a stroke patient's life-style. If he or she can be equipped with some device, or have certain key muscles re-educated by exercises, so as to achieve greater independence at toilet, eating, walking or even turning the pages of a book, life will become more bearable. The stroke patient should not be allowed to vegetate and die like a wounded animal.

After the first two weeks, when the stroke is "completed," further work-up may be advised to determine whether the attack was caused by plaques in the carotid arteries. Reaming them out, even at this late stage, may prevent further extension of the paralysis. Always ask about that possibility.

KEY FACTS TO REMEMBER

Interference with the blood supply of the brain causes stroke. This can happen when an artery to or in the head ruptures and hemorrhages or is obstructed by a clot or arteriosclerotic plaque. *The most important cause of strokes is untreated high blood pressure.* Certain disturbances of cardiac rhythm can result in embolism to the brain—and stroke. Predisposition to the latter may require anticoagulants.

A stroke may occur suddenly or may be heralded by warning symptoms referred to as transient ischemic attacks. When premonitory evidence does occur, treatment with aspirin may reduce the likelihood of a full-blown stroke by about 50 percent.

Stroke symptoms, unless massive, usually clear up or improve after a few days. When they do not, aggressive management and imaginative rehabilitation techniques are required.

Decisions about how to investigate stroke patients so as to prevent recurrences and whether or not to operate should always be made in consultation with an expert neurologist or neurosurgeon.

▼

16

PARKINSON'S DISEASE—
MANY TREATMENTS,
NO CURE—YET

If you happen to be interested in Parkinson's disease—for whatever reason, either because you yourself suffer from it or someone you care about does—here are some key facts of which you should be aware.

This disorder cannot be cured, but it *can* be treated.

It is a progressive disease, but the rate of deterioration is unpredictable. Half of those stricken have no real disability for as long as ten years after the appearance of symptoms.

It is a serious disease, and often a crippling one, but life expectancy is not reduced, thanks to modern therapy.

For all these reasons, if you have Parkinson's disease and things are not going well, it behooves you to ask for a second opinion from a good neurologist, preferably one with a special interest and expertise in this affliction.

Although the appearance of individuals with long-standing, established Parkinson's disease is classic and diagnostic, there is a spectrum of symptoms, some of which, for example, tremor, may be due to other causes.

TREMBLING—WITH FEAR

Not a week goes by without my getting a panic call from a patient complaining that "my hands are trembling. I'm afraid

I have Parkinson's disease." Much more often than not, they're wrong. Tremor can be due to many causes that have nothing to do with Parkinson's disease. You may, for example, develop a transient, residual shaking when you are chilled, excited, angry or otherwise emotionally upset, or have just finished some very strenuous physical exercise. Tremors also run in families (benign familial tremor) and have nothing to do with Parkinson's disease. Interestingly, this latter symptom often disappears after a drink or two, with the result that individuals so affected may end up with an alcohol problem. Some forms of liver disease, multiple sclerosis, chronic alcoholism, drug addiction (especially during the withdrawal phase) and a hyperactive thyroid gland all frequently cause tremor too.

YOU NEED GOOD CONTACTS

In order to grasp the rationale for the diagnosis and treatment of Parkinsonism, you need to understand the chemical abnormalities within the brain that result in this disorder. Note that I refer to "Parkinsonism," and not Parkinson's disease. The former term refers to a group of symptoms that can occur either in the specific disorder we call Parkinson's disease or in several other conditions that mimic, but are not, Parkinson's disease. So it's very important to be absolutely sure whether the "Parkinson's" you have is the "disease" or the "ism." The symptoms of the former are permanent and progressive. The latter may be reversible.

Normal brain function requires a balance among myriads of chemicals, hormones and other biological substances. The two most important ones with respect to Parkinsonism are dopamine and acetylcholine. Persons with Parkinsonism have a deficiency of dopamine and a relative excess of acetylcholine. Treatment of such patients attempts to restore the balance between the two, that is, to get more dopamine into the brain and/or to neutralize the effects of too much acetylcholine.

Dopamine deficiency occurs as a result of a reduction in number of or damage to the specialized cells in the brain that normally produce it. Anything that hurts the brain, for example, a virus infection, toxic drugs or chemicals, physical trauma, tumors and several neurological diseases, can adversely affect these dopamine-producing cells. Sometimes, the amount of dopamine is perfectly adequate in Parkinsonism, but the brain loses its ability to utilize it. This is usually due to some medication like reserpine (still used to some extent in the treatment of hypertension and certain emotional disorders), phenothiazines (widely prescribed agents in psychiatry), the very popular drug Compazine (for nausea) and haloperidol (Haldol, a tranquilizer).

Although Parkinson's disease is primarily an affliction of older persons, it can occur in middle-aged individuals. One form of the disease followed the worldwide pandemic of encephalitis in 1919, and affected young and old alike. Whatever the cause, Parkinson's should not be considered an inevitable or integral part of the aging process.

MAKING THE DIAGNOSIS

Let's assume that in your case the drug and viral causes of Parkinsonism have been excluded. You are told you have the disease itself. What can you expect in the years to come?

The severity of Parkinson's disease varies widely. It is usually insidious in its progression and may not cause significant disability for years. For example, its only manifestation may be a slight tremor, or perhaps some difficulty in coordination; there may be some slowing of muscular activity or a tendency for the limbs, and especially the fingers, to be rigid. When full-blown, however, Parkinsonism presents a fairly typical picture. Patients have a deadpan expression; they don't blink their eyes very often; they drool at the angles of the mouth, which remains slightly open at all times; they have trouble walking, and they seem to lurch forward, slightly bent at the trunk, as if running after their center of gravity; the arms do not swing. Such patients also have a characteristic tremor of the thumb, making it look as if they are always rolling a pill. However, when they reach for an object, the tremor is markedly reduced, and it disappears during sleep. The tremor itself may first affect one arm, then both; and as the disease progresses, the legs, jaw and neck may begin to shake too. Speech becomes slow and monotonous or difficult to understand. One of the more troublesome symptoms is a tendency of the blood pressure to drop precipitously, causing the patient to faint after suddenly standing up from the recumbent or sitting position.

Another common manifestation is akinesia—a generalized slowing of movement. One can often suspect the diagnosis just looking at the handwriting, which in persons with Parkinson's disease is characteristically very small.

Interestingly, despite the blank facial expression, the drooling, the poverty of movement, patients with Parkinson's disease usually remain intellectually intact. Many, of course, are depressed, and who can blame them? Unfortunately, treatment programs sometimes fail to take such depression into account.

A HAPPIER OUTLOOK

I don't want to minimize the tragedy or severity of Parkinson's disease and leave you with an unrealistic picture of what's involved. The good news, however, is that treatment and outlook have changed dramatically in recent years, and continue to improve. Not so long ago death from Parkinson's was three times that of the general population. Today, survival is that of the population at large, and the quality of life is much better than it used to be.

The greatest threat to patients with Parkinson's is not any specific aspect of the disease itself, but some injury resulting from it. For example, because they have difficulty getting about, due to spasm, tremor, muscle rigidity and poor coordination, they often fall and fracture a hip. In old age, that spells trouble. Other Parkinson's patients have difficulty swallowing, so that the food "goes down the wrong way"—into the lungs instead of the stomach—and may result in aspiration pneumonia. That used to be fatal, but with today's new antibiotics and pneumonia vaccine, the number of such deaths has been very much reduced.

HOW TREATMENT STARTED

More than a hundred years ago, atropine (belladonna), a drug that even then had been around for a very long time, was found almost accidentally to modify some of the symptoms of Parkinson's disease. (Atropine is the same antispasmodic agent that until fairly recently was the most widely prescribed medication for peptic ulcers. It is also administered before anesthesia to dry the respiratory passages.) A French physician decided to try it to reduce drooling in patients with Parkinson's disease. He found that it not only dried the mouth but, more important, also reduced tremor and rigidity. And so for the next hundred years, until quite recently, various kinds of belladonna preparations (as well as antihistamines) formed the mainstay of treatment for Parkinson's disease. (Antihistamines also have a drying effect—which is why we use them for colds and runny noses.)

The belladonna drugs exert their beneficial effect in Parkinson's disease not because they replenish the missing dopamine (that treatment was to come much later). Their action is *anticholinergic*, that is, they reduce the relative excess of acetylcholine in the brain. They also probably make better use of the small amount of dopamine that is available. The anticholinergics (Artane, Kemadrin, Parsidol, Congentin, Pagitane and Akineton) and antihistamines remain useful in the treatment of Parkinson's disease. They relieve rigidity and tremor. However, they also make the mouth dry and affect bowel function, causing either constipation or diarrhea. They may also create heart rate and rhythm problems in patients with cardiac disease. So they are by no means ideal. Scientists continued to search for some better therapeutic approach.

A REVOLUTIONARY
TREATMENT—AND HOW IT WORKS

The introduction of L-dopa (levodopa) in 1970 totally revolutionized the treatment of Parkinson's disease. L-dopa acts by partially correcting the dopamine deficit. It works because it is the chemical forerunner of dopamine. When taken by mouth, it makes its way to the brain, where it is converted into dopamine. Why not give dopamine directly instead of beating around the bush with L-dopa? Because the brain does not allow any foreign dopamine into its tissues.

Today, most patients respond well to the modern formulation of this drug. The improvement is so great that many bedridden individuals can now feed themselves, dress and move about without help. About 20 percent are so strikingly benefited that they can barely be recognized as having the disease.

The original L-dopa preparation has been succeeded by Sinemet (in the United States) and Madopar (in Europe). In addition to L-dopa, these agents contain carbidopa, which renders them more effective with fewer adverse symptoms.

Although levodopa is the wonder drug of Parkinson's disease, it has its problems—and you should know about them. First of all, patients usually begin to develop "tolerance" to it anywhere from three to five years after starting it. So the longer you can hold off taking it, the better. If you're given this drug right off the bat, as soon as the diagnosis is made, before trying some other agent, ask for a second opinion.

L-dopa also has significant side effects, the most troublesome of which is the "on-off" phenomenon. You take the pill, it works fine, and then abruptly, and without reason, there is a sudden reappearance and worsening of symptoms. If this happens while you're driving a car, for example, it can be disastrous.

L-dopa can also cause nausea and vomiting and a variety of psychiatric or behavioral disorders, including paranoia (persecution complex). But the addition of carbidopa permits a 75 percent reduction in the dosage of L-dopa, and hence a corresponding decrease in toxicity.

A useful tip that doctors do not always give patients with Parkinson's disease is to avoid vitamin B_6 (pyridoxine), which is found in so many over-the-counter multivitamin preparations. Pyridoxine blocks the action of L-dopa, so that if you take it, your Parkinson's symptoms may become worse.

SERENDIPITY IN THE SOVIET UNION

Another drug developed for use in Parkinson's disease has an interesting history. It is called amantadine (marketed in the United States as Symmetrel) and is widely used in the treatment and prevention of influenza A.

Russian doctors treating their flu patients with amantadine noticed that those who also had Parkinson's disease had a significant improvement in their symptoms. In analyzing the properties of amantadine, they found it to act very much like L-dopa (less effectively, perhaps, but with fewer side effects). Many patients with early, mild Parkinson's disease benefit from amantadine.

The practical implications of this discovery are that if you have been on the antihistamines or belladonna-type drugs, which are usually tried first, and now require something more effective, you should ask about amantadine. It is better not to "graduate" to L-dopa before you really have to. Also, if you can't tolerate L-dopa in any form, amantadine may be a useful alternative.

Bromocriptine (Parlodel) is another relatively new agent in the treatment of Parkinson's. It works by helping the brain make better use of whatever dopamine is available. Most neurologists prescribe it before giving L-dopa. Unfortunately, large doses of bromocriptine can cause psychiatric disturbances.

Several new drugs related to bromocriptine, but which promise to be even more effective, are soon to be released. Their generic names are pergolide, lergotrile, lisuride—and others. Watch for them.

It is important for relatives of patients with Parkinson's disease to appreciate the fact that many of its symptoms are aggravated by anxiety, depression and stress. So antidepressants and properly designed physical exercise programs are key ingredients to every treatment regimen.

The management of Parkinson's disease requires knowledge and experience. If things aren't going well for you, do not hesitate to ask for help from an expert.

THE ROLE OF SURGERY

In the days when drug therapy for Parkinson's disease was really inadequate, several operations were devised to help control the tremor and muscular rigidity that made life miserable. They often helped, particularly when tremor was the major complaint. But such surgical procedures now are rarely necessary. It is not likely that they will be recommended to you. If they are, ask for a second opinion.

KEY FACTS TO REMEMBER

Parkinson's disease is only one of many different causes of tremor. The diagnosis should always be confirmed by a neurologist. Patients with this disorder (which is not a disease of aging) have rigidity and spasticity of their muscles in addition to tremor.

The treatment and outlook for Parkinson's disease have improved greatly in recent years, since the discovery of L-dopa. But patients using this drug may develop side effects from it and become either tolerant or intolerant to it. It should, therefore, not be prescribed before one of several other available medications has been tried. The combination of L-dopa and carbidopa (Sinemet) represents a major advance in therapy. In any patient not responding to therapy, a second opinion from a neurologist experienced in the management of this disease should be obtained.

17

MYASTHENIA GRAVIS—NEW HOPE FOR AN OLD DISEASE

In medicine, statistics have very little immediate application to a specific patient. For example, if you are told that the risk of dying from a heart bypass operation is now well under 2 percent and you lose a loved one during such a procedure, the excellent figures for the rest of the population are of small comfort to you. So, by the same token, although myasthenia gravis in not a common disease, it is of great importance to every single one of the twenty or thirty thousand individuals stricken every year in this country.

A SERIOUS DISEASE OF MUSCLE

Myo means "muscle," *asthenia*, "weakness" and *gravis* "serious." So *myasthenia gravis* is a "serious disease characterized by muscle weakness." The clinical scenario may vary from patient to patient, but this disorder usually presents as weakness after performing some activity that had never caused any problems before—such as swimming a lap or two or a previously invigorating morning walk. The disease may also have its onset as double vision, due to involvement of the eye muscles. Initially, symptoms clear up after a brief rest. But in time fatigue results from less and less effort, and persists for a longer time. Then one day you may find one or both eyelids drooping as you look in the mirror while shaving or applying makeup. Head and neck muscles are most commonly involved at first, but then other parts of the body become weak too. Eventually you may tire just brushing your hair or chewing meat. The ultimate crisis occurs when you have trouble swallowing or breathing. Although most untreated patients gradually become worse in time, some, especially young women, do improve spontaneously. Such remissions, however, are rarely permanent.

MAKING THE DIAGNOSIS

Some of the symptoms of myasthenia gravis can be caused by other neurological conditions, such as a stroke. Early in the course of the disease a routine physical exam may be normal. Unless your doctor thinks about the possibility of myasthenia gravis, he may attribute your weakness to overwork, or even emotional stress. He will then reassure you, give you vitamins, and if you continue to have symptoms, possibly send you to a psychiatrist. I remember one patient, a man in his seventies, who was told that his profound, generalized lack of strength was due to premature aging and "softening of the brain." Before making arrangements for custodial care in a nursing home, his son asked for a second opinion from a neurologist, who made the correct diagnosis of myasthenia gravis. The patient was given the proper medication and now, in his eighties, is living a virtually normal life.

When your doctor suspects the possibility of myasthenia gravis, he can confirm it very easily by injecting a medicine called Tensilon into the veins. This instantly eliminates all symptoms, but only for a few minutes.

WHO IS VULNERABLE—WHY AND HOW?

Myasthenia gravis can strike individuals of any age—newborns, especially those whose mothers have the disease, teenagers and other persons under forty (mostly women), as well as adults of both sexes over the age of forty.

We understand the mechanisms of myasthenia gravis and the biochemical interactions responsible for its symptoms. This is how they come about: A muscle fiber contracts in response to stimulation by nerves. Where the nerve ends within the muscle, a certain chemical is released, enabling muscle contraction to take place. This chemical, upon which muscle contractility depends, loses its ability to function normally in myasthenia gravis. It does so because of the formation of antibodies found only in patients with this disease. As a matter of fact, when the diagnosis is in doubt, one can test the blood for the presence of these antibodies. If none are present, you probably do not have myasthenia gravis.

YOUR TREATMENT OPTIONS

The basis for the treatment of myasthenia gravis is medication that potentiates the critical chemical interaction at the nerve-muscle junction.

There are several drugs available that can do this. Although they are very much alike chemically, they do differ in their potency and duration of action. The most widely used medications in this country are Mestinon, Prostigmin and Mytelase. (Tensilon, referred to earlier, has a very rapid onset and equally short duration, so it is useful only as a diagnostic test. Your eyelids droop. Your doctor wants to be sure of what's causing this. He injects a little Tensilon. Moments later, the eyelids pop up but remain normal for only a few minutes. So Tensilon cannot be used for treatment.)

The drugs referred to above are called "anticholinesterases," and often produce such side effects as excessive salivation, intestinal upset, nausea and vomiting, a drop in blood pressure and a slow heart rate. Atropine, used in the treatment of Parkinson's disease, is often prescribed to alleviate the side effects of the anticholinesterases.

Medications for myasthenia gravis permit most patients to lead normal lives for years. Unfortunately, as the disease progresses, some tolerance develops to the therapeutic agents, so that progressively higher doses are required. When this happens, switching preparations doesn't do much good, although stopping treatment for a few days may restore the efficacy somewhat. Usually, however, at this point, other therapeutic approaches become necessary.

STEROID HORMONES

If the anticholinesterase drugs become ineffective, steroid hormones provide a second option, and often result in dramatic improvement.

Unfortunately, during the first week or two of steroid treatment, myasthenia gravis patients may suddenly become profoundly weak, and have trouble swallowing or breathing. So they should be hospitalized when such therapy is started in order to manage a serious complication, should it occur. Also, anyone receiving steroids for more than a few days should be protected with an antiulcer regimen consisting of antacids and acid-formation blockers (Tagamet, Pepcid, Zantac). Once myasthenia symptoms begin to improve, the lowest possible dosage of steroids should be used.

IMMUNOSUPPRESSANT AGENTS

The abnormal antibody produced in myasthenia gravis is believed to represent some alteration in the body's immune system. And so immunosuppressant drugs, usually Imuran, are now widely used in the treatment of this disease. Unlike the response to anticholinesterases, which occurs in anywhere from minutes to days, or to steriods, which may take two to three weeks, treatment with immunosuppressants may have no visible results for months. This therapy is therefore reserved for those patients who have failed to respond to everything else.

REPLACING THE PLASMA

Patients with myasthenia gravis have another treatment option—plasmapheresis, the exchange of about 2 liters of their plasma three times a week for an equal volume of a solution made of salt and albumin. This removes the antibodies thought to be responsible for causing or aggravating the disease. Plasmapheresis works, but only temporarily, and is most useful to tide patients over an acute crisis in their disease.

REMOVING THE THYMUS— BENEFIT VERSUS RISK

There is also a surgical approach to the therapy of myasthenia gravis and it has an interesting history. In 1938, a patient with this disease was noted to have a tumor of the thymus (a gland in the lower part of the neck, not to be confused with the thyroid gland). When the tumor was removed, the myasthenia symptoms virtually disappeared. This suggested that malfunction of the thymus might be responsible for at least some cases of myasthenia gravis. In the ensuing fifty years, many patients with this disease have had their thymus gland removed. Patients under age fifty respond best to this surgery, and improvement is observed in over 75 percent of such cases (although it may take as long as five years for it to become apparent). The earlier the operation is done, the better the results. Also, if, after it is taken out, the thymus is found not to have a tumor within it, the outlook is better than when it does. So, if you are *under fifty*, have myasthenia gravis, and are *not* offered thymus surgery, ask for a second opinion from a qualified neurologist.

The operative risks of this surgery for those in their seventies and eighties usually outweigh the advantages. So, if you are *over fifty* and surgery *is* recommended, ask for another opinion. Always solicit input from a specialist who has particular expertise in this disease.

About 15 percent of patients with myasthenia gravis have tumors of the thymus gland. Most of these "thymomas" are clinically silent. You never know you have one until it is picked up on a routine chest X ray or a CT scan. When diagnosed, these tumors should be removed because a small percentage of them can become malignant. I believe that every patient with myasthenia gravis should be evaluated for the presence of these thymomas since they occur in 3 percent of such individuals.

SKIP THE GIN AND TONIC

In addition to knowing about what treatments help myasthenia gravis, you should also be aware of what may worsen the condition. Four commonly used heart medications—quinidine, procainamide (Pronestyl), lidocaine, Inderal (and other beta-blockers) can all do so.

There are other substances, often taken unknowingly and unnecessarily, for example, quinine, that can aggravate myasthenia gravis. If you happen to take a gin and tonic (the latter contains quinine), your symptoms may worsen. Certain antibiotics, particularly the "mycins"—gentamicin, kanamycin, neomycin, streptomycin and Achromycin—should also be avoided.

I remember one of my patients with myasthenia gravis, who, unbeknownst to me, decided to try a course of procaine therapy in Rumania—in his quest for eternal youth. He had been responding quite well to mestinon, but wanted more "pep." Unfortunately, the physicians who administered the procaine treatment were unaware that this drug has an adverse effect on myasthenia gravis. My patient was returned to the United States by ambulance plane, unable to swallow and with a respirator. He required intensive treatment with high-dose steroids for many months.

MYASTHENIA AND PREGNANCY

From time to time I am asked by women of childbearing age with myasthenia gravis whether they should adopt children rather than bear them. They worry not only about the risks to themselves of pregnancy, but also about the possible effects of the drugs they require on the unborn child.

Here, in a nutshell, is what you should know.

Myasthenia gravis and pregnancy are not necessarily incompatible. Some patients are unaffected, others improve, and an equal number become worse during pregnancy. A pregnant woman whose myasthenia gravis is under good control with medication can have a normal delivery and does not need a cesarean. She may continue to take her pills. Infants do not inherit the disease, although some 10 percent may be born with a mild weakness that clears up within six weeks. Myasthenia gravis mothers taking anticholinesterase medication should not breast-feed their infants since these drugs are found in the mother's milk.

We have come a long way in our understanding and management of myasthenia gravis. It is no longer the dread disease it once was. Because of modern treatment alternatives ranging from long-acting anticholinesterases to thymus operations, steroids and immunosuppressant agents, many patients today can lead virtually normal lives.

KEY FACTS TO REMEMBER

Myasthenia gravis is not a common disorder. It is characterized by interference with the response of muscle to the stimuli of nerves that normally make it contract. The result is poor muscle function and weakness. When untreated, this disease eventually becomes generalized and ends in death. Most patients can be managed by the expert use of certain drugs, including steroids and immunosuppressants, removal of the thymus gland and plasmapheresis. Decisions concerning medical versus surgical treatment should be made only after consultation with a specialist who has considerable experience with this disease.

▼

18

INFERTILITY, CONTRACEPTION AND ABORTION

Birth control, how *not* to have a baby, gets all the publicity. We are deluged with ads and articles promoting a better "pill," thinner condoms and better diaphragms, and the reversible vasectomy. Our society is also deeply immersed in the debate about abortion, and much of the world struggles to attain zero population growth. Despite all this antipregnancy activity, there are many thousands of women who yearn to have at least one child of their own—but can't.

The large and growing number of adoption services in this country are unable to satisfy the demand for babies, because almost 20 percent of married couples in the United States are unable to conceive. They try their luck at fertility clinics, where they subject themselves to myriads of tests. If and when the cause of infertility is identified, they may then be told there is nothing to be done about it anyway. So the barren couple, sad, anxious and vulnerable, is ripe for exploitation by quacks peddling false hope and expensive, unnecessary testing and therapy. If you are among those who go from doctor to doctor and clinic to clinic because you are infertile, you owe it to yourself to know when to stop, and when *not* to ask for yet another opinion.

THE STERILE MALE CHAUVINIST

Traditionally, at least as far back as biblical times, women were always blamed for a barren marriage. We now know that in as many as 40 percent of couples who cannot conceive, the problem lies not with the female, but with her mate. Whereas it is usually time-consuming, complicated and expensive to determine whether or not a woman is fertile, it is relatively quick, cheap and easy to check her partner. All it takes, at least initially, is a look at his sperm under the microscope. So it makes good sense for any woman to demur if she is advised to have exhaustive fertility testing before her partner is evaluated.

GET IT TO THE LAB ON TIME

In order to study sperm for fertility, the ejaculate must be examined within two hours. First we measure its volume. A fertile man produces between 2 and 5 cc (cubic centimeters) of fluid per ejaculation—but not, of course, when it's the third time around in one day. We then determine how much of this volume is fluid and how much is actually sperm. A minimum of twenty million sperm in every cubic centimeter of ejaculate are required to ensure fertilization of one egg! But there is more to it than numbers alone. We examine the sperm under the microscope to see if they are normal in appearance and whether or not they are moving about actively. Half of them should be. If the ejaculate volume is adequate and there are enough energetic sperm of normal shape, then and only then should the female partner of the sterile couple undergo a fertility evaluation.

SEXUALITY VERSUS FERTILITY

It is often difficult to convince a male that potency (the ability to achieve and maintain an erection) and virility (the ability of the sperm to fertilize an egg) are not necessarily related. I know many men who complained of chronic premature ejaculation from an organ that was rarely ever more than semierect. Yet, they had all fathered one or more healthy children. Although they hardly qualified as great lovers, they were nevertheless fertile, because they could deliver the right amount of healthy sperm to a waiting ovum. And that is what counts when you want to make a baby. By the same token, a Don Juan may find himself in the anterooms of fertility specialists—because, despite the magnitude of his potency and sexual appetite, his sperm are inadequate. I know of one such man who was so outraged when told that he was infertile, he set about to disprove it. And he did. Unfortunately, it was his girlfriend, not his wife, who became pregnant! How to explain it? I suppose his sperm concentration was probably just borderline, not quite enough to impregnate his wife, but adequate for a lucky strike with his girlfriend (who was younger than his spouse and probably more biologically receptive to boot).

HEALTHY MEN WITH SICK SPERM

What can "weaken" the sperm of an otherwise healthy, sexually active young man? Damage to the testes, whose function it is to make vigorous sperm in adequate numbers, for example, direct injury, infection (mumps in adult life is the classic example) or some other type of insult. This effect may only be temporary, in which case testicular function bounces right back. But sometimes the injury is permanent and irreversible. Occasionally, at birth, one or both testes remain in the abdominal cavity instead of descending into the scrotal sac. When that happens, they don't make sperm. They can sometimes be brought down surgically, more for cosmetic reasons than any other, because, unfortunately, a testis that didn't get there on its own hardly ever works right afterwards. Also, since an undescended testis sometimes becomes cancerous, it is almost always removed. If you are told to leave an undescended testis alone, get another opinion.

Drugs, including some used in the treatment of cancer, ulcerative colitis and peptic ulcers (cimetidine), can interfere with sperm production too. So if your sperm count is too low, review with your doctor the medications you are taking before you submit to a more sophisticated investigation of the problem.

The testes make the healthiest, most active sperm in a cool environment, so that chronic fever may result in an abnormal sperm. If your sperm production is borderline, avoid taking hot baths before you try to make a baby.

In addition to local trouble in the testes themselves, you may have a hormonal disorder elsewhere that affects them secondarily. For example, when the thyroid gland (in the neck), the adrenal glands (which sit on top of both kidneys) or the pituitary (in the brain) is not working right, sperm production in the testes may be defective, because the hormones produced by these other glands influence testicular function.

Although the focus of the consequences of diethylstilbestrol (DES) has been on the daughters of women who took this "fertility" hormone, it is now apparent that their sons may also have been affected. In one study, infertility was noted in fourteen of seventeen young men whose mothers had taken that medication when pregnant.

Finally, it appears that some 5 to 10 percent of men have antibodies against their own sperm. These antibodies immobilize the otherwise healthy sperm by causing them to clump together. When infertility is due to such antisperm antibodies, treatment with steroids may be helpful.

GOOD SPERM WITH NO FUTURE

Some men make perfectly healthy sperm, but have a mechanical problem that interferes with their delivery. For example, there may be an obstruction somewhere in the various ducts through which the sperm must pass en route from the testes. Chronic infection and scarring of the genital organs can result in such blockage. A simple operation often solves the problem. Varicose veins of the scrotum (*varicocele*) are also associated with an increased incidence of infertility.

So, if your sperm are normal, but you are nevertheless unable to make a baby, it is a good idea first to be checked out by your urologist, who can evaluate all the possible mechanical factors.

RETROGRADE EJACULATION— "WRONG WAY CORRIGAN"

There is an interesting situation in which you may fail to deliver sperm "on target" despite normal hormone function, adequate sperm production and an intact physical delivery system. In this condition, called *retrograde ejaculation*, the sperm go backward from the testes and empty into the urinary bladder instead of coming out of the urethra. This reversal of flow frequently occurs after prostate surgery, but may also be caused by certain drugs, particularly Aldomet (used in the treatment of high blood pressure).

NO MAGIC IN HORMONES

Treatment of the infertile man will obviously depend on the cause of his problem. If he is lucky and the trouble is only mechanical, like a varicocele, surgical repair is easy and will do the trick. Also, if the testes have been injured physically or by some infection, the condition may clear up on its own. Hormones are not the magic cure-all for infertility, except when they are lacking. The indiscriminate administration of testosterone by mouth or injection will rarely benefit the infertile male if glandular function is normal—with one exception. Occasionally, for reasons that are not understood, testosterone injections may increase the motility or activity of the sperm. If this treatment is going to work at all, it will be apparent after three months. There is no point in continuing the medication beyond that time. If you are advised to do so, ask for a second opinion from an endocrinologist.

COMMON SENSE MAY BE ALL YOU NEED

If you are told that your sperm count is borderline and "not all that bad," a few simple procedures may improve your chances of making a baby. First, be sure to take advantage of the best times (from a fertility, rather than a social, point of view) to have intercourse. Try to deliver the sperm when the egg is right there, waiting to be fertilized—approximately mid-cycle. Then make sure that your partner remains in bed for a while after intercourse with her knees slightly bent and her hips on a pillow, giving the sperm the best chance to get where they should go. Finally, remind her not to douche for several hours.

If a complete analysis of your sperm reveals that they are just not up to snuff and there is nothing to be done, think positively. Consider adoption.

THE EFFECT OF ENVIRONMENT ON YOUR SPERM

The inability to produce healthy sperm may be due not to any disease or disorder of your reproductive system, but to environmental pollution. In 1929, the average sperm count per ejaculation in the United States was ninety million per cubic centimeter (remember, you need at least twenty million to impregnate an egg). By 1974, the median sperm count had dropped to sixty-five million. In a study of 132 students at Florida State University in 1975, the average value was sixty million, with 23 percent having fewer than the critical twenty million. And every one of these samples contained an abnormally high concentration of chemical contaminants from the environment (DDT, hexachlorobenzenes and polychlorinated biphenyls, or PCBs). In addition to being carcinogenic, PCBs reduce the sperm count in experimental animals.

THE INFERTILE WOMAN

Let us suppose that in our barren couple, the male has been found to be fertile. It is now the woman's turn to be evaluated. Infertility in the female is usually due to any of the following causes: (a) hormonal imbalance (one third of cases), in which a gland somewhere—the pituitary, adrenal, thyroid or the ovaries themselves—is not working right; (b) mechanical problems (half the cases) in which something interferes with the passage of the egg and prevents its rendezvous with the sperm (typical examples are a scarred Fallopian tube, an abnormal position of the uterus and the angle at which the cervix projects into the vagina); (c) in about 15 percent of women the cervix—the portal through which the sperm must pass in order to get into the uterus—is "hostile," that is, there are local chemical changes that prevent entry of the sperm.

Evaluation of female infertility consists of investigating these three obstacles to pregnancy. However, if ova (eggs) are not being made by the ovary, there is no point in testing the patency of the tubes or the chemical environment of the cervix. So first make sure that your ovaries are producing eggs. This is something you can do yourself—simply by taking your temperature. If it is elevated for four or five days at mid-cycle, that's presumptive evidence that you are ovulating. The failure to conceive must then be due to some fault in the physical or chemical environment of the egg.

If you are ovulating normally, here is the sequence I suggest you follow: (1) check out the possibility of a "hostile" cervix; (2) look for mechanical problems interfering with egg transport; (3) have your hormones analyzed.

THE HOSTILE CERVIX

The *postcoital* test is used to check the mucus around the cervix in order to see whether it is hostile—that is, impenetrable—preventing the sperm from reaching the uterus. Here is how it's done. Have intercourse while you are ovulating, then see your gynecologist anytime in the next two to sixteen hours. The doctor will collect a specimen of the mucus from your cervix, examine it under the microscope and evaluate the sperm it contains. If the mucus is clear, and the sperm within it are moving about normally, then your cervix is "friendly." But if the mucus is cloudy and the sperm are clumped together and sluggish, they have been trapped and can go no further. This "barrier" may be the reason for your inability to conceive. If so, your gynecologist will prescribe medical measures that can modify the chemistry of the cervical environment.

MECHANICAL CAUSES OF INFERTILITY

As we continue our diagnostic work-up in the search for causes of infertilty, we may find structural abnormalities in the uterus and tubes that can interfere with the passage of the sperm. These can often be detected in the routine gynecological examination without the need for complicated tests, and they are frequently amenable to surgical correction.

If the uterus itself is normal, we check the Fallopian tubes, in which the egg passes from the ovary to the uterus, to make sure they are open. It's not enough to ovulate normally. The egg must be able to get into the tube in order to unite with your partner's sperm. It cannot do so if the tube is obstructed by scar tissue. The patency of the Fallopian tubes can be determined in several ways. The simplest is with an X ray (unless you are allergic to the dye)—a procedure with the tongue-twisting name *hysterosalpingography*. Another technique, devised many years ago and still widely used, involves blowing carbon dioxide gas into the tubes and then taking X rays to see if they are open (Rubin test). There are other methods, but they are more complicated, uncomfortable and invasive—as, for example, looking directly into the tubes through a lighted instrument (culdoscopy), or into the pelvis (laparoscopy). Have those done last.

MEDICINES AGAINST INFERTILITY

Sometimes low-grade gynecologic infections, especially by *Chlamydia*, cause infertility, and these usually respond to antibiotic therapy. But if there is no infection, and the cervical mucus is normal and there is no physical barrier to pregnancy, you must undergo a battery of blood and urine tests to determine whether all your glands are working properly. Hormonal imbalance often can be corrected. Recently, bromocriptine, used in the treatment of Parkinson's disease and painful female breasts due to excessive secretion of a hormone called prolactin, has also been found to increase fertility. Vitamin B_6 suppresses prolactin too, and in one study, when this vitamin was given to fourteen previously infertile women with high levels of prolactin, twelve of them were able to conceive. Ask your doctor about it. Another drug called danazol, used in the treatment of a painful gynecological condition called endometriosis, has also been found effective in some cases of unexplained infertility, as has clomiphene (Clomid, Serophene). In women who cannot conceive because of a specific ovarian disorder called polycystic ovarian syndrome, the drug Metroden may help.

MAYBE IT'S ALL IN THE MIND

If your entire gynecological work-up reveals nothing abnormal, collect all the data that have been accumulated thus far and consult one more infertility specialist. If he can't help you, then call it quits.

But before you abandon hope and decide that you simply "cannot" have a baby, look into the possibility of some psychological, rather than physical, explanation. I don't profess to understand how emotional problems interfere with conception, but many experienced obstetricians and gynecologists tell me they do. I know of several couples who tried for years without success to have a baby and finally adopted one. Then, a few months later, perhaps because of the absence of all the tension and frustration during their infertile years, they were able to conceive. So, it is a good idea, after you have consulted the urologists, endocrinologists and gynecologists without success, to consult a psychiatrist or psychologist.

FERTILE BUT UNWILLING— THE ART OF CONTRACEPTION

Contraceptive techniques include withdrawal of the male organ just before ejaculation (coitus interruptus—enough to make a nervous wreck out of any man and woman) and natural family planning (if you are religiously inclined). But most couples rely on the pill, the intrauterine device, the condom, the diaphragm or other barrier contraceptives. Chinese scientists have come up with gossypol, an oral contraceptive for men, made from cottonseed oil. It is apparently effective, dropping the sperm count to zero in about twelve weeks. Its safety is still being evaluated, but of some concern is the fact that when it is stopped, some 20 percent of the men who have taken it fail to make sperm again. American investigators testing it think that it has promise—but it is still years away from approval in this country. Another new contraceptive, this one for women, administered in a nasal spray, is being evaluated in Sweden. Effective and convenient, it must be taken every day.

The effectiveness of each of the contraceptive techniques varies somewhat, and you should know about all of them before committing yourself to any one. The stakes, if you miscalculate, can be high, especially if pregnancy can endanger your life because of some cardiac disease, blood disorder, kidney trouble or other serious medical problem.

WHEN TO GO TO A MOVIE INSTEAD

If you definitely don't want a large family, but your religious beliefs do not permit medical or mechanical means of contraception, you should practice natural family planning. Physicians are, of course, unenthusiastic about this method from the scientific viewpoint, although we realize that there are many persons who choose to rely on it. The available statistics indicate that if you do, the failure rate with the method may be as high as 27 percent, depending on how careful you are and how regular your periods happen to be.

There are two techniques that couples who follow family planning must learn. The first is the *ovulation method*, in which the woman comes to recognize the appearance of the mucus from the vagina and cervix as an indicator of ovulation. The second method is called *sympto-thermal*. In addition to watching the mucus, the woman records daily temperature readings to determine the time of ovulation. The trick is to identify and avoid sexual relations on those days in midcycle when one is most fertile. In order to do that, keep track of your last ten or twelve cycles. See how long each lasts, then subtract eighteen days from the shortest cycle and eleven days from the longest. For example, if your cycles vary between twenty-seven and thirty days, subtracting eighteen days from the shortest puts you at day nine; eleven days from the longest cycle would be nineteen. Between those two dates, watch TV, read or go to the movies—but abstain from sex. The problem with this method of birth control lies in those last few words.

AN INTERRUPTED AFFAIR

Coitus interruptus, the oldest form of contraception, is still commonly relied upon in a chance encounter, when sexual union was not expected, and neither participant came "prepared." Under these circumstances, the male has no alternative but to withdraw. This decision, made at peak passion, takes tremendous willpower, determination and, to be honest, fear. Even if you act in time, the risk of pregnancy is still about 15 percent for the casual encounter, and 30 percent in couples who regularly practice coitus interruptus. Even when you withdraw with "lots of time to spare," there is almost always some sperm leakage—which can be enough, Dad.

CONDOMS—WHAT THE WELL-DRESSED MAN SHOULD WEAR

Condoms have been around for centuries. They are now the most widely used form of birth control after the pill. The rise in their popularity is largely the result of increased worry about sexually transmitted diseases, especially AIDS and herpes. They were originally made from sheep's gut; then thin rubber was used; and today most brands are plastic (even though they are still called "rubbers"). Not unlike a new suit, condoms come in a selection of colors and styles.

Patients seek advice about various contraceptive techniques, especially the pill, but no one has ever yet asked how to use a condom. Men think there is nothing to it—just slip one on, and away you go. But when using a condom, you must be sure to leave about one half to one inch free at the tip in order to accommodate the pressure and volume of the ejaculate. If you put it on too tightly, it may burst. Also, don't let your ego get the better of you. Use a condom only if you

SECOND OPINION

have substantial erections, so that the condom is tight and leakproof at the top. Remember, too, not to dally after ejaculation, because as the penis shrinks, the contents of the condom may escape into the vagina. Hold on to it when you withdraw after coitus, otherwise it may slip off, a reasonably good way of ensuring pregnancy. For all these reasons—breakage, leakage and improper use—regular condom users, especially careless ones, run a 5 to 15 percent risk of inducing pregnancy.

The condom should be used by every man on the move, not only as a contraceptive, but also for protection against venereal infection. This is especially important if you go from partner to partner, including some whose credentials are uncertain. Many women now carry them too, and offer it to their mate in the event he forgot to bring one along. And quite wisely, they also use spermicidal jelly or foam as an extra measure of protection.

NO PROTECTION FROM A DOUCHE

Some women still believe that *douching* immediately after intercourse constitutes effective contraception. In practical terms, "immediately" usually means five to ten minutes. That's too late, because within two minutes, the sperm are well into the cervix on their way to uniting with the egg. So if you want to douche for hygienic or esthetic purposes, that's fine. As a contraceptive, forget it.

THE DIAPHRAGM—
WHAT THE WELL-DRESSED
WOMAN SHOULD WEAR

The *diaphragm* is about as safe as the condom. Just as the condom can slip off, leak or break, the diaphragm can fail. It will not protect you if it is fitted incorrectly or inserted improperly. And even when it is the right size and put in as directed, it may be dislodged by a vigorous thrust during intercourse.

A diaphragm is somewhat inconvenient in that it must be

276

inserted *before* intercourse. That's acceptable for a couple living together, but not the ideal contraceptive for the unpredicted sexual encounter. For example, if you are being coy, or are "surprised" to find yourself in a vulnerable situation, the presence of a diaphragm on your person will "expose" you. The diaphragm also requires the use of a spermicidal preparation, which some couples may find distasteful, especially those who indulge in oral sex. What's more, should you decide to have another go at it, you must put additional jelly into the vagina. Remember to leave the diaphragm in place for at least six hours after its last use.

THE PILL—FIFTY MILLION WOMEN CAN'T BE PREGNANT

The *pill* has had a profound effect on our life-style, the role of women in our society, our social standards, our economy and our politics. More than fifty million women throughout the world are currently taking it; they were preceded by the same number who are now beyond the childbearing age and who no longer need it. There have been substantial changes in the composition of oral contraceptives since their introduction, and they continue to be more than 98 percent effective when properly used. Despite adverse publicity, the pill remains the number 1 method of contraception in this country.

NO EGG—NO BABY

The basic ingredient of the pill is estrogen. This (female) hormone prevents the release of the egg from the ovary—and without an egg, you can't have a baby. But estrogens, especially in large doses, can produce side effects. They raise the blood pressure in some women, they predispose to clotting within the veins (phlebitis) or arteries (resulting in heart attacks and strokes), they can raise the blood sugar (diabetes mellitus), and increase the fat levels in your blood, making for greater vulnerability to arteriosclerosis. In addition to these major potential consequences, estrogens often give troublesome "minor" symptoms such as nausea and migraine headaches (if you have had these headaches before, they may become worse). Estrogens may transiently affect liver function (which returns to normal when the hormone is stopped); they make you vulnerable to fungus infections of the vagina and suppress your normal menstrual cycle.

You might wonder, looking at this list, why on earth anybody would take such a pill. The fact is that these adverse effects occur in a miniscule percentage of cases in relation to the total number of people taking the medication. Even then, they are very much dose-related—the less you take, the fewer and milder the side effects. There is a level, however, below which one cannot reduce the estrogen without substantially compromising its contraceptive effect. Most preparations also contain another hormone called *progestin*.

There are some thirty-five different formulations of the pill currently marketed in the United States. When your doctor prescribes one for you, ask about its composition. The dosage schedule (and side effects) for each pill depends on its ingredients, but most are usually taken for twenty or twenty-one days, then stopped for the next seven or eight days.

WHEN IT'S BETTER NOT TO USE THE PILL

What else should you know about the pill? What should you tell the doctor about yourself when he prescribes it? What should he bear in mind when you agree to take the pill?

If you are thirty-five or older, you are better off using some other form of contraception—especially if (a) you smoke cigarettes, (b) you are overweight, (c) you have high blood pressure (or a tendency to it), (d) your cholesterol level is abnormally elevated, (e) you have fibroids of the uterus, (f) you suffer from migraine headaches, or (g) you are epileptic. It has been observed that women in this age group with these risk factors have a slightly higher incidence of heart attacks, strokes and other complications when they take the pill. Mind you, the risk is statistically small, but it is better not to chance it.

There are some women who should not take the pill *at any age*. This includes those who have had cancer of the breast (or in whose family there is a strong history of breast cancer), suffer from any kind of circulatory or liver problem, or are prone to vaginal bleeding. Some doctors still feel that diabetes and the pill don't mix, but more and more are prescribing it for their diabetic patients. If you are black and have sickle-cell anemia or sickle-cell trait (3 percent of the black population in the United States are affected by this disorder), the pill may produce clotting problems. If you have had bad varicose veins and/or have suffered attacks of phlebitis in the past, your chance of developing either phlebitis or some other clotting abnormality while taking the pill is increased some five to ten times. (The incidence in normal women is three per hundred thousand.)

An area that is sometimes overlooked is emotional vulnerability. If you are being treated for depression or are prone to it, the pill may make you worse. Prolonged bed rest for whatever reason predisposes to blood clot formation, so if, for example, you have gone skiing, broken a leg and are going to be off your feet for any length of time, stop the pill temporarily. (Besides which, in bed with a broken leg, you don't have too much use for a contraceptive. If you do, use a diaphragm.)

One other caveat. Soon after a pregnancy, one is naturally eager to resume sexual relations after the long period of abstinence. It is best not to use the pill at that time if you are breast-feeding, because not only do the hormones affect the quality of the milk, they are also consumed by the baby. Finally, it is best to stop the pill about two weeks before any scheduled surgery, in order to reduce the possibility of clot formation or embolism, either during the operation or in the postoperative period.

INTRAUTERINE DEVICES (IUDs)—LARGELY A MEMORY

The *intrauterine device* (IUD) was until recently the preferred contraceptive for millions of American women. It did not require the discipline of a dosage regimen, and it lacked the inconvenience of the diaphragm and the mess of vaginal jellies, foams or suppositories. Once in place it was about 90 percent effective.

Despite these advantages, the IUD is less popular than it was ten years ago. This is due to several reasons. Women were becoming disenchanted with these devices because of the mounting evidence that chronic use might lead to infertility or result in tubal pregnancy. When these and other complications occurred, there were many lawsuits against the manufacturers. Today, all IUDs but one have been withdrawn from the market. The remaining product, Progestasert, has a built-in hormone that is released slowly over the period of a year, after which the device must be replaced.

WHEN TO HAVE IT INSERTED

If you have decided to use an IUD, your gynecologist will find it easier to insert it during your period, when the cervix (into which the device is placed) is more widely open to permit the outflow of menstrual blood. Also, if it is fitted at any other time, there is the possibility that you may already be pregnant (which you are not likely to be if you are menstruating). It is not safe to have an IUD in a pregnant uterus because of the greater risk of bleeding, infection and abortion.

STERILIZATION TECHNIQUES

Sterilization techniques for the permanent prevention of pregnancy include *hysterectomy* (removal of the uterus) and *obliterating the Fallopian tubes* (so that the egg cannot get from the ovary, where it is produced, to the uterus, where it is fertilized). Don't confuse sterilization with contraception. The latter is temporary—effective only as long as you want it to be. Sterilization, on the other hand, is usually permanent, although many vasectomies and some tubal ligations can be reversed.

WHY REMOVE A HEALTHY UTERUS?

I believe it is unnecessary and undesirable to remove a healthy uterus to effect sterilization. I have discussed this question with several gynecologists whose opinion I value, and few of them consider it an acceptable procedure for that purpose. A hysterectomy, after all, is real surgery—with all the risks, pain and cost of any important operation. But, more than that, the uterus is also a symbolic organ for most women. Its extirpation may have a psychological impact that is not always fully appreciated by men, be they husbands, lovers or gynecologists.

Why perform a hysterectomy when sterilization can be achieved just as effectively by cutting or tying the tubes? The answer offered by those doctors who still recommend it is that, once done, it is final, irreversible and prevents pregnancy forever. It also eliminates the possibility of ever developing uterine tumors and cancers. Removing the uterus, they argue, also permits one to take estrogen replacement therapy after the menopause without fear of getting cancer.

The final decision about how to be sterilized, if that's what you want or need, is up to you. But if a hysterectomy is advised, ask for another opinion.

THE SOMETIMES REVERSIBLE VASECTOMY

Of course, some women prefer their mates to have any sterilization surgery that is to be done. *Vasectomy* is the male equivalent of tying the Fallopian tubes. Sperm, which are produced in the testes, make their way up from the scrotum and out through the penis via a system of tortuous tubules. One of the ducts through which the sperm must pass is called the *vas deferens*. In a vasectomy, the vas is cut and divided, so that the sperm has no route out. More than a million such male sterilizations are done every year in the United States. It is a simple procedure that can be performed in the urologist's office. It is effective and reversible in most cases due to recent advances in microsurgery.

IT'S SIMPLE, BUT
HOW SAFE IS VASECTOMY?

At one time questions were raised about the safety and long-term consequences of cutting the vas deferens in healthy men. No harmful effect has thus far been observed in humans.

Despite the reversibility and safety of vasectomy, I still advise my patients that if they have *any* intention of having children in the future, however remote the likelihood, they should not have it done. I have known several men who, although ostensibly "finished with raising a family," later either divorced or became widowers and ended up marrying younger women who wanted to have children. An earlier vasectomy made that possibility uncertain.

ABORTION—WHAT COULD
HAVE GONE WRONG?

You have been watching the calendar with some anxiety. You are worried because you have always been regular in the past—periods every twenty-nine days, like clockwork. But suddenly you are almost three weeks late. How could you possibly be pregnant? You never missed inserting your diaphragm when necessary (although you didn't coat it a second time one night). What other explanation could there be? You are not on the pill or any other hormone that might interfere with your cycle. You have not been taking any tranquilizers or sleeping pills (they can upset your menstrual rhythm). There has been no recent illness or emotional shock. You do remember that once, a long time ago, when you went on a crash diet and lost a lot of weight quickly, you missed a period. But nothing like that has happened this time. What's more, you had your routine checkup only a few weeks before, and everything was just fine, including your thyroid tests.

So now you are almost sure you are pregnant. You think of buying one of those do-it-yourself pregnancy testing kits in the drugstore, but decide that this is too important a decision for an amateur to fool around with. And you don't want to go through the experience one of your girlfriends had. A home kit test indicated that she was "positive." She worried herself sick for weeks until she went to her doctor, who found it was all a mistake.

After waiting a few more days in the hope that something will happen, you finally summon the courage to visit your gynecologist. He uses a technique called the radioreceptor assay, which can tell him in just a few hours whether you are pregnant—as early as ten days after your last missed period. He takes some blood (or collects some urine), and before long you get the results. You are pregnant.

IS IT MS., MISS OR MRS. JONES?

If your religious and personal principles permit, you may want an abortion because even though you are *Mrs.* Jones, you already have more children than you can cope with— physically, emotionally or financially. If you are *Miss* or *Ms.* Jones, becoming a mother at this particular time may not be convenient for a host of other reasons. On the other hand, married or single, you may actually want a baby very much, but have been advised against it by your doctor. He may think that the stress of pregnancy and delivery are not advisable at this time because of some underlying illness. Perhaps, too, there is a strong possibility that your child will be born seriously deformed because of some genetic traits in your family or an infection contracted during pregnancy (toxoplasmosis, German measles).

For whatever reason, then, you may begin to think about how, when and where to terminate the pregnancy. Despite all the marches, bombings and protests these days for and against, any woman may still lawfully obtain an abortion on the basis of her own wants, needs and preferences. In fact, more than one million women have been doing so every year in the United States since 1973, when the Supreme Court made it legal, and there are more abortions being performed in this country (and in England) than appendectomies. But remember, making it legal doesn't guarantee its safety.

YOUR ABORTION—
WHERE, WHEN AND HOW?

What's involved in an abortion? Must you enter a hospital? Can the procedure be done safely in your doctor's office? (That would save you the cost of hospitalization—an important consideration if the state in which you live or your insurance policy does not pay for abortions.) Must it be done as a "scraping," using a sharp instrument, or can the unwanted contents of your uterus be "sucked out"? And suppose that you really haven't yet decided what to do and need more time to think it over. How long can you safely wait? I have known many women, both married and single, who were in a rush to terminate a pregnancy, only to regret it later.

TIMING—THE KEY FACTOR

Think of the ten lunar months or forty weeks of pregnancy in terms of three thirteen-week periods, each of which is called a *trimester* (three months). The best time to have an abortion is during the first trimester or twelve weeks. After that, the procedure becomes more complicated and the risk increases. Also, abortion is illegal in the third trimester, that is, after the twenty-fourth week, when the fetus can survive in the outside world. According to the law, abortion at that point is tantamount to murder since the fetus is now viable. Of course, the pregnancy may legally be terminated at any time if it is determined that the fetus is already dead or if continuing the pregnancy constitutes an absolute risk to the life of the mother. However, in the latter circumstances, when the pregnancy is aborted, every effort is made to save the prematurely born infant.

THE FIRST TWELVE WEEKS—
SUCTION OR SCRAPING?

In the first trimester, there are two abortion techniques available. The doctor can either *scrape* out the uterine contents or he can employ *suction curettage*. In the latter technique, the tip of a syringe is inserted through the cervix into the lower part of the uterus, and the contents aspirated. In either method, you need not be put to sleep. The surgeon applies a local anesthetic to the cervix.

Most doctors prefer the suction method for the following reasons. Curettage with a metal instrument may perforate the uterus, which, since it is pregnant, is now softer than normal. (In the diagnostic dilatation and curettage, or D and C, done to determine the cause of bleeding, the risk of perforation is much smaller, because the wall of the nonpregnant uterus is firm and thick.) Also, the pregnant uterus is congested with blood in order to nourish the fetus, so there is always the chance that instrumentation will result in hemorrhage. Since bacteria thrive in an environment rich in blood, poking about a pregnant uterus can cause infection too. Finally, the possibility of adhesions (scar tissue) forming within the uterus is also greater after metal curettage.

Although most gynecologists use suction in the first twelve weeks, some—usually because of habit or convenience—still prefer to scrape. Discuss with your doctor which method he plans for you. But remember, even suction is not without complications, and it too can cause hemorrhage. A more important drawback of suctioning is the possibility that the contents of the uterus will be incompletely evacuated. I know one woman who underwent a suction abortion. Eight months after the procedure she delivered a healthy baby boy. She had attributed her weight gain after the curettage to overeating! I read of another woman who was born with not one but two uteri! One of them became pregnant, the other did not. The gynecologist emptied the wrong one. So if you have a suction curettage, insist that what is removed be examined carefully to make certain the pregnancy has not been left behind.

THE SECOND TRIMESTER— THE RISK INCREASES

The risks to the mother are somewhat greater when the abortion is done in the second trimester, that is, between the twelfth and twenty-fourth weeks. Unfortunately, in the United

States about 15 percent of abortions are performed that late, as compared to Denmark and Japan, where only 3 percent are done in the second trimester. No woman who has decided on an abortion should have to wait until the second trimester. But some still delay because of ignorance, failure to accept the facts or the hope that the pregnancy will somehow "go away." For others, philosophical or religious torment prevents them from going through with it during the first three months. The poor have other problems. Abortion services they can afford are not always easy to find, and some legislators have succeeded in making it more and more difficult for the indigent to have an abortion safely, easily and inexpensively. Delay due to economic factors accounts for at least one quarter of the abortions being done in the second trimester. Finally, a few are performed later because the medical grounds did not exist or were not apparent earlier. If all abortions were done in the first twelve weeks, the number of deaths in the United States from this procedure, small as it is, would be halved.

So here you are, really pregnant—fifteen or more weeks along—and you still want out. If, when you are examined, the doctor can hear the fetal heartbeat, you can be sure the fetus is at least eighteen weeks old, no matter how carefully you have calculated. Although some doctors will abort you by means of a curettage as late as fifteen or sixteen weeks, this technique should rarely be used at that late stage, even by a very skilled surgeon. By that time, and certainly beyond sixteen weeks, metal curettage is hazardous because the pregnant uterus is now very soft. What about suction? This far along, the products of conception are often too large to be sucked out but not yet really big enough to warrant a surgical approach through the abdominal wall. To be absolutely sure that the fetus is in fact too big to be aspirated, sonography (an echo test) can be done on the pregnant patient. If the uterine contents are found to be small enough, then suction can still be used. It is somewhat safer than the alternative techniques described below.

WHEN IT'S TOO LATE
TO SUCK OR SCRAPE

In most cases, this late in the game, abortions are performed by injecting a drug or solution into the sac (the amniotic sac) that contains the fetus. The substance used will depend on your doctor's preferences and your own physical condition. You have a choice among a simple salt solution, a hormone called prostaglandin and urea.

INJECTING SALT

Injecting salt into the amniotic sac is the method currently used in about two thirds of cases after the sixteenth week of pregnancy. We are not sure how or why this brings on the abortion, but it does so in about a day and a half. It is a proven and effective technique, has few failures and rarely results in a living fetus. However, salt injection, despite its widespread use, may produce some undesirable side effects and is not entirely without risk. You will see why in a moment.

PROSTAGLANDINS—
NOW AND IN THE FUTURE

Your doctor may choose to inject *prostaglandin* into the amniotic sac, rather than salt. Prostaglandins are a large group of naturally occurring hormones produced in different parts of the body; they affect the function of many organs and systems. They not only initiate labor, they also have something to do with causing high blood pressure, heart attacks, inflammation, resistance to infection and a host of other processes. As a matter of fact, aspirin, with its myriad effects ranging from pain control and fever reduction to anticoagulation, appears to work through the prostaglandin system. New prostaglandins are being identified all the time, and the more we learn about them the more fascinating they are.

For purposes of inducing an abortion, a specific prostaglandin (in this instance PGF2a) is injected into the amniotic sac after the sixteenth week. It causes the pregnant contents to be expelled in twenty to twenty-six hours. This method has fewer side effects than salt and is safer. However, it does occasionally permit the birth of a live fetus—something that rarely happens with saline.

UREA—MORE THAN A WASTE PRODUCT

A substance called *urea* can also be introduced into the amniotic sac. This is a naturally occurring chemical found in varying amounts in everyone's blood. It is an end product of liver metabolism and is excreted into the urine by the healthy kidney. When injected into the amniotic sac, it terminates the pregnancy safely and effectively. Furthermore, it almost never results in a live fetus. All things being considered, this is probably the best way now available, for women with normal kidneys and liver, to have a late abortion.

There are several additional techniques for inducing abortions now being developed and tested, some of which may soon be available. These include a vaginal suppository containing prostaglandin. It will eliminate the need for any procedure, operation or injection; you'll simply insert it yourself and wait for things to happen. Another method involves an injection of prostaglandin not into the amniotic sac but into your backside, just like a penicillin shot. This technique is still in research. An oral preparation that terminates pregnancy as soon as it occurs was developed in France and made available in Europe in early 1987. It has not yet been approved for use in the United States. This drug, if it fulfills its promise, may have as great an impact on abortion as the pill had on contraception. This "post-ovulatory contraceptive," RU-486, can presumably be taken monthly, terminating any pregnancy, even when a women is not aware she has conceived. It acts by blocking progesterone, the hormone that prepares the uterus to receive the fertilized egg.

TIME FOR A GOOD GOING-OVER

In order to decide which injection technique to use in the second trimester, your doctor should give you a thorough medical evaluation. Be sure to disclose to him all the pertinent facts in your medical history. For example, if you have high blood pressure or a tendency in that direction, it is not a good idea to have salt injected, because some of it may be absorbed and further raise your blood pressure. The same is true if you have a cardiac condition, in which case the added salt may result in fluid retention and heart failure. If your kidneys are not functioning properly, neither urea nor salt should be used (elimination of urea from the body requires a healthy kidney). If you are asthmatic or have emphysema, prostaglandins should be avoided because they can induce spasm of the bronchial tree and an acute wheezing attack.

You see, then, why abortion is not a matter to be taken lightly, and why it is important to avoid having it done in an "abortion mill." You need a doctor who will examine you carefully and assess your overall physical condition before he performs the procedure, especially in the second trimester.

IN A HOSPITAL OR A DOCTOR'S OFFICE?

Where should abortions be performed—in the hospital, outpatient clinic or your doctor's office? While it *must* be done in a hospital after the first trimester, you do have a choice during the first twelve weeks. Most states, however, have regulations concerning the minimal requirements of a legal abortion facility. For example, in New York, abortions may be performed only where blood transfusion is immediately available (because of the risk of hemorrhage or perforation of the uterus). The law also states that your blood type must be determined *before* the abortion is done. It must then be cross-matched, that is, the actual blood you would need in an emergency must be earmarked for you and held in readiness.

Now, think for a moment. Does your own doctor have that capability in his office? Probably not. So for that and other reasons, he is more than likely to recommend that you come into the hospital, perhaps overnight, even if you are still in the first trimester. That usually is good advice, although more and more doctors are terminating pregnancies in their offices before the *eighth* week, using the suction technique.

In any event, it is a good idea to double-check and get a second opinion if you are advised to have your abortion done anywhere but in a hospital or a well-equipped clinic.

DON'T JOIN THE "UNDERGROUND"

Unfortunately, there is a large group of doctors who used to do abortions "underground" before legalization. If you should happen to visit such an "old-timer," he may urge you to have the procedure done in his private facility. In the old days, you had little choice but to do so; today you do. While it is true that some of these abortionists are experienced and capable surgeons, they may nevertheless not meet modern legal and medical standards. So, if you choose to go into one of their private clinics, make sure that it is equipped to handle the kinds of emergencies that occasionally occur, and is clean and well staffed. Remember that infection is a risk in any abortion, despite all the antibiotics at our disposal. While it is true that there are only five deaths (due to infection, hemorrhage, rupture of the uterus) for every two hundred thousand abortions performed in the first trimester, that statistic does not tell the whole story—the complications short of death, the suffering, pain, prolonged hospitalization and sterility—that can occur when an abortion is done improperly or in the wrong facility.

AFTER THE ABORTION

After abortions became legal, many reputable clinics sprang up where the procedure could be done properly, easily and at reasonable cost. These centers are usually run by trained professionals who are able to perform abortions on an outpatient basis. After the uterine contents are aspirated, you rest for an hour or two, and if everything is all right, you can go home. Most women can resume normal activities the next day, but they should avoid douching, tampons or intercourse for at least one week. Also, you should expect to have some bleeding for a week or so after the abortion, very much as you would in the last few days of a normal menstrual period.

INFERTILITY, CONTRACEPTION AND ABORTION

An abortion can be physically and emotionally stressful, so it is a good idea to get plenty of rest afterwards, and to take iron supplements to prevent anemia due to the blood loss.

KEY FACTS TO REMEMBER

Some 20 percent of married couples in the United States have an infertility problem. They are often the victims of repeated and unnecessary testing and quack remedies.

When a couple is unable to conceive, the fault lies with the male in about 40 percent of cases. Since evaluation of male infertility is usually simpler and less costly than that of the female, no woman should undergo such testing until her mate has been checked out first.

Male infertility may be due to defects in sperm quantity or quality, hormone imbalance or some mechanical problem that interferes with the exit of the sperm from the male genitourinary system. The latter condition can frequently be corrected surgically. Several medications and toxic substances in the environment may interfere with normal sperm production. When male infertility is suspected as the cause of the failure of a couple to conceive, a urologist should be consulted first and then, if necessary, an endocrinologist. If you are found to have an undescended testis, remember that it has the potential for becoming cancerous. If you are advised to "leave it alone," a second opinion should be obtained. If you continue to be given testosterone shots for infertility for longer than three months without results, ask for a second opinion from a urologist or an endocrinologist.

Infertility in the female is usually due to hormonal imbalance, mechanical problems due to scarring resulting from chronic infection of the reproductive organs, or abnormal chemical changes in the cervix. Consult your gynecologist first and then, if necessary, see an endocrinologist. Simple diagnostic measures should be exhausted before more painful and costly tests are done. There is a growing number of medications available for infertility due to hormonal abnormalities. When no apparent cause for the inability to conceive can be found after appropriate testing of both partners, a psychiatrist should be consulted, since emotional factors may play a role in infertility.

If *sterilization* procedures are recommended for a woman, a second opinion should be sought from another gynecologist, especially if a hysterectomy is planned. Tying the tubes is less complicated, cheaper and equally effective. It is usually irreversible. Removing a healthy uterus is not usually desirable. In males, vasectomy is simple to perform, but this procedure is not always reversible.

There are several *contraceptive techniques* available. Their efficacy depends on proper use. Selection of the appropriate technique should normally be made by you and your gynecologist. However, your family doctor or internist may need to be consulted if the pill is being considered, since there are several medical circumstances when it should be avoided.

Abortions are either voluntary or medically necessary. In the latter event, if you want the baby, but have been told that the pregnancy must be terminated for your own good, get a second opinion. There have been major advances in the management of pregnant women with diabetes and heart disease that now permit them to have a family.

The best technique for performing an abortion depends on how soon—or late—it is being done. During the first twelve weeks, suction or scraping methods can be used, but suction is generally preferred. If suction is not recommended to you, discuss it with your gynecologist or get another opinion. If the suction technique is selected, make sure that what was removed from the uterus is examined to determine that the pregnancy was, in fact, terminated by the procedure.

At some point between twelve and twenty-four weeks it becomes too late to suction or scrape. There are then three different methods of aborting, each with certain advantages or disadvantages. Discuss with your gynecologist which one is best for you. The technique finally selected should be checked with your internist to make sure that it is safe for you. There are certain medical disorders that may lead you to choose one procedure over another.

Most abortions should be done in a hospital or a specialized clinic. If it is suggested that you have it performed in your doctor's office, make certain that legal requirements are met. You may want to have another opinion to see if it is indeed the best way to go about it.

▼

19

IMPOTENCE—IT MAY
NOT BE ALL IN THE HEAD

WHEN NOTHING HAPPENS

Everyone knows why Richard Nixon resigned the presidency and the Shah of Iran renounced his throne. The Bible tells us that King David abdicated for totally different reasons—he could no longer achieve an erection. Mind you, he didn't quit without trying. It was only when, as the ultimate stimulus, a fair young virgin prescribed by the wise urologists of biblical times failed to evoke an appropriate response that the King decided it was time to go.

AND YOU COULDN'T CARE LESS

Impotence—the inability to achieve and/or maintain an erection and sometimes not caring whether or not you do ("frankly, I'd rather play golf")—is one of the most common problems doctors encounter in daily practice. And it's not always men in their seventies or eighties who are so troubled. For example, just the other day a forty-seven-year-old man came to me, ostensibly for a checkup. He was dynamic, vigorous and healthy, and he still found his wife as attractive as the day they met. The real reason for the visit was a decrease in his sexual desire. He was puzzled by the fact that whereas he had formerly anticipated and enjoyed intercourse three times a week (and more on vacations), he could now "take it or leave it." And when he decided to "take it," it often didn't work out. You will see in a moment how his problem might be approached diagnostically and therapeutically.

Before you identify with either King David or my impotent patient and begin to panic, be assured that male sexual performance is not always predictable on command. Every normal man occasionally "fails." He may be tired or bored—or both. However, anyone who doesn't come through two or three times in every four attempts should consult a doctor. One of the first questions he will ask is whether the difficulty occurs only at home. I remember one man who complained to me because he couldn't achieve an erection. When I asked him if he also had the problem when he "cheated," he looked at me incredulously and answered, "Of course not!" That's one way to distinguish psychogenic impotence (the kind that is in your head) from the organic form, that which is based on some "real" physical impairment.

In this latter category drugs may play an important role. Many medications doctors give their patients can cause impotence. These include Aldomet, Inderal and other beta-blockers, various diuretics, Aldactone, reserpine (all used in the control of hypertension), alcohol, antidepressants and sleeping pills.

Smoking has also been implicated, presumably because it constricts the blood vessels to the penis.

Normal erections depend not only on an intact blood flow to and within the penis (see below), but also on the integrity of the nervous system, which coordinates and delivers all the complex messages involved in the sexual act. Since diabetes can impair both the vascular supply and nerve function, impotence may be an early clue to the diagnosis of diabetes. If you've always functioned normally in the past and gradually begin to lose your sexual vigor, have your blood-sugar level checked.

After pharmacological causes have been excluded, the next step is a routine physical exam. You will be checked for diabetes, for low thyroid function and, indeed, for the presence of any hitherto unrecognized disease or disorder. If nothing is found, most doctors then simply tell the patient that it is all psychological and that he'll be "all right" —eventually. However, if such reassurance doesn't do the trick, don't stop there. Ask to see a urologist. He will do special tests and measure the testosterone (male hormone) level in the blood, looking for some hormonal basis for your complaints. If the testosterone level is low or borderline, you will in all likelihood be offered injections or oral preparations of this hormone. Sometimes it works, but not very often. Prolonged administration of testosterone can hurt the liver, or worsen a small hidden cancer of the prostate that has not yet declared its presence—and might ordinarily never do so.

One of the procedures the urologist will use is an evaluation of "nocturnal penile tumescence." Several different recording devices applied to the penis during the night indicate whether or not erection occurs. This usually separates psychological from physical causes of impotence. In the former, erections occur during rapid eye movement (REM) sleep.

THE DEPRIVED PENIS

Recent research indicates that about half of the men who can't "perform," especially those with diabetes or high blood pressure, have a *measurable* decrease in blood flow to the penis. These data were obtained by using the Doppler technique, which measures blood flow in small blood vessels such as those found in the penis. A tiny blood pressure cuff is wrapped around the (limp) organ. A Doppler probe on its surface determines the volume of blood flowing into it. Remember, an erection depends on *more* blood getting into the penis. Even if you are emotionally stable, without that extra penile blood supply, you'll never "get it up."

In addition to reduced blood supply *within the penis itself*, the larger blood vessels, like the aorta in the abdomen, that deliver the blood to the penis may be arteriosclerotic, further decreasing the circulation to it.

EFFECTING AN ERECTION

If the impotence can be shown to be due to vascular obstruction within the large arteries, the problem often can be corrected surgically. However, if the trouble is local, that is, within the penis itself, surgery is not very successful and I do not recommend it.

WHEN YOU PASS THE PHYSICAL—BUT STILL CAN'T

If you are obviously fatigued, overworked, depressed, worried or bored, altering your life-style may be all that is necessary to restore your sexual prowess. Stress impotence is especially common after business reverses, disappointments, difficult decisions and crises. "Workaholics," totally preoccupied with their life's goals, may also find no capacity for or interest in sex. Men (and women) who have had a heart attack and who worry that sexual activity may be dangerous also frequently lose their sex drive and potential. But remember, despite all the media hype about the splendor of old age, performance and libido do taper with the years. Don't expect to perform at sixty-five as well as you did at thirty.

If simple reassurance is not enough, then—from a practical point of view—some doctors will prescribe testosterone injections or pills, even though the blood level of this hormone is found to be normal. If that works, it's probably a placebo effect. If you are given this treatment for any length of time, ask for a second opinion. It's not without its risks. A much more reasonable approach is to try yohimbine. This is a substance derived from the yohimbé tree. For centuries, extracts of its bark have been credited with aphrodisiac qualities. There is ongoing research into the possible mechanisms of its effect, and some very plausible theories have been formulated. Some researchers claim to have found it effective in impotent diabetics. Others say it also works in men with normal blood sugar. In any event, it appears to be well tolerated, so ask your doctor to let you try it.

If the impotent man is not found to be taking some medication to explain his problem, and no physical cause is found, then he may be referred to a trained psychologist, psychiatrist or sex-counseling clinic, where psychological problems can be probed intensively and in depth. Various treatment techniques may be tried, including short-term psychotherapy, counseling, analysis, hypnotism and biofeedback. I am not impressed with the success rate of any of these modalities, but if all else fails, they should certainly be tried.

The most innovative, imaginative approach to impotence, when all other treatments fail, is the insertion of a rigid or semistiff prosthesis into the penis. Several different devices of this sort are now available and widely used. There are essentially two types. The first is a rigid rod that functions like a gooseneck lamp. Although it does make intercourse possible, it keeps the penis in a state of near erection at all times. That is not as good as it sounds. Think what you would look like in your bathing trunks! One way to deal with this problem is to keep the penis up against the abdomen with a "jockstrap" and release it at the appropriate time.

Most urologists recommend the rigid prosthesis, but some prefer to insert two cylinders, one on each side of the penis, which can be inflated (surreptitiously) at will and deflated when the job is done. The pump that supplies the cylinders usually is inserted into the scrotum, while the fluid is stored in a reservoir just under the abdominal wall. One good squeeze results in the release of fluid into the rods, rendering the penis erect. The entire maneuver, when skillfully done, can be unobtrusive. In fact, in one survey, some of the female partners were not even aware that their mates had been surgically endowed. Unfortunately, this system sometimes breaks down because of some trouble in the pump, valves or tubing.

Interest in penile prostheses is increasing. They are now among the most important topics at national and international urological conferences. If you think you may be a candidate for one, ask your doctor about it. If he is not aware of work in the field, get a second opinion from a urologist who is. Don't be shy about it, either. After all, we insert prosthetic joints, limbs and heart valves and implant pacemakers all the time. There is no reason to treat the phallus any differently. If you are offered such a device, be sure to ask about the possible complications and their incidence. For example, there is the risk of infection—not great, but ever present. Also, if you are a man who still happily awakes from time to time with an erection, and you have an implanted prothesis, the combination of the natural and artificial erection may be painful. But that will soon disappear, because when a rod is inserted into the erectile tissues of the penis, it usually permanently destroys those tissues, together with your ability ever to get a natural erection in the future. The important thing to remember about prosthetic devices is that you should not have one inserted until other treatment possibilities have been tried.

KEY FACTS TO REMEMBER

Do not confuse impotence with *infertility*. The former refers to the inability to obtain an erection, the latter, the failure to father a child.

Impotence formerly was almost always attributed to psychological problems. While these are, in fact, very important, we now appreciate the role of hormonal and circulatory factors. Every otherwise healthy male who complains of impotence should be checked by a urologist to rule out local disease in the genitourinary tract and a deficiency in testosterone (the male hormone). The adequacy of blood flow to and within the penis should also be determined. Several causes of impotence are treatable, even curable. Local infection can be treated, testosterone can be given orally or by injection, and interference with the blood supply to the penis can be surgically corrected. When these measures are not successful, or when definite psychological causes cannot be resolved, there is the very practical alternative of prosthetic penile devices.

▼

20

THE HYSTERECTOMY—
OUR MOST UNNECESSARY
OPERATION

UNNECESSARY—LIKE THE TONSILLECTOMY?

Whenever and wherever the subject of unnecessary surgery is raised, the operations most likely to come to mind are the tonsillectomy and the hysterectomy (removal of the uterus). We are leaving more and more tonsils and adenoids alone because the alleged benefit from their removal has been seriously questioned. But despite the evidence that hysterectomies are too often performed without good reason, they continue to be done more frequently than ever.

IS YOUR GYNECOLOGIST
A MALE CHAUVINIST?

I don't consider myself either a feminist or a male chauvinist. However, I do believe that too many gynecologists (the great preponderance of whom are men) are insensitive to the psychological impact of removing a uterus. This operation is even the subject of "humor." "A hysterectomy removes the baby carriage but leaves the playpen." I've never met a prospective surgical patient who found this "joke" funny.

THE SYMBOLIC UTERUS

Unlike the tonsils, appendix or gallbladder, the uterus is a symbolic organ, synonymous with fertility and femininity. Its extirpation, even when necessary, may have profound psychological implications on most women to which doctors are not always attuned. First of all, to someone still in her childbearing years, it means that she can no longer become a natural mother—in itself a devastating fact. It is one thing to engage in contraceptive techniques that you can discontinue when you decide to have a baby; it is quite another matter to have your fertility so drastically, completely and permanently terminated. And although some women are relieved at the new sexual freedom that a hysterectomy confers, many view their sexuality as having been compromised.

LOOKING OVER YOUR
GYNECOLOGIST'S SHOULDER

How often do gynecologists perform hysterectomies without justification? This crucial question was studied by representatives of the medical profession itself in Saskatchewan, Canada. Review committees there redefined the circumstances under which the operation *should* be done. Using these new criteria, they concluded that 23.7 percent of all hysterectomies were unnecessary. They then publicized the new standards and indicated that henceforth all such operations would be monitored for compliance. In the first year alone, the percentage of unjustified hysterectomies dropped to 7.8 percent. So if you are living in an area where such formal guidelines have been neither enunciated nor enforced and you are advised to have a hysterectomy, it goes without saying that you should get a second opinion from another gynecologist.

THE ADVICE MAY BE RIGHT OR WRONG

In most cases, your doctor will advise you to have a hysterectomy when it is an absolute must. But, as we know from the statistics, you are also likely to be sent to surgery even when you shouldn't be. Following are some guidelines to which you should refer if you find yourself in such a situation.

WHEN TO AGREE TO A HYSTERECTOMY

Suppose that you consult your doctor because of vaginal bleeding or pelvic pain. After he performs the necessary studies (pelvic exam, Pap smear, sonography), he finds a cancer of the uterus. The uterus then must almost always come out. It's not a bad idea to ask for a second opinion to make sure that the diagnosis of cancer was correct in the first place.

If your uterus contains a large fibroid (a benign uterine tumor) pressing on neighboring organs in your pelvis, and causing chronic pain, most gynecologists will recommend surgery.

If you have constant pelvic pain because your Fallopian tubes are scarred by chronic infection, and antibiotics don't help the situation, hysterectomy is usually the best recourse.

If you wet your pants whenever you cough or sneeze because repeated pregnancies have left your vaginal walls or muscles too weak to control urination, your doctor will then need to repair and strengthen the flaccid structures. If you are beyond childbearing age, he may well also recommend a hysterectomy because unless the uterus is removed, it will continue to exert pressure on the lax vaginal walls, bladder and rectum, and the operation will not be entirely successful.

Finally, if you have an ovarian tumor that needs to come out, and you are over forty-five years of age, the uterus should also be removed. It has no physiological function without the ovaries and can develop cancer later on, especially if you are taking estrogens, so there is no point in retaining it. (I also recommend removal of the *unaffected* ovary at the same operation, since cancer of the ovary is the third leading cause of cancer in women, after malignancy of the lung and the breast.)

WHEN TO SAY NO

Too many doctors still recommend a hysterectomy when they find small uterine fibroids in the course of a routine examination. If you have no pain, bleeding, pressure or other symptoms, don't allow it, especially if you would like to have children in the future. Ask for a second opinion from another gynecologist.

THE "USELESS UTERUS" SYNDROME

An "abnormal" Pap test does not always indicate cancer. It may also be due to inflammation or infection. Even if a few malignant cells are found, the problem usually can be managed by surgery or local radiation without removing the entire uterus. Yet there are doctors who tell their patients in this situation that "you might as well have *all* of the uterus taken out." This "might as well" psychology is not in your best interest. Always check it out with another doctor.

Some gynecologists are too quick to remove the uterus in women with chronic pelvic infection, or in those whose periods are always very painful. Medication and hormones should always be tried first. Never submit to such surgery until all your nonsurgical alternatives have been considered.

There are other circumstances under which the uterus should definitely not be removed, one of which is *unexplained* vaginal bleeding. Such bleeding, when not due to tumor, is usually the result of some hormonal imbalance. This problem takes time and patience to solve, and some gynecologists may recommend a hysterectomy as an "easy way out." That's bad medical practice and equally bad advice. If it is given to you, don't hesitate to request a second opinion.

Nor should you have your uterus removed in order to be made sterile—if that is what you want. Although some doctors still recommend it, most don't. The objective of sterility is to prevent an egg from mating with sperm. That can be done just as effectively by cutting or tying the Fallopian tubes (where the ovum travels from the ovary to effect its rendezvous with the sperm). Tubal ligation is a lot easier for you and makes more sense than undergoing a major operation to remove a perfectly healthy organ.

I know of patients who have had the uterus taken out simply because it was retroverted (tilted backward), or because they complained of backache or persistent vaginal discharge. One wonders whether they would have been so advised had the gynecologist been a woman.

Much as I deplore the needless hysterectomy, I must say, in all fairness, that the blame does not always lie solely with the doctor. Too often, the patient herself (or her husband) will insist on having an operation so as to avoid repeated office visits for the control of bleeding or other symptoms. It is essential that *both* you and your doctor appreciate the undesirability of the unnecessary hysterectomy, which carries with it a certain amount of risk, suffering and expense.

KEY FACTS TO REMEMBER

Surgical removal of the uterus is commonly done without good reason. Whenever this operation is recommended, another opinion should be obtained. In addition to unnecessary pain, risk and cost, hysterectomy may have an undesirable psychological impact. There are, however, clear-cut indications for this operation. These include cancer of the uterus, large fibroids that cause pressure symptoms and/or bleeding. Chronic infection of the Fallopian tubes, resulting in pain that is otherwise unmanageable, may also justify hysterectomy. When cancerous ovaries are removed, the uterus is also frequently excised as well. However, hysterectomy should be resisted when done solely for purposes of sterilization, bleeding due to hormonal imbalance, or for treatment of "backache."

21

PEPTIC ULCERS—
DOWN WITH THE DIET

A HOLE IN THE WALL—
STOMACH VERSUS DUODENUM

An ulcer is an erosion or hole in the lining of any organ. You can develop one in your eye if you injure it or on your skin if you burn it. The word *peptic* is derived from the Greek *peptein* (to cook, to digest) and is used as a prefix when the ulcer is located in either the stomach or in the beginning of the small intestine. Ulcers in these two sites are not quite the same disease. Their symptoms, complications, management and outlook differ substantially. A brief review of anatomy will help you understand why this is so.

The stomach is a J-shaped organ that narrows at its end to lead into the small intestine (duodenum), where three quarters of all ulcers occur. The first major difference between stomach, or gastric, and duodenal ulcers is that the latter are *never* malignant. However, gastric cancers often masquerade as ulcers. In practical terms, this means that once the diagnosis of a duodenal ulcer has been made either by X ray or endoscopy (looking directly into the affected area), the response to treatment can be judged more or less by how you feel. Repeated studies, especially X rays, are neither necessary nor desirable. On the other hand, if you have what appears to be a *gastric* ulcer, your doctor, preferably a gastroenterologist, should watch it very closely regardless of symptoms until he has *proved* that it is completely healed. A gastric ulcer that fails to respond to therapy within a few weeks may in fact be a malignant tumor. To be absolutely certain that this is not the case, your physician will want to perform gastroscopy (also called endoscopy). This involves your swallowing a thin, very flexible tube with a light at the end of it that is then passed directly into the stomach. The ulcer is actually seen and, if necessary, a biopsy specimen is taken and examined under the microscope.

ACID IS BAD—MUCUS IS GOOD

Acid is secreted by the stomach to help the process of digestion. But in some vulnerable individuals, this acid eats away the lining of the gastric and duodenal walls, creating ulcers. Mucus secreted by the intestinal and stomach walls normally coats this lining and helps prevent erosion by acid. The mucus in ulcer-prone persons varies in amount and quality. Acid-resisting properties of the cells lining the stomach and intestinal walls may also vary from person to person. Finally, the *amount* of acid produced by the stomach is critical too. This is very much influenced by the food we eat but also by the activity of a nerve called the *vagus*. An overactive vagus results in greater acid secretion by the stomach. That is why for years the basic treatment of ulcers consisted of drugs (antispasmodics) to reduce vagal activity. When that failed, we severed the nerve surgically.

The symptoms of gastric ulcers differ from those of duodenal ulcers. For example, food usually relieves the gnawing hunger pain of a duodenal ulcer, but may aggravate a stomach ulcer. Before the advent of modern drugs, treatment varied considerably too. That is no longer usually the case. Patients with duodenal ulcers are usually between twenty and fifty. Those with gastric ulcers are likely to be older, in their middle sixties.

SEX DIFFERENCES TOO

Interestingly enough, as in arteriosclerotic disease, a pre-menopausal woman is much less likely to develop a duodenal ulcer than is a man of the same age. Men are presumed to be more vulnerable to both conditions because they lack some protective factor present in women, perhaps a female hormone. This theory was the basis for some experiments a few years ago, in which men suffering from severe and recurrent duodenal ulcers were given estrogens. But, as in heart disease, this intervention made no apparent difference.

Peptic ulcers were much more common in the United States forty or fifty years ago than they are today. In 1940, for example, one American in ten could expect to develop an ulcer sometime before the age of sixty-five. Why this common malady is now on the wane is a mystery. In the decade of the seventies, hospitalization for duodenal ulcer dropped by 43 percent and for gastric ulcer by 10 percent. Deaths due to ulcers are declining too at the very impressive rate of 5 percent per year. I'm sure that better diagnosis and more effective treatment have a great deal to do with these statistics. Now for the bad news. Ten thousand people still die every year in this country from the complications of ulcers—hemorrhage (when the ulcer erodes a blood vessel), a perforation (when it bores a hole in the wall), obstruction (when the intestinal tract is scarred from cyclical ulceration and healing), and penetration (when the ulcer burrows through the wall of the gut and involves an adjacent organ like the pancreas).

ANXIETY, FRUSTRATION AND ANGER

No one is surprised when the stereotyped personality develops an ulcer—the harried, angry, high-powered executive (or doctor), the tense television producer, the anxious stockbroker or the aggressive, frustrated politician. Although there is some evidence that these "types" are somewhat more ulcer-prone, many of my ulcer patients are placid, even withdrawn, and certainly not aggressive. Maybe they don't show their stress, or react differently to it. It is certainly true that many persons engaged in "stressful" work, like surgeons performing delicate operations every day (and worrying about the results the night before and the night after), combat personnel, key executives and hostages, may suffer from ulcers. But many of their colleagues do not, so in addition to exposure to stress, there must be other factors involved.

A strong family history of ulcers, as well as certain other diseases—for example, cirrhosis of the liver, emphysema and rheumatoid arthritis—may also leave you ulcer-prone.

HOW TO MAKE AN ULCER

Personality and occupation aside, if for any reason you would like to have an ulcer of your very own, you can make your dream come true by doing any of the following: smoke cigarettes, drink too much, and take lots of aspirin or one of the newer nonsteroidal anti-inflammatory drugs like Indocin, Clinoril, Motrin, and Naprosyn, or continue dosing yourself with large amounts of steroids (prednisone, cortisone, Medrol) for weeks or months.

MAKING THE DIAGNOSIS

Suppose, then, that you complain to your doctor about a chronic "hunger pain" in the midportion of the upper abdomen, which is relieved by food, milk or some antacid. Two or three hours later (after the food has passed through the stomach and is no longer buffering the acid) the pain starts up again. You also remember having similar symptoms last spring, but they cleared up on their own. The pain has begun to interfere with your sleep, and it awakens you between midnight and three o'clock (but never, curiously enough, just before you would normally get up, like six or seven in the morning).

As you describe these symptoms, your doctor will immediately think "ulcer." When he examines you and presses hard on your abdomen just above the belly button, it will hurt. After the physical, he will ask for a stool specimen and analyze it for the presence of blood. Blood from high up in the intestinal tract—that is, originating in the stomach or the duodenum—is usually black by the time it appears in the stool, because it has been chemically altered in its travels down the gut. (But remember, Pepto-Bismol or iron supplements also will make your stool black.) Finally, to establish the diagnosis (which he already strongly suspects from your history and physical exam), he will either send you for an X ray following a barium drink or for a direct look at the area by endoscopy. Either procedure will usually reveal the ulcer. The X ray may fail to locate the lesion when it is tiny or buried in one of the folds of the stomach wall. If the ulcer is in the duodenum, you are free and clear as far as cancer is concerned. If it is in the stomach, the lesion may resemble an ulcer but actually be malignant. In that case your doctor will surely recommend endoscopy if he didn't do so originally. During this procedure biopsy specimens can be obtained to make absolutely sure that an early, curable cancer is not being missed. Even if the first biopsies taken with the gastroscope show a benign ulcer, you should be restudied in six to eight weeks after treatment—just to be certain.

Remember then, if you have a gastric ulcer, you should insist upon (a) an X ray, (b) endoscopy with biopsies, and (c) repeated evaluation until the ulcer has been shown to have disappeared.

INDIGESTION DOESN'T KILL

It's 3 A.M. You wake up with an uncomfortable pressure in the lower chest. Chances are you'll call it indigestion, heartburn or ulcers. You may well be right. You may also be wrong. Attributing such symptoms to a nonexistent ulcer or indigestion can be dangerous, especially when they are due to heart disease. I remember one patient who frequently developed chest pain when he went for a walk after eating. He refused to believe my diagnosis of angina pectoris even though his symptoms were typical of that disorder. He was fixated on the fact that the pain occurred only after eating. He insisted that he could walk to his "heart's content" as long as his stomach was empty, so he decided to go for X rays of his upper gastrointestinal tract (GI series) to prove to himself (and to me) that he did not have heart trouble and that everything could be explained either by an ulcer or a hiatus hernia. After his first swallow of barium at the radiologist's office, he suffered a massive heart attack. So remember, if you have any upper abdominal or chest pain or pressure, especially if it is worsened by emotional stress, walking or some other physical activity, check with your doctor to make sure that the trouble is not in your heart, even though the symptoms appear to be related to food intake.

YOUR CHOICES OF ULCER TREATMENT

Since peptic ulcer is due to erosion of the lining of the gut by acid, the first step in treatment is neutralizing that acid. Many people believe that *antacids* are inert, that it is safe to take as much of them as you want—indefinitely. Ulcer patients often walk around with their pockets full of antacid tablets, swallowing or chewing them every few minutes, especially when they're under stress or drinking too much. Antacids in excess are neither harmless nor inert. Furthermore, there are significant differences among the various brands available. For example, some contain calcium, which in large doses can cause kidney problems. Other preparations, like baking soda, have large amounts of salt, which is bad for anyone with high blood pressure or heart failure. Some antacids will constipate you or, if they have magnesium hydroxide, give you diarrhea. Finally, if you're taking antacids containing aluminum for any length of time, your bones may lose calcium and phosphorus and break easily. Postmenopausal women, who are prone to developing osteoporosis, are particularly vulnerable to this complication.

Because of these potential untoward effects, commercially available antacids are frequently made up of several different ingredients, each of which offsets the adverse side effects of the other. For example, they may contain equal amounts of a substance that tends to constipate you and one likely to cause diarrhea, the net result being neither. The most widely advertised antacids are Maalox, Gelusil, Mylanta, Di-Gel, Titralac and Riopan—not to mention Tums and Rolaids. Although the tablet form is more convenient, the liquid is better for an active ulcer because it neutralizes acid more effectively. Also, to ensure a longer duration of action (up to four hours) be sure to take antacids *after* meals. They work for only twenty to thirty minutes on an empty stomach.

Do you remember when patients with peptic ulcers consumed large quantities of milk and cream to relieve their pain? Unfortunately many still do, and shouldn't. For not only can such a rich source of cholesterol enhance the risk of arteriosclerosis in some people, it can actually *increase* the amount of acid produced by the stomach.

THE H_2 BLOCKERS—
A MAJOR BREAKTHROUGH

In recent years, a new group of antiulcer drugs has been developed that work in a totally different way. These include Tagamet (cimetidine), Zantac (ranitidine) and most recently, Pepcid. Most doctors now rely on these agents as the mainstay of treatment because they are so effective and so easy to take. Patient compliance has been excellent since all three drugs control the ulcer with once-a-day dosage. Tagamet, Zantac and Pepcid are all H_2 receptor blockers. They work by actually preventing formation of acid by the stomach cells. No acid means no ulcer.

I have not found any significant difference among these three H_2 blockers in my own practice. Tagamet was the first one on the scene, and initially doctors prescribed it three or four times a day. Zantac came next and its major advantage, as far as I could tell, was that you needed only two a day. Most recently Pepcid was introduced as a breakthrough because one pill per day had the desired effect. But experience has shown that by increasing the dosage, all three are effective when taken once, usually at night. So now, which one you choose will depend on its cost.

When Tagamet was introduced, we were uncertain about how long it was safe to continue taking it. The more our experience with these agents grows, the more comfortable we are about their prolonged use. At the present time there is no real problem continuing them for at least a year, and indefinitely if serious ulcer symptoms cannot be controlled in any other way.

Side effects can occur, as with any drugs, but are not usually dangerous. The most common complaints I hear from patients are gastrointestinal in origin—diarrhea, nausea, constipation, bloating and dry mouth. Neurological symptoms may also occur—drowsiness, slurred speech and, in older people, confusion. These symptoms clear up when the drug is stopped.

Be careful if you're also taking other medications like Coumadin (the blood thinner), Inderal (and other beta-blockers), certain tranquilizers like Valium and theophylline (for asthma)—whose dosage may have to be adjusted because of interaction with the H_2 blockers.

A BAND-AID FOR YOUR ULCER

A drug called Carafate (sucralfate) is also available to *treat* ulcers (but unlike the H_2 blockers, not to prevent them). It has an interesting mode of action. It neither neutralizes acid nor reduces its formation. When taken by mouth, it coats the ulcerated lining of the stomach or duodenum, thus protecting the injured area from further acid action. It is not absorbed into the body and so has no side effects. It hangs on for about six hours, then peels off, is passed down the gut and excreted. So every six hours you need to take another dose. Never do so on a full stomach because the food prevents the drug from attaching itself to the ulcerated area. Also make sure not to swallow other pills with Carafate, because it may neutralize their effect. It's best to take other medication one hour before Carafate, and food one hour after.

YOU MAY EAT WHATEVER
YOU WANT (WELL, ALMOST)

Not too long ago the most important part of ulcer treatment was a very strict diet. That's because we were very short on effective drugs. You were allowed to eat only bland food, forced to drink lots of milk and cream and forbidden anything you really enjoyed. But that is all a thing of the past, just like prolonged bed rest or compulsory retirement after a heart attack. Now, even when your ulcer is acute, you may eat virtually anything you want. *Bland foods do not promote healing of the ulcer, and a normal diet does not aggravate it.* Despite this new knowledge, many hospitalized ulcer patients are still being prescribed severely restricted diets. If your doctor so advises you, discuss it with him. If he insists, get another opinion from a gastroenterologist.

The facts are that you may safely and comfortably eat whatever you wish so long as you avoid alcohol (which stimulates the formation of acid and irritates the raw ulcer) and all caffeine (coffee, tea and cola drinks, which increase gastric acidity). Incidentally, decaffeinated coffee, popularly thought to be permissible, seems to have the same adverse effects on an ulcer as does regular coffee. So it's not only the caffeine, but something else in coffee that irritates the ulcer.

Aspirin and related drugs (Tylenol is OK) and cigarettes (which promote acid formation) should be avoided.

ULCERS, TRANQUILIZERS AND PSYCHIATRISTS

Doctors almost reflexively tend to prescribe tranquilizers for ulcer patients to "help you relax." A sedative is useful if you are nervous, apprehensive and on edge, but not otherwise. Tranquilizers do not in themselves promote ulcer healing. By the same token, don't consult a psychiatrist simply because you have an ulcer. Psychotherapy is of no help to the ulcer itself and may make things worse by provoking more anxiety. In fact, it is usually better not to get started with a psychiatrist during the acute phase of the disease unless there is some obvious compelling reason to do so.

Research and development in antiulcer treatment is ongoing and very active. There are several promising new agents on the horizon, one of which has already been approved. It is a prostaglandin analogue (misoprostol), one of several naturally occurring substances that are present in virtually every organ system in the body (and which is discussed briefly in the chapter dealing with abortion). Its major advantage is that it permits patients with active ulcers to take other medications such as aspirin, which they may need, and which ordinarily might cause bleeding or delay healing.

KEY FACTS TO REMEMBER

Ulcers of the stomach (gastric) and duodenum are on the wane, but they still account for several thousand deaths each year in the United States alone. However, anyone with recurrent "indigestion" should make certain that the symptoms are not due to heart disease.

Duodenal ulcers are virtually never cancerous; gastric ulcers may be. Treatment of an uncomplicated duodenal ulcer is simple and straightforward. Gastric ulcers, however, require sophisticated diagnostic follow-up and should be managed by a gastroenterologist. Most gastric ulcers require gastroscopy and biopsy.

Stress may contribute to ulcer formation but does not always do so. Psychiatric care is usually not necessary for ulcer patients unless there are specific unrelated emotional problems. Such treatment may be undesirable in the acute stage of the ulcer.

The mainstays of ulcer treatment are H_2 receptor blockers, of which Tagamet is the prototype, antacids and Carafate. Diet restriction (except for caffeine, alcohol, aspirin and aspirin-related drugs, and cigarettes) is usually unnecessary and should be avoided.

22

VIRAL HEPATITIS— AVOIDING A JAUNDICED VIEW

THE SEAT OF THE SOUL

The ancients called the heart "the seat of the soul." Most people think the brain should have been so designated. I take exception to both nominations. In my mind, there is no question that the liver deserves this signal honor—for it is at least as complex as the brain, as vital as the heart and is responsible, to boot, for a multitude of body processes. No wonder then that a Frenchman, whenever he is feeling sick or just out of sorts, invariably blames his liver.

IT GIVES YOU HEPATITIS

Ask any child what the heart does, and he will answer quite properly that it sustains life by pumping blood to the rest of the body. Who doesn't know that the brain controls our every movement and thought? It is common knowledge that the kidneys make urine in which the waste products of the body are excreted. But when I asked several people recently what the liver does, none of them really knew—except one woman who answered, "It gives you hepatitis."

The liver, of which, incidentally, we have only one, performs a staggering array of very sophisticated functions. It is important that you know what they are because only then will you appreciate what can go wrong when your liver is sick.

ALBUMIN AND GLOBULIN— KEY PROTEINS

Let us begin with the synthesis or manufacture of scores of different kinds of proteins. The liver, using as its building blocks the basic elements in the food we eat, reconstitutes them into complicated proteins like albumin and globulin.

Albumin is fundamental to our survival. Attached to this protein and transported by it is an array of minerals and hormones, each of which is released by the albumin wherever and whenever needed. Albumin also maintains the balance of pressure between the fluid within the blood vessels (veins and arteries) and that in the surrounding tissues. When there is not enough albumin around, as happens in severe liver disease, fluid seeps out of the blood vessels and results in generalized swelling of the body.

Globulins are the cornerstone of our body defenses. They make all kinds of antibodies, which help us resist infection and possibly even cancer.

There are scores of other, less well-known proteins, all of which are extremely important to the maintenance of our health and biological status quo. For example, have you ever considered what prevents you from hemorrhaging internally? It is the many proteins that are made by the liver, which maintain the exquisite balance between the clotting and bleeding mechanisms—fibrinogen, prothrombin and a host of other "factors." A deficiency of only one of these factors can be responsible for a serious bleeding disorder, for example, hemophilia.

The liver also builds up, rearranges and breaks down many other protein molecules, like a child with his Erector set or building blocks. Most important in its function as molecular architect is what the liver does to amino acids, a large group of essential body proteins. It constantly changes their composition from one to another.

The liver also converts ammonia, an end product of protein metabolism, into harmless chemicals. Unless this is done, ammonia, derived from the protein in your diet, will accumulate in the body. Enough of it will render you unconscious. That is the mechanism by which chronic alcoholics and patients with other forms of cirrhosis go into coma and die.

FIFTY MILLION FRENCHMEN CAN'T BE WRONG—CAN THEY?

The literally hundreds of chemical reactions in which the liver is involved are usually mediated through enzymes. The liver is responsible for everything from digesting the food we eat to making sure our blood clots and flows properly. It makes bile, which it sends to the gallbladder for storage and to the gut for digesting the fat in our diet. How much cholesterol and triglycerides we have, whether we develop "low blood sugar" or not, the fate of so many of the pills we take (why they just don't keep accumulating as we take one or two every day)—all this is determined by the liver. It stores substances, detoxifies them, eliminates them or changes their chemistry so that they don't poison us. You name it, the liver does it. As I reflect on this myriad of functions, I'm beginning to think that the French are right about their "mal de foie."

Just as the liver has so many critical roles to play, so is it vulnerable to a wide variety of disorders ranging from physical injury to viral infection. You can poison your liver with alcohol or cleaning fluid; some disease process or other can interfere with its blood supply; the bile-carrying ducts that interconnect it with the gallbladder and intestine can become obstructed by stone or tumor, giving you jaundice (the bile backs up into the liver and bloodstream); it may develop a cancer of its own or play host to one originating elsewhere in the body. These are just a few examples of what can go wrong with the liver. Fortunately, this complex organ has a large reserve for the jobs it does. With the exception of cancer, native to it or "imported," and a few of the more serious infections and toxic agents, the liver can take a lot of abuse before it really gets its back up.

DIFFERENT KINDS OF HEPATITIS

Hepar means "liver," and *itis*, "inflammation" or "infection." *Hepatitis*, therefore, refers to inflammation or infection of the liver caused by any of a wide variety of insults—chemical, bacterial, parasitic (such as when a worm from the gut invades the liver), alcohol and viruses. However, I will limit this chapter to viral hepatitis, a group of very common disorders that affect many thousands of people each year. You should be aware of the new and important information about their diagnosis and treatment.

The liver is made up of several different kinds of cells, each involved in its own particular way in the many functions of this organ. When attacked by the specific viruses that cause hepatitis, these cells stop working properly, and you begin to feel sick. You will likely develop a fever, start to itch all over, lose your appetite, experience continual nausea for a few days and even vomit. You find yourself tired, having a feeling of soreness over the liver (in the right upper portion of the abdomen) and then become yellow (jaundiced). Smokers completely lose their taste for tobacco. It is not unusual, especially in one of its forms, hepatitis B virus (or hepatitis B), to have aches and pains in all the joints—a form of arthritis. These symptoms, which may come on abruptly in a matter of a few days, or insidiously over a period of weeks (depending on the particular virus infecting you), last for about four to six weeks in uncomplicated cases. But how sick you get and how quickly you recover depends, in part, on your age (older, fragile persons tolerate the infection less well) and the severity and the nature of the infection itself.

A, B AND NON-A, NON-B— WITH MORE ON THE WAY

We currently recognize three types of viral hepatitis. Each is transmitted, identified, treated and prevented differently— and has a different prognosis (outlook). They are called hepatitis A virus (HAV, formerly called infectious hepatitis),

hepatitis B virus (HBV, formerly called serum or transfusion hepatitis), and Non-A, Non-B (NANB).

Hepatitis B and NANB resemble each other clinically and have a similar mode of transmission, which differs from that of hepatitis A. They are also potentially more serious than is hepatitis A. (Both A and B viruses can be identified by tests or "markers" in the blood.) The existence of NANB hepatitis (which may actually be due to more than one virus) is assumed when neither the A nor B viruses can be identified. If the hepatitis is neither A nor B, what else can it be? Obviously Non-A, Non-B.

Although there is some clinical overlap, the basic differences among these three viruses are as follows: HAV is primarily harbored in the gut, and is transmitted by that route (fecal-oral). For all practical purposes, you contract hepatitis A from food (usually shellfish) or water contaminated by sewage. Therefore, this type of hepatitis is found in largest numbers where public health measures are primitive or inadequate and sanitation control poor, or where there is overcrowding, such as in jail or army barracks. It occurs most commonly among the young, is rarely fatal, and hardly ever ends up giving you chronic liver disease. Its symptoms tend to develop rather quickly, and you are most contagious to others during what is called the prodromal state—after you have been infected but are still not feeling sick with the disease. This incubation period usually lasts between twenty and forty days, and patients remain infective to others for about twenty-one days after symptoms begin. The hallmark of all hepatitis is jaundice, although it may not develop in very mild cases. Once the yellow hue appears, the patient is no longer infective. So if you are close to someone who has developed jaundice and worry about whether you too will get hepatitis, think back on the nature of your contact *before* the jaundice became apparent.

HOW THEY'RE TRANSMITTED

While virus A inhabits the intestinal tract and is transmitted primarily by fecal contamination, HBV and NANB are found in the blood. You "catch" these latter two diseases from someone else's infected blood. How might that happen, assuming that you are not a vampire? The most obvious way is via a transfusion of blood donated or sold by someone who has the disease. Such blood can be screened to eliminate infection by B virus, but we cannot yet detect NANB virus, which causes 80 or 90 percent of all *transfusion hepatitis*. In addition to transfusions, you can also get hepatitis B or NANB when your skin is broken (transcutaneous route) by a needle that was used in drawing blood from someone with the disease and was not properly sterilized. (Unfortunately, disposable needles are not yet used everywhere.) And that can happen in such respectable places as your dentist's chair, or in questionable situations like tattoo parlors. Another obvious reservoir of infection, one that is of great and growing concern, is the drug addict. If he is a virus B carrier or is incubating the disease, he will give it to everybody with whom he shares syringes or needles. Medical and paramedical workers who are in contact with scalpels, other instruments, patients' blood (as for example, in dialysis units) and tissues of various sorts are especially vulnerable to this disease and have a high incidence of it. Finally, hepatitis B (but strangely enough, not NANB) is also spread by the venereal route. The incubation period of the B virus is longer than that of the A virus, usually 60 to 110 days, while the incubation of NANB is somewhere between the two (35 to 70 days). Hepatitis B, because of the way it is transmitted (blood, needles and sexual contact), is more apt to involve the elderly and homosexuals.

Although hepatitis A is transmitted differently than hepatitis B and NANB, the clinical distinction among the three is not always clear-cut. Also, from time to time we come across patients who have either hepatitis B or NANB in whom we simply cannot elicit any history of infection by the needle or blood route. It is more than likely that in these cases, the viruses were spread in some other way. This is supported by the finding of the B virus in mother's milk, in semen, gastric juices and even in urine and feces (usually the hunting ground of the A virus). So, from the point of view of prevention, the nursing care of a patient with hepatitis B or NANB should focus primarily on the sterilization of any needles involved in his or her testing or treatment and normal hygienic attention to the disposition of stool and urine. Oral and other intimate contacts should also be avoided during the infectious stage in all patients with any type of hepatitis.

Whereas hepatitis A is almost always benign, hepatitis B and NANB can lead to prolonged illness and death. So if you contract "hepatitis," make sure to ask what type it is, something that's easily determined by a blood test.

TOO MUCH REST

Despite the difference between virus A hepatitis and the other two forms, the treatment for all three is basically the same—supportive. There is no cure for any of them—no medicine or antibiotic you can take to destroy the viruses. We simply recommend plenty of rest and proper nutrition until the disease runs its course. But too much of a good thing is not desirable either, and that's what we used to do in the treatment of hepatitis. Patients were advised to stay in bed until all liver tests had returned completely to normal and/or until the jaundice had disappeared. Also, the diet was very restrictive—no fats, limited proteins and lots of carbohydrates—a very boring menu, which didn't help to ensure adequate nutrition (at least 2,000 calories per day), or stimulate an appetite that was poor to begin with.

THE ARMY TO THE RESCUE

We are indebted to the military for the modern treatment of viral hepatitis. As you might expect, the Army is not keen on pampering its personnel, tucking them into bed for months and feeding them special diets. So they decided to see whether prolonged bed rest really made any difference to patients with hepatitis. They found, after very careful studies, that it did not. Neither did special diets. On the basis of these and later studies, we now recommend that you remain in bed only as long as you have a fever and the liver tests are getting *worse*. You may safely move about and even return to work even while you are still slightly jaundiced—as long and as soon as you *feel* better, your temperature is normal and your liver function tests begin to return *toward* normal. And from day one you may eat whatever agrees with you, but you should abstain from alcohol in any form for at least six months.

Suppose someone with whom you have had close contact (roommate, lover, parent or child) comes down with infectious hepatitis. Can you do anything to prevent contracting this illness? If the hepatitis is due to virus A, a shot of human immune serum globulin (ISG) will substantially reduce the risk if you take it within the first two weeks after exposure. Should you develop hepatitis anyway, it will be less severe. This gamma globulin probably also affords some protection against NANB hepatitis, but is of no use in type B prophylaxis. For the latter, a new immune globulin, marketed in the United States as HEP-B-Gammagee, provides you about three- to tenfold protection for two months. If you have been infected accidentally—by a needle scratch, as might occur in a hospital worker—you will need two shots of this immune globulin, the first as soon as possible, but no later than seven days after exposure, and the second in about one month. This vaccine is made from the blood of patients who have had hepatitis B and therefore contains natural antibodies against that virus. Unfortunately, it is still very expensive, about twenty times the cost of standard gamma globulin.

PROPHYLACTIC GAMMA GLOBULIN

If you are going to an area with poor hygiene, where you run the risk of contracting virus A hepatitis from the food or the water, get a shot of gamma globulin before you leave home. It will protect you for up to six months. In some countries, the gamma globulin supplies themselves have been reported to be contaminated with virus B. This could protect a person from hepatitis A but give them the potentially more serious hepatitis B!

HEPATITIS B VACCINE—FINALLY

The most exciting development in the field of hepatitis is the availability of a vaccine to prevent the B virus infection.

Make sure you get it as soon as possible if you are a practicing homosexual (in whom 48 percent of all cases of hepatitis B are found), if you do work that exposes you to infected needles or blood or if you are a drug addict.

The first hepatitis B vaccine was made from the blood products of patients who had contracted the virus and whose immune system responded by making antibodies against it. Although this vaccine was very effective, there was considerable resistance to taking it because it came from the blood of hepatitis B patients who might also harbor the AIDS virus. Actually the vaccine was prepared in such a way as to inactivate *any* virus that might be present, but this reassurance was not enough for many individuals. Happily, hepatitis B vaccine is now made by recombinant DNA techniques, another feat of genetic engineering. Since no human blood products are involved, this preparation is completely safe, both actually and theoretically. It should be taken by every doctor, dentist or paramedical worker in possible contact with hepatitis B patients, by homosexuals and by drug users.

AFTER THE ACUTE ATTACK

If you get sick with hepatitis A because you ate some contaminated raw clams, you will be fine once the acute illness is over and you can be virtually certain that you will not develop chronic liver trouble. But it is a different story with hepatitis B and NANB. Five to ten percent of patients with hepatitis B are plagued with a chronic form of the disease, and become carriers. In NANB cases, the incidence is even higher. Chronic hepatitis may be either *persistent* or *active,* and there is a world of difference between the two, in terms of both outlook and treatment.

If you develop chronic, *persistent* hepatitis, you will be mildly sick, but you will recover. Just keep away from alcohol. In a few months your symptoms will disappear and your liver tests will return to normal no matter what life-style you follow.

In contrast, chronic *active* hepatitis is a serious illness that often causes progressive liver destruction, and some 50 percent of patients die within five years. Treatment is not predictably effective. We formerly administered steroid hormones, but their usefulness, especially over the long term, is very questionable. Most doctors, if they prescribe these drugs at all, do so for a very limited time only. Interferon and other antiviral agents are still being evaluated in the treatment of chronic active hepatitis. (Interferon, a normal constituent of the body found in certain types of white cells, is also being tested as a potential antitumor agent.) Although it is too early to predict its effect in the management of chronic active hepatitis, initial reports are encouraging.

The diagnosis as to which form of chronic hepatitis you have can be made only by a liver biopsy. That means sticking a needle into the liver through the abdominal wall. It takes only a few minutes, and it is relatively easy to do—provided that it is done by an experienced gastroenterologist. If you are being given potent medications for "chronic hepatitis," ask what kind it is. The chronic *active* form is the only type that warrants such treatment, and even then, it's wise to obtain a second opinion.

KEY FACTS TO REMEMBER

The liver is one of the most complex and important organs of the body. It is vulnerable to a host of disorders, including poisoning from chemicals and alcohol, bacterial infections, parasites, tumors, injury and viruses.

Viral hepatitis is a common and often serious disease worldwide, with three important forms thus far identified. They all have similar symptoms—jaundice, weakness, low-grade fever, lack of appetite and "malaise." Their mode of transmission, however, differs. Hepatitis A is basically food-borne, while hepatitis B and Non-A, Non-B are transmitted primarily by infected blood. Homosexuals and drug addicts have an especially high incidence of hepatitis B. Most cases clear up spontaneously, without specific treatment. A few of the blood-borne types, however, may end in serious liver damage and death.

The major pitfalls of therapy for the mild, garden variety hepatitis are overtreatment and unnecessary dietary restrictions. A vaccine to *prevent* hepatitis B is now available and should be taken by anyone potentially exposed to the disease *before* the exposure occurs.

23

GALLBLADDER DISEASE—A VARIETY OF TREATMENT OPTIONS

THE FIVE F'S AND THE THIN SPINSTER

As a medical student, I was taught that those most likely to have gallstones are characterized by the five F's—fat, female, fertile, fortyish and flatulent. It's one of the few maxims I learned that remains true many years later. The fatter you are, the more vulnerable. The incidence of gallstones among women, especially those who have had children, is twice that in men. It is a disease of adult life, and its major symptom is gas. So much for the five F's. But if I had suspected the diagnosis *only* in those persons, I would have missed an awful lot of gallbladder disease over the years—in men, in thin spinsters and even in children.

Gallstones are very common in this country; they are present in some fifteen million women and five million men. One million new cases are discovered each year and five hundred thousand cholecystectomies (operations for gallbladder removal) are performed annually. If you are an American Indian, your chances of developing gallstones are seven out of ten! If you have rheumatic heart disease, especially of the mitral valve, or take the "pill," you are also more prone to them than is the rest of the population. Atromid-S (clofibrate), a drug for the reduction of cholesterol and triglyceride levels, is also associated with a higher incidence of gallstones.

Bile, which is required to digest the fat we eat, is made in the liver and stored in the gallbladder. Fat in the diet passes from the stomach into the small intestine, where its arrival signals the gallbladder to send down some extra bile. The normal gallbladder then contracts and squirts out the amount necessary to digest the fat in the gut. A sick or nonfunctioning organ fails to do so, and the undigested fat leaves you feeling full, bloated and gaseous.

The usual symptoms of gallbladder disease are the feeling of fullness, bloating, discomfort or pain in the right upper portion of the abdomen or under the lower part of the breastbone after eating cabbage or fried or fatty foods.

THE GALLBLADDER X RAY

A gallbladder X ray (oral cholecystogram) not only reveals any stones within it, but also indicates whether the organ itself is working properly—that is, squirting on demand. So when you have this procedure, in addition to taking dye pills the night before, you also have a fatty drink in the morning to see whether the gallbladder contracts normally in response to it. Although the presence of stones indicates disease or inflammation of the gallbladder, their absence does not necessarily mean that it is functioning normally.

SONOGRAPHY, THE MODERN ALTERNATIVE TO THE GALLBLADDER X RAY

If your gallbladder needs to be evaluated and you hesitate being exposed to more radiation than is absolutely necessary, there is an alternative—sonography. This is an accurate, relatively inexpensive, painless and noninvasive test that can be done in the radiologist's office. There is no radiation involved. Whenever there's a question of gallstones, and a gallbladder X ray is advised, indicate your preference for the sonogram. It has several advantages. The obvious one is that it obviates exposure to radiation. You also don't have to take any dye pills the night before (which can cause diarrhea and nausea the following morning). You needn't fast for six hours, and the whole procedure takes only five minutes when done with the newer real-time scanners. But traditions die slowly in medicine, and many doctors still opt for the X ray first. There is no real justification for doing it that way.

SILENT STONES

Every now and then, in the course of a routine checkup, we find gallstones in persons who have no symptoms whatsoever. What should you do if you are incidentally found to have gallstones in the course of a routine X ray examination? Before you make any decision, there are some facts of which you should be aware. About 65 percent of persons with stones have no trouble from them, and that includes those who have already had one gallbladder attack. Among those who do develop symptoms, most will improve by simply following a low-fat diet. So there is usually no need to rush to surgery. Even if the gallbladder flares up, there is almost always enough time to act. Remember that in every operation, no matter how trivial, there is some risk—from the anesthesia, an unforeseen complication during the operation, a blood clot afterward or infection. And gallbladder surgery is by no means trivial! Diabetics in particular should, if possible, avoid "elective" operations. Recent data indicate that such patients are at particular risk from this operation.

WHEN TO OPERATE—UNDER THE SWORD OF DAMOCLES

This is what I advise my own patients with gallbladder disease. Anyone who continues to experience attacks of pain, despite a conscientious attempt to adhere to a diet, should have the gallbladder out. This is especially true if there are many stones and they are very small. A tiny stone can pass from your gallbladder into one of the bile ducts, blocking it and leaving you jaundiced. If you have such small stones, you may suddenly develop "biliary obstruction," a surgical emergency. Why risk finding yourself in some remote area, hours away from good care, in such circumstances? But if you have had a heart attack recently, it is better to postpone the operation if possible. *Any* surgery done within six months of a heart attack carries with it a greater risk.

Many doctors, especially surgeons, disagree with my position. They believe that, since the presence of stones means disease, you are going to need surgery sooner or later, and so, regardless of symptoms, it is best to have it done sooner, while you are still in good health. If that is what you are advised, consult a gastroenterologist.

DISSOLVING THE STONES

Since 1972, we have known that certain chemicals can actually dissolve gallstones. They are called *chenodeoxycholic* and *ursodeoxycholic acid.*

In order to determine how successful and safe such treatment really is, several large studies have been conducted in the United States and abroad in recent years. Most of the results have been disappointing. Although the drugs are safe, they dissolve stones in relatively few patients, and recurrence is almost the rule. In other words, you've got to keep taking the medication for the rest of your life. These agents work best in women, in thin people, and when the gallbladder contains many cholesterol stones (so that there is a large surface area in contact with the drug). These drugs seem to have no effect on frequency of pain or the need for surgery.

If this therapy is recommended to you, get a second opinion. It would, at the moment, appear to be most appropriate for those who need surgery but in whom the operative risk is high.

Additional alternatives for the management of gallstones have become available in recent years. Others are still in the experimental stage. It seems that the Mayo Clinic in Rochester, Minnesota, is the most innovative in this field. If you have a serious question about how to manage your own gallbladder problem, you may want to consult one of their specialists.

A new technique to dissolve gallstones now being used at the Mayo Clinic involves injecting an ether solution through the abdominal wall directly into the gallbladder. When stones are stuck in the bile duct, a chemical can be introduced into the duct from the intestine. Neither technique involves an operation. Finally, the people who brought us the lithotriptor, the machine that shatters kidney stones by sending sound waves at them, are now recommending a similar treatment for gallstones. This procedure is now being evaluated in the United States and may very well become available in the near future.

KEY FACTS TO REMEMBER

Gallbladder disease may exist with or without the presence of gallstones. But stones, even in the absence of symptoms, indicate a diseased gallbladder. Sonography represents a more desirable method of diagnosing gallstones than does the traditional X ray.

Gallstones are very common in the United States, particularly among American Indians. Certain drugs and diseases predispose to their formation.

Doctors disagree about how to manage "silent" stones, discovered incidentally. Some recommend early prophylactic removal of the gallbladder even in the absence of symptoms. Most now advise a wait-and-see attitude. Before making a final decision, consult a gastroenterologist, especially if you're a diabetic.

In a small percentage of patients, gallstones can be dissolved chemically. If surgery is desirable but not urgently required, ask your doctor about this treatment, especially if you are a thin female who has many stones and your blood cholesterol level tends to be high.

24

THE BOWEL—
WHEN AND HOW TO
TREAT ITS SYMPTOMS

BELLYACHERS—YOUNG AND OLD

If you were to take a poll every time you sat in your doctor's waiting room, you would almost certainly find at least one patient with symptoms originating somewhere in the gut. Most Americans have bowel trouble sometime or other— you name it—indigestion, bloating, cramps, constipation, "gas," diarrhea, mucus or blood in the stool or the TV catchall of "irregularity."

When your bowels "act up," and you consult the doctor for help, he will listen to your symptoms, examine you and then arrange for whatever tests he thinks are necessary. The work-up will almost always include a rectal exam in which the doctor feels for growths in the anal area. You will have to provide a stool specimen, which, depending on your story, will be analyzed for blood, bacteria, parasites, mucus or chemical composition. Sometimes proctoscopy (in which the doctor looks through an instrument inserted into the rectum for tumors or other evidence of disease), sigmoidoscopy or colonoscopy (using thinner, more flexible tubes, which go up much higher) needs to be done. Frequently, a barium enema X ray is necessary for an assessment of the large bowel.

An *upper* gastrointestinal series (you drink the barium

instead of having it inserted into your rectum) is required to clarify any problems in the esophagus (food pipe), stomach and small bowel. A sonogram (sound waves are directed into the abdomen and the reflected echo reveals the presence of fluid or a growth) may also be ordered. A CT, or CAT, scan (the computerized X ray that visualizes the abdominal contents without barium) may be required. The doctor may also want to perform endoscopy (you swallow a thin tube with a tiny light at the end, which permits him to look directly at all parts of the upper intestinal tract from esophagus to small intestine and to snip off a piece of any suspicious-looking tissue). If the answer is still not forthcoming, and disease is seriously suspected, MRI (magnetic resonance imaging) may be ordered. This procedure reveals information not only about any physical abnormalities in the area under investigation, but about how the tissues are actually functioning.

After any or all of the above tests have been completed, your doctor will almost always come up with the answer to your problem. If you are unlucky, he may find that your symptoms are due to a growth (either benign or malignant) somewhere in your bowel. Or he will conclude that you have picked up a virus or some other infection. Again, you may turn out to have "inflammatory bowel disease," a term used to denote a chronic condition also called ulcerative colitis, or a disorder called regional ileitis (Crohn's disease, named after the doctor who first described it).

MAN MAY NOT BE ABLE TO LIVE BY BREAD (AND MILK) ALONE

A particularly common cause of diarrhea, cramps, gas, bloating and discomfort of which you should be aware is lactose intolerance. Many normal persons are deficient in lactase, the enzyme that breaks down lactose, a sugar found in milk and milk products. Failure to digest milk products causes the symptoms mentioned, which clear up when you eliminate lactose from your diet.

Nor is lactose the only substance that can upset your digestion and elimination. There are several foods to which one can be "allergic" and which can cause an array of intestinal complaints ranging from cramps to diarrhea. A common one is gluten, found in grains. As with lactose, when the offending substance is eliminated, symptoms usually disappear. So even foods that are symbolic of healthy nutrition, like bread and milk, may be harmful to some of us.

THE GROWLING BOWEL

Most people with chronic "indigestion" end up with the diagnosis of *irritable bowel syndrome,* in which there is no apparent structural abnormality. There is nothing to see on the X ray, no infection, no trauma, no anything. All you have are symptoms, chief among which is chronic constipation.

In such individuals, movements usually consist of hard little pellets accompanied by lots of gas. But at other times, they are loose, with mucus on the stool (but never blood). You may experience lower abdominal pain after eating, and the gas is perennial. As many as 79 percent of people who go to a gastroenterologist with bowel complaints of one kind or another suffer from an "irritable bowel."

YOU'RE NOT NECESSARILY NEUROTIC

Most patients are relieved when told that all they have is an irritable bowel (synonyms are nervous stomach and spastic colitis), and not cancer, Crohn's disease or ulcerative colitis. However, such reassurance alone is usually not enough to make them feel better. Given this diagnosis, with the words "irritable," "nervous" and "spastic," both you and your doctor may now conclude that your trouble stems from your personality type. While it is true that tension may aggravate a "nervous" bowel, many people with an irritable bowel are apparently able to cope with their problems. I am further impressed by the facts that the increase in the incidence of this disorder in the United States seems to parallel our greater consumption of refined sugar since 1900, that it is most frequently seen in countries where the diet is similar to our own, and that eating bran improves matters somewhat, no matter what the personality pattern happens to be. So, don't buy the "neurotic" diagnosis as the sole or most important cause of your spastic colon.

"RELAX"—THE IMPOSSIBLE PRESCRIPTION

Anyone with an irritable bowel is immediately told to relax. That's more easily said than done. There is no more frustrating advice. There are, however, real and tangible things you can do, *practical* measures that will make you feel much better. For example, avoid laxatives when you are constipated. They will only further aggravate an already irritated bowel, which needs a rest, not stimulation. Take antispasmodic medications when necessary to reduce intestinal spasm; never ignore the urge to move your bowels; schedule a regular time for elimination, and stick to it—no matter what. You'll probably never be cured, but you will feel a whole lot better.

AVOID OLD-FASHIONED DIETARY WARNINGS

The key to management of the irritable bowel lies in the kind of food you eat. We have learned a great deal in recent years about what is good and what is bad for you. We used to prescribe bland, pureed diets. That was wrong. What you need is bulk, which you can get in a high-fiber diet with lots of bran, other cereals, fruit and vegetables. I grew up thinking that bran was good for constipation but made diarrhea worse. That too is wrong. Diarrhea, which is part of the irritable bowel syndrome, usually improves with a high-fiber diet. Also, eating bran regularly will give you a more definite urge to "go" when the time is ripe because the increased bulk stretches the rectal wall and makes the signal to empty it stronger and more difficult to ignore. Soon after you start eating bran, you may have a lot more "wind." This will pass (no pun intended) with time. And if such a diet alone doesn't do the trick, you may use stool softeners (wetting agents), some of which come with additional bulk in them, like Metamucil, Konsyl, Colace, Surfak and Modane. Prunes or prune juice in the morning is also good.

THE "MUSICAL" FOODS

What *shouldn't* you eat if you have an irritable bowel? Foods like cabbage, beans and cauliflower ferment in the gut, giving you lots of gas. Avoid them. Tea and coffee may also aggravate diarrhea in some patients. (That may surprise your grandmother and Maria, my South American housekeeper, both of whom believe that hot tea is the best treatment for whatever ails you.) Exercise is good for the bowel and for your own sense of well-being. Long walks will make you feel better—so will jogging, if you've been given cardiac and orthopedic clearance.

Some doctors simply don't have the time or patience to give you the practical advice you need for coping with a spastic bowel. Instead, they may send you for psychotherapy. Unless you have some other reason to go, don't head for the couch just because you occasionally have to rush to the head. If your doctor treats you like a psychological misfit because you have a spastic bowel, seek a second opinion from a gastroenterologist.

Remember that the irritable bowel is a chronic problem, something that you will have to live with. Resist *repeated* X rays to "make sure" that there is nothing else going on. Excessive dependence on the diagnostic X ray is the crutch of an insecure doctor, and one that may be dangerous to you.

DIVERTICULITIS—AS COMMON AS HIATUS HERNIA

Diverticulitis is another common condition of the lower intestinal tract. If I were randomly to accost a hundred people over fifty years of age on the street and invite them in for a barium enema, I would probably find *diverticula* in more than half. These are little outpouchings from the bowel—

fingerlike projections—which usually don't cause symptoms. When we see them in the course of a routine X ray and they are not giving you any trouble, we say that you have *diverticulosis*. But if and when they become inflamed (which, by the way, doesn't always happen), you develop a painful, tender belly, constipation and fever. When that occurs, your diverticul*osis* has become diverticul*itis*. We used to think this was the result of irritation of the little sac by a seed or piece of nut, in short, something you ate. I'm not sure that theory is correct. Acute diverticulitis is probably due to infection and in some cases, even perforation of a diverticulum.

Diverticulosis is a relatively "new" disorder in our society, but one that is becoming more and more common. The records of the Mayo Clinic are a good place to look for changing trends in disease in the United States. "Mayo" is synonymous with the checkup, which at least until recently often included routine X rays of the bowel. In 1930, only 5 percent of persons above forty years of age so studied at Mayo had diverticula. Today, in the same age group, the incidence is 30 percent. (In persons over seventy years, the figure may be as high as 60 percent.) Something in our environment is giving us these diverticula. Our diet is the culprit.

DIVERTICULOSIS—A MATTER OF THOROUGHLY MODERN MILLING?

What change in the American diet may be responsible for the increase in diverticulosis? The lack of fiber. We eat much more fat and sugar, which now provide twice the amount of calories they did in the diet of the 1800s. We are consuming fewer potatoes and less bread, both of which contain fiber. What's more, the bread we eat has had 99 percent of its wheat fiber removed by modern milling processes. One hundred years ago, that undigested fiber was left intact. If we compare the incidence of diverticulosis today in this country with that of other populations, we find that in Africa, for example, where the natives eat six or seven times the amount of fiber we do, diverticular disease (and spastic colon too) are very uncommon. But when Africans move from the village to the city and begin to eat like we do, the incidence of both these disorders begins to approximate our own.

For more than fifty years we prescribed a low-residue diet for patients with diverticulosis. Old myths die hard. Many patients (and some doctors) still follow this treatment. As with irritable bowel, it is wrong. The key here is roughage. The richest sources of high fiber are cereals, whole-grain flour or bread, green vegetables, nuts and berries. Fiber makes the stool heavier and more bulky, requiring less pressure for it to be moved along the bowel. It also distends the wall of the gut, which further reduces the pressure within it. This decreased pressure lessens the likelihood of the little pouches or fingers (diverticula) herniating through weakened areas of the bowel wall.

If you have repeated attacks of diverticulitis, try adding two teaspoons of unprocessed bran to your soup or your usual breakfast cereal. This may well give you relief. Roughage can, however, make for some gas. This is not bad for you physiologically, but is socially embarrassing. (But who knows? Perhaps as our diet becomes richer in fiber, expelling gas may become an acceptable custom, just as belching was the thing to do after a Roman feast.)

TURISTA OR TRAVELER'S DIARRHEA

A major challenge to travelers, doctors and pharmaceutical manufacturers is the prevention of diarrhea occurring on visits to "exotic" lands. You may be offered the time-honored advice "Drink only bottled water, avoid raw vegetables, and don't let the bartender put any ice in your cocktail," and prescribed medications to be taken during and/or after your trip.

There have been several recent interesting observations apropos of this problem. The first is that Pepto-Bismol, which has been around since 1906 for the treatment of heartburn, effectively prevents and controls traveler's diarrhea. We thought it was because of the bismuth it contains, but that can't be the whole story, since if you take bismuth alone in some form other than Pepto-Bismol, it is not nearly as effective. Well, why don't we simply load up with Pepto-Bismol on our next trip to diarrhea country? Because the amounts necessary to do the job would require taking a suitcase full of it.

The antibiotic doxycycline (marketed in the United States as Vibramycin) can prevent traveler's diarrhea, and this protection lasts for about five weeks after you stop the drug. You take it the day you leave for your destination and continue it until you return. Sounds easy, except that this agent may have undesirable side effects in some people, like nausea and various sensitivity reactions, especially to the sun. More recently Bactrim or Septra, sulfa-based antibacterials, have become the agents of choice for the prevention of turista (except if you're allergic to sulfa). They are effective and well tolerated for long periods of time.

NO TREATMENT THE BEST TREATMENT?

What causes traveler's diarrhea, and are these things we do to prevent and treat it really necessary or desirable? Most cases are due to an ordinarily harmless bug called *E. coli*. *Turista* is usually not life-threatening, just a nuisance. Of course, in some people—the elderly and the chronically ill— even mild diarrhea can be serious if it persists. But for the rest of us, it is not. More and more doctors now believe that drugs that kill the relatively benign *E. coli* organisms also eradicate many of the other bacteria that normally inhabit the healthy bowel and whose function it is to protect us against more serious infection. When one takes any antibiotic to eliminate the *E. coli* in order to prevent simple diarrhea, the growth of more sinister agents, which can produce dysentery or amebiasis, is facilitated. The latter are more serious, more persistent and harder to treat. So, think twice about trying to prevent ordinary traveler's diarrhea with drugs. Take some gamma globulin against hepatitis before you leave, be very careful about what you eat and drink, keep your fingers crossed and your hands clean. Quite frankly, that's what I do. And it works!

WHEN DIARRHEA MAY
ACTUALLY BE GOOD FOR YOU

Suppose that you get diarrhea on one of your vacations. The tendency is immediately to take something to stop it, like

Kaopectate, Lomotil, Imodium or another obstipating drug. Believe it or not, that may not be the right thing to do. Diarrhea is, after all, nature's way to rid your bowel of irritants and infectious materials. If you suppress the diarrhea, these agents are retained. So the current attitude is to let the diarrhea run its course (so to speak) for a few days. Only if it persists should one intervene.

When you return from a trip anywhere and have *chronic* diarrhea, don't keep dosing yourself with home remedies and over-the-counter obstipants. Have your doctor analyze your stool in order to identify the specific infectious agent that is giving you the symptoms. Once the diagnosis is made, the proper treatment will result in a cure.

INFLAMMATORY BOWEL DISEASE—ULCERATIVE COLITIS AND CROHN'S DISEASE

The intestinal tract has three major divisions: an upper portion consisting of the esophagus, stomach and small bowel; a middle section, the large bowel; and a terminal portion, the rectum and anus. The suffix *itis* means "inflammation." Thus, inflammation of the stomach lining is called *gastritis,* and of the duodenum, *duodenitis.* When the large bowel, or colon, is involved, you have *colitis.* There are two major kinds of bowel inflammation—ulcerative colitis and Crohn's disease. Together, they account for several thousand new cases every year in the United States. Their cause is unknown, but probably involves some disorder of the immune system. You should know about these two conditions because they are common, their respective treatments differ and their long-term outlook is also dissimilar.

CROHN'S DISEASE—A NORMAL SIGMOIDOSCOPY IS NOT ENOUGH

Crohn's disease is an inflammation predominantly of the large bowel (but not infrequently of portions of the small intestine too) that involves the full thickness of its wall. (Ulcerative colitis, on the other hand, is more superficial, affects only the lining and rarely goes through and through.) Crohn's is most commonly seen in persons between twenty and forty years of age. Because it strikes all layers of the bowel, it often penetrates the wall, causing adhesions of and tracts to other intestinal structures like the bladder and even the skin. Unlike ulcerative colitis, which, as you will see later, often has an explosive onset, Crohn's disease may smolder for a long time before ever being recognized. In fact, the average patient waits five years before seeing a doctor about it. The chronic fatigue, anemia, aching belly, constipation, diarrhea and loss of appetite, all characteristic of Crohn's disease, are often attributed to an irritable bowel.

When the doctor is finally consulted and he does sigmoidoscopy, it may be normal, because the sigmoidoscope reaches only twelve inches up the bowel, and this disease is usually situated higher up than that. *The diagnosis of Crohn's disease requires a barium X ray. Negative sigmoidoscopy results do not exclude it.* Colonoscopy, on the other hand, a procedure that reaches much further up, can help establish the diagnosis. Chances are, however, that you'll still need to have the X ray.

ULCERATIVE COLITIS— THE CONTRAST WITH CROHN'S

Symptoms of *ulcerative colitis* appear at about the same age as those of Crohn's disease, but ulcerative colitis has some interesting racial and religious predilections. For example, if you are Jewish, your chances of getting it are two to four times greater than those of the rest of the population; if you are white, your vulnerability is four times that of nonwhites. It also seems to hit certain families more than others, and more women have it than men.

Ulcerative colitis will probably impel you to see your doctor sooner than you would if you had Crohn's disease, usually because of pus or blood in the stool. Diarrhea doesn't usually set in until later. The severity of the symptoms is often a harbinger of whether the disease will become a serious threat to you, or just annoying. In most people, they are

THE BOWEL

mild. In contrast to Crohn's disease, the trouble is usually much lower in the bowel, so that sigmoidoscopy is often the best way to make the diagnosis (even though the barium X ray should also be done). But remember, if you are having *acute* symptoms—with fever, blood or pus in the stool and abdominal pain—the barium enema, sigmoidoscopy or colonoscopy may be hazardous. Wait until you have responded to palliative measures, and *then* have the tests done.

TREATING INFLAMMATORY BOWEL DISEASE

Once the diagnosis of ulcerative colitis or Crohn's disease has been made, there are medications to relieve its symptoms, but they do not influence the underlying disease processes. Lomotil and other obstipating agents help control diarrhea; Azulfidine (sulfasalazine), a combination of sulfa and aspirin, helps too, but it may have unpleasant side effects. Interestingly, the drug was first developed in 1942 for the treatment of rheumatoid arthritis. It didn't work for that disorder. By accident, however, it was noted that the bowel symptoms of those patients who had ulcerative colitis as well as rheumatoid arthritis improved. Since then, Azulfidine has remained an effective treatment for ulcerative colitis.

When symptoms are severe in patients with ulcerative colitis or Crohn's disease, cortisone-type drugs become necessary. In the former, we try it in enema form first. If that doesn't work, the cortisone is given by mouth. As many as 90 percent of patients will improve on this therapy, after which the dosage of steroids is gradually reduced and Azulfidine is resumed. In many cases of Crohn's disease, maintenance cortisone therapy is required. When that fails (about 60 percent of cases after five years), surgery becomes necessary. The sad part is that the disease recurs in the majority of these patients a few years after surgery.

Diet does not appear to play an important role in the management of inflammatory bowel disease, as it does in the irritable bowel or diverticulosis.

Patients with Crohn's disease may suffer serious complications, such as perforation of the bowel and mechanical obstruction. The most dreaded risk of ulcerative colitis, on the other hand, is cancer. In fact, one third of the deaths from ulcerative colitis are due to cancer. The longer you have the disease in its continuously active form and the more extensive it is, the more likely you are to develop a malignant tumor of the bowel.

The question naturally arises as to whether the involved portion of bowel in ulcerative colitis should be removed *before* cancer develops. There is no easy answer. Statistically, total removal of the bowel becomes necessary in about 25 percent of patients with ulcerative colitis in the first five years of their disease. If this operation is recommended to you for whatever reason—because of bleeding, adhesions or an abscess, get another opinion from a competent gastroenterologist. There are many specialists who now feel that such surgery is often unnecessary and that intensive medical treatment should be tried for a longer time.

But if surgery cannot be avoided, you may end up with a colostomy or ileostomy, depending on which part and how much of the bowel is removed. You will then have a pouch on the outside of your abdomen into which you move your bowels. There's no reason to get unduly depressed about that. The pouches these days are plastic, nonodorous and very easy to use. They are clean, flat, adherent to the skin and are no longer a social disaster.

IT'S PROBABLY NOT A MATTER OF PERSONALITY

It is almost always assumed that patients with colitis have some kind of personality or behavior problem. There are still doctors who will straightaway send patients into psychotherapy once the diagnosis is made. There are even stereotype personality descriptions of persons with colitis. They are said to be intelligent, to suppress their anxieties and conflicts and to be very passive. They "let go," so to speak, with their bowels. Recent observations have not substantiated any psychological basis for colitis. Your emotional profile does not explain the racial differences in the disease, nor why it may be found in the course of routine proctoscopy among persons with no symptoms at all. So if you are referred to a psychiatrist *pro forma,* simply because you have colitis, think twice about going.

KEY FACTS TO REMEMBER

Gas, cramps, indigestion, constipation and diarrhea plague most of us sometime or other, depending on what we eat and where we've been. In many cases these complaints are "functional"—that is, without underlying physical bowel disease. But some cause can frequently be found and treated.

Most bowel symptoms are due to diets lacking in bulk and fiber. Others are due to unsuspected food "allergies," notably to milk and milk products or gluten (a grain constituent).

Diverticulitis is a common condition, probably due to our diet and the way in which our foods are processed. We used to treat it with a low-residue diet. We now know that roughage is what is needed.

Most cases of *traveler's diarrhea* are due to a harmless bacteria. Left alone, the infection usually runs its course without complications. The overenthusiastic use of antibiotics and antidiarrheals may do more harm than good.

Inflammatory disease of the bowel encompasses two different disorders—ulcerative colitis and Crohn's disease. The latter is an inflammation of the full thickness of the wall of the large bowel; the former affects only the lining of the gut. Ulcerative colitis can almost always be diagnosed by looking into the bowel (sigmoidoscopy), while the diagnosis of Crohn's disease usually requires an X ray. Diet is not an important factor in their management, but there are several drugs, including cortisone, that may alleviate symptoms. The question of surgery in both these diseases is of great importance and should be answered only in consultation with experienced gastroenterologists. Since severe, long-standing ulcerative colitis may become cancerous, the decision about removing the affected bowel prophylactically is one that should be made only after the input of several experts.

25

THE PROSTATE GLAND—FROM INFECTION TO TUMOR

AN EDUCATED FINGER

The function of the prostate gland is to provide nourishment for the sperm and fluid in which they can travel. Suspect a prostate problem when the force of your urinary stream is reduced, when you have trouble starting it and dribble when you finish, and when you find yourself getting up several times a night to empty your bladder. Your doctor's educated finger is the simplest way to confirm the diagnosis.

HOW IT ACTS UP

There are several kinds of prostate trouble. The normal-sized gland can become infected or inflamed (prostatitis) at any time during adult life (but more commonly as you grow older). It also enlarges with the passing years. Or it can develop a malignant tumor (that likelihood too increases with age). In fact, when we examine tissue from a "benignly" enlarged prostate removed from men in their seventies or eighties, we often find tiny islands of malignancy buried deep within the normal tissue. These had gone unnoticed and undiagnosed, and probably would never have caused any problem had they been left alone.

DIAGNOSING PROSTATE INFECTION

Occasionally, the prostate becomes congested or infected after too much sexual activity—or too little. Whatever the cause, prostatitis makes you urinate frequently and is associated with discomfort in the lower back and genital areas. When you have to "go," you really need to get there quickly. (We call that urgency.) When you actually pass the urine, it burns. You also find that you have to empty your bladder at night for no apparent reason (you haven't been taking a lot of liquor, wine or other fluids at bedtime). You may or may not have any fever.

So you visit your doctor. He examines your urine, which usually, but not always, shows evidence of infection and may contain a little blood, particularly as you finish voiding. When your doctor does a rectal exam and fingers the prostate, he will find it boggy—*you* will find it tender. When he massages the gland, pus cells are forced out and appear in the urine. The doctor will then "culture" the specimen—that is, incubate it, to see what organisms, if any, grow out. But very often (in contrast to kidney infections), no bacteria are identified in prostate "infections." If there was any blood in the specimen, a portion of it will also surely be sent for a Pap test to exclude the possibilty of a malignancy.

HOW IT'S TREATED

There is no problem in treating prostatitis. You will be given an appropriate antibiotic, told to drink plenty of fluids (non-alcoholic) and take hot baths. You will soon feel better. But if you don't, and the infections keep recurring, ask to see a urologist. There may be some special reason why you are having the trouble, over and above simple infection.

With regard to antibiotics, be sure to tell your doctor if you are allergic to the penicillin family of drugs, the sulfas or tetracycline, because these are the agents most widely used in treating urinary tract infections.

THE BIG PROSTATE, AND WHY IT MAKES YOU "GO" SO OFTEN

Urine made in the kidney is delivered via a long duct called a ureter (there is one leaving each kidney) to the urinary bladder, where it is stored. After a certain amount of urine has accumulated in the bladder, the wall of that organ is stretched, signaling you that it's time to "go." Urine then leaves the bladder through another duct called the urethra, which runs through the penis.

When the prostate gland enlarges, it compresses the urethra, causing obstruction to the outflow of urine from the bladder. The stream becomes narrow, you end up dribbling and develop the other symptoms of prostatism. Urine backs up into the bladder, whence it came, distending it like a balloon. Because of the obstruction of the urethra caused by the large prostate, a greater pressure is required for the urine to be passed through it. As a result, there is always some left in the bladder (residual urine). The bladder dilates progressively to accommodate the extra volume of urine. Finally, when it can dilate no further, it overflows, forcing you to the toilet—fast. The stagnant residual urine in the bladder becomes a fertile breeding area for any bacteria that happen to be around. This leads to the infection so common in prostatism.

AT SOME POINT IT NEEDS TO COME OUT

Surgical removal is really the only way to treat an enlarged prostate. The timing of the operation depends not only on your symptoms but also on certain objective evidence. You will need to have an intravenous pyelogram (IVP), in which dye is injected into the bloodstream via a vein in your arm. It travels to the kidney, then to the urinary bladder and out through the penis. This contrast material shows both kidneys (indicating whether or not they are enlarged), as well as the ureters, which carry the urine from the kidney to the bladder (locating any obstruction there). Also, when you are finished voiding and think your bladder is completely empty, the IVP reveals whether there is, in fact, any urine left behind. A large amount of residual urine in the bladder indicates that you are likely to develop acute and total urinary obstruction and require surgery sooner than later.

But even if the residual volume is not all that large, you may still feel enervated from getting up every hour or two during the night. Many men with this problem are chronically tired for want of a good night's sleep. But before you consider surgery, ask your urologist about a drug called *Dibenzyline*. (If you have a heart condition, be sure to tell the doctor about it. A urologist may not be aware of it.) This drug frequently reduces the number of times you have to empty your bladder. So may prazosin (Minipress), used in the treatment of high blood pressure, when taken in small doses at bedtime.

OF PROSTATES AND HERNIAS

Suppose that you suddenly notice a lump in your groin that is diagnosed as a hernia. If you are fifty years of age or older, the hernia may be due to an enlarged prostate, which has made you strain when passing urine. So if you come to your doctor expecting to be sent for a hernia repair and he tells you to have your prostate gland fixed first, he is probably right. Puzzled, you are likely to go for an unnecessary second opinion.

ROTO-ROOTER SURGERY

Once the decision to operate is made, you should know that there are two different ways to do it. In the *transurethral* approach, an instrument is inserted through the penis like a Roto-Rooter and the enlarged prostate is literally scraped out or "shaved." This approach is easier and safer than an abdominal incision, takes less time and is preferred, especially if you are old, have heart disease or are otherwise a poor surgical risk. But it can't be done if the prostate is very large. Also, after several years, the gland, which was not completely removed in the first place (but merely reamed out), may grow back, making a repeat operation necessary.

The second technique involves making an incision in the lower abdomen and cutting the prostate gland away under direct vision. If you have been told that you need a prostatectomy, you should discuss with your urologist which procedure he plans to use.

CANCER OF THE PROSTATE

Cancer of the prostate is usually detected during a rectal exam. Your doctor will note that portions of the gland feel hard and irregular. A needle biopsy, done by a urologist, is necessary to confirm the diagnosis (just as a lump in the breast is almost always biopsied before any treatment decision is made). A prostate biopsy is fairly simple. The needle is introduced from the outside, between the scrotum and the rectum, directly into the suspicious area. A core of tissue is obtained and looked at under a microscope.

Treatment, discussed in greater detail in Chapter 27, depends on whether the malignancy has spread, either within the prostate or to distant tissues like bone and lungs.

KEY FACTS TO REMEMBER

The prostate gland may become infected, enlarged or cancerous. Most infections are easily treated with antibiotics, but if they recur, you should consult a urologist to determine why you're having them. The basic treatment for an enlarged prostate causing symptoms is surgical removal. Surgery can be done in two ways, one of which, the transurethral approach, is simpler and safer than the other. Before having such surgery, it may be wise to consult a second urologist. Cancer of the prostate, which is discussed in Chapter 27, may be treated surgically, by radiation, with hormones, or by benign neglect, depending on the stage of the disease.

26

HEMORRHOIDS— NO LAUGHING MATTER

WHEN IN THE SEAT OF POWER

We all know what varicose veins in the legs look like. They are dilated, enlarged and sometimes painful vascular cords. Hemorrhoids are the same kind of varicose veins situated inside or outside the anus. Although they are not life-threatening, they are uncomfortable and troublesome. Occurring in the seat of power, they have on occasion affected the course of history. It is said that Napoleon changed his battle plans for Waterloo when he couldn't sit on his horse. President Carter's bout with hemorrhoids, on the other hand, made headlines, not history. Anyone suffering an acute attack of hemorrhoids will not find puns and flippant comments at all funny.

Ads in subways, buses and the media constantly remind us that hemorrhoids are very common. By middle age, at least 50 percent of all people have them. They may be internal or external, and can result from any condition that increases pressure on the veins of the anus and rectum. Chronic constipation, straining at stool, a tumor in the pelvis or abdomen and pregnancy are the most common causes. You can reduce the risk of developing hemorrhoids by eating plenty of roughage and fiber, avoiding constipation, not straining at stool, and fostering regular bowel habits.

Engorged hemorrhoidal veins may be painful. Inflamed clots frequently form within these dilated blood vessels, just as they do in thrombophlebitis of the legs. But unlike the latter situation, there is no risk here of the clot traveling anywhere else in the body. You merely suffer from local pain and bleeding.

Hemorrhoids, however small or painless, can result in blood loss, anemia and weakness. Moreover, when bleeding is detected, there is always the danger of attributing it to the obvious hemorrhoids and overlooking another, more ominous and simultaneous cause of the blood loss—a cancer higher up in the bowel. *Never be lulled into a false sense of security when you see blood in your stool simply because you know that you have hemorrhoids.* Everyone with "bleeding piles" should have a bowel evaluation. If you are young and the bleeding is clearly hemorrhoidal, once may be enough. But if you are over fifty, and the bleeding occurs from time to time, you need to be checked at intervals—just to be sure there's no tumor lurking higher up in the bowel. The best way to do that in my opinion is with colonoscopy, rather than a barium enema. I have had several patients in whom I found chemical evidence of blood on a routine stool analysis. I was often tempted to attribute the findings to "obvious" hermorrhoids, only to discover a cancer or polyp in subsequent testing.

PREPARATION "THIS AND THAT"

How should bleeding, painful hemorrhoids be treated? Stool softeners and roughage in the diet are helpful—as is the bidet, found in most European countries; there is nothing like sitting in one and bathing the inflamed area with soothing warm water. Since you are not likely to have a bidet, you will have to settle for sitting in a warm tub for twenty to thirty minutes a couple of times a day.

Creams and ointments that contain a local anesthetic, like benzocaine and Novocain, will often ease the pain. Or, you can insert a rectal suppository or foam containing small amounts of cortisone to reduce inflammation and swelling. In most cases, such local measures suffice.

Never rub hemorrhoids with dry tissue after a bowel movement. Use lubricated or moistened pads. And don't dally on the toilet.

Occasionally, hemorrhoidal bleeding and pain require more definitive treatment. I remember during my internship assisting in several hemorrhoidal operations. They were brutal and bloody in those days, and kept you in the hospital a week or more. We used to give patients large doses of pain-killing narcotics, which left them constipated, thus preventing them from moving their bowels and further irritating the operated area. Such procedures are infrequently done anymore. So if it is proposed to you, double-check with an expert, irreverently referred to in the profession as a "rear admiral."

THE RUBBER BAND

If you are told you need an operation—any operation—to fix your hemorrhoids, ask about the "rubber band." This technique involves tying the dilated veins with a rubber band. It is performed in the doctor's office; it does not require anethesia; it shrinks the hemorrhoid by cutting off its blood supply.

Dilating the anus may also yield good results. If your doctor doesn't know about it or demurs, consult a proctologist or rectal surgeon.

Another (not so hot) way to approach the problem without surgery is to freeze the hemorrhoids—cryosurgery. It is not as effective as the rubber band, which most proctologists prefer.

Many doctors still inject the hemorrhoid directly with a substance that "scars" it. But if it can be injected, it can be tied off, and you are better off with the latter technique.

KEY FACTS TO REMEMBER

Hemorrhoids ("piles") are dilated, inflamed varicose veins in the anus, which usually result from chronic constipation and/or multiple pregnancies. Unlike such veins elsewhere, notably the legs, they are rarely dangerous, but can cause pain and bleeding.

A diet containing roughage and fiber and healthy bowel habits are the best protection against developing hemorrhoids.

Never automatically attribute blood in the stool to hemorrhoids, even if you have them. This may divert attention from a tumor in the bowel.

Treatment of bleeding or painful hemorrhoids may consist of ointments and suppositories, injections, tying off the engorged veins with the rubber band technique, or surgery. Which course to follow may require the opinion of an expert in the field.

27

CANCER—NEW HORIZONS, NEW HOPE AND MORE OPTIONS

HOW TO APPROACH IT?

Books and articles about cancer deal with the subject in a variety of ways. They may focus on *causation*. What role do viruses, personality, genetics and pollution play? The *epidemiology* of cancer is of great interest to society. We are concerned with the safety of our environment—what we eat (does increased fat in the diet really cause more cancer of the bowel, breast and prostate?), drink (do artificial sweeteners increase the risk of cancer in humans as well as in rats?), and breathe (do cigarettes really play so important a role in cancer of the lung and of the cervix?) We are concerned about the additives in our cosmetics, our clothes and our children's toys. Hardly a week goes by without reports claiming that some substance—a medication, food or pollutant—is carcinogenic.

Then there is the matter of cancer *diagnosis*—how to detect it early enough to cure it. There are books dealing with the *treatment* of cancer—X ray, surgery, drugs and immunotherapy. There are texts discussing the *psychology* of the cancer patient—how do you cope when you have it and how can you help others do so? Do depression and bereavement predispose? There are even volumes now on the management of terminal cancer cases when cure and remission are no longer possible, as exemplified in the hospice movement.

THE KEYS—EARLY DIAGNOSIS AND TREATMENT

It is not possible for me to cover in depth all the ramifications of cancer in one chapter. But I do want to present to you some basic facts about the modern approach to the treatment of malignant disease. Above all, I want you to know why and where to get proper care in time. In cancer, *getting the correct diagnosis and knowing where to go for treatment are of the essence.*

As a result of recent and continuing advances in the field, several kinds of cancer, if discovered in time, are now curable. A larger percentage than ever are manageable—that is, the duration of comfortable survival is significantly prolonged. For these reasons, perhaps more than in any other field of medicine, *it is extremely important to get the best and most up-to-date opinion from an expert in the field about how to treat any malignancy as soon as it is discovered.*

IT'S BETTER TO KNOW

Many people skip over any article dealing with cancer. There are those who won't even utter the word, a kind of superstitious denial mechanism. Healthy persons would rather not discuss it for fear of spoiling their luck. Those who suspect or are afraid that they may have cancer but are not really sure don't want to read anything that might confirm their fears. In other words, they believe that what they don't know won't hurt them. That attitude can only end in disaster.

NOT ALL TUMORS ARE CANCEROUS

The word *tumor* means "growth." Some growths are benign. They hardly ever kill. Removing them at any stage of their development usually results in complete cure. Other growths, however, are malignant and will kill if left alone. But many of the latter, if detected before they can spread, can be cured, or at least controlled for substantial periods of time. Unfortunately, there are still some cancers that continue to resist all the currently available forms of therapy, no matter how early we find them.

PESSIMISM IS OFTEN UNWARRANTED

There are still too many patients (and doctors) who are not attuned to the times, and who remain unrealistically pessimistic when dealing with cancer. Families of a loved one so stricken will plead for nothing vigorous, "heroic" or experimental to be done. Patients in good health want me to sign notarized promises that, if they develop cancer, I will hasten the end. Not long ago I discovered lung cancer in a woman in her early eighties. She was coughing, had chest pain and was short of breath. The family made it clear to me that they wanted her given no therapy whatsoever. "Just let her die as soon as possible." I explained that while I could not cure their mother, I could make her more comfortable in the time she had left. But that would require treatment, in this instance, radiation (X-ray techniques are now so sophisticated that very substantial doses can be administered with minimal or no side effects). I thought that this would shrink the tumor and decrease the obstruction to the air passages—which was causing most of the symptoms. The family agreed, albeit reluctantly. My patient did well for seven months. During that time, she was more comfortable, required fewer narcotics and was able to enjoy her family, particularly her grandchildren. Furthermore, she remained at home, where she was happier than she would have been in a hospital, and where she did not dissipate her life's savings.

WHAT IS THE TRUTH?

The other question raised by this woman's family was what to tell her about her disease. She was intelligent enough so that I would lose my credibility if I did not tell her the truth. But does truth demand using the word "cancer," a term synonymous with pain, suffering and death?

In this case, I informed my patient that she had a *tumor* that would be treated vigorously by every available and appropriate means, and that we would hope for the best. That reassurance was enough for her, as it is for most patients. And it *is* essentially true because no doctor can tell for certain how long a patient will live, and no one can predict what advances will be made during the time that has been "bought" by the treatments now available.

"SHOULD I SETTLE MY AFFAIRS?"

But shouldn't a patient be given enough information to settle his affairs? In these days of complicated tax and estate laws, it is often vital that certain legal aspects be attended to—in fairness to both the patient and the family. In my experience, that can be handled in an effective, sympathetic way, without removing all hope—by stressing that just as healthy persons should have their wills and business affairs in order, so should those who are sick, regardless of the disease or its prognosis. Most cancer patients get the message and act on it, without asking the doctor to spell out all the grim details. There is an art to doing it. Make sure, if a loved one of yours is involved, that the doctor running the case knows how to handle that aspect of it. Rehearse exactly what the patient will be told. If it comes out harshly or insensitively, have someone else do it. Also make sure about the consistency of the presentation by all concerned. Patients should never lose faith in the credibility of their doctor or their loved ones.

IT'S A VERY BIG FIELD—
AND THERE'S MUCH TO KNOW

If you are told that you have cancer, regardless of its type or location, no matter what outlook you are given, you must get an opinion from an expert oncologist. Your family doctor, internist, and even *one* cancer specialist may not be enough.

Knowledge in this field is changing from day to day. Your doctor cannot be expected to know about every recent breakthrough, especially if he is not a specialist, and sometimes even if he is. There are several subdivisions in the field of oncology itself. Some institutions and physicians are expert in treating cancer of the bone, others the blood (leukemia), or the breast, or prostate or lungs. No one oncologist knows the latest and the best in every area.

AND NONE OF THEM DIED

I could fill this book with accounts of how important it is to be sure that you are getting the last word in treatment. One involves a close relative of mine. About fifteen years ago, while in his early seventies, he was found to have a malignant condition called *myocosis fungoides.* This is a form of cancer that manifests itself initially as a skin rash. His internist, a competent clinician, called to tell me he had reviewed the current literature and could find no specific effective treatment for this disorder. Patients afflicted with it, he said, survive for an average of "a couple of years." But he assured me that he would do everything to make the patient comfortable and would not "prolong his agony."

I discussed the problem with several colleagues working in this field, and they referred me to an oncologist in Philadelphia specializing in mycosis fungoides. I referred the patient to him. He was treated for ten days with immunotherapy, a brand-new concept at the time, and chemotherapy. After a few weeks, the skin lesions disappeared and the patient was cured. He died many years later in his eighties from heart disease.

In another instance, a friend living in a large city called to tell me that his eleven-year-old son had just been found to have Ewing's sarcoma (a highly malignant tumor of bone) in the leg. Local specialists were pessimistic about the child's chances for survival and recommended immediate amputation. Again, I made inquiries and learned that there was a team at New York's Memorial Sloan-Kettering Hospital especially interested in this particular tumor and working on a novel treatment approach to it. The boy was brought there forthwith and thoroughly studied. These doctors did not think amputation was at all necessary. Instead, they removed only a small piece of bone containing the cancer, and began therapy with drugs and radiation. They gave the boy a 75 to 80 percent chance of cure. It is now eight years later, and the lad is completely well. The specialists who had seen him first were competent. They simply did not have the expertise to treat this particular tumor at that time.

I know many women who, with advanced cancer of the breast, had been "given up." Years later they are still alive and comfortable as a result of new treatment for that disease.

Cancer cannot be treated with kid gloves. It is a disease in which your life is on the line. Given that diagnosis, regardless of the pessimistic or nihilistic attitude of friends, family or physician, you must immediately obtain an opinion from a qualified oncologist. Call the National Cancer Institute in Bethesda, Maryland, or the American Cancer Society, which has local units throughout the country. Or ask your doctor to do so. Tell them what kind of cancer you have and ask where they recommend you go for specialized treatment.

On the basis of such inquiries for my patients, I have sent them to various centers throughout the country, each particularly expert in a specific type of tumor—Memorial Sloan-Kettering Cancer Center in New York City; the M. D. Anderson Hospital in Houston, Texas; the Mayo Clinic in Rochester, Minnesota; Stanford University in Palo Alto, California; Roswell Park Memorial Institute in Buffalo, New York; the Dana-Farber Cancer Institute in Boston; New York Hospital–Cornell Medical Center and the Mt. Sinai Hospital in New York City. And there are others.

THE LOCAL CANCER SPECIALIST

There are many expert oncologists who, practicing in smaller communities, do not yet have access to every new piece of equipment or medication. The good ones will make sure that you somehow get it, since most smaller hospitals have some affiliation with larger centers. So living away from the medical mainstream does not necessarily mean that you are deprived of the benefits of the knowledge explosion in this field. The key is your ability to discuss with your own doctor the need for consultation—and his willingness to cooperate.

THE MAGNITUDE OF THE PROBLEM

One in three Americans develops some kind of cancer. Almost 800,000 new cases are diagnosed every year in the United States, and the patient dies in about 440,000 of these. One in three cancer patients will be alive five years after their disease is discovered. These figures do not include the 500,000 innocuous cases of localized skin cancer, which are easily cured by simple removal. Nor does it embrace the 40,000 women who each year are found to have the very earliest stage of cancer in the Pap test, and who also are cured by surgery or radiation.

THE BREAKDOWN

Among the 800,000 new cases of life-threatening cancer each year, 218,000 affect the digestive system, 144,000 are in the lungs alone, about 20,000 in bone and skin (of which almost 15,000 are malignant melanomas, among the most highly and rapidly fatal of all cancers); there are 125,000 breast cancers, some 165,000 malignancies of the genital organs (86,000 cancers of the prostate, 60,000 of the uterus and 19,000 of the ovaries), 60,000 cases of cancer of the urinary tract (including roughly 40,000 in the bladder and 19,000 in the kidney), 11,000 brain malignancies, and about 9,000 cancers of the hormonal glands, mostly thyroid. In addition to these tumors of "solid" organs, there are some 25,000 new cases every year of blood cancer (leukemia) and about 33,000 cases of lymphoma (tumors of the lymph glands). These data all add up to the fact that cancer is the second leading cause of death, outranked only by diseases of the heart and circulation.

So much for the statistics of the disease. Now what *is* cancer?

THE CANCER PROCESS

The millions of cells in a given organ normally grow in an orderly fashion. When the tissue becomes cancerous, these cells, previously so well behaved, suddenly begin to multiply wildly, totally out of control. As the cancer expands and extends, it presses the life out of surrounding organs and structures. In the lungs, for example, a malignancy might start as a tiny nubbin. The wildly growing cells eventually spread out every which way, blocking the air passages and invading blood vessels, which they then use as a conduit to all parts of the body. Wherever they lodge, they resume their crazy growth. In so doing, they choke off and replace the normal components of whatever organ they strike.

When cancer develops among the red blood cells (polycythemia vera) or white blood cells (leukemia), they multiply and spread into the lymph glands, bone marrow, liver and spleen, interfering with normal blood function and formation.

WHY DO THE CANCER
CELLS GO CRAZY?

What causes a cell that has previously been well balanced suddenly to lose control is the key question to which nobody really has the answer. Is a virus responsible? Probably, in certain types. Is the trigger some chemical irritant in the environment, like asbestos or tobacco smoke or X rays or uranium? It no doubt is in some instances. Is it some other air pollutant, an additive in our food, a hormone that we are taking for one reason or another? It may be any of these, or even a combination of them all. No one knows for sure. And there is a host of other unanswered questions. For example, why do Egyptians have so much bladder cancer? Why does cancer strike the Chinese in the esophagus so often? Why do the Japanese have so great a predisposition to cancer of the stomach? Why is there so much cancer of the liver in Africa? Why did one community in New Jersey recently report an unusual number of cases of leukemia? What is going on in the genes of one family I treat in which the maternal grand-mother, mother and two daughters all had breast cancer?

Genetics is an area of major interest at the present time, since the exciting discovery of oncogenes, genes within our cells that have the potential for making them malignant. Identifying oncogenes, determining what activates them (a virus or a pollutant?) and why, is the focus of intense research.

FIRST YOU'VE GOT TO MAKE SURE

So much for speculation about the cause. Suppose that you are told you have a cancer. It may have been found in a routine physical exam; in a chest X ray, during colonoscopy, or in a blood test taken because you had some bone pain. Before proceeding any further, *you must have the diagnosis confirmed.* Regardless of the tissue or organ involved, have another expert evaluate the evidence.

STAGING AND SEARCHING

Once the diagnosis of cancer is ascertained, a specialist should then "stage" the disease—that is, determine how "wild" the cells are and to what extent, if any, they have already spread. This means looking elsewhere in the body, away from the original site, for evidence of tumor activity. Such spread, when it occurs, is called *metastasis*, or *metastatic disease*.

The search for metastases involves doing blood tests and examining literally every part of the body by means of con-ventional X rays, radioactive scans of the liver or bone, sonograms, a CT (computerized tomography) scan or magnetic resonance imaging. The number and extent of the diagnostic tests required will depend on which organ was primarily involved. Cancers in different tissues spread predictably to favored sites.

How the cancer is to be treated and the outlook for your recovery will depend on whether it is still localized—that is, remains where it began—or whether there is demonstrable evidence of spread. If it is still localized, cure is possible, usually with surgery, radiation, chemotherapy or all three. (By cure, I mean that you are finished with it; it will not recur.) On the other hand, if the cancer has already spread, effective control may still be possible for varying lengths of time. In some cases, as in malignancy of the ovary and testes, cure is possible even after dissemination. But before any course of treatment is selected, there should be consultation with an expert oncologist.

RADIATION—HOW AND WHY IT WORKS

It is ironic that despite all the adverse publicity concerning the cancer risk of excessive and unnecessary radiation, it is one of the most effective ways to treat many malignancies. When trying to cure a disease that may kill in a matter of months, there is not much point to wondering about possible adverse effects fifteen or twenty years later.

Radiation therapy (radiotherapy) can be administered to vulnerable or radiosensitive tumors either by powerful X-ray equipment or by radioactive materials like cobalt or radium, which emit gamma rays similar to X rays. These penetrate the wildly growing cells, altering the genetic substance within them, preventing their multiplication and ultimately destroying them. When the tumor is small enough, sufficiently localized and radiosensitive, such treatment may be as effective as surgery. But when the mass of cancerous tissue is large, some cells survive the onslaught of radiotherapy. Those that do then continue to multiply, requiring more and more radiation to effect control.

The equipment originally available for the X-ray therapy of cancer was primitive by today's standards. We were unable to focus on the small area we wanted to destroy, and so normal tissues were also damaged by the treatment. In order to direct enough radiation into the cancerous material, we had to administer so much that it made the patient sick and nauseated. The side effects were frequently worse than the symptoms of the disease itself. Today, however, there are linear accelerators and cobalt generators that can deliver powerful, concentrated radiation, pinpointed to and penetrating limited areas of the body without even burning the overlying skin.

Radiation is effective in the treatment of virtually every kind of cancer—in the brain, lungs, uterus, skin, prostate, bladder and other areas. It is especially useful when the tumor is deep and intertwined with other tissue, so that it is difficult or impossible to remove surgically, and when the risk of operation is great, as in elderly or debilitated patients.

CHEMOTHERAPY—ELIMINATING THE STRAGGLERS

Since it is always possible that some residual microscopic cancer cells have been left behind after either radiation or surgery, we now add chemotherapy and/or immunotherapy, just to be sure. Such adjuvant therapy is like an insurance policy against any remaining tumor tissue, even if none is apparent to the naked eye.

The concept of chemotherapy originated in 1941, when it was observed that the administration of female hormones caused regression of prostate cancer. Hormones were subsequently tried in the management of breast cancer, and here too an effect was noted. In 1943, nitrogen mustard was found to possess definite activity against certain lymph gland tumors. In 1947 it was demonstrated that other drugs produce short remissions in some forms of childhood leukemia.

In the years since these first observations were made we have identified several cancers that can be cured with chemotherapy. These include Hodgkin's disease, Wilms's tumor in children, certain forms of leukemia and other lymph gland malignancies. So this is no time to have a negative attitude toward cancer or chemotherapy.

COMBINATION THERAPY— A JOB FOR A PRO

Chemotherapy interferes with the multiplication (or division) of abnormal cancer cells. Ideally, these drugs are toxic to the malignant cells, but do not harm healthy tissue. Although chemotherapy can cure some cancers, more commonly its net effect is to control them, that is, hold them in check. To understand how it does so, you must know a little about cell biology. There are different stages in the life cycle of every living cell. First, there is the phase during which DNA is synthesized. This is followed by a "resting" period, and then by the stage of mitosis, during which the cell divides. The more than thirty different anticancer drugs in current use act at different times in this cell cycle. Some are more effective during DNA synthesis, others during mitosis, and the remainder only when the cell is resting. Since the cells in any tumor mass are in various phases at any given time, administering a single drug will affect only a portion of the tumor, leaving intact all those cells in a different stage of biologic activity. But to cure cancer, *every* abnormal cell must be destroyed. Even if only one remains, it has the potential to continue the malignant process and ultimately kill the patient. For this reason, the experienced cancer specialist uses *combinations* of anticancer agents, to cover as much of the cells' life cycle, and thus destroy as many cells as possible in any one treatment.

There are four main categories of drugs available for cancer chemotherapy. *Antimetabolites* (for example, 5-FU, 6-MP, methotrexate) are actually poisons but chemically resemble nutrients or vitamins. The cancer cell gobbles them up, but then dies when the antimetabolites interfere with vital cellular processes. *Antibiotics* (bleomycin, adriamycin) interfere with the cancer cell's ability to make protein. *Alkylating agents* (Cytoxan, L-PAM, Myleran) act on cell division. *Steroid hormones* probably prevent the function of the cancer cell's enzyme systems. When used in combination, these agents can hit hard at the malignant cells in a variety of ways.

An important drawback of chemotherapy is that it not only destroys malignant cells, but also may hurt normal ones as well. Treatment, therefore, is administered in cycles, so that normal cells (which recover from injury more quickly than do sick cancer cells) can bounce back, before the abnormal ones have gotten over the effects of the medication. This permits another treatment course to be started safely. Knowing which combination of drugs to use against a specific tumor and in what dosage requires skill and experience. For that reason, in cancer chemotherapy, you should always consult an expert.

COPING WITH SIDE EFFECTS

The side effects of chemotherapy are myriad and vary in severity and duration. The most common are nausea and vomiting, rashes, loss of hair, disturbances of heart rhythm, damage to the heart and interference with bone marrow function (so that the number of red cells, white cells and platelets is reduced). Such side effects may become intolerable.

If you develop severe reactions and are advised to terminate or reduce treatment substantially, ask for a second opinion from an experienced chemotherapist. Side effects can frequently be controlled by various ingenious techniques. For example, the anticancer drug adriamycin often causes severe hair loss. Some very observant nurses working in a tumor clinic found that when they applied ice packs to the scalp at the time of the administration of the drug (it was given by vein), the loss of hair was minimized. Today, such ice packs are standard treatment. The cold application constricts the local blood vessels so that less blood, and hence less adriamycin, is delivered to the scalp area. That's all right if the tumor being treated is in the ovary, but not if it's in the head.

Marijuana also reduces the severity of nausea and vomiting, sometimes permitting chemotherapy to be continued in greater comfort. For this reason it is now legally available for cancer patients in several states and is available by prescription.

Frequently, certain elements within the blood, like platelets, white cells or red cells, are destroyed by chemotherapy. When that happens, other drugs can be substituted and treatment continued.

TREATING CANCER IN THE TEST TUBE

There is a new and exciting experimental technique in the planning stage of which you should be aware. Normally, the oncologist selects an anticancer drug on the basis of the origin, size and stage of the malignancy. This choice is based on the track record of that agent in similar cancers in which it has been used. But the fact that it worked in one patient doesn't necessarily mean that it will be effective in another. Now an attempt is being made to tailor the treatment to the individual patient. An analogy may be made in the way we manage infections. There is a process called "culture and sensitivity" to determine the best antibiotic agent against a given bacterium. For example, when you have a sore throat, we swab it and incubate the material in a series of test tubes. To each of these we add a different antibiotic and later look at the results. Where the antibiotic has destroyed the organism, the test tube is clean, with no evidence of bacterial growth. Where it was ineffective, the infection continues rampant in the culture medium.

A similar technique for treating cancer was developed at the University of Arizona. A small piece of tumor, a sliver, is taken from the patient, and its cells are grown in the laboratory. Then various anticancer drugs are applied to them, just as antibiotics are administered to bacteria. The effect of each agent is assessed outside the body. If this technique proves to be reliable it may, in the future, save a great deal of time, money, inconvenience, side effects and even danger to cancer patients by allowing the best drug to be given first, without speculation and trial and error.

IMMUNOTHERAPY—DEALING WITH THE BREAKDOWN IN LAW AND ORDER

When you are given a vaccine to protect you against a particular infection, your body manufactures specific antibodies against that organism. The vaccine may contain live viruses or killed ones. Your immune, or protective, system doesn't care which it is. The vaccine triggers complex biological defenses to be available and mobilized should the *live* pneumonia, smallpox or whooping cough organism ever strike. Your body is then able to ward it off. In other words, vaccines stimulate your immunity. Many scientists believe that cancer represents a breakdown in the body's defense or immune system and that immunotherapy may restore that capability.

The efficacy of the immune system diminishes with age.

That's why cancer is basically a disease of the elderly. It would, therefore, seem logical to try to enhance resistance to cancer, just as we do against infection. To that end, the effectiveness of several anticancer vaccines is now being studied. For example, BCG vaccine, which confers immunity against tuberculosis, is effective in bladder cancer. Other drugs that enhance immune function may have a beneficial effect on cancer of the breast. *Immune stimulation,* though it may not cure the malignancy, may prolong remission and survival when used with other forms of therapy.

DIFFERENT FORMS OF IMMUNOTHERAPY

There are several different forms of immunotherapy currently available. The first is called *active, nonspecific* immunotherapy, in which some "messenger of immunity" like interferon (an antiviral protein) or a vaccine (like BCG) enhances the immune response. In *active, specific* immunotherapy, extracts of your own tumor cells are reinjected into your body so that it will manufacture specific antibodies against those cells (monoclonal antibodies). Another approach called *adoptive* immunotherapy involves the administration of substances (immune RNA, thymosin) derived from defense cells (lymphocytes) in the body. Then, there is *passive* immunotherapy, in which antibodies from animal sources or from patients who had a cancer identical to yours, and from which they were cured, are injected to act against your tumor cells. Finally, there is *local* immunotheraphy, in which agents are inoculated directly into the tumor.

FEEDING THE CANCER

Patients with advanced cancer lose weight and are gaunt, pale and fragile. I have always wondered how a cancer, sometimes smaller than one's thumb, can wreak such havoc on the rest of the body. It apparently does so by producing a specific substance called cachectin, which is responsible for this wasting.

Hyperalimentation is a fairly recent approach to the management of cancer. Vitamins, minerals and other nutrients, administered intravenously, can provide a cancer patient with as many as 4,000 calories a day. Such enhanced nutrition may increase the effectiveness of other forms of therapy.

CANCER OF THE LUNG

This year approximately 145,000 new lung cancers will be diagnosed in the United States and almost 130,000 of us will die from it. It remains the leading cause of cancer deaths among men and women. It is responsible for one of every three cancer deaths in this country. A male child born today has an 8 percent chance of eventually dying from lung cancer. For female infants that figure is 4 percent. As compared with forty years ago, twenty times the number of people now die from this disease. Nor is treatment very successful. Despite all we can do, only 13 percent of patients with lung cancer will be alive five years after the disease has been discovered. Although lung cancer still strikes men more frequently than women, and absolute numbers are increasing for both sexes, the male-female difference is narrowing as more and more women use cigarettes. Indeed, lung cancer in women is now of epidemic proportions.

YOU CAN BE TOO RICH OR TOO THIN

A few years ago, a fifty-year-old woman consulted me because she was troubled by palpitations. As happens so often, these "extra beats" were especially frequent after drinking too much coffee, taking an extra martini or smoking cigarettes. I was able to persuade her to switch to decaffeinated coffee and cut down on the alcohol, but she simply would not do anything about the thirty or forty cigarettes she was smoking every day. "It's not really a habit," she told me. "I can quit anytime, but if I do, I'm afraid I'll gain weight. One can't be too rich or too thin."

I continued to warn her about the relationship of tobacco, heart disease and lung cancer, but without success. She continued to smoke—and endured not only her heart pounding but her "morning cough" as well. She used a mouthwash to mask her tobacco breath and wore nail polish to cover the nicotine stains on her fingers. In her mind, these were only minor inconveniences of remaining elegantly thin.

One day, while on a trip to China, she contracted "pneumonia." She was treated with the appropriate antibiotics, and improved. When she came back we obtained a routine chest X ray. It revealed cancer of the lung. (Lung cancers frequently present as pneumona because of the obstruction and infection associated with the tumor.)

Despite all our efforts—surgery, radiation, chemotherapy and immunotherapy—she died two years later, rich and very, very thin.

PREVENTION AND EARLY DETECTION

This story highlights two very important points: (a) the outlook in lung cancer is still bleak—the disease is almost always in an advanced stage by the time the diagnosis has been made; (b) tobacco is a major cause in most cases. At the present time the only hope for successful treatment lies in the earliest possible detection. Forty percent of lung cancers are diagnosed by chance, that is, in a routine chest X ray. In sixty percent of cases the tumor is seen on a film taken because of a cough or other respiratory symptoms. By that time, it's almost always too late to cure. At highest risk are those who smoke more than one pack of cigarettes a day and certain industrial workers. I advise annual chest X rays for all such persons. With respect to prevention, the elimination of tobacco from our society would significantly reduce the incidence of this dreaded affliction.

WILL SURGERY REALLY HELP?

Although the only chance for cure in cancer of the lung is its early removal, if an operation is suggested to you, get another opinion. It may be too late for surgery, and an operation may only add unnecessary pain and suffering. The conventional chest X ray cannot always be depended on to help you make that decision. A CT scan of the chest in expert hands is the most revealing diagnostic technique to determine whether or not the lung cancer has spread within the chest cavity.

The basic treatment of lung cancer is either surgery or radiation, or both, depending on the particular cell type, location and extent of disease.

CANCER OF THE KIDNEY— A BAD ONE TO HAVE

The only hope for curing cancer of the kidney is to discover it very, very early. That is usually difficult, because this particular malignancy remains "silent" for so long. The experience of one patient highlights that fact. A musician, he was on a ship to South America, where he was scheduled to perform. While at sea, some twenty-four hours from port, he suddenly found himself unable to pass his urine. The ship's surgeon introduced a tube (catheter) into the bladder, drained the obstructed urine, and left the catheter in place. The cause of the trouble was a big prostate that needed immediate removal. My patient canceled his performance and took the next plane back to New York. He was immediately admitted to the hospital for the necessary operation.

But before prostate surgery is performed, several routine tests and X rays are almost always done. These include an intravenous pyelogram, which, in this case, indicated a "shadow" in the right kidney. A sonogram (sound waves directed at the mass) revealed that it consisted of solid tissue and was not a cyst. Cysts of the kidney (sacs containing fluid) are almost always benign, while solid masses are usually malignant. What was to have been a simple prostate operation ended in exploratory surgery on the kidney, as a result of which cancer of that organ was found. Happily, it had not yet spread. The kidney was removed, and the patient was cured.

When cancer of the kidney is not found accidentally, as it was in this case, it usually makes its presence known through blood in the urine. The only treatment for renal cancer is surgical removal. Although chemotherapy is also administered, it is done so more out of desperation than out of hope. To date, the cure rate and even the incidence of response are very low, because by the time the affected kidney has been removed, the cancer has often spread.

TESTICULAR CANCER—NOW CURABLE

Testicular cancer is the most common malignancy among men between the ages of twenty and thirty-nine, even though there are only five thousand cases diagnosed each year. This tumor is very highly radiosensitive and can often be cured with radiation alone, although surgery is frequently required as well. The big breakthrough in treatment, however, is chemotherapy, which can effect a high percentage of cures, especially when radiation and surgery have not been completely successful. Combinations of such drugs as bleomycin, cisplatinum and vinblastine can permantly eradicate testicular cancer even after *it has already metastasized.*

So, if you develop a testicular malignancy, ask to be referred to a major cancer center and inquire whether you are a candidate for this chemotherapy, in addition to whatever radiation and/or surgery are administered.

In terms of prevention, every male with an undescended testis at birth should have it brought down surgically by two years of age because it can become malignant. In any event, if one is discovered later in life, the operation should be done before the age of fifty. Beyond that it is generally not recommended.

BLADDER CANCER

Cancer of the bladder strikes about 40,000 people a year and kills about 11,000. It is three times as frequent in men as in women, and its peak incidence is between the ages of fifty-five and sixty. The incidence is increasing worldwide by 3 or 4 percent a year. Cigarette smoking and exposure to toxins in the rubber, dye and leather industries appear to be the major factors.

There is nothing vague or silent about cancer of the bladder. Other neoplasms (the medical term for cancer) may remain undiagnosed for months because the symptoms they cause are nonspecific, like fatigue and insidious weight loss. Bladder cancer, however, declares itself early, usually with the appearance of blood in the urine, frequent or painful urination, or the need to empty your bladder urgently once you get the signal. If you come to your doctor with these symptoms, especially if you're middle-aged, male and a smoker, he will suspect bladder cancer. His work-up will include a Pap test of the urine to look for tumor cells. He will also order an IVP (kidney and bladder X rays after injection of dye) followed by cystoscopy, in which the urologist will actually look into the bladder through an illuminated scope. He will biopsy any growths he sees and then cauterize them, that is, burn them away with an electrical current. If the cancer is small and detected early enough, that may be all that is necessary in 50 percent of cases. Even so, you will have to come back every three months for the first year, then every four to six months thereafter to make sure that the cancer has not started up again. If it has, it may either be burned away once more, or various drugs can be instilled directly into it. These agents include BCG vaccine, doxorubicin and thiotepa.

When the cancer is so deeply embedded in the bladder that cautery alone will not remove it, you will need a major operation to remove the entire bladder and almost all the tissue around it. Without your bladder, you will pass your urine through a small tube emerging from your abdomen. Although the penis will remain intact, sexual function will be compromised because of all the surgery done in the pelvic area. At this late stage, there is still a 40 percent survival. When mestastases occur to other parts of the body, chemotherapy with cisplastin is employed, but then survival rarely exceeds two or three years.

The key to successful management of cancer of the bladder, as in so many other locations, is early detection. *Never ignore blood in the urine.* You may get the providential warning only once.

CANCER OF THE BREAST

Cancer of the breast is the most prevalent malignancy in women, although lung cancer causes more deaths. There are about 125,000 new cases each year in the United States, and cures are obtained in half of them. About 7 percent of American women can expect to develop breast cancer in their lifetime. We now have a better understanding of how the disease spreads and the best means available to treat it. In the following pages you will see why it is extremely important to get a second opinion after one doctor's evaluation of a lump in your breast.

EXIT THE TRADITIONAL
RADICAL MASTECTOMY

In the past, virtually every woman with proven breast cancer routinely underwent an extensive operation (radical mastectomy) in which not only the breast itself was removed, but muscles, nerves and fatty tissue all the way into the armpit were dissected. Such surgery resulted in disfigurement, frequently left the patient feeling depressed and sexually inadequate, sometimes threatened marital relationships and often left the woman with pain, stiffness and swelling in the arm on the affected side.

The rationale for this extensive procedure was the belief that cancer of the breast usually spreads by direct extension, encroaching gradually on adjoining tissues. So if a lump was found in the breast, it seemed logical to cut away as much of the surrounding structures as possible—all the lymph glands from the breast to the armpit, the pectoral (chest wall) muscles and connective tissue—to make sure that the advancing edge of the tumor was excised. If at the time of operation, the cancer was found to have involved the lymph glands, radiation therapy was administered.

Over a forty-year span, however, as we looked at the results of such extensive surgery, we realized that it did not yield a lower death rate than did more conservative procedures. Doctors then began to question the need for radical

mastectomy, with all its adverse physical and emotional consequences. Less drastic surgical approaches were then
introduced.

YOU THINK YOU'RE
CURED—AND THEN SUDDENLY

Here is the important new knowledge that has influenced
the modern treatment of breast cancer. Its spread is not primarily by extension, as we once thought. Even in the smallest cancers, the cells migrate to various parts of the body,
not necessarily by direct extension to the lymph glands, but
via the bloodstream. Many of the malignant cells that dis-
seminate in this way are destroyed by the body's defense
mechanisms. Those that are not, and theoretically it takes
only one, seed the cancer at another site. This metastasis to
distant organs such as the lungs, bones or brain may be
clinically silent for several years, during which time these
microscopic foci, with their ominous potential, lie dormant.
Then, suddenly, five, ten or even fifteen years later, long
after the patient was considered cured, she (and occasionally *he*, for men develop breast cancer too) develops bone
pain, or finds a lump somewhere. This late and unexpected
manifestation of cancer is due to the *early* spread of tumor
cells, a phenomenon not prevented by the radical mastectomy. Such surgery is akin to locking the barn door after the
horses are gone. Why, then, remove all that tissue—muscle,
sinew and fat—when the malignant cells may have already
escaped from the primary tumor by another route?

THE MODIFIED RADICAL MASTECTOMY

This appreciation of how cancer of the breast spreads has
led to a modification in treatment. Most surgeons now recommend a *modified radical mastectomy,* in which only the
breast and the lymph glands are excised. Others think that a
simple lumpectomy, that is, removal of the visible portions of
the tumor with a little more tissue around it to spare, is
enough. A major advantage of these less complicated opera-

tions is that they permit reconstruction of the breast so that it can assume an almost normal appearance. (More about that later.) After the surgery, some cancer specialists follow up with radiation to the affected breast if the excised lymph nodes fail to reveal any evidence of cancer. This radiation is prescribed in order to kill off any possible residual tumor cells in the area. Some specialists even rely on radiation alone if the tumor is very small. They cite statistics showing equivalent survival rates in comparison to the more complicated approaches.

SURGERY ALONE IS NOT ALWAYS ENOUGH

Although it is still too early to be sure, the data so far suggest that these more limited surgical approaches (sometimes followed by radiation therapy) have the same cure and relapse rates as the more aggressive surgery. Of critical importance is the evidence that follow-up (adjuvant) chemotherapy with anticancer drugs and/or hormones, after the visible tumor has been removed, is effective in delaying the appearance of metastases that may have already been seeded. Whatever the treatment, the main determinant of the future outlook with breast cancer is how many glands in your armpit turn out to be involved. The greater the number, the less rosy the outlook.

PLANNING THE BIOPSY

When a lump is discovered in your breast, your doctor will usually perform a biopsy to determine whether it is malignant. That can sometimes be done by freezing the area locally and sucking out the contents with a needle. But more commonly you are taken to the operating room and anesthetized while a piece of tissue from the growth is sent for analysis. If the pathologist reports back that the tumor is malignant, the surgeon will usually want to proceed with the surgery then and there. Should you give him carte blanche to do so?

THE MEANING OF INFORMED CONSENT

The law states that no patient should have *any* operation unless he or she (or a legal representative) understands what is going to be done—and agrees to the procedure in writing. That is especially pertinent in breast surgery. If a breast biopsy reveals a malignancy, you have two alternatives with regard to the next step. The first—and the one that I usually recommend—is to request the surgeon *not* to proceed with the operation. The next day you, your husband and your surgeon can discuss the nature of the surgical approach that he proposes. That may be a good time to get a second opinion. This field is changing so radically and opinions are so divergent that you may benefit from another competent viewpoint. The disadvantage of this approach is that you end up with two operations (and two anesthesias) instead of one. Some women prefer to settle it all beforehand. Whichever course you choose, your consent to surgery should be fully informed.

Aside from giving you some time to think it over, delaying your final decision has other advantages. The analysis of the tissue removed is more accurate when studied with conventional staining techniques than in the frozen section done at the time of the biopsy while the surgeon waits with scalpel poised; also, a malignant tumor can be more accurately staged—that is, the extent and degree of its spread can be more carefully assessed. If it is determined, after such careful work-up, that other sites are already involved, there is much less reason to do extensive local surgery on the breast.

THE IMPORTANCE OF CHEMOTHERAPY

Researchers in several countries have for years been accumulating data about the effects of different combinations of anticancer drugs for breast tumors, and the results reported are most impressive. There are now several regimens available to you using different combinations of drugs. Be sure to discuss all your options before deciding with your doctor which is best for you, since therapy is usually continued for six to twenty-four months.

WILL YOU NEED HORMONES TOO?

Another important observation affecting treatment of breast cancer involves "estrogen receptors." The cancerous breast tissue that has been removed is tested to determine whether it accepts, or "binds," estrogens. If it does, then the patient may respond better after surgery to hormones than to chemotherapy. Such estrogen binders do especially well with prolonged remissions in premenopausal women. The most effective agent is an *antiestrogen* called tamoxifen.

If the cancer does not have estrogen binding sites, then chemotherapy is likely to be of greater benefit than hormones. So we can now predict, with reasonable accuracy, who is apt to respond to which treatment and why.

WHEN THE CANCER IS ADVANCED

When breast cancer has spread throughout the body, even if it is of the positive estrogen receptor type, it may be too late for hormones alone. Your doctor may recommend removal or destruction of the pituitary gland in the brain, the adrenals, located atop the kidneys, or the ovaries. Before you agree to any of these measures, always ask for another opinion from a specialist in breast cancer to determine whether such therapy is really necessary.

THE ROLE OF IMMUNOTHERAPY IN BREAST CANCER

As I indicated earlier, cells may escape from the breast cancer and lie dormant in various parts of the body for months or years, waiting for the right moment to resume their explosive growth. Some of these are destroyed by the body's immune mechanism before they begin to multiply. Those that remain perpetuate the disease. So it stands to reason that anything we can do to help the body cope with these malignant cells may improve the outlook. There is evidence in several different cancers, including that of the breast, that enhancement of immune capability may be of help even *after* spread has occurred. Such therapy is now available in several centers on an experimental basis.

A SECOND LOOK AT MAMMOGRAPHY

When and how often should a woman have mammography? Some years ago, after Betty Ford and Happy Rockefeller were found to have breast cancer, there was a stampede for mammography in the United States. The demand was so great that patients sometimes had to wait weeks for an appointment. Since then, we have taken a hard second look at this procedure, because it does involve radiation, and the less you get of that, the better. The newer X-ray equipment significantly reduces exposure to acceptable amounts.

I believe a baseline mammogram should be obtained between thirty-five and forty years of age. Thereafter, you should have a mammogram every year or two in the following situations: if you are over fifty years of age; if your breasts are large and difficult to examine, so that they may conceal small cancers, even from your own fingers or those of an experienced doctor; if you have had cancer of one breast and are therefore more vulnerable to developing it in the other; if there is a strong family history of the disease—as, for example, when your mother or sister has had breast cancer.

THE "LUMPY BREAST" DIET

An observation comes to mind that may interest women with benign lumpy breasts. According to one recent report, abstinence from coffee, tea and cola drinks seemed to result in the disappearance of the lumps. If your breasts are lumpy, why not follow such a diet for about four weeks and see what happens? It certainly can't hurt.

Other doctors claim success in treating lumpy, painful breasts with 600 units of vitamin E daily. I am not impressed with the results obtained in my own practice.

GYNECOLOGICAL CANCERS

This year in the United States we expect to detect about 75,000 new cases of ovarian and uterine cancer. Some 22,000 women will die from these malignancies, over 50 percent of them from cancer of the ovary (11,600).

IS YOUR LIFE WORTH $2,000,000—TO YOU?

Not too long ago saving even a single life, regardless of cost, was a paramount societal goal. That was in the days of cheap energy and the promise of an increasing standard of living for everyone. All that has changed. We are now preoccupied with *efficiency* in medical care. The major concern of politicians, health administrators, insurance actuaries and, yes, even some doctors today is *cost effectiveness.* Their argument goes something like this. About 50,000 proctoscopies must be done to detect just one curable cancer of the bowel or rectum. Since each proctoscopy costs $25 or $30, we are spending almost $2,000,000 to save one life—and in their view, that is simply not worth it. They hold that the money would have had a greater impact on the health of more people were it spent in some other way. With the current explosion of HMOs and corporate medicine, and their emphasis on cost cutting, the decision about having $2,000,000 worth of proctoscopies to save your life may soon be made by someone other than you or me.

What does this have to do with gynecological cancers? A great deal. The cost-cutting "experts" feel that the Pap test (which involves scraping the cervix to look for early cancer cells) constitutes an unnecessary expense. According to them, early localized malignancies detected by this test don't often spread. They think it's perfectly safe to wait until the symptoms of cancer appear, before instituting treatment.

I don't agree. The death rate from cancer of the uterus has dropped to one third of what it was forty years ago because of earlier detection resulting from the widespread use of the Pap test. (Some gynecologists believe that circumcision has something to do with it too, since mates of circumcised men have less cancer of the cervix than those of uncircumcised males. The foreskin may harbor a virus or other agent responsible for inducing cervical cancer.) In my own practice, I recommend Pap tests annually to the age of sixty-five years.

CANCER OF THE UTERUS

Uterine cancer may involve either the main portion or "body" of that organ, the lining of its walls (the endometrium, which is shed every month during your period), or its "neck" (the cervix).

HORMONES, HEARTS
AND BROKEN BONES—
THE ESTROGEN SAGA

American women have been on an estrogen yo-yo for years. "Yes, the hormone should be taken." "No, it shouldn't." "Yes, estrogens cause breast cancer." "No, they don't." Even today, you're apt to get conflicting opinions on ERT (estrogen replacement therapy) from your family physician, gynecologist, endocrinologist and favorite TV doctor. What follows are my own opinions and recommendations—admittedly controversial.

Humans are the only mammals with a menopause. Except for *Homo sapiens,* all other females continue to menstruate until they die. Menstruation begins when estrogen levels are high enough. Menopause has its onset when those levels fall. The question is whether this drop in hormone concentration is a natural, normal phenomenon, not to be tampered with, or an aberration of nature to be corrected. Without impugning any divine design, I support the latter viewpoint.

In my opinion, women on ERT feel better and look younger, and their vaginal vaults are moist enough to permit comfortable sexual activity. Even more important, there is impressive evidence that estrogens help prevent the two leading causes of death in postmenopausal women—heart attacks and osteoporosis. This more than compensates for the increased risk of uterine cancer resulting from estrogen supplements. Scores of thousands of females die from coronary heart disease and the complications of osteoporosis. Only 3,500 succumb each year to uterine cancer, a figure that can be further reduced by adding ten days of progesterone to the cyclical estrogen therapy, and routine examinations and Pap tests twice a year in women taking estrogens.

So my advice is this: Unless you have (a) some previous history of cancer, especially of the breast or uterus, (b) a disturbance of your blood clotting mechanism that has caused phlebitis or thrombosis in a blood vessel in the past, or (c) liver trouble, discuss with your doctor the advantages of ERT. Don't wait for hot flushes to justify such supplements. And if you've had a hysterectomy, all the more reason to take the estrogens.

There is no convincing evidence that estrogens increase the risk of breast cancer, but just to be sure, get a mammogram every year, examine your breasts every month, and insist that your doctor do it at every visit to his office.

You may, however, want to consider a compromise position if you're leery about taking estrogens over a long period of time. Not every postmenopausal woman is totally devoid of this hormone. Some produce small amounts, not enough to continue their periods, but perhaps enough to prevent some of the complications of estrogen deprivation. This can be determined by your gynecologist on the basis of a vaginal smear. If it reveals an acceptable level of estrogen activity, you may be able to forgo ERT.

TREATING CANCER OF THE UTERUS

Treatment of uterine cancer depends on its stage, and whether the tumor is still localized or has already spread. Before committing yourself to any therapeutic plan, always confirm the diagnosis with another gynecologist. I have seen several patients whose "cancer" turned out to be a benign fibroid after review by someone else. Even if it is malignant, chances for cure are as high as 75 percent, especially if the tumor remains confined to the pelvis.

As much of the growth as possible should be removed. If it is too advanced for that, or not completely accessible to operation, radiation is necessary. Finally, chemotherapy with several agents in combination—drugs like cyclophosphamide, bleomycin, 5-FU, doxorubicin and methotrexate, as well as certain hormones, are also available to slow tumor growth and possibly prolong life.

OVARIAN MALIGNANCY—THE SECOND LEADING CAUSE OF CANCER DEATHS IN WOMEN

The incidence of ovarian cancer, second only to malignancy of the breast, is increasing very rapidly, and nobody really knows why. It has been suggested that cosmetic talc in powders, deodorants, soaps, textiles, and on condoms and diaphragms may sometimes be responsible, but this is largely speculation.

Until recently treatment of ovarian cancer was not nearly as effective as therapy for uterine cancer, but now through combinations of chemotherapy, cures can be obtained in as many as 50 percent of the cases, even after the cancer has spread within the abdominal cavity. As in uterine malignancy, as much of the tumor as possible should be removed, regardless of the extent of spread. Ovarian malignancies are not usually radiosensitive. The effectiveness of therapy can be monitored by CT scan, but after several months, a second "look-see" operation is desirable. If you are advised that because the tumor has spread, it is too late to operate, obtain a second opinion.

CANCER OF THE DIGESTIVE TRACT

The digestive tract starts in the mouth and ends at the anus— and any part of it is vulnerable to cancer. The incidence, as well as the location, of such malignancies varies from country to country. For example, in China, there is a great deal of esophageal cancer, while in Japan the big killer is cancer of the mouth and stomach.

The most important cancer in the United States is that of the lung, but when you put them all together, malignancies of the digestive organs account for the highest number of cancer deaths in the United States. There are about 218,000 new cases every year, and 120,000 deaths. Some of these tumors are more deadly than others, the worst ones being esophageal, pancreatic and liver. By the time a cancer is recognized in any of these organs, it is often too late to effect a cure. By contrast, if you are alert to the danger signals of cancer of the bowel (98,000 new cases per year), early diagnosis and surgery will yield a 50 percent chance of cure. So if you have an unexplained pain in your belly, find blood in your stool or notice a change in your bowel habits (sudden constipation alternating with diarrhea, or the appearance of narrow, ribbonlike movements), have yourself checked right away. Colonoscopy, CT scanning and ultrasonography, as well as conventional X rays (particularly double contrast barium enemas) can often detect these cancers in time. But you do need a high index of suspicion.

SURGERY IS THE KEY

The key to the treatment of intestinal cancer is surgery. Complete removal of the malignant growth offers the best chance for cure. One of my patients, who lived abroad, consulted me because of bloody diarrhea, which developed after he had eaten some "bad roast beef" somewhere in the Far East. I found nothing abnormal in a complete physical examination—and that included a careful finger rectal probe. In pursuing the history in greater detail, however, I learned that these symptoms really had begun months earlier. I then arranged for a sigmoidoscopy. This didn't appeal to the patient (it never does—to anyone) but he agreed to go through with it anyway. We found a cancer of the lower bowel, situated just beyond the reach of my examining finger (that is why the rectal exam was normal). The rest of the story has a happy ending. At surgery the cancer was found not to have spread. The patient made an uneventful recovery and is alive and well eighteen years later.

BUT RADIATION MAY BE NECESSARY

Radiation therapy becomes necessary when an intestinal cancer is too extensive to eradicate by surgery. Unlike its effect on some other malignancies, radiation is virtually never curative in the bowel. It may, however, prolong life when combined with chemotherapy.

Frequently, especially when the tumor is situated very low in the bowel, the surgery that can cure you may necessitate a colostomy, that is, an opening of the bowel externally through the abdominal wall. Patients dread this prospect and some even tell me that they would rather be dead. That attitude is foolish these days, when colostomy bags are odor-free, lie flat on the abdomen and are quite easy to manage. One can adjust very well and lead a virtually normal life. Colostomy is a small price to pay for a cancer cure.

Chemotherapy after removal of a tumor apparently has no impact on the subsequent clinical course. Some doctors recommend it anyway. Most do not.

CANCER OF THE PROSTATE

There are about 86,000 new cases and 26,000 deaths from cancer of the prostate every year in the United States alone. For some reason, American blacks have the world's highest incidence of this disease. Equally perplexing is the fact that the lowest rate is in Asiatics. Would that we understood the genetic or environmental factors that give Japanese men so much cancer in the stomach and so little in the prostate.

HOW IT'S DISCOVERED

Believe it or not, most cases of prostate cancer are not detected when the patient is alive! At autopsy, in 70 percent of men dying of other causes, small cancers are found buried deep within the prostate gland. There they apparently remained for years without spreading or otherwise making their presence known. What causes such cancers to remain in place in some men and spread in others is anyone's guess.

SURPRISE, SURPRISE!

You may also learn you have prostate cancer after undergoing a routine prostatectomy for enlargement and symptoms of obstruction; the pathologist, in looking at the tissue that has been removed, finds little islands of cancer, usually surrounded or walled in by completely normal tissue. At that point it is at what is called Stage A. Such foci of cancer so frequently found in older men are nothing to worry about. Under the microscope, they almost always appear well *differentiated,* that is, the cells, though malignant, are fairly orderly in appearance. If a number of such cancer "islands" are present, you will likely be advised to have a "radical prostatectomy," that is, get the whole gland out, because of the possibility that some cancer cells may be left in the remaining tissue. That is good advice. If you are not given it, get a second opinion. Failure to clean out all the cancer leaves you one chance in five of developing a serious prostate malignancy within two years.

"SILENT" PROSTATE CANCER

Your prostate cancer may also be detected during a routine checkup. A careful doctor will always do a rectal examination, regardless of symptoms, at least once a year on every male patient forty-five or older. At that time, if you have a "silent" prostate cancer, one that is not giving you any symptoms, he may find a suspicious area that feels irregular and harder than the rest of the prostate. A needle biopsy must then be done. This is a fairly easy procedure in which a needle is introduced from the outside (through the skin) into the gland. The only problem here is that occasionally the needle may miss the cancer, especially if it is a small one. Before undergoing such a biopsy, however, you might ask the doctor to try a course of antibiotics first. Occasionally, chronic infection can cause a little swelling that feels like a cancer. If, after a couple of weeks, the suspicious area does not disappear, then you must have the biopsy. Waiting two weeks won't make any difference in the outlook.

If the biopsy confirms the presence of cancer, you are in what we call Stage B. The tumor is large enough to feel, but is still within the gland and has not yet spread. At this point you have the choice of surgery or radiation, and not all urologists agree which is better. Statistically, surgery yields a higher rate of cure, but radiation may be safer if you are very old or a poor operative risk.

Stage B prostate cancer can also be treated by pellets of radioactive iodine implanted surgically into the gland. Ask your urologist about the necessity or desirability of this technique if radiation has been decided on in your case.

WHEN YOU'RE IN TROUBLE

Suppose that, in the course of the rectal examination, your doctor finds a tumor not only in your prostate but also in neighboring tissue (local extension); however, it has not yet spread to your bones, liver or lungs. You are now in Stage C of the disease. At this point, as much of the prostate and tumor tissue as possible is removed, especially if the enlarged gland is causing obstruction to urine outflow. But since it is now virtually impossible to remove the entire cancer, surgery at this point is palliative, rather than curative. Radiation is now advisable in order to destroy as many of the remaining cancer cells as possible.

New X-ray equipment like the linear accelerator makes it possible to pinpoint high doses of radiation to the affected area and so control the disease for years. Another method of delivering radiation is by implanting radioactive iodine seeds locally, as is done in Stage B. This requires a long and difficult operation, but the malignant tissue can be irradiated very accurately, since the radioactive material is placed directly into it under direct vision. If radiation is suggested, ask your doctor about this particular technique. It is a sophisticated procedure, which should only be done by an experienced surgeon.

Most doctors do not prescribe female hormones or "antimale" hormones at this stage, unless radiation is unsuccessful.

ADVANCED PROSTATE CANCER

This brings us to Stage D cancer of the prostate. You probably got that far by avoiding a routine checkup, when Stages B and C might have been detected (and more successfully treated). If it is any comfort to you, 50 percent of prostate cancers are not diagnosed until this late stage. What began as a "silent" nodule has now metastasized—spread to the lymph glands and other organs in your body. The most common symptom at this stage is bone pain, usually in the spine. Your first reaction is to ignore it or attribute your discomfort to arthritis of the spine. When it gets worse you consult your doctor. When he examines you, the astute physician will check the prostate before focusing on the area of pain in the spine. He will feel a rock-hard gland, very irregular and diffusely enlarged. Blood tests will indicate the presence of enzymes that have seeped from the cancerous bones (elevated acid phosphatase), while X rays and radioactive scans of the skeleton will confirm the spread of the cancer.

You are now in serious trouble, but all is not yet lost. At this point it is too late to obtain a surgical cure, and an operation should not be done unless the gland is so big that it obstructs your urinary outflow. So if you are voiding satisfactorily and are advised to undergo surgery, get another opinion. At this stage, you still have a 70 to 80 percent chance of improvement. Your pain can be lessened, and the rate of spread of the malignancy can be slowed, but you cannot be cured. Such palliation can be achieved either with hormones or by having your testicles removed. In either event, forget about having any more erections. Your main objectives now are survival and freedom from pain.

The hormone usually now prescribed is still estrogen, which should be taken in the smallest amount necessary, because cardiovascular complications (clots in various blood vessels) may develop at higher dosages. And remember, you need surgical removal of the testes (orchiectomy) or hormones. There is no evidence that doing both is any better than either alone.

In recent years, another substance called LHRH has become available for the treatment of advanced prostate cancer, especially with bone involvement. Ask your doctor about it.

LITTLE PLASTIC BALLS

Many men are psychologically (and understandably) distraught when their testes are removed—at any age. To help them cope, at least in the locker room, the surgeons can insert little plastic balls or even some of the patient's own tissue from elsewhere in the body into the scrotal sacs to create the appearance and feel of normalcy.

CANCER OF THE GLANDS AND BLOOD

No discussion of cancer is complete without mention of the lymphomas (tumors of the lymph glands) and leukemias (malignancy of the bone marrow and the blood). These are both variations of cancer that affect all age groups and both sexes.

LYMPHOMAS

Lymph nodes are collections of tissue found throughout the body. Their function is the regional defense against infection of the area in which they are situated. They filter fluid passing through them, remove harmful bacteria and entrap any circulating tumor cells that may happen by. Normally, when not inflamed, infected or infiltrated by cancer cells, lymph glands cannot be felt. Any gland you or your doctor can detect is, by definition, already enlarged. Infected lymph glands are usually swollen and tender. When they have become malignant, however, they are generally hard and almost painless.

In lymph glands that have developed *lymphomas* (Hodgkin's disease is one type), the cells, normally orderly and well behaved, have become malignant. The disease process usually involves most of the glandular system, so that enlarged lymph nodes can be felt in many areas of the body. Untreated, lymphomas are ultimately fatal.

Cancer specialists classify the lymphomas into various categories, which need not concern us here. More than 70,000 such cancers are diagnosed every year in the United States, and result in about 25,000 deaths—a serious business.

When I graduated from medical school, these disorders were virtually always fatal. That's no longer the case. For example, Hodgkin's disease, which accounts for about one quarter of all lymphomas, was then lethal. It can now be cured in 80 percent of cases. Modern treatment can induce long remissions and cures in several of the other lymphomas as well.

A lymphoma may be discovered in the following way: While shaving, or putting on your makeup or deodorant one day, you find some swollen glands, usually in the neck or armpit. They are painless and feel hard and rubbery. You may delay seeing your doctor because they don't really bother you, and besides which, you know that most swollen glands are harmless and disappear spontaneously. Later you may notice that when you have a cocktail, the gland aches a little. (Alcohol-induced pain is characteristic of some lymphomas, for reasons that are not clear.) When the glands persist and enlarge even more, you usually decide to ask the doctor about them.

If he suspects infection, he will prescribe an antibiotic and wait for a week or two. After that time, if the enlarged glands persist, he will recommend a biopsy. Some infections mimic cancer cells under the microscope and are not always interpreted correctly. If it comes back "lymphoma," get a second opinion before you allow any treatment to be instituted.

The basic therapy of localized lymphomas, when only a single gland or one area is involved, is radiation. The new high-powered mega-voltage machines are able to pinpoint delivery of the rays and focus a very high concentration to the specific target without unduly injuring adjacent healthy tissue. Make sure, again, that the facility where you are receiving this treatment has the most modern equipment available. A second opinion from a qualified radiotherapist can assure you of that.

After radiation, some patients are given chemotherapy. One currently used combination in Hodgkin's disease consists of nitrogen mustard, vincristine, procarbazine and prednisone. Chemotherapy and/or radiation can effect a cure in most cases of Hodgkin's disease and will control and sometimes cure other lymphomas as well. In addition to chemotherapy there is new work with concomitant immunotherapy. The results, however, are still inconclusive at this time.

THE LEUKEMIAS

The prefix *leuk* means "white"; *emia* refers to "blood." So *leukemia* means "white blood." The term embraces a group of malignant diseases in which the white corpuscles, normally numbering from 6,000 to 10,000 per cubic centimeter of blood, go "crazy"—values as high as 50,000 to 100,000 or more are found. When we look at these cells under the microscope, not only are they overabundant, but they look very abnormal too. There are about 25,000 new cases every year and about 18,000 deaths.

White blood cells are made in the bone marrow, and are normally released into the bloodstream at a controlled rate when they are fully matured. In patients with leukemia, the process controlling the growth of these cells and the rate at which they are fed into the blood breaks down. As a result, immature blood cells, not fully formed, are released prematurely into the circulation, where they can be detected.

One of the main functions of the white blood cells is to counter infection. But that is a "man's job" (for mature cells), which the juvenile ones can't perform. (All they do is clog the circulation, invade other organs of the body and finally cause death.) As these immature white cells pack the marrow, they replace other elements that should be formed there—elements that have important roles to play. For example, platelets are responsible for normal clotting; red cells carry oxygen. In leukemic patients we find anemia (not enough red cells) and hemorrhage (due to platelet deficiency). Also, infections are rampant in leukemic patients because the abnormal white cells can't cope with bacterial invasion as do their healthy counterparts.

NO LONGER ALWAYS FATAL, BUT BE GOOD TO YOUR BROTHERS AND SISTERS

Not so many years ago, leukemia was uniformly fatal. Today, however, it is curable in about 55 percent of children. But that requires treatment planned and executed by highly skilled specialists. Management now consists of chemotherapy and radiation, and there is a great deal of interest in the potential of immunotherapy. In special circumstances, after destroying the leukemia cells, we now transplant normal bone marrow into leukemic patients, if compatible donors (almost always brothers or sisters) can be found.

While the outlook for adults with acute leukemia is not as good as for children (the cure rate is only 15 percent), they often enjoy long remissions with the same kinds of treatment. As I have repeatedly said in these pages, it is critical to buy time, because nobody knows what new therapy will bring as early as tomorrow in any area of cancer—especially in the field of leukemia.

KEY FACTS TO REMEMBER

The news about cancer is both good and bad. The good news is that improved methods of diagnosis and treatment have resulted in increasing numbers of cures and more prolonged survival. The bad news is that with a few exceptions, the overall incidence is increasing.

The major points to remember about cancer are:

1. The diagnosis should always be confirmed by an expert specializing in the field (oncologist) before further steps are taken.

2. Not all cancers are fatal, and not all tumors are malignant.

3. Early diagnosis and treatment are critical.

4. Techniques of managing and controlling cancer are changing rapidly; therefore, your doctor must constantly be aware of what is new and available and so should you. Major approaches to the treatment of most cancers consist of surgery, irradiation, chemotherapy and immunotherapy. The rule of thumb to follow is that a cancer should be completely removed surgically whenever possible. The decision to use other forms of treatment in addition to, or in place of, surgery is based on many considerations and should be made by experts in the field.

CANCER OF THE LUNG

Cancer of the lung is the leading cause of cancer deaths in the United States. Though still more common in men, its prevalence in women is increasing in epidemic numbers, presumably due to changing smoking habits. Although a small number of cases, if detected early enough, can be cured, for the most part, cancer of the lung remains incurable.

CANCER OF THE KIDNEY

Cancer of the kidney, except when detected very early, is highly malignant and usually refractory to all treatment.

CANCER OF THE TESTES

Testicular cancer, formerly fatal, is now frequently curable by a combination of surgery, chemotherapy and radiation—even after it has spread.

CANCER OF THE BLADDER

Bladder cancer usually declares itself by the appearance of blood in the urine. It is basically a disease of males. Treatment consists of cauterizing the tumor where possible, or instilling BCG vaccine or chemotherapeutic agents into the bladder. Reexamination at regular intervals is necessary to detect evidence of recurrence. When the malignancy is advanced, complete excision of the bladder itself is usually required.

CANCER OF THE BREAST

Cancer of the breast is the most prevalent malignancy in women. The traditional radical mastectomy is much less frequently done now, having been replaced by the modified radical, in which only the breast and involved lymph glands are removed. Muscles, tendons and connective tissue are spared. Some doctors limit surgery to excision of the cancer itself (lumpectomy). A few depend solely on radiation. Whichever combination of these approaches is suggested for you, always ask for a second opinion.

Since breast cancer spreads not only by direct extension to neighboring tissues, but also via blood and lymph channels to distant sites, surgery should almost always be followed by chemotherapy and/or hormones and, in some cases, immunotherapy. The best combination of drugs should be decided in consultation with an expert oncologist.

Mammography should be performed routinely in women over the age of fifty. In younger women, except for a baseline study at age thirty-five, it is required only when there is particular vulnerability to the disease, as might be evidenced by a strong family history or a history of cancer in the other breast.

CANCER OF THE UTERUS

Cancer of the uterus is a common form of malignancy, whose risk is increased by the use of female hormones (estrogen). These should always be taken together with progesterone as prescribed by your gynecologist, if you have not had a hysterectomy. If estrogens are required for whatever reason, routine pelvic exams and Pap tests should be done every six months. Cancer of the uterus is best treated with surgery and radiation.

CANCER OF THE OVARY

Cancer of the ovary is an important cause of cancer deaths in women, after lung and breast cancer. Treatment is basically surgical, followed by chemotherapy and radiation. Cures can be expected in about 50 percent of cases.

CANCER OF THE DIGESTIVE TRACT

Cancer of the digestive tract, in aggregate, is the most common malignancy today. Wherever it is found, gastrointestinal cancer should be surgically removed, when possible.

CANCER OF THE PROSTATE

Cancer of the prostate is a very common disease of older men. The early forms are often accidentally discovered, easily removed and curable. Although the outlook is less good after local extension or distant spread has occurred, prolonged survival is still frequently possible. Treatment consists of surgery, when possible, followed by radiation (external or by means of implanted radioactive iodine seeds) and hormone therapy. An alternative to the latter is removal of the testes.

LYMPHOMAS AND LEUKEMIAS

Lymphomas and leukemias are malignancies of the lymph glands, blood-forming tissues and blood constituents. Once uniformly fatal, several types are now curable, including certain childhood leukemias and Hodgkin's disease. The mainstays of treatment are chemotherapy and radiation.

28

ARTHRITIS—AVOIDING A LAISSEZ-FAIRE APPROACH

COMMON, COSTLY AND CHRONIC

You are not likely to take arthritis seriously or consider it a very important disease unless you actually suffer from it yourself. It is not as dramatic as a stroke, as threatening as a heart attack or as devastating as cancer. What's more, joint aches and pains are so common, they are often lumped into the "arthritis" category and taken for granted as the inevitable wear and tear of living. In actual fact, however, more than twenty million people in the United States have arthritis that is troublesome enough to require medical care. This is not a disease of old age. Ten percent of all those *disabled* by arthritis are under forty-five years of age. To paraphrase Winston Churchill, "Never have so many suffered so much for so long" as do these patients. Over and above the pain it causes, arthritis also exacts an enormous economic toll. Absence from work and loss of productivity due to this group of disorders cost this nation billions of dollars annually.

Because of its chronicity, too many patients with arthritis do not take advantage of newer concepts, drugs and treatments that can make life much more bearable, if not actually cure the disorder.

Arthritis means "inflammation of a joint" (from *arthron,* Greek for "joint," and *itis,* a medical suffix derived from Latin and meaning "inflammatory disease"). Used alone, it is not a specific diagnosis, because the causes and anatomical locations of such inflammation are legion. They include simple wear and tear (osteoarthritis); infection (gonorrhea, hepatitis); a generalized disease (rheumatoid arthritis), which involves, in addition to the joints, many other systems in the body (the heart, arteries, muscles and other internal organs); a disorder of the joints traditionally attributed to "high living" (gout); and allergy. Each of these forms of "arthritis" requires different treatment and has a different outlook. So if you are told, with a shrug of the shoulders, that "all you have is arthritis," make sure that you understand precisely what kind it is and that everything possible is being done to help you. If you are in doubt, see a rheumatologist—he's an internist with special training and expertise in the various types of arthritis.

RHEUMATOID ARTHRITIS— THE WORST KIND

Rheumatoid arthritis (RA) is usually the worst kind you can have. It is three times more common in women than in men and strikes most frequently between the ages of twenty-five and fifty. Although RA can involve many different joints of the body, it is usually most apparent in the small ones, like the fingers. It is generally symmetrical—that is, it affects both sides of the body. Joints are swollen, stiff, painful and warm to the touch. In most patients, attacks are mild, and there are periods of remission during which symptoms are either slight or absent. Such letups occur frequently and may persist for months. In other instances, the disease may progress relentlessly to the crippling stage. Because this is a generalized disease striking other organs of the body as well as the joints, you feel pretty miserable with it. You lack energy and tire easily, your appetite is poor, you lose weight and may run a low-grade fever.

Treatment of rheumatoid arthritis must be aggressive and have as its major goal relief of joint pain and swelling and prevention of joint deformity and destruction.

HELPFUL MEDICATIONS

The most useful drug to try first is aspirin. But you will have to take it in large doses—twelve or more a day. Aspirin can be irritating to the gastrointestinal tract and cause bleeding from the stomach or bowel if you take large doses for any length of time. Use the enteric-coated preparations to forestall this problem. If you have ever had a peptic ulcer, make sure to tell your doctor. Also, ask for several Hemoccult cards to check for blood in the stool. Every few weeks, you smear a tiny film of stool on a card and add a few drops of chemical to it. They will tell you if the specimen contains any blood. Continue to do this as long as you take aspirin regularly. And remember, blood in the stool is not always visible to the naked eye.

Aspirin alone is often all you will need if your rheumatoid arthritis is mild. Since symptoms are usually worse in the morning, so that you awake with pain and stiffness of the joints, take time-release or long-acting aspirin at bedtime, which will be working when you get up.

Despite the veneration in which aspirin is held (and for good reason), there has been a good deal of active research to produce salicylate drugs that create less gastric irritation. There are now available two such preparations that I have found as effective as aspirin. They are marketed in the United States as Disalcid and Trilisate. Their advantage lies in the fact that they need be taken only two or three times a day, rather than every two or three hours.

WHEN SALICYLATES AREN'T ENOUGH

When salicylates either don't work or are not well tolerated, another group of drugs is available for control of symptoms of RA. They are called nonsteroidal anti-inflammatory drugs (NSAIDs), and dose for dose are more effective and cause less gastrointestinal upset than does aspirin. They go under such trade names as Indocin, Motrin, Naprosyn, Tolectin, Nalfon, Feldene, Clinoril, Dolobid, Anaprox and others. None is the "magic bullet" for rheumatoid arthritis. There is no evidence that using them in combination is any more effective than prescribing them singly. The response of any given patient to any one of these drugs is unpredictable. You may benefit from one and not from another, and it's often a matter of potluck.

MAKE SURE YOU DON'T GET HOOKED

An important principle for you to follow, especially in the early stages of RA, is to avoid taking narcotics for pain relief. None of the drugs mentioned above will make an addict out of you, but I know of several tragic cases of patients with rheumatoid arthritis who, racked with pain, pleaded, cajoled, insisted and finally persuaded their doctors to give them codeine, Dilaudid, Demerol, Talwin, Percodan or other controlled substances. If you use them regularly, you may well get hooked. That may not be an important consideration in late-stage cancer; but in RA, after the disease goes into remission, you may have a drug problem on your hands for the rest of your life.

BEWARE OF THE RIP-OFF ARTISTS

Suppose you have tried all the above medications without success. At this point, it is easy to fall prey to forms of quackery. Some of it is innocuous, like the copper bracelet, to which I have no real objection. (Although some patients swear it works, I know of no scientific evidence to prove it.) Since it is decorative, and the worst it can do is give you a green wrist from the oxidation of the copper, by all means wear it if you think it helps.

While copper bracelets are harmless, the same can't be said for some of the "arthritis clinics" that operate barely within the law. Here you will be given combinations of drugs that, at best, don't help, and frequently are dangerous. And there is no special diet, either, that is likely to make one whit of difference to your disease. (Just be sure to eat balanced and nutritious meals containing plenty of protein and foods rich in iron.)

THE GOLD RUSH

If none of the medication mentioned thus far has helped, instead of looking for a miracle, you should consider gold therapy. Properly administered, gold will bring on a complete remission or result in significant improvement in 50 to 60 percent of patients. The full course of treatment takes up to twenty weeks. Although not without risk, gold therapy should be tried if your symptoms are progressive and severe. But remember, not every doctor is experienced with this technique. If yours isn't, ask him to recommend a rheumatologist. Because of its potential toxicity, the administration of gold is not something to be taken casually, either by you or your doctor. Formerly available only in the injectable form, gold can now be taken by mouth.

Your next option is a drug called penicillamine (don't confuse it with penicillin, of which it is a synthetic relative). Penicillamine is not an antibiotic; it is, like gold, a potent chemical with potentially serious side effects and should be administered only by experienced specialists. If you are given penicillamine, don't expect immediate results; it may take as long as two or three months before you begin to respond. During the entire time you are on the drug, you have to be watched very carefully for toxicity. Only one patient in four is able to tolerate it, the major problems being kidney trouble, rashes and gastrointestinal symptoms. If you have a preexisting kidney condition, chances are that you will not be eligible for this therapy.

When penicillamine works, it not only acts on the joints, but attacks the underlying disease process too, so that you will feel a whole lot better generally, with less fever, improvement of appetite and a sense of well-being. We are not quite certain how it works. Perhaps it enhances the body's own defense mechanism, the so-called immune system.

If penicillamine doesn't help, the next step may be antimalarial drugs (chloroquine, hydroxychloroquine), which in some cases have a salutary effect on rheumatoid arthritis. They are not very popular because of the frequency with which they damage the eyes. Think twice before accepting this treatment.

THE UBIQUITOUS IMMUNE SYSTEM

A word about the *immune system* here. When you are in-fected by a bug or virus of some kind, the body develops antibodies to neutralize or destroy the invader. But some-times this defense mechanism gets all mixed up. It forgets who's who and what's what, and begins to attack the body itself instead of, or in addition to, the "enemy." In the case of rheumatoid arthritis, healthy joints become its target. The rationale for treating rheumatoid arthritis with immunosup-pressant drugs is to tone down such inappropriate actions. Sometimes these measures are effective. The trouble is that when we suppress the aspect of the immune system that has gone wrong, we also impair its other vital mechanisms that protect against real threats to the body. So use of immuno-suppressive agents can be hazardous, in that they may lower natural protection against other disease. For this reason, anyone taking these drugs, of which Imuran is the prototype, must be monitored very closely.

THE HAZARDS OF STEROIDS

You and your doctor should try to resist the temptation of steroid (cortisone) drugs for rheumatoid arthritis. Their long-term use in large doses (and we usually have to use progres-sively larger amounts to obtain the same effect) can produce threatening or otherwise undesirable complications. Corti-sone repeatedly injected into a joint may eventually cause its destruction, just as surely as will the disease itself. The temporary benefit of oral steroids is short-lived and you usu-ally pay heavily for it. You become more vulnerable to infec-tion, you may develop a peptic ulcer, your bones may lose their calcium and become so thin that they fracture sponta-neously and you may develop diabetes or high blood pres-sure. Despite the dangers and drawbacks, there *are* special circumstances when severe complications of arthritis, such as inflammation of the blood vessels in the heart, brain or liver, make the use of these hormones necessary. Consult with a rheumatologist before deciding to take them.

THE UNFORTUNATE FEW

Remember that, despite all our efforts, a substantial number of patients with RA do progress to the crippling stage of the disease. In that case, long-term management involves more than pills and injections. While drugs help to control pain, we must address ourselves to the mechanics of the joints themselves. Adequate rest is essential, but too much will eventually leave the joints rigid and immobile. Heat should be liberally applied because it increases the range of joint motion. Supervised exercises prescribed by professional pysiotherapists or experts in rehabilitative medicine may prevent loss of motion and strengthen the muscles around the joints. Specially fitted splints may be required to prevent deformity. The most important part of physiotherapy is a home exercise program, which is your responsibility to follow.

WHEN TO CALL THE SURGEON

In special circumstances, surgical removal of the lining of the diseased joint may reduce pain and slow the progress of RA. But it takes a skilled rheumatologist to know when to call for the surgeon. Occasionally, pain is so severe in the moving joint that you may have to undergo a fusion operation. Here we deliberately sacrifice joint mobility for comfort. You may even be a candidate for complete joint replacement. These are all decisions that must be made from time to time in the management of your disease, and should not await arbitrarily set appointments at six- or eight-month intervals.

LITTLE TIPS CAN HELP
BIG MEDICATIONS

Many patients with rheumatoid arthritis are able to lead productive lives. A wise, experienced doctor can give you useful little tips in addition to big medicines. For example, there is the question of sexual activity. Your doctor should instruct you in coital positions that are comfortable enough to make sexual relations enjoyable. I remember one woman in her late forties who had moderately severe rheumatoid arthritis. There were many days when she felt "lousy," with a low-grade fever, pain and stiffness of the joints and beginning deformity of her hands and knees. She was extremely depressed, for which she was given various mood-elevating drugs. It took just a few minutes talking together for me to discover that her depression was due not only to the pain, but also to the fact that she believed she was sexually undesirable to her husband. So she withdrew from any sexual relationship, not wishing to "force herself" on him in this "deformed and ugly state." The fact was that he loved her and, despite her arthritis, wanted her. *He* did not wish to force himself upon *her* for fear of aggravating her symptoms. When it was all straightened out, she no longer needed the antidepressants and adopted a more realistic outlook on her disease.

The treatment of arthritis is changing rapidly. Keep in touch with the Arthritis Foundation, which has branches in most large metropolitan areas. To find the one nearest you, write to the Arthritis Foundation, 1314 Spring Street, N.W., Atlanta, Georgia 30309. They will send you all the latest literature and tell you where to find the special counseling services that can help you live with this disease.

OSTEOARTHRITIS

Let us assume that you have consulted the doctor about pain, stiffness and a little swelling of some of your joints. You are worried about the possibility of unrelenting or progressive deformity. But the doctor tells you that you have *osteoarthritis,* the noncrippling disease, and not rheumatoid arthritis. (He will probably have taken X rays, which help to differentiate the two, as well as blood tests.) Unlike rheumatoid arthritis, which is a generalized disease, osteoarthritis affects only the joints.

EVEN IN DINOSAURS

Osteoarthritis is not a new disease of civilization. We see evidence of it in dinosaur skeletons representing life 200 million years ago, as well as in the bones of the Neanderthal man of 40,000 years ago. Most doctors refer to osteoarthritis as degenerative (as opposed to infectious or inflammatory joint disease), because it is believed to result from simple wear and tear on the joints over the years. So, you would expect to find this form of arthritis predominantly in athletes, parachutists and others who impose repeated, abnormal strain on their joints. In fact, many persons who lead ordinary lives also develop osteoarthritis.

CONTROLLING PAIN

The mainstay of pain control, as in RA, is aspirin. Here too you may need a lot of them—six, eight, ten or more a day— and you must be constantly alert to the risk of gastric irritation or ulceration. If you now have, or ever have had, a peptic ulcer, aspirin in such large doses may constitute a problem. As mentioned earlier, there are several new salicylates, like Trilisate, that are as effective as aspirin, and since they need be taken only twice a day, may irritate the stomach lining less.

The new nonsteroidal anti-inflammatory drugs discussed in reference to rheumatoid arthritis are also useful in osteoarthritis. Physiotherapy and the occasional injection of small amounts of cortisone into the affected joint can help too. Again, try to avoid oral medication containing cortisone or narcotics for relief of pain. If you are given any, get another opinion from a rheumatologist.

MY OWN NONOPERATION

Not too long ago I had a firsthand experience that highlights the need for a good second opinion. I began to notice pain whenever I rotated my right wrist. I consulted a good orthopedic surgeon, who first splinted the wrist. After ten days, all I had to show for my effort was a stiff joint. The pain persisted. My doctor then suggested a surgical procedure to excise one of the small wrist bones that he firmly believed was giving me all the trouble. I was about to submit; but since I practice what I preach, I discussed the matter with another colleague. He was very much opposed to surgery and referred me to a physiatrist (that's an M.D. who specializes in physical and rehabilitation medicine), who also thought that surgery was unnecessary. Instead, the physiatrist recommended exercises to stretch the tendon in my wrist. I performed them faithfully for a week. He then injected the joint with a tiny amount of steroid. That cured me—at least my wrist has been free of pain for the past eight years. So even in a matter as relatively trivial as a little arthritis of the wrist, a second opinion spared me the pain and cost of an unnecessary operation.

MECHANICAL MEASURES

In addition to injecting something *into* a joint to obtain relief, you may also benefit from the *removal* of fluid that has accumulated in it (for example, "water on the knee"). Physiotherapy too can yield very gratifying results in osteoarthritis. Unfortunately, it is underutilized, largely because it is time-consuming and there are not enough well-trained people around to treat everybody who needs it (about 50 percent of the population over fifty is troubled by some form of osteoarthritis). As in rheumatoid arthritis, physical measures must be tempered with daily rest periods. When weight-bearing joints are involved, a cane, crutch or other support may be helpful during the acute phase.

Doctors often don't have the time to discuss with you the details of your life-style. Many symptoms can be minimized by avoiding unnecessary stair climbing, wearing proper shoes to correct the line of weight bearing, improving your posture, and losing weight if you are obese. (The heavier you are, the greater the stress on your weight-bearing joints.) When you have pain in a limb or a joint, you tend to favor it. This results in the muscles around the affected joint becoming thin or, as doctors say, atrophied. Also, remember that osteoarthritis can produce pain at a distance from the actual site of involvement. For example, the bony spurs that develop when you have arthritis in the spine may press on nerves that emerge from it to go to other parts of the body.

So if you have arthritis of the neck, you may awaken one morning with chest pain and think you have had a heart attack. Under these circumstances, traction (which eases the pressure on the affected nerve) or even a soft, fitted collar can be of help.

PHYSIOTHERAPY FOR SPASM CONTROL

Much of the discomfort that you experience when your spine or shoulders are involved by osteoarthritis is due to spasm of the muscles in the affected area. Muscles are nature's splints. If you have arthritis in the bones of your spine, the muscles in the area become tense and rigid in order to prevent the bones from moving too much. But in so doing, the muscles themselves become painful, and you end up with a "bad back." So good physiotherapy to relax the muscles, prescribed by somebody who understands the relationship between joint and muscle structure and function, can be enormously helpful. I have known many patients who were spared disc surgery by an intensive program of physiotherapy. *Whenever surgery is recommended for osteoarthritis, make sure that you have exhausted all the nonsurgical alternatives* (exercise, heat, bracing and drugs for pain relief).

REASSURANCE IS NOT ENOUGH

If your osteoarthritis is severe, you need proper treatment. Reassurance that you are not going to be crippled is not enough. Moreover, some cases do indeed end up with deformities. If that happens, you may ultimately require braces or an operation either to stabilize or replace the involved joint.

The most important breakthrough in this area has been the ability of surgeons to replace a painful, deformed hip. Patients who only a few years ago would have been virtually crippled are now leading normal lives because of this incredible surgical procedure. So if you have been limping along with pain because of arthritis of the hip and are living on painkillers, ask whether you are a candidate for *total hip replacement*. The risk is very small when the operation is done by an experienced team.

We are now able to replace not only hips, but knees, elbows and other joints as well.

As remarkable as the joint replacement technique is, it is not an operation you should have without a second opinion—first, to make sure that it is needed, and then to determine whether the surgical team that is doing it is sufficiently experienced. Remember, however, if you have *any* artificial prosthesis inserted, whether it be in the heart or in the hip, be sure to take prophylactic antibiotics whenever you have dental work done, or any invasive diagnostic procedure or operation. You must take the same precautions as if you had a rheumatic heart valve.

GOUT—THE RICH MAN'S DISEASE?

No one with gout is amused by the traditional cartoons depicting that disease—the corpulent man with bulbous nose, who has obviously indulged to excess, sitting with outstretched leg while a valet ministers to his acutely inflamed big toe. Although this disorder may be precipitated in vulnerable subjects by prolonged, excessive consumption of alcohol, the use of diuretics, overweight and diets rich in animal organs (liver, brain, pancreas, kidney), it also plagues those who are moderate both in their incomes and life-styles—men much more often than women.

FACT AND FANTASY

What is fact and what is fantasy in this disease? Gout results from impairment in the way the body handles certain chemical processes. This results in an excess of *uric acid* in the body, because either too much is produced or it is not eliminated properly. Gout develops when uric acid crystals form in the joints and inflame them. The most commonly affected site is the big toe, but gout can involve other joints—the knee, elbow, wrist, heel and so on. The attack is occasionally mild, but more often so exquisitely painful that you cannot bear even the slightest pressure, such as a bed sheet, on the affected area.

A TRICKY DIAGNOSIS

The diagnosis of gout is not always easy to make; the disease may be confused with several other conditions ranging from gonorrhea to osteoarthritis, all of which may cause a joint to become inflamed. What further complicates the picture is the fact that the uric acid level in the blood is not always elevated. One of my patients was a seventy-eight-year-old man who developed acute swelling of both knees. It is unusual for gout to strike more than one joint at a time. The fact that his uric acid level was normal also made the diagnosis of gout unlikely. It looked just like acute osteoarthritis. Aspirin was of no help; neither were Motrin and Clinoril. Because the patient was so uncomfortable, I admitted him to the hospital with the diagnosis of "arthritis of unknown origin." Only when we withdrew some of the fluid from the swollen joint, analyzed it under the microscope and actually saw the urate crystals in the fluid were we able to confirm the diagnosis of gout.

Over the years, we have learned how more effectively to prevent and treat gouty arthritis. You should be aware of this new knowledge, because the manner in which the acute attack is handled is important to your comfort. Modern therapy may eliminate recurrences in most patients, often permitting them to eat and drink what they like.

WHEN THE CURE IS
WORSE THAN THE DISEASE

Colchicine is the specific medicine for the acute attack of gout. Not so long ago this was the only drug we had for that purpose. You take it at the onset of symptoms and continue taking one tablet every hour until either relief is obtained or you are so sick from the treatment that it has to be stopped. Some patients find the abdominal cramps, diarrhea, nausea and pain in the belly due to colchicine almost as bad as the gout attack itself. There are some old-time physicians who still use this treatment. It is effective, mind you, and it also has the advantage of being diagnostic. In other words, if you suddenly develop acute pain in a joint and neither you nor your doctor are sure what kind of arthritis it is, relief with colchicine is virtually certain evidence that it is gout, for this drug does not influence the pain from any other form of arthritis.

In my opinion, once the diagnosis of gout has been established, colchicine is not the best drug to use. I prefer Indocin, an anti-inflammatory agent that has fewer side effects than colchicine, but which can irritate an empty stomach. So always take it after meals.

HOW TO PREVENT RECURRENCES

After the acute gout attack has subsided, your next objective is to prevent a recurrence. Most patients don't like to take medication indefinitely, but that is what you will probably have to do if you are vulnerable to gout. Simply changing your life-style is no guarantee against future attacks. For example, even if you lose weight, watch your diet and abstain from alcohol, the risk of acute gout is somewhat reduced, but not eliminated.

You will need preventive maintenance medication in addition. Those most widely used include *allopurinol* (marketed as Zyloprim in the United States, Zyloric in Europe), Benemid or Anturane. Zyloprim prevents gout by decreasing the amount of uric acid the body produces; Benemid doesn't interfere with the manufacture of uric acid, but increases its excretion in the urine. Anturane (sulfinpyrazone) works much like allopurinol.

Should patients with gout ever drink? In moderation, alcohol is not likely to give you any trouble. But if you are a heavy drinker, even if you take prophylactic medications, your life is likely to be punctuated by attacks of gout.

WATER PILLS AND GOUT

Many thousands of individuals regularly take "water pills" for one reason or another—because they have high blood pressure, heart failure or retention of fluid due to liver or kidney disease. Virtually all diuretics increase the uric acid level. If they are prescribed for you and you have had problems with gout in the past, you should, in addition, take allopurinol or one of the other preventives.

THE BAD BACK

A "bad back" may be due to several different causes—an infectious process, a birth deformity, erosion of the bone structure, osteoporosis (especially common in postmenopausal women), an old injury that has caused disruption in the normal alignment of the bones in the spinal column, or the common, garden variety of "arthritis." Because the bad back is so common, those who suffer from it tend to accept it as inevitable and just "live with it." Either that, or they become so desperate that they submit to management that is too aggressive—ranging from heavy braces to unnecessary surgical procedures.

WHOM TO SEE FIRST—AND LAST

At the first sign of back trouble, see your internist. The problem may not be orthopedic. It may, for example, reflect a kidney problem. Only when other medical causes have been excluded should you consult an orthopedist or rheumatologist. If it is confirmed that you have a bad back due to strain or arthritis, go to a physiatrist. Many general hospitals now have departments of physiatry, or rehabilitation medicine, where patients can be given significant relief of symptoms by learning exercise programs that can be performed at home.

THERE'S A LOT THAT CAN BE DONE

There are many ways to obtain relief of back pain due to orthopedic causes or arthritis. These include a judicious balance between rest and specific, appropriate exercises (depending on the muscle groups involved), heat therapy, Novocain injections, splinting or bracing, wearing properly fitting shoes, correction of posture, physiotherapy, medication and finally, but only as a last resort, surgery. Unfortunately, too few internists or family practitioners have the time, patience, interest, facilities or skill to treat a back problem and to stay with it. Orthopedic surgeons are busy setting broken bones and dealing with other *acute* surgical problems, and are not usually enthusiastic about embarking on a long program of supportive measures for the patient with backache.

WHEN IT'S A DISC

Discs are the pads between the spinal bones that cushion the friction between those bones. When they wear out or are displaced, the nerves that leave the spinal cord on their way to various parts of the body are impinged upon. When a nerve is thus compromised, the muscle groups it supplies are weakened, and the irritation of the nerve itself produces pain. The most common example of symptoms from such nerve pressure is sciatica, in which the sciatic nerve emerging from the lower spine is damaged by spurs from the vertebrae themselves or by a displaced disc.

If the disc is causing sufficient pressure on one or more nerves in your back, so that there is muscle weakness or loss of sensation, then surgery may be required.

THE CONTROVERSIAL
ALTERNATIVE TO DISC SURGERY

The traditional approach to a displaced disc is its surgical removal, which 250,000 patients undergo each year. However, there is an alternative to this procedure—the injection of chymopapain (derived from the *Carica papaya*) into the disc space. Chymopapain is an enzyme that digests protein. When injected into the damaged disc, it dissolves some of it, thus reducing the pressure on the nerve roots responsible for the pain and weakness. Most orthopedists prefer the definitive surgical approach. A few recommend chymopapain. You should at least be aware of your options before deciding which route to follow if you have a disc that needs treatment.

THE EPIDURAL INJECTION FOR SCIATICA

If you can't decide between surgery and chymopapain, you have one other choice. You stand a 50–50 chance of improvement for at least one year by having an injection (epidural) of cortisone into the area where the nerve leaves the spinal cord. Cortisone reduces inflammation and swelling of the irritated nerve. If your own doctor has no experience with it, ask him to refer you to someone who does.

AFTER THE MENOPAUSE

After the menopause, the calcium content of bone is decreased for reasons that we really don't understand, and the bone becomes brittle—a phenomenon called *osteoporosis*. This thinning of the bone in women is almost universal after the menopause and accounts for the large number of hip fractures in older females. In any event, the older woman, now lacking in calcium, suddenly develops severe pain in the back for little or no apparent reason. Occasionally, it happens after she takes a bumpy car ride or steps down hard because of a missed stair; the jolt causes the fracture of a vertebra in the spinal column. Whatever the mechanism, the symptoms lead to a vicious circle. The pain keeps the patient in bed. But that causes the skeleton to lose even more calcium, so that more fractures may ensue. (This is one of the reasons for getting up early and exercising after an illness or operation, in order to prevent demineralization of the skeleton; another is to prevent blood clotting.)

When the vertebrae fracture, they become compressed and

so our female patient becomes shorter. The term "little old ladies" derives from the fact that osteoporosis occurs primarily in older women, after the menopause, and results in compression fractures that shorten the spine and reduce height. The spontaneously fractured bones in the spine may become distorted as they heal. The result is that many of these elderly women develop back deformities, leading to the term "widow's hump" or "dowager's hump."

OSTEOPOROSIS AND ESTROGENS

Estrogens constitute the most effective preventive against osteoporosis. They decrease the reabsorption of bone and thus the number and rate of fractures. As indicated earlier, I believe that every postmenopausal woman who is estrogen deficient should receive replacement therapy, unless there is some overriding reason not to do so (previous cancer of the breast, clotting abnormalities, liver disease). Estrogens should be accompanied by progesterone for ten days each month. If you do take estrogens, you should have regular gynecological exams and Pap tests every six months, and immediately report any vaginal bleeding to your doctor.

In addition to estrogens, extra calcium is also helpful. You should take about 1,500 mg per day after the menopause, together with about 400 mg of vitamin D. Some doctors are now beginning to question this emphasis on calcium, but unless you've had trouble with kidney stones, I'd certainly supplement your intake of this mineral.

The final treatment (and preventive) for osteoporosis is weight-bearing exercise. Make sure, however, not to do too much if your bones are already brittle.

MALE HORMONES FOR WOMEN?

What about giving male hormones to osteoporotic women? The evidence favoring it is much less convincing than that for estrogens. In addition to putting hair on your face and endowing you with other male characteristics, male hormones taken by mouth can also hurt your liver. So, whether in combination with estrogens or alone, male hormones really have no place in the treatment of osteoporosis. You should get a second opinion if you are told to take them.

KEY FACTS TO REMEMBER

Arthritis, or "inflammation of the joints," is not a single disease, but may be due to several different causes—infectious, chemical, traumatic, mechanical and "unexplained." So always find out what kind of arthritis you have.

Rheumatoid arthritis (RA) is the worst type. Although it is often mild, chronic and insidious, it may be painful, progressive and crippling. It is a generalized disease of the body that makes itself most apparent in the joints, but affects internal organs as well. Treatment goals should be directed at pain control and prevention of joint deformity and destruction.

The most useful medications in the treatment of RA are salicylates (aspirin) or some of the newer antiarthritis drugs, gold, penicillamine and, in resistant cases, steroids. Physiotherapy is extremely important and, in some cases, surgical correction of the joints becomes necessary.

Osteoarthritis is the wear-and-tear form of arthritis. It is not usually as crippling or debilitating as rheumatoid arthritis, but it also requires adequate control of pain, physiotherapy and, when the joint is severely damaged, surgical replacement.

Gout is a disease of metabolism that affects various joints, classically the big toe. It can now be prevented by maintenance medication, and the acute attack can be treated effectively. Severe dietary restrictions are usually not required.

The *bad back* is usually due to arthritis, bone deformity or muscle spasm. It can often be managed by heat, rest, analgesics and exercise, but occasionally disc surgery is required. The injection of an enzyme called chymopapain into the disc space, an alternative to operation, is still a matter of controversy.

Osteoporosis, or thinning of the bones, is a frequent cause of fractures in women who are beyond the menopause and are calcium deficient. The management of this disorder involves supplementing the diet with calcium, estrogens and exercise.

REFLECTIONS

THE WARY PATIENT

Public education about medicine is a good thing. Understanding the nature of a disease and its treatment helps us to take better care of ourselves, and in many cases provides the motivation to follow doctors' orders more intelligently, conscientiously and effectively. But remember that the medical establishment does not speak with one voice on many fundamental medical questions—cholesterol, hysterectomies, coronary bypass surgery, vitamin supplements and literally hundreds of other practical matters. Regardless of what your doctor tells you about almost anything, if you look hard enough, you can always find an opposing view—one that you would prefer to hear, but that may not be in your best interest. On the other hand, you should be aware of all your legitimate options when you are confronted by an important medical decision. I have tried to present some of these options in this book.

WHEN DOCTORS DISAGREE

Disagreement among scientists is not new, but in the past, when doctors argued at their conventions, the door to the public was closed—and locked. Outsiders were not privy to these "family" disputes. Most doctors felt that laymen had no business being there. When an unauthorized reporter managed to sneak into a convention, medical jargon, like the unintelligible Latin prescription, shielded the profession against his prying. Part of this attitude by "organized medicine" was admittedly sheer arrogance, but there was also the fear that "civilians" might misunderstand and therefore distort the meaning of the technical deliberations.

How times have changed! Science reporters—astute, enthusiastic and well trained—are not only allowed into medical conferences, they are actually invited. And they work fast. Whereas it takes months for an important piece of news to reach the doctor in the medical journals, it is announced in the media worldwide the very same day.

WHEN WHAT YOU READ OR HEAR IS WRONG

How do doctors feel about this widespread availability of medical information? We have learned to live with it, but not always happily. It is confusing enough for us when conflicting data appear in the scientific literature, but all hell breaks loose when these reports are carried in the lay press before we have heard about them or had an opportunity to evaluate and discuss them among ourselves. Suppose, for example, while casually browsing through your morning newspaper, you read that a pill your doctor has prescribed is bad for you. This report may be correct, but it may also turn out to be either wrong or valid only in circumstances that don't apply to you. I remember three of my own patients with severe angina pectoris, in the hospital and awaiting bypass surgery, reading in the newspaper that according to a Veterans Administration study the procedure was of no benefit. This conclusion was subsequently shown to be in error. But in the meantime, one patient had me cancel his operation, and the other two were wheeled to surgery not with the hope and optimism so important when one is sick, but feeling like sheep being led to slaughter. (Tragically, the man who backed out died three weeks later. The other two are fine.)

So the medical profession is in constant competition with *Time, Newsweek,* the *National Enquirer,* TV and Diane Sawyer—a contest the doctor doesn't always win.

YESTERDAY'S REMEDY— TODAY'S POISON

Don't let your confidence in your doctor be shaken by the fact that his advice seems always to be changing. Do you remember when the best treatment for a heart attack was prolonged bed rest, followed by forced retirement from work? Available knowledge *at that time* suggested that was the best thing for you to do. Today we have you virtually dancing with the nurse in the coronary care unit as soon as your chest pain subsides, and then sign you up for a vigorous physical rehabilitation program after you return to your old job. That is because we *now* know that such activity is good for you. We didn't then.

So you are now aware of some of your treatment options, at least for the specific symptoms and diseases discussed in the preceding pages. That does not mean that you must challenge *any* advice your doctor gives you. He should, however, be able and willing to discuss alternative approaches that appeal to you. Remember, too, that simply because your own doctor favors a specific course of action with which some other physician disagrees, he is not necessarily wrong. There is usually more than one way to skin a cat in medicine.

The best recourse for you, the patient, is to try to keep abreast of those advances in medicine of particular relevance to you—not in a posture of challenge, criticism or suspicion, but with the spirit of partnership, which is what a good patient-doctor relationship is all about.

INDEX

A

Abdomen
  aneurysm and, 239–41
  pain in, 331
  see also Stomach
Abortion, 282–91
  care following, 290–91
  key facts on, 292
  legality of, 283, 284
  location for performing, 289–90
  medical evaluation before,
    288–89
  pill for, 288
  pregnancy tests and, 282–83
  prostaglandins for, 287–88
  reasons for, 283
  risks of, 285–86
  salt injection for, 287
  scraping for, 284–85
  second trimester techniques,
    285–89
  suction curettage for, 284–85
  timing of, 284
  underground, 290
  urea for, 288
  vaginal suppository for, 288
Accutane, 113–14
ACE (angiotensin converting
  enzyme) inhibitors, 146, 199,
  218, 223

Acelylcholine, 251–52
Acetaminophen, 14, 119
Acetohexamide, 71
Acne, 109, 110–15
  causes of, 111–12
  diet and, 112
  key facts on, 120
  myths about, 112
  treatment of, 112–15
Acoustic nerve, 90, 91
Acquired Immune Deficiency
  Syndrome, *See* AIDS
Acylovir, 119, 127
Addiction
  to drugs, 222, 319
  to exercise, 174–75
  to smoking, 154
  see also Alcoholism
Addison's disease, 224
Adenoids, removal of, 88–90, 93
Adrenal gland, 217, 268, 270, 375
Adriamycin, 363
Aged. *See* Elderly
AIDS, 121–24
  condoms and, 275
  hepatitis and, 322
  key facts on, 135
AIDS-related complex (ARC), 122
Akinesia, 253
Albumin, 315
Albuterol, 100

Alcohol, 170, 235–36, 312
Alcoholism, 80, 83, 316
Aldactone, 220
Aldomet, 221
Allergen, 99
Allergy
  to antibiotics, 343–44
  asthma and, 95, 96
  desensitization, 99
  food, 99, 300–31
  hearing loss and, 92–93
  intestinal discomfort and, 331
  nasal decongestants and, 86–87
  to pets, 96–97
  sinusitis and, 84
Allopurinol, 406
Aluminum, 309
Alkylating agents, 362
Amantadine, 256
American Diabetes Association, 74
American Heart Association, 164, 170
Amiodarone, 35, 203
Ammonia, 316
Amniotic sac, 287–88
Amoxicillin, 131
Ampicillin, 85, 131
Amputation, 234
Analgesic creams, 119
Anemia, 36, 388
Anger, 215
Angina pectoris, 29, 168–81
  coronary spasm and, 186
  drugs for, 175–81, 221
  exercise and, 172–75
  key facts on, 210
  pain and, 234, 308–309
  sexual activity and, 198
  surgery for, 184–86
  thyroid function and, 40
Aneurysm, 238–41
Angiogram, 19, 172, 182–84
Angioplasty. See Percutaneous
  transluminal angioplasty
Angioplasty, balloon, 188, 195, 238
Antacids, 309–10
Antiarrhythmetic drugs, 200–204
Antibacterial gel, 113

Antibiotics
  allergy to, 343–44
  asthma and, 100, 103
  cancer and, 362
  colds and, 12–15, 103
  diarrhea and, 336
  gonorrhea and, 128–33
  hearing loss and, 91, 92
  heart disease and, 141, 149–50
  sinusitis and, 85
  resistance to, 129–30
  side effects of, 263
  see also specific drug name
Anticholinesterases, 260
Anticoagulants
  aspirin and, 245–46
  embolism and, 16–17, 148
  heart surgery and, 148
  phlebitis, 18, 19–20, 228, 229
  stroke and, 148, 243, 245–46
  see also specific drug name
Anticholinergics, 254
Antihistamines, 86–87, 91, 254
Antidiabetics, 47, 71–72
Anti-inflammatory drugs, 100, 307, 406
Antilopas transfusion, 123
Antimalarial drugs, 397
Antimetabolites, 362
Antispasmodics, 332
Antithyroid drugs, 41–42, 44, 45
Antiulcer drugs, 310
Antral window, 85
Anturane, 406
Apresoline, 146, 222
Arm
  circulation and, 233
  phlebitis of, 225, 226
Arteries, 232–41
  alcohol and, 235–36
  aneurysm of, 238–39
  blockage, 236
  carotid, 244–45
  cerebral, 243
  injuries and, 236–37
  key facts on, 241
  plaque, 245, 246, 248
  smoking and, 235
  spasm of, 235, 236

Arteries *(continued)*
  surgery and, 237–38, 245, 246
  vertebrobasilar, 244–45
  see also Arteriosclerosis; Circu-
    lation; Vascular System
Arteriogram, 183–84, 237–38
Arteriosclerosis, 151–52
  aneurysm and, 238–41
  cholesterol and, 157–61, 162
  collateral circulation and,
    234–35
  diabetes and, 65–66
  exercise and, 165–67
  hypertension and, 156–57, 217
  key facts on, 241
  obesity and, 167
  oral contraceptives and, 277
  smoking and, 153–54
  triglycerides and, 161
Arthritis, 393–411
  back pain and, 407–409
  copper bracelet and, 396
  drugs for, 395–98, 401
  gold therapy and, 397
  gonorrhea and, 128
  key facts on, 411
  physiotherapy for, 401–402, 403,
    407
  rheumatoid, 394–400
  spinal, 232–33, 403, 407–409
  surgery for, 399, 403–404
Arthritis Foundation, 400
Aspartame, 75
Aspirin
  anticoagulants and, 245–46
  arthritis and, 395, 401
  asthma and, 96
  cataract prevention and, 55
  fever and, 14
  hearing loss and, 92
  heart disease and, 186–87
  herpes and, 127
  prostaglandins and, 287
  shingles and, 119
  stroke and, 244
  ulcers and, 312, 313, 395, 401
Asthma, 94–103
  causes, 95–97
  in children, 95, 98, 101–102
  death and, 94
  desensitization and, 99
  diagnosis of, 98–99
  environmental factors and, 98
  extrinsic *vs.* intrinsic, 95–96
  heart disease and, 178–79
  inhalator for, 101–102
  key facts on, 103
  steroids and, 102
  treatment for, 100–103
  types of, 94–95
  vaccines for, 99
Atenolol, 178
Atrial fibrillation, 243
Atromid-S, 324–25
Atropine, 254, 260
Azulfidine, 339

B

Baby Fae, 139
Back pain, 407–409, 411
Bactrim, 336
Barium X ray, 329, 338
Barlow's syndrome, 140
Barnard, Christiaan, 207
BCQ vaccine, 365, 370
Belladonna, 254
Benemid, 406
Benzocaine, 348
Benzoyl peroxide, 113
Beta-adrenergic antagonists,
    100–101, 102
Beta blockers
  asthma and, 100
  heart disease and, 140, 178–80,
    200, 201
  hypertension and, 218, 220–23
  psoriasis and, 107
  side effects of, 233, 263
  thyroid gland and, 42, 44
Betoptic, 179
Bile, 325, 326
Biliary obstruction, 327
Birth control. *See* Contraception
Bladder
  cancer, 365, 369–70, 390
  catheterization of, 149

Bleeding mechanism, 315
Blindness. *See* Eyes
Blood
  cancer, 388–89
  in intestines, 307–308
  in stool, 338–39
  transfusions, 123, 319
  in urine, 368, 370
  vaginal, 302, 410
  volume, 219
  see also Hemorrhage
Blood pressure, high. *See*
    Hypertension
Blood pressure, low, 194, 223–24,
    253
Blood thinners. *See* Anticoagulants
Blood vessels. *See* Vascular
    system
"Blue baby," 138
Bone
  cancer, 355–56
  thinning, 409–10
  see also Osteoarthritis;
    Osteoporosis
Bowel, 329–41
  cancer, 340, 348, 381–82
  diagnostic testing of, 329–30
  diverticulitis of, 333–34
  inflammation of, 337–41
  irritable, 331–33
  key facts on, 341
  perforation of, 339
Brain
  circulation and, 233
  damage, 35
  hemorrhage, 243
  Parkinsonism and, 251–52
  tumor, 25–26
  wave test, 37
  see also CT scan
Breast
  cancer, 30, 278–79, 356, 361,
    371–76, 390–91
  enlargement in men, 39
Bromocriptine, 256, 272
Bronchial tubes, 94, 99, 102
Bronkosol, 100
BuSbar, 140
Bypass surgery, 184–86, 189–90

C

Cachectin, 365
Caffeine, 312
Calamine lotion, 119
Calcium, 309, 409, 410
Calcium channel blockers, 180–81
Capoten, 146, 218, 222–23
Cancer, 351–92
  AIDS and, 122
  bladder, 365, 369–70, 390
  blood, 388–89, 392
  bowel, 340, 348, 381–82
  breast, 30, 278–79, 356, 361,
    371–76, 390–91
  causes, 358–59
  cell biology and, 361–62
  cervical, 126, 377–78
  chemotherapy for, 361–63
  diet and, 376
  digestive tract, 380–82, 392
  incidence of, 357
  key facts on, 389–92
  kidney, 368–69, 390
  lung, 154–56, 353–54, 358,
    366–69, 390
  lymph gland, 361, 371, 372, 392
  mechanism of, 358
  ovarian, 301, 360, 375, 377, 380,
    390
  prostate, 346, 361, 382–87, 392
  radiation therapy for, 360–61
  radioactive iodine and, 44
  shingles and, 118
  skin, 109, 115–17, 357
  smoking and, 154–56, 366–67,
    369
  staging and searching, 359–60,
    374
  testicular, 360, 369, 390
  test tube treatment for, 363–64
  thyroid, 33, 34, 47, 48–50, 109
  tonsillectomy and, 89
  ultraviolet radiation and, 109–10
  uterine, 281, 377–80, 390
  vaccine, 364–65
  weight loss and, 365–66
Captopril, 199, 222–23
Carafate, 311

Carbamazepine, 119
Carbidopa, 255
Carbon monoxide, 153, 155
Cardiac catheterization, 145–46
Cardilate, 177
Cardioversion, 193
Cardizem, 180–81
Casts, 236–37
Catapres, 221–22
Cataracts, 51–62
  formation of, 53–54
  key facts on, 61–62
  "second sight" and, 52
  surgery for, 56–62
  ultraviolet radiation and, 109
CAT scan. See CT scan
Ceclor, 85
Cell biology, 361–62
Cephalosporin, 85
Cerebral hemorrhage, 243
Cerebrovascular accident, 248
Cervix
  cancer of, 126, 377–78
  infertility and, 271
Charley horse, 234
Chemosurgery, 117
Chemotherapy, 361–63, 374–75, 380
Chemodeoxycholic acid, 327
Chest
  pain, 308–309
  X-ray, 144, 367
Chicken pox, 118
Chicken soup, 13
Children
  asthma in, 95, 98, 101–102
  cataracts in, 54
  diabetes in, 64–65, 73, 76
  heart disease in, 137–39, 142–43, 153
  herpes in, 125
  leukemia in, 388–89
  passive smoking effect on, 156
  sore throat in, 88, 90
  thyroid problems in, 35, 44, 48
  tonsillectomy and adenoidectomy for, 87–90
  see also Puberty
Chlamydia, 124, 132–33, 272
Chlorpropamide, 71

Cholesterol, 157–61, 170–72
  diet and, 157–58, 160–61, 170
  drugs for, 158, 171
  diuretics and, 220
  hearing loss and, 92
  lipoproteins and, 162–63
  minority viewpoint about, 158–59
  normal levels, 160
  NHLBI project about, 158, 159
  oral contraceptives and, 278
  stroke and, 243
  thyroid function and, 36
  triglycerides and, 161
Cholestyramine, 158, 171
Choloxin, 171
Churchill, Winston, 51
Chymopapain, 409
Cigar smoking, 157
Cigarettes. See Smoking
Circulation, 232–41
  alcohol and, 235–36
  casts and, 236–37
  collateral, 234
  diagnostic evaluation of, 234
  in legs, 16–20, 233–36
  oral contraceptives and, 279
  smoking and, 235
  treatment for, 235–36
Cirrhosis, 316
Cisplatinum, 369
Cleomycin, 369
Clindamycin, 113
Clofibrate, 159
Clomiphine, 273
Clondine, 221–22
Clots, 225–26
  see also Embolism; Phlebitis
Coal tar, 108
Codeine, 119
Coitus interruptus, 275
Colchicine, 405–406
Cold, common, 12–16, 103
Cold extremities, 233
Colestid, 171
Colestipol, 171
Colitis, 338–41
  key facts on, 341
  psychotherapy and, 340–41

Colitis (continued)
  symptoms, 338–39
  treatment, 339–40
Colon. See Bowel
Colonoscopy, 329, 339, 348, 381
Colostomy, 340, 382
Coma, diabetic, 69, 74
Commisurotomy, mitral valve, 147
Compazine, 252
Complete Medical Exam, The (Rosenfeld), 191
Condom, 127, 275–76
Constipation
  antacids and, 309
  diverticulitis and, 334
  hemorrhoids and, 347
  irritable bowel syndrome and, 331, 332
Contact lens, 58, 61
Contraception, 273–82
  coitus interruptus, 275
  condoms, 275–76
  diaphragm, 276–77
  douching, 276
  intrauterine device, 279–80
  key facts on, 292
  ovulation method of, 274
  pill, 111, 114, 131, 277–79
  post-ovulatory, 288
  spermicides, 127, 276, 277
  sterilization, 280–81
  sympto-thermal method of, 274
  types of, 273–74
  withdrawal, 275
Copper bracelet, 396
Cordarone, 203
Cornea surgery, 60–61
Coronary artery disease, 23–24
  angina and, 169
  arteriosclerosis and, 151
  cholesterol and, 170
  heart attack and, 182
  personality type and, 167–68
  testing for, 145
Corticosteroid, 87
Cortisone, 54, 108, 113, 339, 348, 409
  see also Steroids

Cough, treatment of, 15–16
Coumadin, 19, 311
Cramps, leg, 219, 234
Crohn's disease, 337–40
  key facts on, 341
  symptoms, 337–38
  treatment, 339–40
Cromolyn, 101, 102
Cryotherapy, 117
CT scan
  for aneurysm size, 240
  for bowel problems, 330
  for digestive tract cancer, 381
  for lung cancer, 368
  for stroke clot, 246, 247
Culdoscopy, 272
Curettage, 284–85
Cyclosporine, 207
Cryosurgery, 349
Cyst, thyroid, 48
Cytellin, 171
Cytomel, 38

D

Dacron graft, 238
Danazol, 273
Dandruff, 106
Dead Sea, 109
Deafness, 90–93
  causes, 92–93
  conductive, 91
  key facts in, 93
  sensorineural (nerve), 91
  treatment for, 91–92
Death
  asthma and, 94
  diabetes and, 69
  embolism and, 226
  oral contraceptives and, 279
  thyroid surgery and, 45
  ulcers and, 306
Decongestants, nasal, 85, 86
Dermabrasion, 114
Dermatology, 104–105
Dental work, 149
Desensitization, 99
Deviated septum, 84

Dextromethorphan, 16
DiaBeta, 71
Diabetes mellitus, 63–77
  adult-onset (non-insulin dependent), 65–66, 69
  beta cells and, 64, 76
  coma and, 69, 74
  complications of, 65–66, 72
  death and, 69
  definition of, 63–64
  diet and, 66–67, 69, 73–75
  eye changes and, 55, 60
  gallstones and, 326
  hearing loss and, 92
  heart disease and, 178
  home testing for, 75–76
  impotence and, 294, 296
  insulin-dependent, 64–65, 69, 74
  juvenile (insulin-dependent), 64–65, 69
  key facts on, 77
  leg pain and, 233
  myths about, 66–67
  oral contraceptives and, 277
  pills for, 69–72
  pregnancy and, 72–73
  Pritikin program and, 164
  research on, 76
  symptoms of, 67
  treatment of, 68–76
  UGDP study of, 70–71
  weight loss and, 68, 69
Diabetic neuropathy, 233
Diabinese, 71
Dialysis, 110
Diaphragm, contraceptive, 276–77
Diarrhea
  antacids and, 309
  cancer and, 381
  diet and, 330–31, 332–33
  traveler's, 335–36
  treatment of, 336–37, 339
Dibenzyline, 345
Diet
  acne and, 112
  cancer and, 376
  diabetes and, 66–67, 69, 73–75
  hearing loss and, 91–92

  heart disease and, 157–58, 160–64, 170, 187
  hypoglycemia and, 82
  intestinal disorders and, 330–31, 332–33, 334–35
  peptic ulcer and, 311–12
  see also Food allergy
Diethylstilbestrol (DES), 268
Digestive tract, cancer of, 380–82, 392
Digitalis, 146, 179, 193, 200–201, 205, 219
Dilantin, 119, 200, 248
Diltiazem, 180
Dipyridamole, 187, 244
Disalcid, 395
Disc, spinal, 408–409
Disopyramide, 202–203
Diuretics, 91, 146, 219–20, 222, 407
Diverticulitis, 333–34
Doctor. See Physician
Dopamine, 251–52, 255
Doppler test, 19, 144, 227, 234, 246, 295
Double vision, 25–26, 39, 57
Douching, 276
Doxorubicin, 370
Doxycycline, 85, 336
Drugs
  name variations of, 38
  resistance to, 129–30
  see also specific drug names
Duodenal ulcer, 304–305, 307
Duodenitis, 337
Dymelor, 71
Dyrenium, 220

E

Ears, 118
  see also Deafness; Hearing
Echocardiography, 140, 144
E. coli, 336
Egg, ovarian, 270–71, 272
Ejaculation, 269, 276
Elavil, 119
Elderly
  cancer and, 361, 365

Elderly *(continued)*
  cataracts and, 52–53
  contact lenses and, 58
  hearing loss and, 91–92
  hepatitis and, 319
  skin cancer and, 117
  thyroid function and, 37, 39–40
  vision loss and, 55
Electrocardiogram (ECG), 143,
  144, 166, 196
  heart attack and, 24
  pacemaker and, 206
  pericarditis and, 23
  thyroid function and, 36
  Wolff, Parkinson and White
    syndrome and, 25
Electroencephalogram, 37
Electroshock treatment. *See*
  Cardioversion
Embolism, 17–18, 148, 226
Embolus, 226, 243
Emotions
  and asthma, 96
  and colitis, 340–41
  and heart attack, 167–68
  and hypertension, 215
  and hyperthyroidism, 40
  and hysterectomy, 299
  and impotence, 24, 199, 294,
    296–97
  and infertility, 273
  and mitral valve prolapse, 140
  and Parkinson's disease, 253,
    256
  and ulcers, 306–307
Enalapril, 222
Endarterectomy, 238, 246
Endocarditis, bacterial, 141,
  148–50
Endoscopy, 304, 305, 308, 330
Enzyme, identification of, 130
Ephedrine, 86
Epilepsy, 278
Epitheliomas, 116–17
Erection problems. *See* Impotence
Erythromycin, 85, 113, 134, 149
Estrogen
  for acne, 144
  in oral contraceptives, 277

receptors, 375
replacement therapy, 281,
  378–79, 410–11
Ethacrynic acid, 92
Ewing's sarcoma, 355
Exercise
  asthma and, 96
  irritable bowel syndrome and,
    333
  heart disease and, 162, 165–67,
    172–75
  osteoporosis and, 410
  physical exam and, 166
  pregnancy and, 165–66
  smoking and, 165
  surgery and, 165
Exercise Myth, The, 166–67
Eyes
  arteriosclerosis and, 151
  bulging, hyperthyroidism and,
    39, 46
  cataracts of, 51–62
  circulation and, 233
  glasses for, 55, 57, 60–61
  shingles and, 118
  surgery, 56–57, 60–61
  vascular changes in, 55
  see also Vision

F

Fallopian tubes, 270–71, 272, 280,
  281, 301
Family planning, natural,
  274–75
  see also Contraception
Farsightedness, 52
Fats, polyunsaturated, 159
Feces. *see* Stool
Fiber, dietary, 73, 82, 331–33,
  334–35, 347
Fibrinogen, 315
Fibroids, uterine, 278, 301, 302
5-FU, 117
Floppy mitral valve, 139–41
Food allergy, 99, 330–31
Freis, Edward, 213

G

Gallbladder, 20–22, 324–28
  diagnostic testing of, 325–26
  key facts on, 328
  liver and, 316
  removal of, 326–27
Gallstones, 20–22, 324–28
  dissolving, 327
  five F's of, 324
  incidence of, 324–25
  key facts on, 328
  silent, 326
  treatment of, 326–29
Gamma globulin, 321, 336
Gastric ulcer, 304–305
Gastritis, 337
Gastrointestinal series. See GI
  series
Gastroscopy, 305
Gemfibrozil, 171
Gender, ulcers and, 306
Genetic factors, 211–12, 307
German measles, 137
GI series, 308–309, 329–30
Glaucoma, 55, 60, 179
Glipizide, 71
Globulins, 315
Glucose
  elevation during pregnancy, 72
  level in blood, 63–64, 80
  tolerance test, 79
  see also Sugar
Glucotrol, 71
Gluten allergy, 331
Glyburide, 71
Goeckerman method, 108–109
Goiter, 34, 46–47
Goitrogens, 46–47
Gold therapy, 397
Gonococcus, 128, 130
Gonorrhea, 127–33
  incidence of, 130–31
  key facts on, 135
  syphilis and, 132, 134
  from toilet seat, 133
  treatment of, 128–33
Gossypol, 273–74
Gout, 220, 404–407, 411

Guaifenesin, 15
Guanethidine, 222

H

Haloperidol, 252
HAV hepatitis, 317–18
Hay fever, 99
HBV hepatitis, 317–18
HDL (high-density lipoproteins),
  162–63, 170, 171, 172
Headache, 25–26
  migraine, 140, 244, 278
  nitroglycerin and, 175–76
Hearing, 90–93
  see also Deafness
Hearing aids, 90, 92, 93
Heart, 137–210
  aneurysm, 239–40
  antacids and, 309
  arrhythmia, 200–206
  artificial, 208
  aspirin and, 186–87
  block, 205
  cardiac circulation and, 182
  cholesterol and, 157–61, 170
  collateral circulation and, 172
  commisurotomy of valve, 147
  congenital disease of, 137–39,
    142–43
  diet and, 157–58, 160–64, 170,
    187
  drugs for, 146, 171–72, 175–81,
    200–204
  electroshock treatment of,
    193–94
  endocarditis of, 141, 148–50
  exercise and, 166, 172–75
  failure, 199
  floppy valve of, 139–41
  gonorrhea and, 128
  graft, 190
  key facts on, 208–10
  lipoproteins and, 161–63, 170
  mitral valve of, 139–41
  murmur, 139, 141, 143
  nasal decongestants and, 86
  pacemaker, 179, 194, 204–206

Heart *(continued)*
panic attacks and, 140
pregnancy and, 137–38, 140, 141, 150, 153
Pritikin program and, 163–64
pump for, 194
rheumatic fever and, 142–43
rhythm disturbances, 200
stroke and, 248
surgery, 138–39, 142, 146, 146–68, 184–96, 189–90
testing of, 140, 144–46
thyroid function and, 36–37, 39–40, 41
transplant, 207–208
Wolff, Parkinson and White syndrome and, 25
see also Angina pectoris; Arteriosclerosis; Coronary artery disease; Heart attack
Heart attack
angina and, 169
blood pressure and, 194, 221
see also subhead hypertension
causes, 151, 182
cholesterol-HDL ratio and, 163
continuing symptoms after, 199–200
emergency procedures for, 191–92
estrogen and, 378–79
exercise and, 165–67
hypertension and, 156–57, 170, 213, 215
impotence following, 296
oral contraceptives and, 278
personality type and, 167
rehabilitation after, 197
retirement and, 24–25
sexual activity after, 197–99
silent, 24
smoking and, 154
surgery after, 327
symptoms of, 188–89, 190–91
treatment for, 193–96
Hemophilia, 315
Hemorrhage
leukemia and, 388
risk during surgery, 45

Hemorrhoids, 347–50
key facts on, 349–50
symptoms, 347–48
treatment, 348–49
Heparin, 18, 19, 229
Hepatitis, 314–23
diagnosis of, 323
key facts on, 323
symptoms of, 317
treatment of, 320–21, 322–23, 336
types of, 317–18, 322–23
vaccine, 321–22
HEP-B-Gammagee, 321
Hernia, 345
Heroin addiction, 222
Herpes simplex virus (HSV), 124–27
causes, 126–27
condoms and, 275
treatment, 127
types of, 124–25
Herpes zoster. *See* Shingles
Heterograft, valve, 148
High blood pressure. *See* Hypertension
Hip replacement, 403–404
Histamine, 99
HIV virus, 122
Hodgkin's disease, 89, 361, 387
Holter monitoring, 196
Homograft, valve, 148
Homosexuals
AIDS in, 122
gonorrhea in, 132
hepatitis in, 319, 322
Hormones
acne and, 111
for cancer treatment, 361, 375
infertility and, 268, 269, 270–71
osteoporosis and, 378–79, 410–11
thyroid, 34–42
see also specific hormone
Hospital, day center, 89–90, 145, 183
HSV (virus). *See* Herpes simplex virus
HTLV-III (virus), 122
H_2 receptor blockers, 310–11
Hydralazine, 222

Hydrocortisone, 107, 108
Hyperalimentation, 365–66
Hyperglycemia. *See* Diabetes
    mellitus
Hypertension, 211–24
  anger and, 215
  antacids and, 309
  arteriosclerosis and, 156–57, 217
  causes of, 217
  compliance and, 215
  definition of, 213–14, 216, 218
  drug side effects and, 86, 87,
    217–18, 277
  genetic factors and, 211–12
  heart attack and, 156–57, 170,
    213, 215
  impotence and, 220, 221
  key facts on, 224
  life insurance and, 214, 216
  oral contraceptives and, 278
  salt and, 219, 220
  strokes and, 156–57, 213, 242–43
  treatment for, 218–23
  VA study of, 213
Hyperthyroidism, 34, 39–46, 47
Hypoglycemia, 78–82
  alcohol and, 80, 81
  causes, 80–81
  definition of, 78–80
  diet and, 82
  functional, 81
  key facts about, 82
  reactive, 81
  treatment for, 82
Hypoglycemics (drugs), 71–72
Hyposensitization, 99
Hypotension, 223–24
Hypothalamus, 34
Hypothyroidism, 34, 35–39, 43, 45,
    92, 233
Hysterectomy, 299–303
  alternatives to, 302–303
  estrogen replacement therapy
    after, 379
  key facts on, 303
  necessity for, 300–301
  psychological impact of, 299
  as sterilization technique, 280,
    281

Hysterosalpingography, 272

I

Ibuprofen, 18
Ileostomy, 340
Immune serum globulin (ISG),
    321
Immune stimulation, 365
Immune system, 122, 398
Immunosuppressive drugs, 118,
    261, 398
Immunotherapy, 364–65
Implanted lens. *See* Intraocular
    lens
Impotence, 293–98
  causes, 220, 221, 233, 294–95
  drug-induced, 294
  heart attack and, 199
  key facts on, 298
  psychological factors and, 24,
    199, 294, 296–97
  treatment for, 296–97
Imuran, 261, 398
Inderal
  antacids and, 311
  asthma and, 100
  heart disease and, 140, 178, 201,
    205
  hypertension and, 218
  side effects of, 233, 263
  thyroid function and, 42, 44
Indigestion, 308–309
Indocin, 107, 139, 228, 406
Indomethacin, 107, 139
Infants. *See* Children
Infarction, 226
Infertility, 265–73
  female, 129, 270–73, 280
  key facts on, 291
  male, 266–70
  psychological factors, 273
Inflammatory bowel disease,
    337–41
  see also Bowel; Colitis; Crohn's
    disease
Insulin, 63–64
  adult-onset diabetes and, 69, 74

Insulin *(continued)*
hypoglycemia and, 80
juvenile diabetes and, 64–65, 69
myths about, 66–67
pregnancy and, 72–73
pump, 76
reaction, 74
Insulinoma, 81
Interferon, 16, 323
Intestines, 329–41
blood in, 307–308
cancer of, 380–82, 392
poor circulation and, 233
see also Bowel
Intraocular lens, 58–60
Intrauterine device (IUD), 131, 279–80
Intravenous pyelogram (IVP), 344–45, 370
Iodides, 35
Iodine
acne and, 112
radioactive, 43–44, 45, 47, 384
in salt, 46
Isordil, 177
Isotretinoin, 113
Isuprel, 100
IUD. *See* Intrauterine device

J

Jarvik artificial heart, 208
Jaundice, 316, 317, 318, 320
Jogging. *See* Exercise
Joints
pain in, 402
swelling of, 400–401
see also Arthritis
Juvenile diabetes. *See* Diabetes, juvenile

K

Keloids, 114
Kelp, 112
Keratosis, 116
Ketones, 68

Kidneys
antacids and, 309
arteriosclerosis and, 151, 159
cancer, 368–69, 390
cholesterol and, 159
circulation and, 233
diabetes and, 71
digitalis and, 201
hearing loss and, 92
hypertension and, 217
urine production and, 344

L

Lactose intolerance, 330–31
Laetrile, 50
Laparoscopy, 272
Laser beam therapy, 188
Lasker, Mary, 213
LAV (virus), 122
Laxatives, 332
LDL (low-density lipoproteins), 162, 171, 172
L-dopa, 254–56
Legs
cramps, 219, 234
diabetes and, 66
pain in, 16–20, 226–27, 229–30, 232–34, 235–36
phlebitis and, 225, 226–27
Lens implant, 58–60
Leukemia, 358, 361, 388–89, 392
Levodopa, 254–55
Levothroid, 38
LHRH (cancer treatment), 385
Lidocaine, 193, 263
Life insurance, 214, 216
Lipoproteins, 161–63
Liquor. *See* Alcohol
Lithium, 35, 46–47, 107, 205
Lithotriptor, 328
Liver
biopsy, 323
diabetes and, 64
estrogen replacement therapy and, 379
gonorrhea and, 128
hypoglycemia and, 80

Liver *(continued)*
    function of, 315–16
    oral contraceptives and, 278,
        279
Lomotil, 339
Lopid, 171
Lopressor, 178, 218
Lorelco, 171
Lourdes, 49
Lovastatin, 171, 172
L-tryptophan, 55
Lues, 134
Lump. *See* Cyst; Tumor
Lumpectomy, 372
Lungs
    asthma and, 98
    cancer, 154–56, 353–54, 358,
        366–69, 390
    embolism of, 18, 226
    fluid in, 144
Lupus erythematosus, 134
Lymph gland, 361, 371, 372,
        386–87, 392
Lymphoma, 386–87, 392

M

Macular degeneration, 55
Madopar, 255
Magnesium hydroxide, 309
Magnetic resonance imaging
        (MRI), 246, 330
Malpractice suits, 29
Mammography, 376
Manic-depression, 47
Mannitol, 248
Marijuana, 363
Mastectomy, 371–73
Masturbation, 112
Mayo Clinic, 327–28, 334
Medications. *See* Drugs; specific
        illnesses
Melanoma, 115, 117
Ménière's disease, 91
Meningitis, 122
Menopause
    acne and, 111
    cancer and, 378–79
    hormone replacement after,
        281, 378–79, 410–11
    hysterectomy and, 281
    osteoporosis after, 409–10
Menstruation
    acne and, 111
    exercise and, 165–66
    oral contraceptives and, 278
    thyroid function and, 35, 39
    varicose veins and, 230
Mestinon, 260
Metaproterenol, 100
Metastasis, 359
Methimazole, 41, 42
Methotrexate, 110
Methyldopa, 221
Metoprolol, 178
Metroden, 273
Micronase, 71
Migraine headache, 140, 244, 278
Milk, 310, 330–31
Minipress, 146, 222, 345
Mitral valve prolapse, 40, 135–41
Motrin, 18, 228
Mouth
    breathing, 88–89
    cancer, 155
Muscle
    myasthenia gravis and, 258–59
    spasm, 233
Myasthenia gravis, 258–64
    key facts on, 264
    mechanism of, 259–60
    pregnancy and, 263–64
    symptoms of, 258–59
    treatment of, 260–63
Myocosis fungoides, 355
Myopia, 52, 60–61
Mytelase, 260
Myxedema, 36
    see also Hypothyroidism

N

NANB hepatitis, 317–18
Narcotics, 222, 363, 396
Nasal decongestants, 85, 86

National Heart, Lung and Blood
Institute, 158, 159, 213
Nearsightedness, 52, 60–61
Neck, murmur in, 246–47
Neck collar, 246
Neomycin, 171, 172
Nicotine, 153
see also Smoking
Nicotinic acid, 91, 171
Nifedipine, 180
Nitrates, 177
Nitrobid, 177
Nitrogen mustard, 361, 387
Nitroglycerin, 146, 175–77, 189, 198
Nitrolingual spray, 176
Nodule. See Cyst; Tumor
Nonsteroidal anti-inflammatory
drugs (NSAIDs), 395–96, 401
Norpace, 202–203
Nose
decongestants for, 85, 86
polyps in, 84, 98
septum, deviated, 84
stuffy, 86, 93
Novocain, 348

O

Obesity
arteriosclerosis and, 167
oral contraceptives and, 278
Obstipants, 337, 339
Omega-3 polyunsaturated fatty
acids, 160, 170, 187
Oncology, 354–55
Orinase, 69, 71
Osmotic agents, 248
Osteoarthritis, 400–404
Osteoporosis, 409–11
antacids and, 309
exercise and, 410
hormone treatment and, 378–79,
410–11
key facts on, 411
smoking and, 154
Ovary
cancer of, 301, 360, 375, 377, 380,
391

infertility and, 270–71

P

Pacemaker, cardiac, 179, 194,
204–206
Pancreas
diabetes and, 64, 72, 76
hypoglycemia and, 80, 81, 82
tumor of, 81, 381
Panic attacks, 140
Pap test, 302, 343, 370, 377–78, 379,
410
Parathyroid glands, 45
Parkinson's disease, 250–57
key facts on, 257
psychological factors and, 253,
256
symptoms of, 252–53
treatment of, 254–57
Patent ductus arteriosus, 138
Patient
fears of physician, 28–29
medical care system, 27
Pauling, Linus, 14
PCBs, 270
Pelvic inflammatory disease
(PID), 124
Pelvic pain, 301
Penicillamine, 397
Penicillin
allergy to, 343
for gonorrhea, 129, 130, 131–33,
134
prophylaxis, 149
for sinusitis, 85
Pencillinase, 130
Penis
bladder surgery and, 370
condoms and, 275–76
discharge from, 129, 132
impotence and, 233, 294–98
prosthesis for, 297
urination and, 344
Pentoxifylline, 236
Pepcid, 310
Peptic ulcer, 304–13
acid and, 305

Peptic ulcer *(continued)*
  aspirin and, 312, 313, 395, 401
  death and, 306
  diet and, 311–12
  drug-induced, 307
  genetic factors and, 307
  key facts on, 313
  mucus and, 305
  psychological factors and,
    306–307
  sex differences and, 306
  smoking and, 307
  steroids and, 307, 398
  symptoms of, 305, 307–309
  treatment of, 309–313
  types of, 304–305
Pepto-Bismol, 335
Percutaneous transluminal
    angioplasty, 187–188, 238
Perforated bowel, 339
Pericarditis, 23
Peritrate, 177
PERK (Prospective Evaluation of
    Radial Keratomy), 61
Persantine, 187, 244
Personality, Type A *vs.* Type B,
    167–68
  see also Emotions
Pets, allergy to, 96–97
Phako-emulsification, 56–57
Pharynx cancer, 155
Phenothiazines, 252
Phenypropanolamine, 86
Phlebitis, 16–19, 225–31
  dangers of, 225–26
  diagnosis of, 226–27, 228–29
  estrogen replacement therapy
    and, 379
  key facts on, 230–31
  oral contraceptives and, 277,
    279
  shingles and, 227
  treatment of, 228
Phototherapy, 109
Physician
  ego and, 30
  loyalty to, 28–29
Physiotherapy, for arthritis,
    401–402, 403, 407

Pimples. *See* Acne
Pipe smoking, 157
Pituitary gland, 34, 270, 375
Plasmapheresis, 262
Pneumonia, 13, 122, 367
Pockmarks, 114
Pollen, 87, 95, 96
Polycythemia vera, 358
Polyps, 84, 98
Potassium, 219
Prazosin, 222, 345
Prednisone, 87, 387
Pregnancy
  acne treatment and, 114
  antibiotics and, 131, 132
  cataract formation in child
    during, 54
  contraceptive use following, 278
  diabetes and, 72–73
  exercise and, 165–66
  heart disease and, 137–38, 140,
    141, 150, 153
  hemorrhoids and, 347
  herpes and, 126
  hypoglycemia and, 80
  myasthenia gravis and, 263–64
  shingles and, 118
  smoking and, 154
  thyroid problems and, 44, 45,
    46–47
  tubal, 280
  see also Abortion; Contracep-
    tion; Infertility
Presbyopia, 52
Pritikin program, 163–64
Probenecid, 132
Probucol, 171
Procainamide, 193, 200, 202, 263
Procarbazine, 387
Proctoscopy, 329, 377
Progestasert, 280
Progesterone, 379, 410
Progestin, 278
Prolactin, 272–73
Propranolol, 42, 178
Propylthiouracil, 41, 42, 45
Prostaglandins, 287–88, 312–13
Prostate gland, 342–50
  cancer, 346, 361, 382–87, 392

Prostate gland (continued)
  drug side effects and, 86, 203
  enlargement, 344–45
  hernia and, 345
  infection of, 342–44
  key facts on, 346
  surgery, 344–46, 383
Prostatectomy, 383
Prostatitis, 342–44
Prostigmin, 260
Protein, manufacture of, 315
Prothrombin, 315
Pseudoephedrine, 86
Psoralen, 109
Psoriasis, 105–10
  causes of, 105–106
  key facts on, 120
  treatment of, 106–10
Psychological factors. See Emotions; Stress
Psychotherapy, 312, 333, 340
Puberty
  acne and, 111
  goiter and, 46–47
Pulmonary embolism, 18, 226
Pump
  heart, 194
  insulin, 76
PUVA, 109–10
Pyridoxine. See Vitamin B_6

Q

Questran, 158, 171
Quibron, 101
Quinidine, 193, 200, 202, 263

R

Radial keratomy, 60–61
Radiation therapy, 47, 48, 360–61, 382
Radioactive iodine, 43–44, 45, 47, 384
Radionuclide angiogram, 182–83
Radionuclide cineangiogram (RNCA), 144

Radioreceptor assay, 283
Rauwolfia, 221
Raynaud's disease, 236
Rectal exam, 329
Reflexes, abnormal, 37
Renin, 212, 217, 218, 222–23
Reserpine, 205, 221, 252
Retina, detached, 60
Retinoic acid, 113
Retirement, 24–25
Reye's syndrome, 14
Rheumatic fever, 142–43
Rheumatoid arthritis, 394–400
  hearing loss and, 92
  key facts on, 411
  symptoms of, 394
  treatment of, 395–400
Roughage. See Fiber
"Rubber band" surgery, 349
Rubella. See German measles
Rubin test, 272
RU-486, 288

S

Saccharin, 75
Salicylate drugs, 395
Salt
  for abortion, 287
  antacids and, 309
  heart disease and, 170
  hypertension and, 219, 220
  iodized, 46
Sciatica, 408–409
Scrotum, varicosity, 268
Seaweed, 112
Sebaceous glands, 111
Sectral, 178, 179, 221
Seldane, 87
Septra, 336
Sexual activity
  AIDS and, 123
  arthritis and, 399–400
  heart attack and, 197–99
  herpes and, 125, 126, 127
  thyroid function and, 36, 39
  See also Impotence

Sexually transmitted disease, 121–35
  AIDS, 121–24
  antibiotics and, 128–34
  condoms and, 275
  gonorrhea, 128–33
  hepatitis, 319
  herpes, 125–27
  key facts on, 135
  syphilis, 134
Shingles, 117–20, 227
Sickle-cell anemia, 211–12, 279
Sigmoidoscopy, 329, 338, 339, 381
Sinemet, 255
Sinequan, 119
Sinusitis, 83–85
  antral window for, 85
  asthma and, 98
  causes, 84
  irrigation for, 84, 85
  key facts on, 93
  treatment, 85
Sinus node, 204
Skin, 104–20
  acne and, 110–15
  cancer, 109, 115–17, 357
  myths about, 116
  psoriasis and, 105–10
  shingles and, 117–20
  tags, 116
  testing, asthma and, 98
  thyroid function and, 35, 36
Sleep, thyroid function and, 36, 39
Slo-Phyllin, 101
Smokenders, 155
Smoking
  addiction to, 154
  asthma and, 98, 103
  cancer and, 154–56, 366–67, 369
  circulation and, 235
  exercise and, 165
  hearing loss and, 92
  heart disease and, 152–56, 162, 170
  hepatitis and, 317
  impotence and, 294
  oral contraceptives and, 278
  passive, 156
  pregnancy and, 154

safety of, 154–55
  stopping, 155–56
  stroke and, 243
  ulcers and, 307, 312
Sodium. See Salt
Sonar technique. See
    Echocardiography;
    Sonography
Sonography
  abdominal, 240, 330, 381
  arterial, 246
  of gallbladder, 21, 325–26
  of thyroid, 48
Sorbitol, 75
Sorbitrate, 177
Spectinomycin, 132
Sperm, 266–70
  adequacy of, 266–67
  deficiency, 267–68
  environmental effect on, 270
  retrograde ejaculation and, 269
  vasectomy and, 281–82
Spermicide, 127, 276, 277
Spinal disc, 408–409
Stanford University, 207
Staphylococcus, 129
Sterility. See Infertility
Sterilization, 280–81, 292
Steroids
  allergy and, 87
  arthritis and, 398, 401
  asthma and, 102
  cancer treatment and, 362
  Crohn's disease and, 339
  hepatitis and, 323
  myasthenia gravis and, 261
  psoriasis and, 107–108
  shingles and, 119
  stroke and, 248
  ulcers and, 307, 398
Stomach
  acid, 305
  inflammation of, 337
  See also Bowel; Intestines;
      Peptic ulcer
Stool
  blood in, 338–39
  softeners, 333

Stool *(continued)*
 viral hepatitis transmission in,
  318, 319
Streptococcus, 129
Streptomycin, 92
Stress
 asthma and, 96
 hyperthyroidism and, 40
 impotence and, 296
 ulcers and, 306–307
Stress test, 166, 173, 183, 196
Stroke, 242–49
 anticoagulants and, 245–46
 arteriosclerosis and, 151
 aspirin and, 244
 circulation and, 233
 heart surgery and, 148
 hypertension and, 156–57, 213,
  242–43
 key facts on, 248–49
 oral contraceptives and, 278
 recovery from, 247–48
 TIA and, 243–45, 247
 types of, 243
Suction curettage, 284–85
Sugar
 hypoglycemia and, 81
 irritable bowel syndrome and,
  331
 see also Glucose
Sugar, blood
 diabetes and, 63–64, 67–68, 71,
  74, 75–76, 220
 hypoglycemia and, 78–80
 triglycerides and, 161
Sugar substitutes, 74–75
Sulfa drugs, 129, 336, 343
Sulfites, 96
Surgery
 aneurysm and, 239, 240, 241
 arterial, 237–38, 245, 246
 for arthritis, 399, 403–404
 blood transfusions and, 123
 bowel, 340
 day centers for, 89–90
 exercise and, 165
 gallbladder, 326–27
 heart, 138–39, 142, 146–48,
  184–86, 189–90

 hemorrhoidal, 349
 hysterectomy, 280, 281, 299–303
 for impotence, 296
 informed consent and, 374
 joint, 399
 Parkinson's disease and, 257
 prostate, 344–46, 383
 thyroid, 44–45, 48–49
 vascular disease and, 237–38
 vasectomy, 281–82
Swan-Ganz catheter, 194–95
Synthroid, 38
Syphilis, 127–28, 132, 134, 135

T

Tagament, 119, 310–11
Tamoxifen, 375
Tartrazine, 96
Teeth. *See* Dental work
Tegison, 110
Tegretol, 119
Tenormin, 178, 218, 221
Tensilon, 259, 260
Terbutaline, 100
Testes, 267–68, 360, 369, 385–86
Testosterone, 269, 296
Tetracycline
 acne and, 113, 114
 allergy to, 343
 sexually transmitted diseases
  and, 124, 131, 132, 134
Thalidomide, 137
Theo-Dur, 101
Theophylline, 101, 311
Thiazides, 219–20
Thiotepa, 370
Throat
 cancer, 155
 sore, 88, 90, 149
Thrombolysis, 195
Thrombophlebitis. *See* Phlebitis
Thrombosis, 243, 379
Thymomas, 262–63
Thymus gland, 262–63
Thyroidectomy, 44–45
Thyroid gland, 33–50
 asthma and, 98

Thyroid gland *(continued)*
  blood pressure and, 224
  cancer, 33, 34, 47, 48–50, 109
  cholesterol and, 159
  drug interactions and, 35
  drug therapy for, 37–39, 41–42
  enlarged, 40, 42
  function of, 34
  goiter and, 46–47
  hormone production and, 34–42
  infertility and, 268, 270
  key facts on, 50
  nasal decongestants and, 86
  overactive, 34, 39–46
  tumor, 34, 47–50
  underactive, 34, 35–39
  surgery, 44–45, 48–49
  see also Hyperthyroidism;
    Hypothyroidism
Timolol, 179
Timoptic, 100, 179
Tobacco. *See* Smoking
Tobacco chewing, 155
Tofranil, 140
Toilet seat, 133
Tolazamide, 71
Tolbutamide, 69, 71
Tolinase, 71
Tonsillectomy, 87–90, 93
Tonsils, function of, 88
Tranquilizers, 87, 91, 140, 216, 312
Transcutaneous nerve stimula-
    tion, 119
Transduction, 129
Trunsfusion, blood, 123, 319
Transfusion hepatitis, 319
Transient ischemic attack (TIA),
    243–45, 247
Transplant, heart, 207–208
Transurethral prostatectomy,
    345–46
Traveler's diarrhea, 335–36
Treadmill. *See* Stress test
Tremors, 250–51, 252
Trental, 236, 237
Treponema pallidum, 134
Tretinoin, 113
Trichomonas, 124
Triglycerides, 92, 114, 161, 171, 220

Trilisate, 395, 401
Tubal pregnancy, 280
Tumor, 352–53
  abdominal, 347
  adrenal gland, 217
  biopsy, 373
  bone, 355
  bowel, 340
  brain, 25–26
  ear, 90
  esophageal, 381
  liver, 381
  lumpectomy of, 372–73
  lung, 354
  lymph gland, 361, 386–87
  ovarian, 301
  pancreatic, 81, 381
  pelvic, 347
  prostate, 342, 384
  skin, 116
  thymus gland, 262–63
  thyroid, 34, 47–50
  uterine, 281
  Wilms's, 361
  see also Cancer
Tylenol, 14, 119
Type A-B personality theory,
    167–68

U

Ulcer. *See* Duodenal ulcer; Peptic
    ulcer
Ulcerative colitis. *See* Colitis
Ultrasound. *See* Sonography
Ultraviolet radiation, 108–110, 115
Uniphyl, 101
Urea, abortion and, 288
Ureter, 344
Urethra, 129, 344
Uric acid, 220, 404
Urination, 343–44, 368, 370
Urine, blood in, 368, 370
Ursodeoxycholic acid, 327
Uterus
  abortion and, 284–86
  cancer of, 301, 377–80, 391
  fertility and, 272

Uterus (continued)
  fibroids of, 278, 301, 302
  removal of, 280, 281, 299–303
  see also Hysterectomy

V

Vaccine
  asthma, 99
  cancer, 364–65
  hepatitis, 321–22
Vagina
  abnormal bleeding of, 302, 410
  hysterectomy and, 301
  oral contraceptives and, 278,
    279
Vagus, 305
Valium, 311
Valve, heart
  artificial, 146, 147–50
  homografts and heterografts,
    148
  infection prevention and, 149–50
  insufficiency, 143
  stenosis, 143
Vanceril, 102
Varicocele, 268
Varicose veins, 18, 229–30
  hemorrhoidal, 347
  oral contraceptives and, 279
  of scrotum, 268
  surgery for, 18, 230
Vascular system
  acne treatment and, 114
  arteriosclerosis and, 151–52
  diabetes and, 66, 72
  diagnostic evaluation of, 234
  phlebitis and, 228
  surgery and, 237–38
  vision impairment and, 55
Vas deferens, 281
Vasectomy, 281–82
Vasotec, 146, 218, 222
VDRL test, 134
Veins, hemorrhoidal, 347–50
  see also Phlebitis; Varicose
    veins
Venereal disease, 124

  see also Sexually transmitted
    disease
Venereal warts, 124
Ventricular septal defeat, 138
Verapamil, 180, 193
Vertebrobasilar system, 244–45
Veterans' Administration (VA),
  213
Vibramycin, 85, 336
Vinblastine, 369
Vincristine, 387
Viral hepatitis. See Hepatitis
Virus
  AIDS, 121–22
  cancer, 364–65
  cold, 12, 16
  hepatitis A and B, 318–22
  herpes (HSV), 124–27
  HIV, 122
  HTLV-III, 122
  interferon, 16, 323
  LAV, 122
  shingles, 117–18
Vision
  cataracts and, 51–62
  causes for impairment, 55
  double, 25–26, 39, 57
  see also Eyes
Visken, 178, 179, 221
Vitamin A, 113
Vitamin B, 255, 272
Vitamin C, 13, 14
Vitamin D, 410
Vitamin E, 376
VLDL (very-low-density lipopro-
  teins), 162
Vocal cords, 45

W

Warfarin, 19, 229
Warts, venereal, 124
Wassermann test, 134
Water pills. See Diuretics
Weight
  cancer and, 365–66
  diabetes and, 68, 69
  heart disease and, 162, 170

Weight *(continued)*
  thyroid function and, 35, 39
  see also Obesity
Wheezing. *See* Asthma
Wilms's tumor, 361
Wolff, Parkinson and White
  syndrome (WPW), 25

gastrointestinal, 308–309
stomach, 304

Y

Yohimbine, 296

X

Xanthines, 101
X rays
  barium, 329, 338
  chest, 144, 367
  Fallopian tube, 272

Z

Zantac, 310
Zinc, 114–15
Zoster virus, 117–18
Zovirax, 119, 127
Zyloprim, 406